The Appraisal
of Personal Property

*Principles, Theories, and Practice Methods
for the Professional Appraiser*

American Society of Appraisers

Patricia C. Soucy, FASA, and Janella N. Smyth, ASA
Co-Editors

Library of Congress Catalog Card Number: 94-072243
ISBN 0-937828-01-7

Printed in the United States of America.

Printed by Automated Graphic Systems, Inc., White Plains,
MD, Mark Edgar, Technical Consultant on printing.
Typesetting by Triangle Office Assistance, Cary, NC,
Carolyn Shaw.

Contributing Editors
Louise Hall, ASA and Mary Sudar, ASA

Contributors

Richard-Raymond Alasko, ASA
John Alico, FASA
David Borodin, ASA
Stephen Caudana, ASA
Jessica L. Darraby, JD
Bernard Ewell, ASA
Carolyn Price Farouki
Louise Hall, ASA
John Housiaux, ASA
Janie King, ASA
Terry King, ASA
Alyn Lacombe, ASA

John Lanterman, ASA
Dexter MacBride, FASA
Terry Melia, CPA
Corinne Richardson, JD, MVS
Maureen Sandstrom, ASA
Barbara Shanley, ASA
Janella Smyth, ASA
Santo Sottilare, JD
Patricia Soucy, FASA
Peter Sorlien, ASA
Mary Sudar, ASA

Personal Property Committee
Richard-Raymond Alasko, ASA, Chairman – 1992-3
June L. Johnson, ASA, Chairman – 1994
Elizabeth Blagbrough, FASA, Advisor
Stephen Caudana, ASA, Parliamentarian
Patricia Soucy, FASA, Immediate Past Chair – Advisor

Personal Property Journal Editors
Editor - Barbara Shanley, ASA, and Managing Editor - Carol Worthington, AM -1994
Editor - Louise Hall, ASA, and Associate Editor - Carolyn Price Farouki - 1992-3

Members (1992-1994 Inclusive):

Corrine Cain, ASA
Dean Fehrman, ASA
Carol Foster, ASA
Louise Hall, ASA
Roderick Hardy, ASA
Emyl Jenkins, ASA
Yvonne Karn, ASA
Janie King, ASA
Terry King, ASA

John Lanterman, ASA
Charles Rosoff, ASA
Victoria Scogland, ASA
Barbara Shanley, ASA
Janella Smyth, ASA
Peter Sorlien, ASA
Mary Sudar, ASA
Frances Zeman, ASA

Acknowledgements

There are a number of people who provided advice and/or assistance in the production of this book and to whom the Editors and Contributing Editors wish to express gratitude. Our thanks go to Elizabeth Blagbrough, FASA; Lee Hardin, ASA; Martha Vacca, AM; Sylvia Wade-Olsen; Roy Morris, FASA; Yvonne Karn, ASA; Charles Rosoff, ASA; Emyl Jenkins, ASA; Elin-Lake Ewald, ASA; Roderick Hardy, ASA; Sharon Kerwick, ASA; Steve Minor, ASA; and Shirley Belz, Public Relations Director for the American Society of Appraisers. Thanks also to the many others, too numerous to name, who contributed in some way to the success of this project.

Editorial Statement

A Handbook On The Appraisal of Personal Property, a landmark publication in the field of personal property appraisals, was originally created by The International Personal Property Committee of the American Society of Appraisers and published in 1989 by the Society.

It was an achievement which was correlated to over fifteen years of academic initiatives on the part of the Society, encompassing the establishment of an unprecedented degree program in Valuation Sciences, the publication of a scholarly journal to serve the needs of professional personal property appraisers, the development of a multi-disciplinary series of Appraisal Education courses, and the continuous offering of educational programs and advanced seminars.

This book has been written to replace that handbook and has been produced under the leadership of the International Personal Property Committee with the cooperation and contribution of Society members and other individuals knowledgeable in legal matters relating to the appraisal profession, all of whom have given unselfishly of their time and expertise to assure the timely publication of this edition.

This book has been written to serve as (1) an instructional guide to professional personal property appraisers for the continuing development of appraisal skills; (2) a reference tool for the practicing personal property appraiser; (3) the statement of policies and standards of the International Personal Property Committee of the American Society of Appraisers; (4) a useful guide for governmental agencies, museums, attorneys, insurance companies, and others who use the services provided by professional personal property appraisers.

This book, with its emphasis on ethics, professionalism, and principles of practice is intended to be particularly helpful to sole practitioners and small firms.

The appraising profession develops reports for and provides services to a number of users, market sectors, courts, institutions, businesses and agencies, each with their own protocols. A rapid sophistication of services in character and requirements has resulted in a wider sense of responsibilities, and, inevitably, a multiplicity of concepts, vocabularies, rules, and methods which as in all professions require refinement. This book was developed with the contributions of appraisers and attorneys based upon their own experiences in professional valuation. More often than not, their vocabularies are consistent and their application or interpretation of concepts and rules may appear unified. Particularly in newer areas of valuation every effort has been made to unify and reconcile phraseology and interrelations of appraisal methods and theories. However, seeming contradictions may remain. The editors believe that the dynamics of our profession require flexibility and they have opted to include those areas even where some disagreement exists. Consequently this book represents the profession as it exists today, not with strict uniformity but with those awkward and sometimes unresolved notions yet to be refined. Particular phrases or interpretations published in this handbook are not designed or intended to be the basis of any civil liability.

Patricia C. Soucy, FASA
Janella N. Smyth, ASA

Table of Contents

Chapter 3 *Established Principles and Methods of Valuation* 12

Chapter 4 *Technical Competence and Professional Skills* 23

Chapter 11   *Business Aspects of a Professional Appraisal Practice* 203

Chapter 1

Value and Market Level Definitions

Appraisal Value Terms and Definitions

An appraisal prepared by a professional appraiser identifies clearly the appraisal question (objective) for the appraisal, the intended use (function) of the appraisal, and the type of value (purpose) being estimated. The appraisal questions or objectives for an appraisal include: estimating the value of the property; estimating the cost of producing, reproducing, acquiring, altering or completing the property; estimating the monetary amount of damages to the property; and forecasting the monetary earning power of the property. There are many functions or intended uses for appraisals, such as insurance, taxation, distribution, and liquidation. The intended use is specified, usually by the client, at initiation of the assignment; an appraisal can have only one intended use. There are many purposes or types of value, and it is the responsibility of the appraiser to select the type of value that is fully relevant and appropriate to the objective and intended use of the appraisal. The determination of the objective leads the appraiser to the appropriate type of value to be estimated which is compatible with the intended use of the appraisal.

Black's Law Dictionary defines an appraisal as "a valuation or an estimation of value of property by disinterested persons of suitable qualifications" and "the process of ascertaining a value of an asset or liability that involves expert opinion rather than explicit market transactions."

It is important for the appraiser to understand the meaning of value terms and their definitions. Those listed below are the most commonly used value terms for the personal property appraiser.

Appraisers need to be aware of contractual terms that reflect the type of value that may be required in the preparation of an appraisal. As examples, the insurance industry uses Replacement Value and Actual Cash Value. The latter is defined as "current replacement cost, less

depreciation." This type value is normally established by an insurance adjuster based on insurance industry depreciation guides.

The Internal Revenue Service requires that Fair Market Value be used for all donation and estate tax purposes, references follow:

Sec. 1.170.1-1(c)	Income Tax Regulations, Rev. Proc. 66-49: Donations
Sec. 20.2031-1 (b)	Income Tax Regulations, Rev. Proc. 66-49: Estate Tax
IRS Publication 561	Determining the Value of Donated Property
IRS Publication 448	Federal Estate and Gift Taxes

The judicial system generally recognizes and accepts the Fair Market Value concept although many jurisdictions adopt insular variations of the more commonly used Fair Market Value, i.e., specifically requiring Market Value or Net Market Value or some other defined value.

Caution should be exercised when utilizing auction prices as a determinant of value. It is difficult to ascertain whether published sales prices represent sales to dealers or to the ultimate consumer. Other factors unique to auctions must also be taken into consideration when auction prices are used as part of the valuation process.

The International Personal Property Committee of the American Society of Appraisers has accepted the following value terms and definitions:

Fair Market Value

Fair Market Value is the price at which the property would change hands between a willing buyer and a willing seller, neither being under any compulsion to buy or sell and both having reasonable knowledge of relevant facts. (Treasury Regulation Sec. 20.2031-1[b])

1

The components of this concept are:
1. Price at which property would change hands
2. Between a willing buyer and willing seller
3. Neither party under compulsion to buy or sell
4. Both parties having reasonable knowledge of all relevant facts as of the valuation date
5. The sale is made to the ultimate consumer in the appropriate market level.

Market Value

Similar to Fair Market Value except that the provision for lack of compulsion to buy or sell is removed and the assumption of a sale within a specified time frame is added.

The federally accepted definition of Market Value as stated in the Definition Section of *USPAP*, is as follows:

The most probable price which a property should bring in a competitive and open market under all conditions requisite to a fair sale, the buyer and seller, each acting prudently, knowledgeably and assuming the price is not affected by undue stimulus. Implicit in this definition is the consummation of a sale as of a specified date and the passing of title from seller to buyer under conditions whereby:
1. buyer and seller are typically motivated;
2. both parties are well informed or well advised, and each acting in what he considers his own best interest;
3. a reasonable time is allowed for exposure in the open market;
4. payment is made in terms of cash in U.S. dollars or in terms of financial arrangements comparable thereto; and
5. the price represents the normal consideration for the property sold unaffected by special or creative financing or sales concessions granted by anyone associated with the sale.

Marketable Cash Value

Marketable Cash Value represents the anticipated net proceeds (or cash in hand) that would be yielded from the orderly sale of a property once all costs of sale were subtracted. It represents the amount not merely obtained (paid in full [including any buyer's premiums, taxes, etc.] by buyer) but retained (received, net, by seller) from sale.

Replacement Value — Comparable

The price in terms of cash or other precisely revealed terms that would be required to replace a property with another of similar age, quality, origin, appearance and condition within a reasonable length of time in an appropriate and relevant market. Intangible provenance value is additive as appropriate.

Replacement Value — Cost New

Cost to replace a property with an equivalent or substitute which is new, using modern materials, techniques and standards which satisfies the description or use of the replaced property. The present cost of replacing the property with one having the same quality and utility.

Replacement Value — Reproduction Cost

Total cost to reproduce a replica of a subject property at current costs. Replacement property would be constructed in a design and with materials consistent with the described piece of property being replaced by a qualified artist or craftsman.

Forced Liquidation Value

The most probable price in terms of cash, or other precisely revealed terms, for which the property would change hands if sold immediately, without regard to relevant market place.

Orderly Liquidation Value

The most probable price in terms of cash, or other precisely revealed terms, for which the property would change hands under required and limiting conditions in an orderly manner, generally advertised, with reasonable time constraints, in an appropriate and relevant marketplace, with knowledgeable buyers.

Value in Use

The value of property which reflects a value to a particular user, recognizing the extent to which the property contributes to the personal requirements of the owner.

Actual Cash Value

The price in terms of cash or other precisely revealed terms that would be necessary to replace a property with another of similar age, quality, origin, appearance, size and condition within a reasonable length of time in an appropriate and relevant market. This definition encompasses the concept of "as is" or "with or without restoration." It is the market value of a property, plus appreciation or less all forms of depreciation.

Appropriate Market Levels

Personal property is commonly bought and sold in or at several market levels depending on the quantity, quality and condition of the property. The purpose and function of the appraisal determines the appropriate market that an appraiser analyzes and reports on, relevant to the subject property at auction, wholesale, retail and liquidation.

Implied in the definitions of Fair Market Value and of Market Value, is the fact that the appraiser knows the appropriate and relevant market level at which a property changes hands under certain circumstances.

The concept of Appropriate Market Level is the corollary in the personal property appraisal discipline to the concept of Highest and Best Use in the discipline of real property appraisal.

The following are definitions of the major market levels:

Immediate Cash Liquidation Market Level

This represents a market in which similar property is regularly sold, for immediate cash, to willing buyers within a very limited time. The buyers typically are antique dealers, auctioneers, auction houses, secondhand dealers, jobbers, wholesalers. Immediate Cash Liquidation Market Level represents a bargain or distress market level.

Major Auction Liquidation Market Level

This represents the most frequently realized price level at major auction, including the buyer and seller premium.

Minor Auction Liquidation Market Level

This represents the most frequently realized price level at a minor regional auction, including the buyer and seller premium.

Orderly Cash Liquidation Market Level

This represents a market in which similar property is regularly sold to willing buyers with time constraints, but in an orderly and advertised manner. This includes, but is not limited to, auctions, auction houses, advertised house, shop, and gallery sales. The buyers typically are antique dealers, secondhand dealers, jobbers, wholesales, collectors.

Retail Market Level

This is the most common retail price at which specific property(ies) and property types are offered for sale in a geographical region.

Wholesale Market Level

This is the price at which wholesalers can buy from the market or sell property to the trade.

3

Chapter 2

Ethical Standards of Professional Appraisal Practice

Introduction

What is Ethics?

The word **ethics** derives from the Greek word *ethos*, which means character or disposition. Contemporary dictionaries define **ethics** as a system of moral principles or values; principles of right or good behavior; study of the general nature of morals and the specific moral choices an individual makes in relating to others; rules or standards of conduct governing the members of a profession.

The essential element of these definitions is value structure and its relation to human behavior. Value structure informs and guides judgment and action. As judgment and action are at the core of human existence, the need for understanding and applying ethics is tremendously important.

What is the Relevance of Ethics and Standards to Professional Appraisal Practice?

John Alico, FASA, in his article "Appraisal Ethics," recognizes the appraiser's prime concern as the estimation of value and the importance of judgment in that estimation. That judgment is informed and guided by ethics and standards.

Furthermore, professional appraisal ethics go beyond rules, obligations, sanctions and discipline. They are a statement of identity, reflecting the changes in appraisal practice that have transformed the vocation from a business occupation to a profession.

Discussion of Ethics and Standards

The intent of this discussion is to articulate in a general way, ethics and standards which inform and guide contemporary professional appraisal practice. This ethical framework is introduced in three sections. The first two sections originate from a point of view within the appraisal profession and focus upon two major value structures: the revised *Principles of Appraisal Practice and Code of Ethics* of the American Society of Appraisers and the Appraisal Foundation's *Uniform Standards of Professional Appraisal Practice*. The final section originates from a legal point of view and addresses the implications of professional ethics, codes of ethics and the appraiser-client relationship.

All three sections emphasize the professional character of contemporary appraisal practice and the continuing challenge to exercise the highest professional and personal judgment in performance of that work.

An Introduction To And Synopsis of the ASA *Principles of Appraisal Practice and Code of Ethics*

What are the *Principles of Appraisal Practice and Code of Ethics*?

The revised *Principles of Appraisal Practice and Code of Ethics* are a set of **authoritative** appraisal **principles** and **code of ethics** specifically designed to address the appraisal of "...all classes of property as well as the complexities of the various appraisal procedures." This broad scope reflects the Society's multi-disciplinary concern with all areas of appraising as well as its pro-bono, public and professional interests.

What are the Goals of Putting Forth the *Principles of Appraisal Practice and Code of Ethics*?

The goals of promulgating the *Principles of Appraisal Practice and Code of Ethics* derive in a straightforward way from ASA's professional orientation and structure. The essential elements that characterize a profession and distinguish it from a trade are (1) a shared body of knowledge, (2) specialized education and training and (3) a code of ethics.

Consequently, the *Principles of Appraisal Practice and Code of Ethics* serve to: (1) articulate the common definitions, theory, objectives, duties and responsibilities of appraisal work; (2) educate and guide practicing appraisers to achieving and increasing competence; and (3) inform and guide both practicing appraisers and the public as to what constitutes ethical conduct and provide for enforcement of that conduct.

Organization of the *Principles of Appraisal Practice and Code of Ethics*

An awareness of the organization of the *Principles of Appraisal Practice and Code of Ethics* can be very helpful in understanding and applying this document as a working reference in daily appraisal practice.

Sections 1 and 2: Basic Theory

Sections 1 and 2, **Introduction** and **Objectives of Appraisal Work** are basic and theoretical — the "what" and "why" of appraisal work. Section 1.2 provides concise definitions of property and appraisal practice; Section 2 provides the objectives and unbiased character of that work. Importantly, practice and its objectives, "the what and the why" of appraisal work, are defined in terms of the classic approaches to valuation.

Sections 3, 4 and 5: The Appraiser's Duty, Responsibilities and Obligations

Sections 3, 4 and 5 articulate the appraiser's duty, responsibilities and obligations. To understand the relation of these essential elements to practice, a visual image can be helpful. This image is that of a radiating, ring pattern created by a stone dropped into a smooth pool of water, with the rings representing levels of the appraiser's duty, responsibilities and obligations.

These responsibilities begin with the primary elements of appraisal practice, the appraisal assignment itself, and extend to the appraiser's relationship to the client, to other appraisers and ultimately to society at large.

Section 3 defines the **Appraiser's Primary Duty and Responsibilities,** which are the basic elements of appraisal practice: to determine and describe the apposite value/cost with competence and due diligence, ethically and with an awareness of fiduciary responsibilities.

Section 4 details the **Appraiser's Obligations to the Client** of confidentiality, competent service, honest testimony and good faith dealing.

Section 5 is directed to the **Appraiser's Obligations to Other Appraisers and Society** to protect the reputation of other professionals and report breeches of ethical conduct.

Sections 6 and 7: (Recognized) Appraisal Methods and Practices v. Unethical and Unprofessional Appraisal Practices

Sections 6 and 7 cover the principles, methods and considerations of appraisal practice and present those elements in strongly contrasting ways. In fact, the sections can be thought of as polar opposites.

Section 6 focuses on those recognized principles, methods and considerations **to be employed** in developing a valid appraisal. These include selection of the appropriate type of value and methodology, as well as consideration of the scope, required expertise and limiting context of the assignment.

Section 7 follows with focus on unethical appraisal practices **to be avoided** in order to establish and maintain client and public trust. Contingent and percentage fees, advocacy, negligence, misleading advertising and misrepresentation of appraiser credentials or responsibility for work invoke censure and potential discipline by the Society.

Section 8: Conclusion: (Components of a Complete) Appraisal Report — The Principles of Appraisal Practice and Code of Ethics *as a Working Reference*

Section 8 concludes the *Principles of Appraisal Practice and Code of Ethics* and summarizes the clear communication of the complete appraisal process that must characterize every appraisal report. Its outline — which specifies descriptions, statements and explanations of the property, objective of the appraisal, limiting context, appraisal method and appraiser disinterestedness, credentials and signature — is a working reference, a checklist to be applied to any report by the thorough appraiser.

NOTE: See **Appendix 1**-"Appraisal Ethics" and **Appendix 2**-*Principles of Appraisal Practice and Code of Ethics* for further discussion and/or clarification.

An Introduction To and Synopsis of the *Uniform Standards of Professional Appraisal Practice* of The Appraisal Foundation

What are the *Uniform Standards of Professional Appraisal Practice?*

The *Uniform Standards of Professional Appraisal Practice (USPAP)* are a comprehensive set of standards that inform and guide the attitude and concept of contemporary professional appraisal practice. The standards specifically address procedures to be followed in the development and performance of an appraisal, review or consulting service, as well as the manner in which the results of that process, an appraisal, review or consulting service, are communicated.

What are the Goals of Putting Forth the *Uniform Standards of Professional Appraisal Practice?*

The purpose of the *USPAP* is to serve as a guideline for appraisers to maintain and practice the highest level of valuation and consulting services and to provide consumers and the public with the means to measure competence and compliance with professional standards. These standards apply to written and oral valuation as well as appraisal review and consulting services for all appraisers and appraisals prepared by candidates and designated members of the American Society of Appraisers.

Contemporary appraisal practice can no longer be defended by the appraiser's statement: "I'm the expert, so trust me." Competent appraisal practice demands documented explanation of what is to be valued, why, and how, in addition to a clearly interpreted result. The beginning appraiser often asks, "Where can I get samples or a guide to writing a good report?" The seasoned appraiser asks, "What can I do so that my report is not misused, misinterpreted, or used for an unintended purpose?" *USPAP* assists and directs both appraisers by providing specific, legally accepted definitions, rules and methodology under which reports are to be prepared.

Origin, Development and On-going Revision of the *Uniform Standards*

The *Uniform Standards of Professional Appraisal Practice* were developed by the Ad Hoc Committee of the Appraisal Foundation, composed of eight nationally recognized American appraisal organizations and one nationally recognized Canadian appraisal organization. *USPAP* is not a static document, nor was it ever intended

to be. The *Uniform Standards* have been reviewed and amended on a regular basis since their inception in 1987 by the Appraisal Standards Board (ASB) of the Appraisal Foundation. With the benefit of input from practitioners, users, and other interested parties, the ASB regularly amends the *Uniform Standards* to assist practitioners and consumers of valuation services. The Standards Board further issues Statements on Appraisal Standards for the express purpose of clarification, interpretation and elaboration of the *Uniform Standards,* as well as Advisory Opinions, which are designed to help the professional practitioner by illustrating the applicability of the Standards in specific situations involving appraisal issues and problems. The *Uniform Standards of Professional Appraisal Practice* are published annually in January, with a mid-year supplement published in July. The ASB developed an internal operating policy establishing effective dates for revisions to the *USPAP*. The policy calls for revisions adopted between each period beginning October 1 and ending September 30 to become effective on the next January 1. A copy of the current edition of *USPAP* may be obtained by contacting The Appraisal Foundation, Suite 900, 1029 Vermont Avenue, N.W., Washington, D.C. 20005, phone (202)347-7722.

How are the *Uniform Standards of Professional Appraisal Practice* organized?

An awareness of the organization of the *Uniform Standards* can be helpful in understanding and applying this document as a working reference in daily appraisal practice. The Standards are set forth in ten rules, prefaced by Provisions and followed by Opinions.

Preamble: Standards Outline and Purpose

The **Preamble** acknowledges the necessary ethical context of appraisal work and outlines the organization of the *Uniform Standards.* That organization reflects the dual concerns that characterize all professional appraisal practice: **process** and **communication**. Consequently, all of the *Standards,* regardless of their specific applicability to a particular appraisal discipline or problem, are presented in a **consistent** manner, emphasizing procedures to be followed in the development of a credible appraisal as well as the way in which the results of that process are reported.

Ethics, Competency and Departure Provisions

Consistent with the importance of the fiduciary responsibilities in appraisal practice, the *Uniform Stan-*

dards begin with an **Ethics Provision.** This provision focuses upon the personal obligations and responsibilities of the appraiser; issues of integrity, objectivity, independent judgment and ethical conduct. It mandates disclosure of the total context of an appraisal assignment, including appraiser interest in the property, non-contingent fees, confidentiality and adequate record keeping. (See Appendix 3.)

A **Competency Provision** follows, situated in the *Uniform Standards* in a way which reflects its immediate responsibility upon the appraiser prior to acceptance of an assignment. Again, disclosure is the operative mandate — disclosure of the limits of appraiser's expertise, as well as steps taken to address those limits and competently complete the assignment.

A **Departure Provision** is also in place, applicable to standards that are classified as specific guidelines rather than binding requirements. This provision allows appraisers to perform an assignment of limited scope, which differs or departs from a specific appraisal guideline, under limited circumstances. It mandates disclosure and extreme caution in determining that the appraisal process and resulting conclusions are not compromised by the limited scope.

Definitions are the shared vocabulary of the profession. While framed from a real property perspective, these are clustered around three subjects: appraising (and its spin-offs, review and consulting), property, and value. Of particular interest to the personal property appraiser is the robust definition of market value with its temporal and financing nuances.

Standards 1-6 deal with the development and communication of credible real property, review, consulting service and mass/ad valorem appraisals. Again, these Standards employ the dual concern structure of emphasizing procedures to be followed in the development of a credible appraisal as well as the manner in which the results of that process are reported. These same issues are addressed from the perspective of personal property appraisal practice in **Standards 7 and 8.** However, it is important to realize that "Personal Property" **Standards 7 and 8** are modeled upon — and contain deliberate, specific references and parallels to — Standards 1-2.

Standard 7 is a restatement of **Standard 1**'s binding requirements of appraisal practice in a personal property context. **Standards Rule (S.R.) 7-1** mandates professional competence in the execution of a personal property appraisal assignment; **S.R. 7-2**, consideration of the appraisal purpose, intended use, appropriate value and valuation method, adequate scope and diligence; **S.R. 7-**

3, relevant issues to be considered in developing a personal property appraisal, including "highest and best" (most appropriate) use of property, market selection and value enhancements or reductions such as maker, materials, quality, condition, origin, age, rarity, provenance, alteration or restoration, etc.

Standard 8 articulates the binding requirements of a personal property appraisal report which clearly summarizes the appraisal problem, process and result. **Standards Rule 8-2** mandates:

- Descriptive identification of the property being appraised
- Identification of the ownership (whether whole or fractional interest) in the property being appraised
- Statement of purpose and intended use of the appraisal
- Definition of value (consistent with stated purpose and intended use)
- Effective date of value and the date report was prepared
- Description of the scope of the appraisal (extent of the collection, confirmation and reporting of data)
- Assumptions and limiting conditions
- Information, appraisal procedures, reasoning that supports the analyses, opinions, and conclusions
- Appropriate comparable sales data, auction results, offers or other statistics
- Explanation and support of the appropriate market
- Highest and Best use; explanation and support placing the subject property within its most appropriate market context
- Explanation and support of the appropriate market
- Explanation and support of exclusion of usual valuation approaches where exclusion is appropriate to the appraisal problem
- Additional information in compliance with permitted departures from **Standard 7.** The answer to the question: "Can I perform appraisals with less than the minimum requirements?" is yes, when done in compliance with the very limited exceptions detailed in the **Departure Provision** and with **full disclosure** of departure from the Standards.
- Signed certification

The above outline encapsulates in checklist form, the binding requirements of all appraisal reports, both written and oral. These minimum requirements are what separates a thorough, supportable appraisal from an incomplete report which is subject to misinterpretation, misuse or use for unintended purposes.

Standards 9 and 10 deal with the development and communication of an appraisal of a business. Again, these standards employ the dual concern structure of emphasizing procedures to be followed in the development of a credible appraisal, as well as the manner in which the results of the process are reported.

Conclusion — *USPAP* Personal Property Standards — An Acceptable Language and Defensible Methodology of Valuation

Appraisals are written or oral reports which communicate value. The descriptions of the appraised property, type of value, and limiting conditions of the value must be understood by **all**, and therefore must be uniform in basis. Valuation terminology must have as its basis common understanding, meaning, and legal acceptability. Appraisers become quickly aware of the clarity of their communication when clients question, challenge and request additional explanation and support. Consequently, the professional appraiser must be precise in defining and qualifying the value required for an assignment. Some say the final test is in the courtroom, where the appraiser defends what was valued. In that adversarial arena, the most defensible work is an appraisal which is characterized by the competence, diligence and clarity that the court expects and *USPAP* has adopted.

As a result of its standards, qualifications, and advisory boards, the Appraisal Foundation has become the recognized valuation profession authority. Appraisers have come to rely upon the *Uniform Standards of Professional Practice* as a guideline to superior valuation practice, a useful tool to educate users of valuation services and a persuasive counter to pressure to perform in a less than objective manner. Adherence of all appraisers, affiliated and unaffiliated, to *Uniform Standards* is one of the profession's greatest challenges and goals. Appraisers who adopt the letter and spirit of the *Uniform Standards of Professional Appraisal Practice* will find the answer to the question, "How can I achieve the recognition and acceptance of my appraisal work?"

The ASA Code of Ethics and the Appraiser-Client Relationship

© 1994 by Jessica L. Darraby, J.D.

What is a Code of Ethics?

A code of ethics establishes professional or organizational guidelines for minimum standards of conduct below which no subscribing member may fall without violating basic group tenets and incurring potential censure. The degree to which codes are enforced and the extent to which penalties are imposed affects the maintenance of group standards and public expectations about identifiable group professionalism.

A Code of Ethics is a Guide

The principles and standards established in a code of ethics serve as general minimum guidelines to members regarding their conduct with clients and others in terms of both performance and communication. It is incumbent upon professionals to conform their conduct to those principles by exercising judgment and discretion in the exercise of their practice and other tasks.

Performance

Professionalism is predicated upon the notion that those with education and training have the superior skills to make informed judgments in their area of specialty. However, the professional cannot simply rely upon the words of a code of ethics in performing professional services. The professional must interpret the meaning and import of a code of ethics and apply that understanding to the particular facts and circumstances of each situation in the context of his or her experience and training.

Communication

Consistent with the *Principles of Appraisal Practice and the Code of Ethics* of the ASA, the appraiser has the responsibility to communicate candidly with the client. Timely and informed communication enhances the appraiser-client relationship, reduces the possibility of legal exposure and may have the added benefit of stimulating new business. Communication, like performance, involves the exercise of judgment.

The ASA *Code of Ethics* Does Not Substitute for Personal Ethics

What should be emphasized at the outset is that neither ASA's *Code of Ethics* nor any legal standard for professional conduct substitutes for an appraiser's moral integrity, personal ethics and professional rigor in the performance of his or her services and the treatment of clients and others. There is neither an organization nor a law that can truly measure the propriety of professional conduct. Consequently, codes of ethics are typically viewed as minimum standards; professionals are expected to act in accord with the highest personal principles, which may well exceed those expressed in a code of ethics.

Compliance with the ASA *Code of Ethics* Does Not Provide Exemption from Legal Process

Acknowledging that the ASA *Code of Ethics* is the repository for principles subject to interpretation by individual appraisers, it should not be surprising that interpretations are subject to interpretation. To determine whether a violation of the ASA *Code of Ethics* has occurred, those charged with enforcement will ask: Did the appraiser act in accordance with the principles, or deviate sufficiently to invoke censure? As stated above, this is the basis upon which ASA and other organizations regulate the conduct of members.

However, it is important to realize that a professional code of ethics is not necessarily the legal standard by which that complex process of professional conduct is evaluated in the event a client files a legal action in court against an appraiser. This is one of the most misunderstood aspects of appraisal ethics, and it is here discussed.

The Appraiser as Professional, A Legal View

What is a Professional?

From a legal perspective, a professional is distinguished from a trade or business person in that its professionals have the following characteristics and attributes: acquisition of extensive formal training; admission to practice by qualifying licensure; regulation by codes of ethics imposing high standards of conduct beyond those that prevail in the marketplace; duties to subordinate financial rewards for social responsibility; obligations to act in professional, and even in nonprofessional matters, as members of a learned, disciplined and honorable occupation.

Are ASA Appraisers Professionals for Legal Purposes?

The ASA unequivocally presents itself as a professional organization. The ASA *Code of Ethics* acknowledges the fiduciary relationship that exists between the appraiser and the client, who relies upon the appraiser's findings and conclusions. ASA members induce clients to repose trust in them based upon their distinctive expertise exemplified by ASA's testing and accreditation.

Accreditation, practice of superior skills and exercise of expertise occur within a subset of appraisal disciplines: real property, personal property, gems and jewelry, machinery and equipment, business and technical valuation. Further, within the disciplines there exist additional areas of specialty, e.g., within personal property there are fine arts, decorative arts, residential contents, etc.

Although all ASA appraisers are bound by the same *Code of Ethics*, there exists, at present, one appraisal discipline that is licensed at the state level and others that are not. Real property appraisers have been held professionals prior to enactment of FIRREA, the federal statute which provides a federalized standard of care in real property appraisal and a system of state licensure for real property appraisers. No reported case to date classifies personal property appraisers, who are not subject to state licensure, as **professionals** per se. However, all appraisers in ASA are bound by the standards of the *Uniform Standards of Professional Appraisal Practice*.

Standard of Care to Which a Professional is Held

All persons ordinarily owe a duty of reasonable care to avoid foreseeable injury to others. Breach of that duty which proximately causes damage is the basis for tort liability. In summary, the standard of care is tested by what a reasonable person would do in like circumstances.

However professionals, by virtue of their special skill and expertise, are held to a higher standard of reasonable care. Professionals are bound to use skill and care in the performance of duties commensurate with the standards and requirements of their profession and specialty. In summary, the standard of care is **not** what an ordinary, reasonable person would do, but rather what another reasonable professional with comparable standing, skill and experience would do in like circumstances.

Distinction Among Appraisal Disciplines Does Not Affect the Duty of Care

The fact that some appraisers are licensed and others are not does not affect the duty of care owed by all appraisers to their clients. All appraisers are held to the higher standard of care the law applies to those who hold themselves out to the public as having the superior skills and training of professionals.

How is the "Reasonable Appraiser" Standard of Care Applied?

Thus all ASA appraisers, realty and personalty, are subject to the "reasonable appraiser" standard: What would a reasonable appraiser with comparable standing, skill and experience do in like circumstances? The comparability of skills turns upon the degree of expertise the appraiser has as well as the manner in which that expertise has been presented to and understood by the client. The law applies this standard in the following, hierarchical way:

Legal Hierarchies of Applicable Standards

The law attaches a hierarchical standard to the expert based upon his or her presentation of skills and knowledge, and tests that presentation upon persons who are similarly situated, with comparable backgrounds.

An appraiser who purports to have no particular specialty is held to a minimum standard of basic knowledge and skill within the general field of appraisal. The "reasonable appraiser" would be a comparably situated generalist appraiser. An appraiser who purports to specialize is held to a higher standard of specialized knowledge and skills. The "reasonable appraiser" would be a comparably situated specialty appraiser, e.g., fine arts. Obviously, the above standards are simplifications; the actual standards applied are meaningful only when interpreted by the court under the facts and circumstances of each particular case.

Duties of Competence Require Specialized Training for Specialized Work

Duties of competence, both ethically and at common law, weigh against undertaking specialized appraisals in the absence of specialized skills. There are instances, however, where the client reposes trust in an appraiser and wants that appraiser to do the work irrespective of his or her qualifications. Those situations are fraught with legal and ethical considerations. The law permits appraisers to limit their expertise. However, it becomes

a "question of fact" at trial as to whether or not the client understood those limitations, as well as a "matter of law" as to whether or not such limitations will be upheld.

How Legal Standards are Presented in Courts of Law

To determine the "reasonable appraiser" standard, testimonial and oral evidence is presented. Evidence offered may or may not be admitted; if admitted, it may be limited as to purpose and value.

Testimonial Evidence

To prove the reasonable appraiser standard, other appraisers may be called as witnesses to testify about what they and other appraisers would do under like facts and circumstances. Witnesses may be asked to testify about ethical standards of appraisers, based upon their experience and codes of ethics. The opposing party has the right to object to testimony itself as well as to admission into evidence of codes of ethics. If admitted, the opposing party can still attempt to limit the purposes for which codes of ethics will be used.

Material Evidence

In addition to witness testimony, documents are offered by the litigants in the form of material evidence. A code of ethics can be an important item of evidence if admitted, but how does it affect evaluation of the appraiser's standard of care toward his or her client? Once again the issue of licensed professionals requires separate analysis.

A Code of Ethics as a Matter of Evidence

What is the evidentiary value of a code of ethics? Codes of ethics have been deemed relevant to show related industry standards of conduct and to provide examples of what conduct is appropriate. Codes of ethics may also be a clear enunciation of the specific standard of care applicable to a particular defendant. Where professional licensure exists, courts have held that codes of ethics establish specific standards. Where professional licensure does not exist, or exists but does not apply to the particular defendant, codes of ethics may be limited to examples of standards but not the sole standard of care.

Conclusion

How should an appraiser regard his or her obligations to the client and consider the ASA *Principles of*

Appraisal Practice and Code of Ethics in terms of discharging those obligations? The professional standards in the ASA *Code of Ethics* are one of many aspects of a multi-dimensional appraiser-client relationship involving trust, competence, diligence, communication and respect. The relationship triggers legal, ethical and moral considerations.

The ASA *Code of Ethics* provides guidelines of minimum standards for the appraisal profession, and no member should fall below those standards. Whether the ASA *Code of Ethics* will be evidentiary of a sole standard of care or limited to one example of many appraisal standards is, as yet, undecided by the courts.

Even if the evidentiary value of codes of ethics is clarified by future judicial decisions, appraisers should be aware that ethical codes and legal standards are aspects of the appraiser-client relationship but not its absolute determinants. The totality of the appraiser-client relationship turns upon the exercise of personal and professional judgment and ethics in the context of each appraisal assignment.

Chapter 3
Established Principles and Methods of Valuation

Theory and Principles

Appraising is both multi-disciplinary and inter-disciplinary. The final intent of any appraisal assignment is to obtain an apposite value conclusion. Valuation is a process concluding in an apposite value based on principles and concepts that are derived from economic theory. There are also traditional approaches and market trade levels of value that come to us through personal property and real estate tradition. Appraisal methodology, as contemporary economic theory, focuses on short and long run market activity and forces. An analysis of appraisal facts leads to a considered apposite opinion of value, and that opinion is treated as professional insofar as it reflects the principles and concepts which influence the market.

The valuation process involves several stages: 1) identification; 2) description; and 3) analysis. Once the subject property is identified and fully described, the appraiser asks several questions: 1) what are its quality features; 2) how does the market react to these features; 3) how is the property related to similar or comparable properties; and 4) how does the appropriate market, or buyers within a market, react to the specific value elements of this property? When all these questions have been answered, an approach to valuing is chosen and applied. The facts are analyzed and a conclusion is reached based upon those facts.

Economic theory suggests that all value concepts fall into one of two general categories — **Value In Use** or **Value In Exchange**. Economic decisions are necessarily tied to how much a buyer is willing to pay (exchange) for the anticipated benefits of ownership.

Value In Use is the value of a property reflecting value to a particular user, recognizing the extent to which the property contributes to the personal requirements of the owner. It is a general category for ways of using things to derive benefits which may be monetary and/or non-monetary. One person may like or want something more than another thing; the same thing may be of more value to someone in one place than another place and at one time over another time.

Value In Exchange is the amount of money or things one can receive for a property. It is usually lower than a purchase price new, i.e., new sofa versus a used sofa. However, it can be more than an original investment, particularly in instances of fine and decorative arts.

Value In Exchange in economic terms means not only that the property is desirable but also implies that its supply is somehow limited. This interaction of the marketplace fulfills the accepted laws of economics, specifically that of supply and demand.

Supply is the amount of a thing that sellers are willing to sell at a given time and price. **Demand** is what buyers are willing and able to pay to possess something. The Law of Supply and Demand governs all market transactions everywhere and at all times as markets seek a balance.

Principles of Value

All principles of value work collectively rather than singly on any particular property. Each focuses on an aspect of the social mechanism which creates and/or influences value. Principles of value are generally grouped in three major divisions, as they apply to 1) market, 2) productivity and 3) identification. Those factors that apply to market help appraisers understand the traditional market and cost approaches to value more thoroughly, whereas those that apply to productivity help in understanding the traditional income approach to value. Finally there are the principles that apply to the property itself, called identification.

Market Related Principles

Market principles are a specific concern to personal property appraisers and include: Progression and Regression, Utility, Substitution, Supply and Demand, Conformity, Change and Competition.

Principle of Progression and Regression states that the value of a property placed in the context of either higher or lesser valued properties will increase or decrease respectively, by association. Lower valued properties generally benefit or increase in value from association with higher valued properties. Higher valued properties tend to suffer or decrease in value when placed in proximity with lower valued properties.

An example of progression would include a major auction offering cookie jars, which sell high in keeping with the overall rhythm and quality of the auction; as a consequence, cookie jars nationwide, of various qualities, would in general subsequently enjoy an increase in value. If a trade magazine features peanut butter jars, then local antique shops may find an audience for the same merchandise they have had on hand for years. An example of regression would be a flea market that will not attract an audience for highly valuable properties. In such an environment highly valuable items suffer in close proximity with much less valuable properties. This principle is related to conformity and helps one with analysis of sales within a market place.

The principle of Marginal Utility states that utils of satisfaction decrease as consumption increases. The more one has of something the more the desire for it decreases. Conversely, the less one has of something the more the desire. A thirsty desert traveler would pay almost anything for that first bottle of water. How much they would pay for a second one would depend upon how much water is needed to get back home. Upon reaching a location with an abundance of water, the traveler would pay much less. So we see then that economic value is related to availability, as well as to what the market will bear.

Once a collector has a fine example of a particular type of property, such as an eighteenth century Philadelphia mahogany Chippendale side chair, he will usually be less eager to buy a second example. Once a collector has fine examples of several eighteenth century Philadelphia pieces of furniture, he will have a decreased interest in acquiring any more. Marginal utility also has to do with additional satisfaction, and there is a strong relationship between scarcity, marginal utility and economic value.

Principle of Substitution states that the value of a replacement property is dictated by the value of an equally desirable substitute property. This principle recognizes that when a property can be easily replaced by another, the value of such property tends to be set by the cost of obtaining an equally desirable substitute property. No prudent buyer is going to pay more for what they consider almost the same thing. Therefore, the one with the lowest price will be in the greatest demand.

A woman who desires and can afford designer jewelry will not buy a reproduction at a lower price. However, she will not pay more for designer jewelry than the price at the local outlet store. "Equally desirable" is the key phrase. Substitution is a principle for comparison that is basic to all approaches to value. This principle drives buyers.

Principle of Supply and Demand states that markets seek a balance between supply — the amount of a thing that sellers are willing to sell at a given price, and demand — what buyers are willing and able to buy. Reiterating, this principle governs all market transactions and is closely related to marginal utility and scarcity.

Principle of Conformity states that value is created and sustained when the characteristics of a property are similar to those demanded by its markets. This principle basically has to do with trends, cycles and general market attitudes. This is particularly true in stable middle markets of decorator antiques and collectibles. In high value properties and materials and in high demand markets, conformity is of less importance. This principle of conformity aids or assists in the analyzing of sales in the marketplace.

Principle of Change states that the choices and actions of consumers, producers, valuators, financiers and people in general continually affect and alter markets. Change is the market principle which recognizes the shifting importance of other principles. It recognizes the interplay of progression and regression, contribution, and competition, thus explaining the cycles of market development, stabilization, decline and renewal.

Principle of Competition states that competition arises from profits and that the reverse is true, i.e., profits create competition. Market demand generates profit, and profits generate competition. Excess profit breeds ruinous competition and that competition dissipates excess profit. The first dealers interested in a new collectible, such as lunch pails in the 1950s, could buy their inventory for very little and make a high profit in selling them. Once other dealers became interested, the cost of inventory became higher, and, with this added competition, profits decreased. Competition reflects supply and demand in all markets.

Productivity Related Principles

Principles of value related to productivity include Anticipation, Surplus Productivity, Highest and Best Use, Increasing and Decreasing Returns, and Production.

Principle of Anticipation states that value is created by the anticipation of the benefits of ownership. All property has a value related to its expected or anticipated use and anticipated benefits of that use and ownership. These benefits can be intangible or tangible. Intangible benefits are often the case with collectibles or the fine and decorative arts. The perceived status of owning certain things drives buyers and markets. Tangible benefits are usually associated with future appreciation in value, explaining why condition is such a strong factor in value.

Principle of Surplus Productivity states that the production left over after a balance between supply and demand is achieved has no value. Balance in productivity is the point where additional expenditure will not add to value.

Artists understand supply and demand, holding surplus works off the market or even destroying them in an attempt to control supply and thus create demand. The expense to create a larger edition of a print will not add value to an inventory if there is no demand for the additional supply. Demand adds value.

Highest and Best Use of a property is the reasonable, probable, feasible and legal use of a property which results in its highest value. For personal property, this often is purchase or sale in the most appropriate market.

This principle recognizes the scope of exposure and the full range of possibilities. An old brooch with several small gemstones and a large mine-cut diamond often will be purchased by a jeweler and dismantled. The small gemstones will be sold off separately; the gold setting will be melted down; and the diamond will be re-cut as a smaller yet more desirable brilliant stone. The gold will be cast in a new mount for a diamond and, when sold, all this results in a considerable profit. One must always consider highest and best use in selecting a market layer relevant to a valuation assignment. A Remington bronze will sell for more in New York at a well-advertised major auction than at a local Mid-Western auction. Utilitarian household goods will sell best at a local tag sale. Personal property is portable and has many different market levels

and values. Highest and best use determines the appropriate market level.

Principle of Increasing and Decreasing Returns states that additional units of production, consumption or investment create an increase in returns or income at first, but eventually at a decreasing rate. A dealer will not buy a chair for $1,000 that is in need of repairs that will cost $2,000 if the probable resale value is $3,000. A prudent collector will not restore, reline and reframe a $1,000 painting at a cost that is more than the painting will be worth. This principle is closely related to that of surplus productivity. There is a point of balance beyond which additional improvement or expenditures will not add to value.

Principle of Agents of Production states that all production results from four agents in balance: Labor, Land or Materials, Capital and Coordination. The loss of balance in any of these makes production inefficient. This principle is basic to the cost approach to value. Labor includes all wages paid except those of upper management. Coordination or upper management is entrepreneurial compensation or commissions. Capital includes construction and equipment costs, material costs, and repayment of loans. Profitability is linked to these being in balance and presupposed demand.

Identification Related Principles

Principles of value relating to identification include contribution, identification and qualitative ranking.

Principle of Contribution states that the value of a component part of a property is the amount it contributes to the value of the whole or the amount by which its absence detracts from the value of the whole. This principle recognizes that comparison between properties that are not exactly the same is possible, and that adjustments can be made. Chippendale chairs with carved knees or carved crests will sell for more than those without, all else being equal.

Principle of Identification states that a genuine article has certain identifying characteristics, traits or marks. If the identifying characteristics of a genuine property match the same characteristics of the subject property, the subject is assumed to be genuine. This principle is a time honored basis for authentication, which is based on previous documentation. Scholarship has documented features of eighteenth century Philadelphia Chippendale chairs allowing identification by carving, construction, size and design. Soft paste porcelain can be identified by its distinguishing features that are different from hard paste porcelain.

Principle of Qualitative Ranking states that a sound opinion of relative quality, or relative value, can be derived from comparison of characteristics and features of the subject property with the corresponding characteristics and features of another property selected as a standard for comparison.

One can rank by quality and value. Usually the characteristics important to quality are important to value and vise-versa, but there may be exceptions. For example, the cookie jars in the Andy Warhol auction realized prices far above the norm for similar quality jars. Provenance was the driving force in this case. In general, however, ranking for good, better, or best is a comparative process that is usually validated in the market by knowledgeable buyers.

Ranking by quality is primarily a question of aesthetic judgment and connoisseurship and is independent of economics and fashion. Ranking by value is primarily a question of fact and has an objective relationship to the marketplace. It is market driven and market generated.

Markets

All principles are derived from the market, meaning not a market as a place or a thing but rather as a concept. The notion of a "perfect market" is an ideal standard. It consists of the following basic elements:

1. existence of numerous buyers and sellers
2. all buyers and sellers who are knowledgeable
3. all buyers and sellers who are free to trade or not trade
4. properties that can be transported to their best market
5. properties that are similar and interchangeable
6. properties that are frequently purchased are small in size and not usually expensive

The most perfect market known is the stock market in which prices cannot be controlled, either by sellers or buyers. Most markets cannot meet the above criteria. We find markets with few sellers, and the sellers then can fix prices. In many markets buyers and/or sellers are unknowledgeable, and therefore imprudent decisions are made. As buyers become more knowledgeable, prices change again. Potential buyers may get information ahead of time and use it to their advantage. An appraiser's responsibility is to interpret and analyze market activity.

In reality most markets are imperfect. Patterns common to imperfect competition are as follows:

1. select or few buyers and sellers
2. buyers and sellers who may or may not be knowledgeable
3. no price competition and barriers to entry and exit
4. properties not transportable, similar or interchangeable
5. properties not purchased in small amounts and may be expensive

In such markets, resources are reallocated in response to supply and demand changes. In general when economists talk about market structure, they are referring to the number and relative sizes of buyers and sellers for specific products and services.

It is critical to any appraisal assignment that the appraiser is knowledgeable concerning the appropriate market for a property. In reality appraisal work is that of reporting the market back to the market.

Creators and Context of Value

The value of a property is affected by the broad forces of Scarcity, Transferability, Utility and Demand.

Scarcity implies there must be somewhat of a limited supply of the product relative to the market demand for it. The principle of scarcity works closely with that of utility.

Transferability is the capacity of any property to change ownership. If a property cannot be sold, demand for it is not effective; thus the property has no market value and is non-marketable and non-transferable.

Economists set a value on properties by measuring the units or utils of satisfaction they generate. If no one wants possession of something, the property has no market value and is not meeting a human want, need or desire. This is known as the principle of Marginal Utility or **Utility**.

To have value, a property must have buyers with the desire to possess it, as well as the financial ability to obtain it, i.e., there must be a **Demand**. Value can be visualized as a table, supported by four legs which represent the above basic elements. To create the condition known as market value, all must be present for an object to have full value. These relationships are complex yet essential, and, while being referred to individually, are inter-related. If this table had only three legs, it would be very unsteady; with two legs it could not stand at all.

These four elements are themselves susceptible to broad economic forces that affect value, specifically political, economical, physical and social forces. **Political forces** include police power, eminent domain, taxation and escheat. Governmental-political-legal actions at all levels, positive or negative, have strong and far-reaching effects on value. The legal climate at any time or place affects the natural forces of supply and demand that create value, as can be seen historically and currently in cultural import laws, the deficit, interest rates, the stock market and regulatory agencies. Specific historic examples include high taxation on mahogany and glass; current examples include import regulations on ivory, emeralds, cultural properties and oil.

The **Economic Force** is a function of the constantly changing "Economic Climate" and its relationship between current and predicted supply and demand conditions and the population's ability to purchase the things it needs, wants and demands. Specific characteristics to be considered are employment opportunities, wage levels, housing and food costs, available credit and interest rates, savings and investment returns, the general state of the economy nationally, internationally and further by geographic area.

Physical or Environmental Forces, man-made or natural, influence value. They can be seen, so they are easier to understand than the other forces. Natural catastrophes, earthquakes, drought, storms and pollution influence value as they physically affect the condition of property.

Natural resources affect personal property as demonstrated historically with coal and wood supplies, and currently with oil supplies. The weather and pollution have most certainly affected the artifacts of the Acropolis. Earthquakes, floods or hurricanes have a devastating result, nationally and internationally, upon market supply and demand, and the geographic location of resources and the cost of recovering them affects value. These and many other forces cause trends which must be taken into account by the appraiser in value analysis.

All social forces affect value. **Social Forces** include characteristics and customs of a people, community or countries and are reported psychographically and demographically. Psychographics or consumer research is the study of factors relating to personality, life style and other values that influence consumer behavior. Demographics or objective market research is the study of economic effects of and changes in characteristics of a population, including size, composition and area of the market and the market's age, sex, income and employment. The demographic composition demonstrates the potential demand of people for specific things. Values are affected by population changes and characteristics as well as by the total spectrum of human activity.

The Process of Valuation

The valuation process should be an orderly, logical procedure answering particular valuation questions and adhering to the structure of a sound argument. Its conclusion is therefore an estimate of value supported by substantial facts. Each valuation question is unique and each valuation conclusion is reached by following specific steps. These steps are presented graphically below and were adapted from *Appraising Real Property* by Boyce and Kinnard, *Fundamentals of Valuation* by Rickert, and are discussed in the fundamental courses of the American Society of Appraisers.

The valuation process is grounded upon economic principles and results in the appraiser's final work product, the Appraisal Document.

The Appraisal Problem

The first task of an appraiser is to clearly and completely understand the appraisal question and valuation issue. Every appraisal is based on the questions to whom, for what reason, when and where. These questions limit and clarify the appraiser's work plan and assignment. This task encompasses the seven steps in Part 1 of the Valuation Process chart.

The first step of this task is to clearly understand the appraisal request in all its complexity. Identify the appraisal issues and property and establish purpose or type of value to be estimated. Consider the effective date of the appraisal and the date of examination. In this step an understanding of the intended use of the appraisal and the terms it will define are considered. The appraisal document enumerates the general and limiting conditions which will affect the assignment; they must be identified at the start of the assignment. Professional fee structure and agreement or understanding with the client should be reached prior to accepting the assignment and followed by a letter of agreement or contract.

Initially, it must be determined what is to be appraised, i.e. oil paintings, Victorian furniture, American art glass, Hummel figurines, an antique gun collection, etc. This determination is a critical part of a work plan and the valuation process. It is critical for the appraiser to evaluate the level of expertise and the qualifications required to appraise the type of property in question.

Secondly, determination must be made of the type of value to be estimated for this particular assignment. What level of value is to be estimated: insurance replacement, donation, estate tax liabilities or liquidation? A new sofa may cost $1,000, but put in a liquidation situation it might sell for only $200. The market level of

Valuation Process Chart

[1] **Define The Appraisal Problem**
   a] Identify the appraisal issue and property
   b] Establish the type of value to be estimated[purpose]
   c] Establish the effective date of appraisal and date of inspection
   d] Establish ownership of the property
   e] Stipulate the intended use of the appraisal and terms of the report
   f] Enumerate other limiting conditions - general and specific
   g] Stipulate fee structure agreement with client

[2] **Plan The Appraisal**
   a] Identify pertinent economic factors
   b] Identify data requirements of market and property
   c] Identify and develop data sources - general and specific
   d] Identify methodology, procedures and bibliography
   e] Design research program
   f] Outline appraisal report
   g] Program work schedule

[3] **Identify The Subject Property**
   a] Description of subject: literal and interpretative
   b] Description of rights to be valued
   c] Application of specific principles of identification, contribution and qualitative ranking
   d] Specification of value-making and unique features
   e] Provenance
   f] Condition

[4] **Data Collection**
   a] General international, national, regional, local market conditions
   b] Economic: trends, projections, demo-/pyschographics
   c] Subject property: appropriate market or highest and best use
   d] Specific: sales, rentals, income

[5] **Analyze Data And Apply The Appropriate Method[s] Of Valuation**
   a] Cost Approach
   b] Market Comparison Approach
   c] Income Approach

[6] **Reconciliation And Final Value Estimate**
   a] Reasonable/logical judgment of facts and circumstances
   b] Weigh data
   c] Weigh approaches

[7] **Value Conclusion**
   a] Determined from the above steps

[8] **The Appraisal Document**
   a] Self-contained, summary or restricted document
   b] Testimony

---

value being sought, as well as the type of property, guides an appraiser to the appropriate marketplace. The type of value and market level is stated as the purpose of the appraisal; they must be given a precise definition within an appraisal report.

Defining the problem necessitates a specific date for the valuation question. The principle of change is ongoing; market trends and cycles are in constant flux. If an appraiser was being asked to estimate the value of a sterling silver tea set as of January 1980, that value would be very different from the same property's value in 1994. At any market level, any appraisal is valid only at a certain point in time

The estimate of replacement value with the intended use for insurance advice differs from the requirements and definition of fair market value with the intended used for estate taxes. The purpose and intended use of the appraisal influences the type of document needed, its length and its scope.

The exact definitions of all valuation terms must be included in a report. The exact definitions 1) frame the document; 2) condition and clarify research decisions concerning the appropriate market, data considered and data not considered; and 3) support the logic of the argument. Definitions are, in fact, general limiting conditions, as is the date of the appraisal. In addition, each appraisal question usually has specific limiting conditions; i.e., was the print examined under glass within a frame; did the appraiser personally inspect the subject property; how was the silver weighed; were kitchen utensils having a cumulative value of under $200 lumped together; was there important information the appraiser was unable to obtain? If any of these or other conditions apply, they should be clearly stated as specific limiting conditions.

The fee structure of an appraisal assignment has important implications. It must be clearly stated in the appraisal report. Any other specific agreements made should also be stated in the report, and the report should include a statement of the appraiser's ethical stance and compliance with the *Uniform Standards of Professional Appraisal Practice*.

Plan the Appraisal

The scope of the appraisal assignment must be previewed in its entirety in order for the completion to reflect the process thoroughly. The steps of the logical argument are generated by gathering facts that lead to an opinion of value. The appraisal plan, description and detail depend on the nature and scope of the specific assignment. Some assignments take only a few hours, others take months to collect all the data needed to analyze and interpret a property or properties and their appropriate market(s). This planning step increases efficiency and accuracy and conforms generally to those steps taken by all researchers. What the assignment is must be previewed in its entirety in order to complete a logical argument for value.

Identification of the Subject Property

In the third step of the valuation process, the subject property must be clearly and accurately identified. The properties being appraised at a particular time should be described in such a way that they are distinguishable from any other similar properties. The vocabulary used by the appraiser must be clear to potential report readers, while still demonstrating familiarity with the material. Literal and interpretive aspects of the description are treated separately in the appraisal report as each elicits specific market responses, especially pertaining to the value-making features and physical condition. In the identification of the subject property, the principles of identification, contribution and qualitative analysis are exercised.

Principle Of Identification, as previously defined, states that if the identifying characteristics of a genuine article have the same characteristics as the subject property, then the subject property is assumed to be genuine. Everything genuine has certain features in common with all other genuine things from the same category; by stating what ought to be there, this principle establishes a norm by saying what a genuine or authentic property is expected to possess. Chairs, for instance, have four legs, a seat and a back. The lack of a back or one of the four legs would alter the "whatness" of a chair and render it a stool instead. All teapots have spouts. Without a spout, there can be no orderly pouring. The "whatness" of the teapot is altered when there is no spout, and it becomes something else. (Babcock 194)

Principle Of Contribution, as previously defined, states that the value of component parts of an subject property depends upon how much the value of their presence contributes to the value of the whole, or how much their absence detracts from the value of the whole. Moreover the Principle of Contribution is interrelated with "identification" and the "whatness" of a thing, but it takes the Principle of Identification and develops it further. Identification establishes the elements of genuineness expected in an authentic piece by creating a kind of "model" against which to measure similarities and dissimilarities and their contribution to the whole. (Babcock 208)

Principle of Qualitative Ranking and Rating, as defined previously, states that appraisers rendering opinions on quality or artistic merit of a property do so by comparing the quality and characteristics of the subject property with those of like properties. The principle states that the quality and characteristics of an appraisal deal with what can be rated, ranked, or graded on a standard scale, such as: excellent, good, average, fair, poor; that is, the rating of the subject property in regard to this qualitative characteristic can be placed in one of these categories. (Babcock 193)

This analysis is useful and effective only when the appraiser possesses the connoisseurship to know a "good" from a "better." The ranking labels can then be linked with the realized prices of other ranked properties to arrive at a more accurate estimate of the subject property's worth, especially when utilizing the market comparison approach to value.

It is with these principles in mind that the appraiser separates rare from common qualities and transmits the difference to the reader, who presumably does not know the subject property or have the appraiser's eye to rank and understand subtle quality differences. In writing an appraisal document an appraiser demonstrates interpretive abilities. Again it must be remembered that these principles are presented as separate entities while, in fact, there is much interdependence and relationship between them through cause and effect.

The Principles of Identification and Contribution require the appraiser to look at components of a whole subject property and come to some general decisions about what attributes to expect to find in such a property. Qualitative Rating brings focus by a weighing and ranking of the quality elements to which the market reacts.

So, to the identification process an appraiser brings a trained eye and a body of art historical knowledge and applies valuation skills in interpreting the marketplace. The data necessary for making a qualitative rating comes from looking at both the subject property and at properties that are identical or equivalent.

Data Collection

An estimate or opinion of value is not a guess but is rather a researched conclusion built on and supported by the facts gathered, analyzed and interpreted from the marketplace. These opinions are often referred to as "market derived facts" and are called market data. They are the glue of an appraisal argument and document. These market data represent the amount and specific kind of data required for a report, depending on the purpose and the subject property. They also include general data from the appropriate market area and level, together with specific market data and prevailing market conditions. This premise in turn investigates the most reasonable, frequent and probable exchange level and location that support the value estimated within the report at the effective date. It generates an opinion based on reasonable and probable data appropriately supported. Most reports require confirmed sales information on properties sold that are comparable with the subject property. Comparable properties are the key element.

This fourth step within the valuation process, data collection, will be addressed in detail in the section on research, and the techniques for location and analyzing specific and general data required for a substantiated document will be fully discussed.

Application of Appropriate Value Estimation Techniques

There are three traditional approaches to value in the appraisal field. While personal property appraisers often utilize only one approach, it is important to have an understanding of all three. The three traditional basic approaches to value include:

1. cost approach
2. market comparison approach
3. income approach

Cost approach basically provides an estimate of the depreciated reproduction, reproduction new, or replacement cost new of property. This approach is grounded in the principle of substitution. No prudent person will pay more for a property than the amount for which they can obtain property of equal desirability and utility. A person will not pay the same amount for a contemporary previously owned diamond that they could obtain it new. The cost approach is particularly valuable in providing a basis for proceeding with another approach to value, especially in determining the marketable cash value of residential contents.

The income or revenue approach to value is applicable to income producing properties. It produces an estimate of present worth of anticipated income. This approach is not practical in the appraisal of properties with no rental market or income potential. It is grounded in the principle of anticipation and uses a process of capitalization to translate an income projection into a present capital value. With this approach, an appraiser researches market attitudes and perceptions prior to critical judgment decisions. The income approach is directly related to investor thinking and motivation. The principle of anticipation is reflected in the present worth of all rights to future benefits accorded to ownership of a property. For example, the print and multiples market reflects this basic value approach with Rockwell prints and Franklin Mint and Boehm limited edition pieces.

An investor in fine arts and antiques would have to anticipate an acceptable return on the investment, as well as a return of the invested funds, in order to justify a claim of "investment." Art objects are not frequently bought and sold on the basis of their income producing potential, the exception being items purchased by a dealer. Since at least the eighteenth century, as Gerald Reitlinger documents in his three-volume work entitled *The Economics of Taste*, certain art has proven consistently both desirable and profitable to collect. However, evidence suggests that, from a purely investment standpoint, art and antiques require a typical holding period of 25 to 30 years before realizing profits comparable to those from other more standard investments, such as stocks and bonds. There are emerging data that indicate playing the investment game requires formidable sums of money focused upon purchasing only the very finest work of a particular artist, period, craftsman or factory.

Unlike the rental market in real estate, the rental market for art and antiques is limited. Most art objects are not analogous to real properties in terms of producing a stream of income over time, thus limiting the use of the income capitalization approach.

The market comparison approach has great weight in the estimate of value in all appraisal work, especially personal property. In market comparison, sales of property similar enough to the subject property to permit detailed comparison are researched and analyzed. Market comparison requires several steps. The first step is to research the appropriate markets to identify similar properties for which pertinent sales, offerings, and listings are available. The second step is to confirm and qualify the prices as to their terms and motivating forces influencing the transaction. The third step compares similar properties and their important attributes to the corresponding features and condition of the property being appraised. Consideration is also given to general factors such as time, location, and conditions of sale. Comparable property as defined by Babcock is a "whole property of the same kind as the subject property and capable of being compared with it." Sometimes the comparable property is actually equivalent to the subject property; other times it is identical. But to be comparable, it does not necessarily have to be either. Different properties can be comparable if their elements or assessable attributes are of like kind. This is the method of value ranking.

Conversely, the fourth step is considering all dissimilarities and their probable effect on the value and how these affect the subject property as a whole. There are no set numbers on the amount of market data required to be utilized in an appraisal report, but the comparables should be described. Thus, from the pattern emerging, one can analyze and arrive at an apposite value being sought.

This approach often has adjustments, and there are techniques for comparing or adjusting market data. Basic procedures would include adjustments in three possible ways: whole property comparison, dollar adjustments, and percentage adjustments. (Babcock 51)

Analysis of market data, adjusted to the property being appraised, is convincing evidence of the appraiser's apposite value estimate. Personal property appraisers most often use the adjusted sales procedure.

The market comparison approach as used in real estate considers current comparable sales of similar properties in the same geographic area. In personal property, the market approach often moves beyond the local scene to the national or international level in order to seek an appropriate market where transactions involving similar properties occur with frequency. Utilization of the principle of highest and best use obliges the appraiser to seek the most relevant and appropriate marketplace.

Comparables used in the appraisal report should be confirmed to determine that they did sell for the published price. It is important for these comparables to reflect the market as close to the valuation date as possible. In special circumstances, it may be necessary to go back further into the market. The appraiser must compensate for this by adjusting the dollar amount for the valuation date.

The comparables must be realistic; if the market reflects an excessive, one-time transaction, this should be eliminated. Comparables from a liquidation sale will reflect duress and should be disqualified if seeking anything other than a liquidation market level.

In conclusion, using the market comparison approach means sifting, analyzing and interpreting the activity of the appropriate marketplace for convincing evidence in the form of actual transactions that reflect the frequency of what consumers in a particular market and at a particular time wanted and were willing to pay for it.

Comparables should be as similar as possible to the subject property, as this strengthens the valuation issue. They can be wholly identical or wholly equivalent to the property in question, but do not have to be either, provided there are common value elements possessed by the subject property and the comparable. For example, the rare exotic bird pattern in Worcester porcelain is an element of value whether it is on a jardiniere or a pair of vases; that element can be compared. Even value elements which are dissimilar can be considered against the model to ascertain the degree to which they enhance or detract from a final value estimate.

For the reader of the appraisal report to feel confident with the comparables selected, the appraiser should describe them thoroughly. As in a physical description of the subject property, description of any comparable should evaluate the rarity, quality, condition, and period of attribution. Once an appraiser has described the degree of similarity or difference between the subject property and the comparables, analysis of data from the patterns identified by comparing the data can be performed.

Factored into these adjustments will be the number of sales which actually transpired, the time span covered by these sales, the typical exposure time for similar objects on the market in that period, the no sales or withdrawn properties, and the instances in which realized price went above or below estimate. The behavior pattern of sellers and buyers toward that class of objects at a particular time will emerge.

Reconciliation and Final Value Estimate

It is at this step in the valuation process that the appraiser in a reasonable and logical manner concludes the final considered opinion of value. If more than one approach to value was used, these approaches are correlated for the final value opinion. This step results in the dollar estimate determined by the methodology prescribed in the above steps.

Value Conclusion

At this point the appraiser presents a professional, researched value conclusion. If all the steps above have been thoroughly accomplished, this conclusion of value is documented and believable to the reader. It is the considered research opinion of a professional appraiser.

The Appraisal Document

The final step in the appraisal process is the written evidence of research and a professional work product. This document represents the appraiser and his appraisal practice. It is prepared for the client and potential third party readers.

An appraisal document leads its reader through its purpose, function, definitions of value used, the approach to value followed, liabilities, specific and general limiting conditions, property(ies) being valued, relevant research, and considered dollar conclusion(s). It is a work product reflecting a logical objective analysis of all relevant facts of the appraisal question or issue using procedures and principles that apply and are communicated in a clear truthful manner. The document can be long, short, detailed or very detailed. The document represents the question asked and the appraiser's professional answer to that question. A research paper consists of standard components, and yet no two are exactly alike. This is also true of an appraisal document.

Personal property report writing places emphasis on the narrative content. For this reason, boiler plates and sample forms can be growth stunting and are not appropriate. The elasticity of the process is lost in a form void of an analytical and interpretive demonstration of the writer's expertise. Often forms stay the same for years, resulting in an appraisal reflecting inventory skills rather than a professional command of valuation methodology and interpretive ability. It is important to understand that an appraiser's signature is implicit of both the conclusive authority of the signer and the professional responsibilities accepted in preparing the report and continuing during the lifetime of the document.

■

Valuation Bibliography

Alico, John et al. ed. *Appraising Machinery & Equipment.* New York: McGraw-Hill, 1989.

Alsop, Joseph. *The Rare Art Traditions.* New York: Princeton/Harper & Row, 1982.

The Appraisal of Real Estate. 10th ed. Chicago, IL: Appraisal Institute, 1992.

Babcock, Henry. *Appraisal Principles & Procedures.* Washington, DC: American Society of Appraisers, 1980.

Barnet, Sylvan. *A Short Guide to Writing About Art.* 3rd ed. New York: Harper Collins, 1989.

Barzun, Jacques & F. Graff. *The Modern Researcher.* 4th ed. New York: Harcourt Brace, 1985.

Barzun, Jacques. *Simple & Direct.* New York: Harper & Row, 1975.

Beasley, David. *How To Use a Research Library.* New York: Oxford University Press, 1988.

Black, Henry C. *Black's Law Dictionary.* 5th ed. St. Paul, MN: West Publishing Co., 1979.

Blackby, James and Patricia Greeno et al. *The Revised Nomenclature for Museum Cataloging.* Nashville, TN: American Association for State and Local History, 1988.

Boulding, Kenneth E. *The Basics of Value Judgments in Economics, Human Values, and Economic Policy: A Symposium.* Sidney Hook (Ed.), New York: New York University Press, 1967.

Bowden, E. V. *Economics.* Cincinnati, OH: Southwestern Publishing Company, 1992.

Cameron, George and Phillip Scaletta. *Business Law.* Plano, TX: Business Publications, 1985.

Commerce Clearing House. *Federal Estate & Gift Taxes Explained.* Chicago, IL: CCH, Annual.

Commerce Clearing House. *IRS Valuation Guide for Income, Estate and Gift Taxes.* Chicago: CCH, 1987.

Duboff, Leonard D. *Art Law.* St. Paul, MN: West, 1984.

Engel, James F. and Roger D. Blackwell. *Consumer Behavior.* Fourth Ed. Chicago: Dryden Press, 1982.

Foreman, R. *Communicating the Appraisal: A Guide to Report Writing.* Chicago: American Institute of Real Estate Appraisers, 1980.

Friedman, Jack. *Income Property Appraisal & Analysis.* Englewood Cliffs, NJ: Prentice-Hall, 1981.

Graphic Artists Guild. *Pricing & Ethical Guidelines.* 4th ed. New York: The Guild, 1982 (30 East 20th Street, NY, NY 10003).

Harrison, Henry H. *Harrison's Illustrated Dictionary of Real Estate Appraisal.* New Haven: Collegiate Distributing, 1986.

Jones, Lois Swan. *Art Information Research Methods and Resources.* 3rd ed. Dubuque, IA: Kendall Hunt, 1990.

Lipsey, Richard, Peter Steiner et al. *Economics.* 9th ed. New York: Harper & Row, 1990.

MacBride, Dexter D., FASA. *Opportunities in Appraisal and Valuation Science.* Washington, D.C.: American Society of Appraisers, 1976.

Reitlinger, Gerald. *The Economics of Taste.* New York: Hacker Art Books, 1982. Three Volumes, Revised.

Rottenberg, Anette. *Elements of Argument.* New York: Saint Martin's, 1985.

Smith, Charles W. *Auctions, The Social Construction of Value.* Berkeley, CA: U. of California, 1990.

Spurgin, Sally D. *The Power to Persuade.* Englewood Cliffs, NJ: Prentice-Hall, 1985.

Weil, Stephen. *Beauty and the Beasts.* Washington, DC: Smithsonian, 1983.

Chapter 4

Technical Competence and Professional Skills

Report Writing

No aspect of the appraiser's vocation is as demanding, no aspect of the appraiser's profession is as important, and no aspect of the appraiser's practice is as significant as composing the appraisal report. It is demanding because it requires the appraiser to articulate the development of the conclusion; it is important because the appraisal records facts and analyses which commit the appraiser to continuing and often unforeseen obligations; and it is significant because the appraisal report places in one document the breadth and capability of the appraiser's expertise.

Two guides are available to the appraiser for the composition of the report; the *Code of Ethics* of the American Society of Appraisers and the *Uniform Standards of Professional Practice* (*USPAP*), promulgated by The Appraisal Foundation. Both of these documents are discussed elsewhere in this handbook. Both are indispensable to understanding the basic features which guide the construction of the appraisal report.

The *Code of Ethics* enumerates the eight requirements of an appraisal report under Section 8 in points 8.1 through 8.8. Those requirements include: 8.1, a description of the property; 8.2, a statement of the objectives of the assignment; 8.3, a statement of contingent and limiting conditions; 8.4, a description of the appraisal method used; 8.5, a statement of the appraiser's disinterestedness; 8.6, a statement of the appraiser's observation of the *Uniform Standards of Professional Appraisal Practice*; 8.7, a statement regarding compliance with the reaccreditation programs of the American Society of Appraisers; and 8.8, the Code's requirement for each appraiser's signature. These requirements are interconnected with the ten points of Section 6 of the *Code* (Appraisal Methods and Practices) and cannot be applied independently.

Similarly, the Standard Rules of *USPAP* governing the practice of the appraisal of personal property, Standard Rules 7 and 8, are interdependent with the Provisions that introduce the *Uniform Standards of Professional Practice* which pertain to ethics, competency and departure from the rules. The introduction to the Standards also includes a statement of Jurisdictional Exception to the Standards which recognizes jurisdictional precedence. While Standard Rule 7 is addressed to the development of an appraisal of personal property, Standard Rule 8 is concerned with the appraisal report. Besides requiring, under Rule 8-1 points (a) through (c) that each report (whether written or oral) not be misleading, contain sufficient information and express extraordinary assumptions or conditions that impact the valuation, the rule also requires, under Rule 8-2 points (a) through (n) that each written appraisal include a description of the property, the identification of the property rights as they are known to the appraiser, a statement of the purpose and intended use, a definition of the value which is consistent with the purpose of the assignment, the effective date of the value, a description of the research process, the limiting conditions which have affected the valuation process and its conclusion, the information used and the reasoning that leads to the conclusion, comparable sales data where appropriate, and also where appropriate, an explanation and support of the concept of **highest and best use** with a description of the **appropriate market** along with a discussion of any exclusion of usual valuation approaches. That rule also requires a statement regarding compliance with or departure from the requirements of Standard 7 and, finally, a signed certification which is outlined under Standard Rule 8-3.

Standard Rule 8-3 requires that each written personal property appraisal report include a set of certifications similar in content to the seven declarations it lists.

These certifications express the appraiser's knowledge and belief in the truth of the statements made in the appraisal, the appraiser's independence in presenting an unbiased conclusion and the appraiser's independence from financial or contingent interests in the subject property — including the fee structure, the appraiser's compliance with the rules of the *Uniform Standards*, the appraiser's personal inspection of the subject property (or not), and finally, the appraiser's own statement of authorship for the appraisal.

While these certifications provide the minimal ground rules for a professional appraisal report, they are not intended to be merely repeated and added to the body of a report as just more "boilerplate." They need to be made alive as part of the fabric of the report and are only useful to the reader if they truly reflect authoritative development by a professional appraiser. Indeed, a repetitive list of certifications which do not have their basis in the report proper might raise questions regarding the appraisal process and the reliability of its conclusion.

Therefore, the guidelines of the Code of Ethics and of the Uniform Standards of Professional Appraisal Practice cannot be looked to as a paradigm. Rather — and together — they are constant and useful reminders of the interdependence of each section of the appraisal. For example, the purpose of a report must be explained in relationship to its use, and the use must be defined in a logical relationship with the type of value defined. The definition of the type of value must be connected in some vital way to the explanation of the method by which the conclusion was developed; the definition of value, particularly in those instances where the value is designated as "Fair Market Value," must be explained in relationship to the concepts of highest and best use, meaning the scope and mechanics of the relevant market. When composed in this manner the appraisal report is not just a rehearsal of a set of lifeless formulas (form without content). Instead, the professional appraisal report is a demonstration of the lively process through which a professional practitioner has exercised particular skills and expertise. The demonstration of those skills and of that expertise makes the signature authoritative and establishes the reliability of the conclusion.

In a large number of instances — usually because of the value, the identity of the subject property, or the intended use of the appraisal — a report will require an extended narrative which provides the reader an understanding and appreciation of the identity of the subject property, an understanding and appreciation of the market(s) in which such property is regularly traded, and then, by consequence, an understanding and appreciation of the value conclusion.

The narrative should distinguish between that information which assists in the identification of the subject property and that information which reports the gathering and analysis of valuation data. Those parts of the narrative that discuss the property's characteristics would place emphasis on the criteria of identification and treat with particular care those characteristics which contribute to or detract from value. In exploring such criteria the information that is typically curatorial is considered. However, the identification section of the narrative, while using the tools and vocabulary of a curator, is most useful when its observations are consistent with the valuation data. If undue or unsupported claims regarding the desirability, rarity, history, or physical condition of a property are advanced without commensurate examples of how such characteristics are **experienced** in the marketplace, then the thrust of the assignment may be weakened or questioned.

The section of the narrative that might be described as the core of the appraisal is the section that explains the what, why, and how of the valuation process. It is in the discussion of the valuation process that sales of comparable properties — or of sales of properties that bear some relation to the subject property but which cannot be considered comparable — are analyzed. The character and qualities of the property which have been identified and ranked or rated against similar properties are now valued on the basis of the identity. It is in this discussion of the valuation process that the interconnected structure of the purpose of the assignment, the type of value sought, and the method used are brought together so that, in concert, they communicate the careful application of fact to circumstance. It is in this discussion of the valuation process that the professional judgment of the appraiser is demonstrated. And it is in this part of the narrative that the requirements of the *Code of Ethics* and of the *Uniform Standards of Professional Appraisal Practice* are most urgent.

All appraisal reports should be approached as arguments in that they offer reasons for or against a conclusion. The reliability of the conclusion is based upon the strength of the relationship between the conclusion and the purpose of the report. The credibility of the conclusion is established by the reasoning used to reach it. Ultimately the test of the report is whether the conclusion is shown as, if not indisputable, at least highly probable.

A well-composed appraisal report can meet such a test head-on only if its format and development reflect the diligence and expertise of its author. That is why no single format or model of a report can stand as a unique example of what all appraisals should be. As the work-product of the appraiser, the report concludes the work of data gathering and analysis and presents the factual and interpretive findings of the appraiser in a way that a reader can comprehend. Consequently, no two appraisals will necessarily be composed in the same order or with the same areas of emphasis, although all features will be present. The best composed appraisals lead their readers from the introduction of the value question, through a description of the property that reports its features of value, to the assembled statistics, into the analysis or **evaluation** proper, toward the value conclusion. In such reports the apposite nature of the value conclusion is articulate and clear.

Well-written appraisals convince their readers through the structural integrity of the report. Such appraisals are organized to introduce, explain, and answer a value question. Therefore the skills needed to compose a report with a focused design and with a cogent argument are as important to exercise as are those of data gathering and analysis.

Although each appraisal assignment requires its own format depending on the value question and the type of property designated, there are essential features in every appraisal:

1. A **Letter of Transmittal** or an **Executive Summary**, which outlines the specifications of the assignment and its conclusion. This introduction encapsulates the scope of the assignment but is not a substitute for the total appraisal report.

2. The descriptions of the **Purpose** or **Type of Value**, **Intended Use**, **Value Definition**, and **Method(s)** make explicit and specific the strategy by which the conclusion was reached and provide an understanding of the apposite character and meaningfulness of the conclusion.

3. A listing of **Limiting Conditions** which have governed the development of the report and which will circumscribe the use of the document details assumptions or circumstances which have affected the parameters of the assignment.

4. The **Liabilities** which must be accepted by the appraiser and those which cannot be borne are stated so that the reader understands the extent of the appraiser's responsibilities. This section defines the understood limits of the appraisal's use

and application and the extent of the appraiser's responsibilities and obligations. These expressed liabilities are not disclaimers.

5. The **Certifications** of the appraiser are the formal expressions of the professional character of the development of the appraisal. The minimal certifications of *USPAP* Standard Rule 8-3 must be included in this list of declarations, along with the effective date of value and those certifications specific to the assignment. These certifications bear the signature of the appraiser as author of the appraisal.

6. In the appraisal of a number of items, the **Descriptive List** of properties itemizes each object in an inventory or schedule. Individual items are described by: (a) artist or manufactory; (b) medium or material; (c) date or period; (d) measurements; (e) quality features; (f) condition; (g) provenance; (h) additional features affecting value.

7. The **Narrative** or **Commentary** describes the property as it would be understood in its most common market. The appraiser comments upon and compares the subject property with related examples and then compares the subject property with those properties which have appeared in the marketplace during the time relative to the effective date of value. It is in this section of the appraisal that the interpretive expertise of the appraiser is demonstrated. The narrative concludes with the appraised value. The valuation process is completed.

8. The **Credentials** of the appraiser describe the particular studies and experiences which have qualified the writer as a **valuer** appropriate to the issues of the assignment. Specific credentials and licentiate which support the authority of the appraiser are stated; curricula vitae and degrees are provided. Members of the American Society of Appraisers are obligated to specify the designations earned and the level of membership attained. Compliance with the reaccreditation program of the American Society of Appraisers must be stated.

These eight basis features of a report are often amplified with (a) a **Title Page** which identifies the project, (b) a **Table of Contents**, (c) a **Glossary** which defines the specialized vocabulary or terms, (d) **Photographs**, **Diagrams**, **Graphs**, or **Charts**, (e) a general **Bibliography**.

Since the appraisal process is an exercise in comparisons, the writing skills of the appraiser should be organized around the essential purpose of the report — to present an authoritative answer to a question of value. In editing the report the writer should be concerned with these questions:

- Has the property been examined and described accurately?
- Does the sequence of the report assist the reader in understanding the writer's authority, attitude, method and conclusion?
- Are the facts presented so that the objectivity of the appraiser and of the appraisal process are clear?
- Are **all** the factors that impinge on value considered?
- Is the vocabulary meaningful and understandable?
- Are references cited accurately?
- Are exhibits, photographs, and diagrams legible?
- Has the report been proofread to eliminate arithmetical or secretarial errors?

As a counterbalance to the development of a report, the writer should consider the points and questions which form the parameters of the Appraisal Review process. These are articulated in *USPAP* Standard Rule 3.

Authentication as a Component of Due Diligence

The public expects much of the personal property appraiser and frequently misunderstands the parameters of the profession. One subject which is frequently confusing to clients and to those who make use of appraisal reports is the responsibility of the appraiser for establishing the authenticity of appraised personal property. The consumer reasons that the appraiser has to be sure of what the property is before rendering an opinion of its value.

With designations in Fine Arts, Antiques, Decorative Arts, Residential Contents and a host of other specialties, personal property appraisers represent themselves as experts and are retained as such to do appraisals and consultations and to provide expert witness testimony in courts of law. It is reasonable to expect that the property identifications they provide in appraisal reports are authoritative. That is certainly what the consuming public assumes they receive, and frequently significant decisions are made on that assumption.

Among the roles of an appraiser — as witness to the existence of the property, identifier of its nature and condition and finally as estimator of its value — one role is noticeably absent, that of authenticator. **As a profes-**sional appraiser, one authenticates implicitly by virtue of valuing any property. Explicitly, however, an appraiser does not authenticate.**

Technically the only person who can authenticate a work of art, antique or other property is the person who made it. If that person is not available, then all that can be offered is the informed judgment of the most credible authorities available. The public generally assumes that appraisers are such authorities. They have been tested and accredited in their fields, and they are professionally obliged to pursue continuing education in order to meet requirements for reaccreditation.

Appraisers work continuously to develop their connoisseurship and expand their valuation knowledge. At what point in their development, however, do they know enough to make credible determinations of authenticity? Only after years of study and familiarity with objects does an appraiser develop sufficient expertise in a particular area to become an expert on that topic.

So, what are the published requirements that appraisers must follow? The *Uniform Standards of Professional Appraisal Practice* of The Appraisal Foundation provide the answer. Standard 7 states: "An adequate identification of property should accurately describe property as understood within its market." In other words, an appraiser identifies property as he believes it would be accepted and identified within the market in which it most often changes hands. Standard 7 also states that an appraiser must "...not commit a substantial error of omission or commission that significantly affects an appraisal," and must, "...not render appraisal services in a careless or negligent manner...."

Just as appraisers don't determine values but rather estimate the value they observe in the market; they also don't make determinations about what a property is, but rather reflect how the knowledgeable market recognizes and treats it. In other words, appraisers primarily act as educated and trained interpreters.

True professionals attempt to go beyond providing merely "adequate" identification. There are, for instance, some types of property which are well known to have been extensively faked or reproduced. When dealing with prints attributed to Marc Chagall, Joan Miró, Salvador Dalí, Erté and many other modern artists, appraisers cannot provide an adequate appraisal without including an evaluation of the probable authenticity of the print. The same is true of Pre-Columbian antiquities, ancient coins, Remington bronzes, eighteenth century American furniture and many other types of personal property. It simply is not acceptable to write in a report that, "if the figurine is a genuine Colima ceramic, then the value is…." If reasonable efforts have not been made to establish the authenticity of the object through research and opinions from recognized experts, the appraiser has not exercised **Due Diligence**.

The concept of **Due Diligence** is not defined in the *Uniform Standards*, nor is it codified in law. It is, however, becoming more clearly established through written decisions in various court cases concerning personal property. Increasingly, judges and juries are holding professionals to higher standards when it comes to investigating the authenticity and clear title of valuable art works they handle or appraise.

Authentication is defined as "establishing authorship or origin conclusively," but in fact, it rarely can be proven conclusively. Rather, a statement of origin is a reasoned judgment by experts who may disagree or change their minds. Courts have held repeatedly that whatever the qualifications of an expert, his opinion is only as credible as the facts on which it is based and the logic with which the facts have been analyzed. A judgment of authenticity must meet the same standard as all other parts of the appraisal agreement, the standard of **Substantial Evidence** is "such evidence as a reasonable mind might accept as adequate to support a conclusion" (*Black's Law Dictionary*), where there is no bias, relationship, emotional involvement or pecuniary interest.

The appraisal report documents due diligence in meeting that standard, either by showing that the necessary experts were consulted and explaining their reasoning, or by showing that the appraiser has the necessary expertise and laying out the results of the research and reasoning.

Authentication is rarely definitive; rather, it is a matter of informed, reasoned opinion subject to revision if additional information becomes available, and subject to disagreement among experts. An argument for authentication is built on the facts, references and opinions available. Its conclusion is phrased carefully to reflect how specifically, and with what certainty, authenticity can be determined. The strength of the argument will be reflected in value.

What then, can an appraiser do in order to demonstrate **Due Diligence**? The first step, obviously, is to carefully consider the assignment and the appraiser's ability to investigate any attributions which might be questionable. If the appraiser is not competent to form and express an opinion, the assignment must be declined. If accepted, the next step is to develop a research plan and pursue whatever paths are necessary to verify the provenance, solicit expert opinions and express professional opinions as to authorship and authenticity.

Due Diligence is a concept which applies to all phases of the appraisal process. There is no guarantee that an appraiser can make a totally credible attribution or that all the information needed for a valuation is available. Appraisers do, however, need to do three things for their clientele and the public consumers of appraisals. The first is to pursue the appraisal process in as complete a manner as possible. The second is to state in the report that the appraiser is giving an **opinion** of authenticity and value based on the process described in the report, rather than making it appear that an attribution in an appraisal is a statement of unquestionable fact. The third is to state the limitations in relevant research, the information or resources available, and, consequently, the opinions expressed. To do less is to fall short of exercising Due Diligence and to perpetuate public misperceptions about what professional appraisers do for their clients.

Alternative Dispute Resolution Methods: Mediation and Arbitration

The active participation of lawyers and their clients in litigation to solve a dispute can entail great expense and lengthy delays and can develop poor relationships and unwanted publicity. When the disposition of a case does not satisfy either party, appeals may be filed causing further delays in the final dispute solution. The nominal winner of a dispute is frequently the real loser in terms of time and money expended.

Mediation and arbitration are two of the most widely used methods of alternative dispute resolution (ADR). Over the years the strategy of "win-win" used collaboratively by labor unions and management to develop collective bargaining contracts and to settle disputes, has found its way into various public and private sectors. This strategy is a viable alternative method to the lengthy and costly adversarial approaches to contract development and dispute settlement.

In the *American Bar Journal* of June 1989, the President of the Bar Association, Robert D. Raven, summarized the relatively recent interest in alternate dispute resolution:

> The justice system in most of our major cities is in crisis. A complex web of factors has made civil litigation too costly, time consuming and uncertain. An overload in criminal cases saps the resources of the entire court system. In this environment, access to justice is not a reality for anyone…poor, middle-class, wealthy and businesses alike.

Improving this situation will require lawyers and judges to develop new approaches and to acquire new skills to resolve disputes. Alternative dispute resolution, or ADR, offers great promise for improving access to civil justice.

Mediation and **Arbitration** are major processes in ADR. They are principal alternatives to adversarial litigation.

Mediation

Mediation is a process by which parties to a dispute voluntarily select an impartial third party to facilitate a resolution of the issues by the parties themselves. Confidentiality, consensus-seeking, and procedural informality characterize the process. A "win-win" potential is emphasized, and settlement by consensus is the objective.

Successful mediation depends on the personal qualities and attributes of the mediator, who must possess and employ diplomacy, tact, perseverance, patience and great energy. The mediator can be appointed through the American Arbitration Association (AAA), Federal Mediation and Conciliation Service (FMCS), various state and local mediation agencies or private mediators.

The mediator reviews the positions of both parties, offers compromise suggestions based on fact finding and possible caucusing. The mediator or "third party" functions as a facilitator who helps the parties focus on the areas of agreement as well as the areas of disagreement. The act of mediation helps to maintain a cooperative climate in which both parties can finally solve their dispute in a "win-win" atmosphere. It develops a sense of ownership of the solution for both parties. Neither party involved in the dispute, however, is obligated to follow the recommendations of the mediator. **In mediation disputing parties retain the power to decide issues.**

Mediation is, therefore, confidential; nothing revealed in the mediation process can be used for or against any party in any future proceedings. If a collaborative agreement can not be reached, the mediation process may end and the parties may submit their dispute to arbitration or litigation.

Arbitration

Arbitration is a quasi-judicial proceeding in which a dispute is submitted to one or more impartial parties for a binding determination made by the arbitrator(s). Submission to arbitration generally emanates from contractual agreement. The parties determine details of the proceedings, such as issues, location of meetings, etc. The process is similar to a conventional trial, requiring introduction of evidence, witness-examination, argumentation, and binding decision. Arbitration offers an alternative method of impasse resolution and adjudication when mediation and fact-finding have proved unsuccessful.

Arbitration, through the efforts of a third party, imposes a binding settlement or "award." **The third parties receive and hold power to decide issues.** The arbitrators are often persons selected from AAA, by appraisers themselves who have generated reports with differing value conclusions, or by the court. These arbitrators possess a high degree of expertise and experience in the field of question.

The arbitrator will make a decision following a private hearing where testimony and pertinent documents are submitted. Witnesses may be questioned and cross examined. The term **voluntary binding arbitration** is used when both parties select the arbitrators. **Compulsory binding arbitration** is the term used when, in following a statute, government or court-appointed arbitrators, not chosen by the parties, impose the award.

Models for mediation and arbitration appear on the following page.

Cases using alternative dispute resolution are becoming creasingly common. The following describes an insurance claim settled by an ASA member using arbitration.

An insurance company was refusing to settle a restoration claim for a new fire truck purchased by a rural volunteer fire department. The insurance company felt the truck, involved in an accident on its second fire call, should not be restored as new but with depreciation. The insurance company was willing to pay only a reduced amount and was "dragging its feet." The volunteer fire department, left without the use of this equipment, proceeded to have the truck repaired. They chose to ship the truck to California, where it had been purchased, believing that this was the best place to have the repairs done. The insurance company refused to pay shipping-related costs and the cost of repairs. Both parties agreed to honor the arbitration clause in their contract and to enter arbitration. An arbitrator from AAA was selected who was a member of ASA accredited in Machinery and Equipment. The arbitrator listened to witnesses from both sides, reviewed pertinent documents, cross-examined witnesses, allowed for rebuttals, and finally issued a decision. The arbitrator decided the insurance company should pay the costs of restoring the truck as a new truck. However, it was the decision of the arbitrator that there were competent repair companies in the immediate area

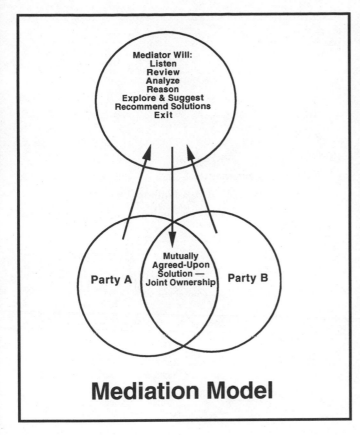

Mediation Model

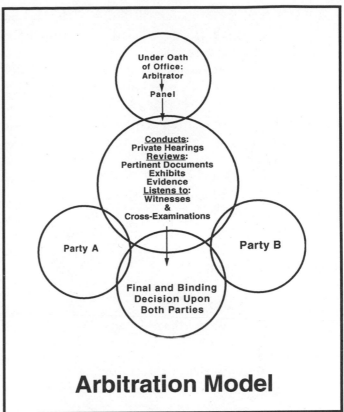

Arbitration Model

and that the costs of shipping the truck to California and of flying people down to retrieve it and drive it back were not justified. The arbitrator therefore disallowed the volunteer fire department's claim for those costs. This claim was settled quickly and without additional legal or court costs. The costs of the arbitration procedure and the arbitrator's fees were paid jointly by the insurance company and the volunteer fire department.

In another example a sterling silver tea and coffee service was stolen from a home. The owner, at the request of the insurance company, had a hypothetical appraisal done from photographs for "insurance replacement value." The insurance company questioned the value given and retained their own appraiser. The two appraisers were ten thousand dollars apart in their conclusions.

The insurance company then invoked their arbitration clause. Both appraisers agreed to arbitration and submitted names of possible arbitrators. They jointly agreed on one ASA appraiser with a designation in Silver and Metal ware.

The arbitrator reviewed both appraisal documents, reviewed the methods, analyses and conclusions as requisite in a review appraisal. Telephone conference calls were initiated for clarification and additional information regarding methodology (a strong reminder that most appraisals are deficient because of information left out of the report) and then began the task of point-by-point contrasting of the reported methods and analyses and deciding which were most convincing. In this case the arbitrator was not given the option of a third opinion, rather the charge was to decide which report was most convincing. Due to the discrepancy in opinions on the age of the silver and the most relevant market between the two appraisal reports, the arbitrator, with independent confirmation of both, gave weight to one over the other. This claim was settled quickly and without additional legal or court costs. The costs of the arbitration procedure and the arbitrator's fees were paid jointly by the insurance company and their client.

Either mediation or binding voluntary arbitration is a viable alternative to a costly law suit. The suggestion by an appraiser to a client, whether an insurance company, business associates or other parties, that they consider either honoring the third party or arbitration clause in their contract or agree to a submission agreement for binding voluntary arbitration is an ethical consulting strategy. Increasingly appraisers will be requested to provide valuation data in the course of a mediation or arbitration proceeding. Such involvement will not require a new appraisal process. Rather, the appraiser will be introduced to the new dispute resolution techniques.

In consequence, the appraiser will be offered new service opportunities which can be fulfilled with existing appraisal procedure and practice.

Every appraiser, regardless of practice discipline, should consider carefully the possibility of a lawsuit arising from some aspect of that practice. The College of Fellows of the American Society of Appraisers, in an opinion noting that "The relationship between client and appraiser involves general fiduciary care as well as contractual specificity" suggests that "…an agreement should precede commencement of the appraisal assignment and should serve as the basis for employment to undertake the assignment." Among the contractual conditions which the College lists for consideration by the appraiser, the following appears:

> In the event of a dispute involving interpretation or application of this agreement, the dispute shall be referred to a neutral third-party Mediation Service. The cost of such mediation shall be borne equally by the parties. In the event Mediation is not successful, the parties agree to submit the dispute to binding Arbitration under the laws of the State of _____.

The prime responsibility of an appraiser is to write appraisal reports using **due diligence** and **moral certainty** in accordance with the *Uniform Standards of Appraisal Practice* and the American Society of Appraiser's *Code of Ethics*. It is through a properly written appraisal report that an appraiser can, at the beginning of a client relationship, establish a firm foundation of apposite value that can prevent adversarial disputes.

The American Arbitration Association and the Federal Mediation and Conciliation Service both provide excellent literature, periodicals, pamphlets, films and videotapes on the rules and regulations governing mediation and arbitration, education and training sessions, and rosters of available experienced arbitrators or umpires. The AAA has at its New York headquarters the Eastman Arbitration Library. This library contains an extensive collection of periodicals, pamphlets, books, manuscripts, clippings and microfiche covering all facets of alternative dispute resolution. A call to either of these organizations will provide information to aid in resolving controversies in business, the construction industry, international commerce, labor-management, insurance claims, securities arbitration and disputes within trade associations and professional societies.

Recommended Resources

(A) American Arbitration Association
140 W. 51st Street, New York, N.Y. 10020-1201
(Offices in major cities; outstanding nation-wide educational programs. ASA has participated with the AAA, since 1971, in training/educational programs for appraisers involved in ADR cases).

(B) American Bar Association
Standing Committee on Dispute Resolution
1800 M Street, N.W., Washington, D.C. 20036
(In the forefront of attorney/judiciary, ADR pioneering)

(C) American Dispute Resolution, Inc.
1502 Central Park Drive; Hurst, Texas 76053-7402
(Innovative networking structure; specializes in Mediation, Arbitration, Conflict Management)

(D) California Department of Consumer Affairs
Dispute Resolution Office
1020 N Street, Room 504; Sacramento, CA 95814
(Supervises participation of state's 58 counties in the "Dispute Resolution Program Act of 1986")

(E) Claremont Dispute Resolution Center
333 W. Foothill Blvd.; Glendora, California, 91740
(Highly effective ADR programs, including Training / Certification; operates under California Dispute Resolution Program Act.)

(F) City of Diamond Bar: Mediation Center
21660 E. Copley Drive, Diamond Bar, California 91765
(Unique "grass roots," community-sponsored, non-profit mediation center, conducted in City Hall, after hours, to accommodate local citizens' hours and needs; in cooperation with Dispute Resolution Center and the County of Los Angeles.)

(G) Harvard Mediation Project
Harvard Law School, Cambridge, Massachusetts 02138
(A major US source of research, investigation, publication *re* ADR; research undertaken with expectation of publication; example, the popular "Getting To Yes" by Fisher and Ury.)

(H) Society of Professionals In Dispute Resolution (SPIDR)
815 15th Street, N.W., Suite 530; Washington D.C. 20005
(Practitioners' professional society; emphasizes seminars, conferences; publications include SPIDR News, annual Conference Proceedings.)

(I) Supreme Court of Oklahoma-ADRS
1915 North Stiles, Suite 305; Oklahoma City, Oklahoma 73105

(Program established under the jurisdiction of the court in 1985; Certifies mediators in all parts of the state; excellent training manual.)

(J) Virginia State Bar
Department of Dispute Resolution Services
8th and Main Bldg., 707 E Main Street, Suite 1500
Richmond, Virginia 23219-2803
(The Virginia Bar, a pioneering Bar in mandating participation in professionalism and Ethics classes, has extended thoughtful recognition to advances in ADR.)

Suggested Further Reading for Mediation/Arbitration Issues

American Arbitration Association. *Dispute Resolution Procedures for Insurance Claims, #139.* Amended 1989. New York: American Arbitration Association. 1993.

American Arbitration Association. *Dispute Resolution Program For Insurance Claims, #141.* New York: American Arbitration Association. 1991.

American Arbitration Association. *Labor Arbitration Rules, #6.* Amended 1993. New York: American Arbitration Association. 1993.

American Arbitration Association. *Resolving Your Disputes, #155.* New York: American Arbitration Association. 1993.

Baer, Walter. *Labor Arbitration Guide.* Illinois: Dow Jones-Irwin, Inc. 1974.

Coulson, Robert. *Labor Arbitration-What You Need To Know.* New York: American Arbitration Association. 1981.

Davey, Harold, W. *Contemporary Collective Bargaining.* New Jersey: Prentice-Hall, Inc. 1982.

Federal Mediation and Conciliation Service. *Dispute Resolution.* Washington D.C.: Federal Mediation and Conciliation Service.

Hagburg, Eugene C. and Marvin J. Levine. *Labor Relations An Integrated Perspective.* New York: West Publishing Co. 1978.

Henderson, James. *Creative Collective Bargaining.* New Jersey: Prentice-Hall, Inc. 1965.

Sloane, Arthur A. and Fred Witney. *Labor Relations.* New Jersey: Prentice-Hall, Inc. 1991.

On Being an Expert Witness

An area into which personal property appraisers may expand their appraisal practice is in the role of expert witness, whereby a professional appraiser has been retained by or through an attorney to represent a client and to present expert testimony in a valuation litigation. To be fully effective in such an assignment, it is necessary for the appraiser to have some understanding of the legal process and terminology, the role of an expert, and the attorney-appraiser team.

Most of what has been written for appraisers in the past on expert witnessing has been presented in a "how to" form, usually with a series of do's and don'ts. This material is by no means comprehensive. It is intended to provide a brief and basic orientation to our system of justice so that the appraiser can better adapt to the legal process. The English system of Common Law is the basis of our legal system. Everything in litigation is based on the law. It is essential that an appraiser who becomes involved in valuation litigation understand the legal aspects of the case.

Valuation litigation arises when there is a serious dispute as to the value of a property which is irresolvable by other means such as negotiation, arbitration or mediation. Almost without exception, the legal procedure involved to resolve a valuation matter takes the form of civil litigation. In such a lawsuit the **burden of proof** is on the **Plaintiff**, and the standard of proof is the **preponderance of evidence**, which is viewed as having proof that is greater than 50 percent in his favor. Contrast this with the criminal standard of proof which is **beyond a reasonable doubt**, usually requiring something greater than a 90 percent proof in order for the Plaintiff to win. In valuation litigation, what wins from an evidentiary standpoint is the preponderance of evidence. The appraiser must be fully aware of this standard in his approach to forensic appraisal services.

Legal Process and Terminology

In the American legal system, civil litigation is a formal dispute resolution procedure that follows the route prescribed by the applicable law. These procedures differ from jurisdiction to jurisdiction but what follows provides a general overview for the appraiser.

Forensic appraisal services encompass a range of professional services provided by an **expert**. So you may ask, what is a **forensic appraisal**? It is an appraisal that has been prepared for litigation purposes and one which has the qualities suitable for presentation in a court of law. Being **suitable** includes the following: the appraisal study has been fully documented and referenced, the property and its value characteristics have been thoroughly researched, and the value conclusion is fully supportable and reasonable. The appraisal work product must be able to withstand both technical and legal attacks and criticism.

The legal process, in general, consists of four **stages**; the pleading stage, the pre-trial stage, the trial stage and the post-trial stage. The appraiser is rarely, if ever, involved in the pleading or post-trial stages. The pleading stage is initiated when one party files a complaint, petition or declaration which alleges in broad terms a cause for action. The pleadings identify the issues which can be raised at trial. **In valuation litigation, usually the only significant issue that concerns the appraiser is the value of the property involved.**

The second stage, the pre-trial stage, does involve extensive participation of the appraiser. It is during this stage that the **discovery** process occurs, and it involves **subpoenas, interrogatories** and **depositions.** Discovery requires mutual disclosure of evidence by both parties.

Subpoenas are usually issued by the clerk of the court and are used to compel a witness to appear at a deposition or trial. You cannot decline to testify if you are subpoenaed. A *subpoena duces tecum* is issued not only to compel your attendance and testimony but also requires you to produce certain documents and materials (for example, your complete work paper file for the appraisal).

Interrogatories are written questions sent to the other side. There factual questions must be answered under penalties of perjury. Interrogatory questions and answers are not easy to formulate and should involve both the attorney and the appraiser. Very specific questions should be asked in order to avoid receiving vague responses that do not yield the information needed.

Depositions consist of oral testimony taken under oath with no judge present. Depositions are taken prior to a trial. A court reporter transcribes everything that is said, and the written transcript of the deposition can be used as evidence during the trial. Discovery and particularly depositions are used to probe the opposition's case, weaknesses in their appraisal study and approach, conclusions and other matters that will be challenged during the trial. The appraiser can be of valuable assistance to the attorney in preparing a line of questions for the opposition's expert, to evaluate the responses and to analyze their case. The deposition transcript can be used during the trial to **impeach** the expert witness if the court testimony varies from the deposition statement. The appraiser when retained as a testifying expert, should always require a personal copy of his deposition transcript and should read it very carefully to edit it for corrections. The appraiser should not waive the right to sign the deposition transcript. It is not unusual for a deposition to last for several days or for as long as a week.

The third and most challenging stage in the civil litigation process is the trial stage. The trial is an adversarial proceeding. In this proceeding the **trier of fact** is either the trial judge or the jury. The trial judge presides and is the gatekeeper with regards to evidence. The appraiser needs to understand what constitutes evidence so as not to omit relevant exhibits and documents. Evidence consists of oral testimony and tangible evidence such as prepared exhibits, appraisal reports, charts, graphs, photographs, and video tapes. Tangible evidence is usually introduced through an expert witness. Evidence is offered by the attorney and its admissibility is determined by the trial judge. The last step of the trial stage is when the trier of fact formulates conclusions based on the evidence admitted. A fundamental rule of evidence is that lay witnesses can only testify to facts to which they have personal knowledge and are not permitted to express opinions or conclusions. However, **expert witnesses** are permitted and expected to **state their opinions** and conclusions, and the stated opinions and conclusions become evidence. The most important aspect of the trial is the presentation of the evidence. Since the testimony of two opposing experts differs, it is the duty of the judge or jury to determine the weight and believability to accord to each. Other procedures that are part of the trial but do not directly involve the appraiser include: jury selection, opening statements, closing arguments, and instructions to the jury. The trial stage is concluded when the judge's or jury's verdict is delivered and the judge directs the entry of a **final judgment.**

However, the case may not necessarily be closed after the final judgment is entered—a post-trial stage may follow. This occurs when either party enters an appeal to an appellate court. Appeals are based on such matters as errors made at the trial court, an excessive award, or for other reasons. From the appraiser's perspective, additional testimony and participation are not involved in the post-trial stage because appeals are based on the record that was made in the trial court.

Role of the Expert

The professional appraiser may be retained as an expert at any point in the first three stages of civil litigation. The role of the expert then depends on the maturity of the case and where the matter is at the time of entry. The two most common roles for an appraiser are either as a testifying expert or as a consulting expert. A consulting expert provides technical assistance and background knowledge to the attorney and the client. The work of a consulting expert enjoys a work product **privilege** and as such is not discoverable. It should also be noted that communications between clients and their attorneys are protected by the Attorney-Client Privilege. The Attorney Work Product Privilege protects working papers prepared by a consulting expert under the direction of an attorney.

The data and information that a testifying expert or expert witness relied on to develop a value opinion and conclusion are discoverable. The role of expert witness in litigated matters is to assist the trier of fact by explaining complex valuation issues and to then express expert opinions and conclusions as they relate to the matter in dispute.

Federal and state rules of court, in general terms, define an **Expert Witness** as a person who by reason of education or special training and experience possesses specialized knowledge in a particular subject area; for our purposes that is appraisal and valuation, in greater depth than the public at large. The expert witness serves the legal process by helping the trier of fact to understand complex valuation matters that are not within the knowledge of the lay person. **An appraiser is not an expert witness until a court of law confers that recognition, which then permits the expert to express opinions and these opinions are evidence.**

One of the qualifications for being an expert is a demonstrated mastery of an appraisal discipline. Qualifying as an expert witness must be done separately for each case. After being sworn in, the witness is first subject to *voir dire*. In this procedure the expert's pertinent credentials are presented through the attorney who engaged him. The expert is then questioned by the opposing counsel whose purpose is to challenge or deflate the expert's credentials and credibility as an expert. Immediately after being recognized as such, the expert witness' direct testimony begins. At this point, the court is anxious to hear from the expert witness. The attorney has built his case for the jury with the fact witnesses. Now the expert witness will discuss the facts, present the valuation interpretation of them and offer opinions and value conclusions. An expert can testify only in the area in which he has been qualified.

One of the most critically important functions of the expert witness is to define the **standard of care** exercised by professionals in the field. As an expert witness, the professional appraiser should define the professional standard so that the court will be able to measure the standard of care exercised by the experts on the other side. Valuation trials can become a battle of the experts. Attorneys want the "best" experts they can afford and being the best includes the appraiser's professionalism. The jury knows that the attorney was hired to be an advocate for his client. Section 7.5 of the *Principles of Appraisal Practice and Code of Ethics* of the ASA declares that it is unethical and unprofessional for an appraiser to act as an advocate in giving court testimony (or in report writing). (*The Principles of Appraisal Practice and Code of Ethics* of the American Society of Appraisers has three sections that relate to testimony, Sections 4.3, 4.4 and 7.5. The *Uniform Standards of Professional Appraisal Practice*, at present, do not include sections on testimony or expert testimony.) The professional appraiser as an expert witness must be independent, objective and forthright and avoid any perception of bias or of being a "hired gun," as an expert witness is sometimes called. Cross-examination by the opposing attorney begins after completion of the direct testimony. The purpose of cross-examination is to question and test the validity of the witness' opinions and to cast doubt on the knowledge, credibility, character and capabilities of the witness. As a trial attorney, the opposing counsel has probably spent a good portion of his professional life training to discredit a witness by cross-examination. The common strategy is to impeach the appraiser's testimony and destroy the appraiser's credibility. An impeachment occurs when there is a contradiction in the expert witness' testimony. The contradiction is between what is said during direct testimony and cross-examination or between the deposition and the testimony given during the court trial. If this should happen, the attorney will conduct a **redirect** examination to correct misinterpretations of answers given in cross-examination and to explain the reasons for the changes which lead to impeachment. The purpose of redirect is to rehabilitate the expert witness' testimony. When there is redirect, **recross** is permitted, but its scope is limited to the areas covered by redirect. It should also be noted that an expert witness for the plaintiff may be called upon later in the trial to testify again in **rebuttal** after the defense presents its case.

As an expert witness, the importance of courtroom decorum, demeanor and dress cannot be over-emphasized. To be persuasive as an expert witness, complete mastery of the technical aspects of your appraisal is not enough. An expert witness' courtroom conduct must in all respects express propriety and good taste in behavior, speech and dress. Impact on the jury by the expert witness will be enhanced by portrayal as an average person, much like the jurors, with some special expertise that will assist them in understanding the case. Testimony by the expert witness, on both direct and cross-examination, must be directed almost entirely to the jury. During the trial, an expert witness is not allowed to speak with any juror or interact in any way, except as part of sworn testimony. A good guideline to follow for attire is to dress in a manner that is in keeping with the image of an expert witness in the mind of the jury. The image of an expert witness will vary, of course, depending on the locale. As difficult as it may be during cross-examination, the witness must be deferential and courteous to the opposing attorney — whose job is to destroy the opposing expert's credibility and to weaken the jury's confidence in the expert's opinion of value.

During the trial, the rule of **sequestration** may be invoked. This rule prohibits witnesses from being in the courtroom while other witnesses are testifying. Under the rule, a witness can only be in the courtroom for his own testimony.

The Attorney-Appraiser Team

An attorney is retained to do the best possible job he can for his client — to be the client's advocate in all of the legal actions involved. Even though the professional appraiser is retained by the same client to represent that client, the substance of the opinions developed should be the same no matter who has retained him. Professionally and ethically, the appraiser cannot and must not be an advocate for the position of his client. Therefore, in considering a forensic appraisal engagement, the most important point for the appraiser to establish before becoming involved is to know exactly what is expected in regards to professional conduct and independence. A fundamental difference exists between the roles of the attorney and the appraiser. These two differing professional interests are teamed together to represent a common client. From the perspective of the appraiser the attorney is the team captain, and the team's objective is to get the best results possible for their client. (The best result possible is not a 50-50 split in the final value.) The attorney is the leader who manages the preparation and presentation of the case.

The role and expectations of what each team member, i.e., the attorney and the appraiser, rightfully expects of the other are summarized below.

The attorney expects the following from the appraiser: professional performance; technical competence; honesty, integrity and a sense of good judgment; preparation of exhibits that clearly communicate the facts and conclusions; the ability to persuasively articulate the value conclusions; the ability to withstand vigorous cross-examination and to be responsive in a timely manner to the attorney's requests for assistance. The appraiser's role from the perspective of the attorney is: to conduct and document the appraisal study and investigation required to produce a virtually unassailable value conclusion; effectively communicate the appraisal principles, concepts and techniques that are involved; analyze the data, exhibits, positions and conclusions of the opposition; an understanding of and the ability to relate to the legal issues involved; to participate in the pretrial stage of the case; to assist the attorney as requested during the trial; and to be a persuasive expert witness during both direct testimony and cross-examination.

The professional appraiser expects the following from the attorney: a complete explanation of the proceedings and issues involved; a clear understanding of the appraiser's assignment and responsibilities; adequate time and money to perform the required study and investigations; recognition of the necessity to formulate value conclusions in an independent, objective manner; and a willingness to listen and learn.

Fulfilling the roles of an expert witness requires diligence and discipline. It is demanding and challenging. Court testimony by an expert has two fundamental purposes: to convince the jury and to make a record for an appeal. The legal process relies on experts to effect justice. If justice is to be realized, it is vitally important that the most competent qualified experts who can deal with complex valuations issues in the courtroom be involved in the legal process. Without their participation, those of lesser competence become involved. An expert witness serves justice. A skilled one is of great value.

■

The Appraisal Expert and The Judicial System

© 1994 by Santo J. Sottilare, J.D.

Personal property appraisers are being involved in litigation testimony with increasing frequency. By the time of eligibility for senior appraiser status, almost every personal property appraiser expert will have been deposed or will have given trial testimony. Appraisers new to the trial and testimony aspects of professional appraisal practice may be unfamiliar with the rules or role they play as expert witness.

The purpose of this essay is to provide some explanation of the procedures the appraiser may expect to encounter in the discovery and trial phases of lawsuits. It is anticipated that recognition of the importance of the role of the personal property witness will assist in development of behaviors appropriate to the professional appraiser as expert witness.

The Litigation Setting

Civil trials between attorneys are under the supervision of a randomly assigned judge who, like the appraiser, is not an advocate and who also subscribes to a code of ethics requiring impartiality,[1] disinterestedness[2] and fairness.[3] Because parties' interests are adverse to one another, however, their attorneys are advocates for them and are not expected to be impartial as are expert witnesses and judges.[4]

At all stages of the proceedings, attorneys use legal doctrines and principles, rules of court and of civil procedure as well as evidence codes and statutes to seek admissibility of evidence favorable to their own clients or to obtain court rulings denying their opponents offerings of evidence. This contest for position, commonly called motion practice,[5] begins virtually as soon as the lawsuit has been filed, and continues with increasing intensity through the pre-trial exchange of facts called the discovery phase, and climaxes with the trial proper where the actual evidence and testimony are presented to the judge or jury as trier of fact.

Its adherents believe that the adversarial, combative nature of trial contests furthers the ultimate discovery of the truth about fact disputes and assists in their resolution by cooling down the emotionalism which accompanies most disputes through this variety of codified safeguards of the interests of justice and the formal etiquette of civilized trial contests.

Rules of American litigation are set in a dual but separate federal-state court system. Each state has jurisdiction over cases arising within its borders and imposes its own statutory law, Rules of Procedure and Rules of Evidence. Federal courts use Federal Rules of Evidence and Federal Rules of Procedure but sometimes use state substantive law. State courts' rules of procedure and rules of evidence may be similar to the Federal Rules or may depart from them in some respects. The appraiser will become more familiar with the different rules of evidence and of civil procedure as he gains more exposure to the process. This report can provide a general framework.

Introduction of Evidence

The Rules of Evidence and the Rules of Procedure are provided to secure fairness in administration, to eliminate unjustifiable expense and delay, to promote growth and development of the level of evidence to the end that truth may be ascertained and proceedings justly determined."[6]

Verdicts are rendered on the issues based on the evidence which comes from the mouths of the witnesses on the stand or from the documents and physical evidence offered before the judge and/or jury during the actual trial itself.[7]

Relevant evidence is admissible and under the rules, relevant evidence means any evidence having any tendency to make the existence of any fact that is of consequence to the determination of the action more probable or less probable than it would be without the evidence. Whether evidence is relevant is decided by the Court in the first instance and irrelevant evidence is not admissible.[8]

Introduction of Testimony

Every person is competent to be a witness (except as otherwise provided in the federal or state rules of evidence); however, in a civil action [in which state law applies], the competency of a witness is determined in accordance with state law, even if the case is being heard in the federal courts.[9]

Preliminary questions concerning the qualifications of persons to be witnesses are determined by the Court in the first instance, and the Court is not bound by the rules of evidence in making a determination as to who is qualified.[10]

With the exception of experts, a witness may not testify to a matter unless evidence is introduced to support a finding that the witness has personal knowledge of the matter.[11]

Under the federal and some state rules, any party to the litigation may attack the credibility of a witness, including the party calling the witness.[12]

At a party's request or on its own motion, the Court may order each witness excluded from the courtroom so that the witness cannot hear the testimony of other witnesses. Corporate parties may keep a representative in the courtroom and, of course, natural parties to the litigation have rights to be present in the courtroom at all times throughout the proceedings.[13]

There are several distinct points along the litigation pathway when the personal property appraiser's qualifications as an expert witness will be questioned, analyzed and disputed between counsel. The first is in discovery.

Pre-Trial Discovery

All courts, state or federal, use pre-trial discovery rules allowing parties to obtain relevant evidence from others. Depositions and other pre-trial discovery procedures are mandated by the Federal or State Rules of Civil Procedure.[14]

All witness testimony may be compelled by the Courts power of subpoena and failure to obey can be punished as a contempt of court.[15]

Evidence and Procedures at Pre-Trial

Depositions take place before a court reporter. The expert witness is sworn in and first questioned by the attorney requesting the deposition, who is permitted to ask any question which may lead to relevant evidence. The questions themselves do not have to be relevant as long as the potential answer might be.

The court reporter records each question and answer and any objections made by the attorneys (to be later ruled on by the judge). At conclusion of the deposition, the expert is informed of the right to review a printed copy of the deposition at the court reporter's office. The expert may not alter the questions and answers but may place an addendum at the end to clarify questions not understood or answers believed to be improperly recorded. After deposition, the witness is offered an opportunity to waive this right but should confer with the client's attorney before doing so because the written deposition will be used for cross examination of the witness at trial, and its accuracy is essential to good trial posture.[16]

Expert Testimony in Deposition

The property appraiser's role should be no less formal and professional in the pre-trial deposition than at his appearance at the trial. It is in the deposition that the attorneys are scrutinizing the expert's witness value for the courtroom contest to come.

The appraiser must be familiar with all elements of the appraisal document, be able to describe the details of the research, its compilation, the methodology of valuation, the reasons for the methodology selection and the value conclusions in a clear and direct manner.

Since depositions are out of court proceedings, the appraiser must rely upon the client's attorney, who is also present, to protect the right to fairness and impartiality, and to intervene if the opposing attorney acts in an unprofessional manner or goes beyond the bounds of propriety. Appraisers not familiar with the deposition scenario should be personally instructed on proper deposition behavior by the client's attorney. Many effective trial attorneys prepare a list of do's and don'ts which they will provide the witness on request.[17]

The witness must never allow one's self to be drawn into an argument with counsel over one's opinion or its bases, as such conduct will be seen as impairing the expert's effectiveness as a courtroom witness.

Months or years may elapse between the date of deposition and the date of trial and memory fades; therefore, it is wise to review the deposition and be familiar with it. Near the time of the trial the appraiser should obtain a copy of the deposition; should review it thoroughly with any document attachments; and should become familiar with the questions, the answers as recorded and the documents attached.

Expert depositions may be, and frequently are, used at trial as witness substitutes or to impeach live witnesses, so it is therefore possible that the appraiser's deposition may be read, in whole or in part, before the jury.[18]

Competent opposing attorneys always read and digest expert depositions, indexing answers for ease of access upon cross examination and the expert must, therefore, be more familiar with the deposition than is the cross examining attorney.

The appraiser may find it helpful to imagine giving deposition responses to a judge and jury, not opposing counsel, and so treat the deposition as rehearsal for courtroom testimony. Bearing and demeanor should be appropriate and professional.

The Trial

Evidence and Procedures at Trial

Lay witnesses are permitted to testify **only** as to facts within personal knowledge and then **only** about facts that are of consequence to the lawsuit. Stated another way, non-expert lay witnesses may not give opinion or inference and may testify only as to facts personally known and which come to them through the five senses.[19] Expert witnesses are allowed much more leeway as to opinion and hearsay than are lay witnesses, merely because they are being questioned about their opinions and must necessarily include all factors, which contribute to the opinions.[20]

The Court may appoint its own experts, call its own witnesses, or interrogate the parties' witnesses. The parties, however, reserve the right, in all cases, to select experts of their own choosing.[21]

The trial court has the responsibility in the first instance of determining the admissibility of expert testimony and the range and scope of subjects to which the expert may testify. If facts are within the ordinary experience of the jury then conclusions are left to them and the expert may not give an opinion or conclusion. Expert testimony from a qualified expert must be distinctly related to some science, profession, business or occupation, so as to be beyond the ken of the average layperson, and the witness must have such skill or experience so that the opinions or inferences will assist the jury in determining the issues at law.[22]

Preliminary Qualification of Expert

Occasionally, with Court approval, the parties may agree that each other's witnesses are qualified experts and testimony may begin without preliminary qualification. More often each party interrogates the other's expert then motions the court to exclude that witness' testimony on the ground that the opposing expert is not sufficiently qualified to render an expert opinion on the issues in controversy.

This preliminary qualifying of the witness is usually done from the witness stand and out of hearing of the jury, concluding with the judge's ruling as to whether the proposed witness is a qualified expert. If qualified, then testimony is permitted and the expert's opinion will be heard and weighed by the jury along with all other testimony.

Qualifying begins with direct examination by the attorney supporting the witness regarding the witness' credentials, background, skill, knowledge and experience followed by the opponent's cross examination to test these same qualifications of the witness.[23]

It has been held on appeal, that although a witness may have been qualified to testify as an expert, the trial court's refusal to permit the testimony was not error where the supporting attorney failed to ask proper questions which would have qualified the witness as an expert.[24]

Trial Testimony

Once the witness has qualified to give expert testimony, the number and sufficiency of facts submitted to enable the formulation of an opinion must normally be decided by the witness because the trial judge would not ordinarily be in a position to know whether the facts are sufficient to permit formation of the opinion.[25]

The jury hearing all testimony can give whatever weight it chooses to give to the evidence called expert testimony.

The line between competency to testify as an expert and weight of the evidence as to values, is not well defined; therefore the expert should be prepared to testify, in detail, supporting the value conclusions even in the qualification stage of the testimony since opposing counsel may seek to prove that it is speculative and conjectural, and therefore affects competency to testify as a witness.

Weight and Sufficiency of Evidence

Usually, wide latitude is granted the expert, once qualified, in testimony concerning opinions, and the facts or data upon which an expert bases an opinion or inference may be those observed by or made known to the expert at or before the hearing. If the opinion is of a type reasonably relied upon by experts in the particular field in forming opinions or inferences upon the subject, the facts or data need not be separately admissible in evidence.[26]

Thus the appraisal expert witness can testify about the methodical compilation of data, phone calls, computer searches, library runs, and other non-admissible forms of evidence which aided in the formation of the apposite value conclusion. However, where comparable market data is the basis for the value conclusion, the personal property appraiser should be able to tell the jury how adjustments were made for value differences in the comparables when determining the estimate of value, and inability to do so can result in the testimony being stricken as speculative and conjectural.[27] Generally, any reasonable method of valuation used by the appraiser is acceptable to the court, and its exclusion is reversible error. The weight to be accorded to the expert testimony of the appraiser, in almost all instances, rests with the trier of fact[the jury].[28]

Throughout the trial, and also now, toward its conclusion, the court, of its own motion, or in response to parties' requests, provides verbal instructions to the jury on the law to use in reaching its decision. These instructions vary with the case and the state but commonly all jurisdictions use standardized instructions regarding the responsibilities of the judge and jury, believability of witnesses including experts, burden of proof and instructions concerning prejudice and sympathy.[29]

The jury is free to accept or reject part or all of the expert testimony placed before it and is so instructed by the judge.

Verdict and Damage Awards

Plaintiff and Defendant conclude presentation of their cases, are given an opportunity to summarize the case to the jury from their perspective, and the judge turns the case over to the jury, with proper instructions, for a decision. How damages are awarded varies from state to state, but in every court the judge decides disputed issues of law, the jury decides the disputed issues of fact, and the written jury decision called verdict is a synthesis of law based on the judge's legal instructions and the jury's fact-finding. The written verdict becomes the determination for that particular case. The written verdict is either for the Plaintiff, naming a sum awarded as money damages or against the Plaintiff stating that the Plaintiff shall take nothing.[30]

The fundamental principle of the law of damages is that a person injured by breach of contract or by wrongful or negligent act or omission shall have fair and just compensation commensurate with the loss sustained and difficulty in proving damages does not preclude recovery if there is some reasonable basis in the evidence for the amount awarded.[31]

The variety of "values" with which the personal property appraiser obtains familiarity, such as replacement value, replacement cost new, reproduction cost, actual cash value, marketable cash value, and fair market value, are concepts which have been or are a part of the law of damages depending upon the litigation context and the relationship between the parties.

Our judicial system attempts to reconcile the ideal of fair and just compensation with the need that there be an end to litigation over damage for future losses. The line between the two is continually shifting as our fifty state courts separately continue to develop and refine the law of damages.

Sometimes income producing features of personalty are legally enforceable and awardable as damages but in other cases are termed speculative or conjectural and are therefore unprotected and unrecoverable.

As for example, a dispute between insurer and insured over insurance contract damages defined as actual cash value will limit the damage award. Courts may accept the insurance contract definition or refuse and substitute a "broad evidence rule" as to how damages are measured. In cases of negligent destruction, the courts may seek "market value on date of loss," as a guide toward "fair and just" compensatory damages.

In an early case of destruction of antiques, the legal measure of damages for total loss was held to be market value on the date of loss where market value could be established, but other values if not. A later case used market value not purchase price or cost. Another case held it to be reversible error for a court to calculate damages based on replacement cost and not market value.[32]

In a case of negligent partial destruction of personalty, damages were measured by the property's before damage and after damage market values, or, at the owner's election, reasonable cost of repair or restoration with allowance for irreparable, permanent loss in value. The Plaintiff in partial loss cases must prove before and after market value.[33]

Because the law of evidence and damages vary from state to state, no general rule may be laid down. The appraiser should always be aware of the fact that the professional appraisal document is an estimate of value as of a specified date but that the jury's dollar award of damages is guided by the legal principles of damage recovery in the local jurisdiction and may or may not be similar in amount to the apposite value conclusion. The appraisal expert deals in valuation issues, not in damage allocation. Expert opinion testimony on value is one part of the evidence, the judge's instruction on the law of damages another part, and other evidence not known to the expert may constitute a third part of the totality called the body of evidence leading to the award of damages.

Appraisal Office Practices

The personal property appraisal experts preparation for testifying begins on the day of acceptance of the professional appraisal assignment. The appraisal document and its supporting evidence should be maintained in a file separate from other files. The original appraisal document and its supports, may become subject to a wide variety of discovery techniques, and should be intact as it was on the day the assignment was completed, uncomplicated by any subsequent correspondence between the appraiser and the client, attorneys, the Courts, or other interested individuals.

This later material can be kept in a separate folder, within the appraisal document folder, or it can be kept separately for handy reference.

It should be remembered that the appraiser's primary assignment concludes with the submission of the appraisal document with a valuation date thereon. In the event of a dispute concerning valuation between the client and third parties, it is that document which must be readily available and easily explained, which process can be complicated by the insertion of later memos, diagrams, descriptions or correspondence.

The appraiser's first indication of possible litigation may come in the form of a telephone call from the client or an attorney or in a letter from these or other sources. The keeping of a separate file recording each of these contacts will enable the appraiser to make appropriate responses, which should be measured and in proportion to the inquiry received, taking into account client confidentiality and the appraiser's ethical obligations. Telephone information requests from persons who claim a fiduciary relationship with a client should be verified by the client, and the appraiser should obtain suitable authorization from the client for the release of information. Receipts for copies of file documents should be maintained when the appraiser, in accordance with the client's instructions, provides client representatives with copies of file materials.

Once the bonafides of the client's representatives have been established and the appraiser has secured acceptable arrangements for compensation for professional time, the appraiser may be subject to a deposition subpoena duces tecum (which directs the subpoenaed person to bring certain documents) conducted by the attorneys.

An updated curriculum vitae should be provided to the sponsoring attorney along with a letter description of the appraiser's experience. It might include years of experience and average number of hours by week, month, or year exposed to the profession. It might include the average number of appraisals completed weekly, monthly or yearly. The combination of education and experience, in its totality, is what determines one's qualifications as an expert. The personal property appraiser should work closely with the attorney in the qualification phase, and, if necessary, provide the attorney with an appropriate question and answer format which will allow the attorney to adequately question the appraiser as to education and experience sufficient to qualify one as an expert.

Personal property appraisers are occasionally engaged to become experts in disputes already in existence. Generally, the request is to prepare an estimate of value as of a specific date, concerning a lost, damaged or destroyed article of value. It is understood that the personal property appraiser will be testifying as a qualified expert on behalf of a party to the litigation. Occa-sionally, however, the client or the client's attorney attempts to specify the valuation approach that the expert is to use. If a conflict arises between the appraiser's ethical obligations under *USPAP* Standards 7 and 8 and the valuation approach directed by the client or by the attorney, then the employment should be declined or the consulting parties should be informed that the proposed valuation approach will not withstand adequate cross examination and/or is contrary to the *Uniform Standards of Professional Appraisal Practice*.

Because of the pioneering efforts of our fellow real-estate appraisal professionals, almost every state legislature has statutorily specified, as a standard by which to judge real estate appraisals, the *Uniform Standards of Professional Appraisal Practice*.[34]

If the attorney you are working with seems unaware of the development, please acquaint him with it. The attorney may be able to use *USPAP* as a guide in examining and cross examining the opposing personal property experts; to quote from *USPAP* or, even to introduce *USPAP* into evidence as relevant to the issues being litigated. Become familiar with the specific statute numbers identifying the *Uniform Standards* in your state for easy reference in your own testimony and always keep a copy of the latest standards for ready reference in testimony.

Conclusions

Personal property appraisal is at one and the same time an art and a science — an art in the judicious application of the connoisseur's eye and experience to the assignment and a science in the rigorous application of value theory and methodology as taught by the American Society of Appraisers.

As our distinguished colleague, Bernard Ewell, ASA, said in an earlier edition of this work,

"The job of an expert witness is not to prove the case presented by any one side in court, but to educate the court in an unbiased manner. It is thus critical that you serve as a totally disinterested person. Anything less compromises your testimony and professionalism and subverts the judicial system."

His words, then timely, now timeless, are spoken with the voice of reasoned experience and should be heeded.

In view of the foregoing, it is important that the expert appraiser not permit appraisal objectivity to be seduced by the siren call of advocacy's drive for a "victory" in court. Rather, the American Society of Appraisers' personal property expert should utilize appearances in the judicial system as an opportunity to educate attorneys, judges, jurors and parties in the appraisal expert's knowledge and methodological use of the *Uniform Standards of Professional Appraisal Practice* as established by The Appraisal Foundation and as subscribed to by the American Society of Appraisers and its constituent members.

By adhering to the *Code of Ethics* of the American Society of Appraisers and the methodology of Standards 7 and 8 in the *USPAP*, the personal property appraiser will create a professional appraisal document fully sustainable in the American court system and a model document to which all other appraisals must be compared.

Endnotes

1. Typically; Canon 3, <u>Florida Code of Judicial Conduct</u>
   A Judge Should Perform The Duties of His Office Impartially and Diligently

   The judicial duties of a judge take precedence over all his other activities. His judicial duties include all the duties of his office prescribed by law. In the performance of these duties, the following standards apply:
   A. Adjudicative Responsibilities.
      (1) A judge should be faithful to the law and maintain professional competence in it. He should be unswayed by partisan interests, public clamor, or fear of criticism.
      (2) A judge should maintain order and decorum in proceedings before him.
      (3) A judge should be patient, dignified, and courteous to litigants, jurors, witnesses, lawyers, and others with whom he deals in his official capacity, and should require similar conduct of lawyers, and of his staff, court officials, and others subject to his direction and control.

2. Typically; Canon 2, <u>Florida Code of Judicial Conduct</u>
   A Judge Should Avoid Impropriety and the Appearance of Impropriety in All His Activities.

   A. A judge should respect and comply with the law and should conduct himself at all times in a manner that promotes public confidence in the integrity and impartiality of the judiciary.
   B. A judge should not allow his personal relationships to influence his judicial conduct or judgment. He should not lend the prestige of his office to advance the private interests of others; nor should he convey or authorize others to convey the impression that they are in a special position to influence him. He should not testify voluntarily as a character witness.

3. <u>City of Miami v. Williams</u>, 40 So2d 205 Fla. Supreme Ct. (1949)

"Judge in conducting a jury trial must administer law fairly and impartially between litigants and in such connection is vested with broad discretionary powers."

Florida Evidence Code
90.106   <u>Summing Up and Comment by Judge</u>
"A judge may not sum up the evidence or comment to the jury upon the weight of the evidence, the credibility of the witnesses, or the guilt of the accused.

4. American Bar Association Code of Professional Responsibility Canon 6, <u>A Lawyer Should Represent a Client Competently</u>.

   <u>E-C 6-1</u>
   "Because of his vital role in the legal process, a lawyer should act with competence and proper care in representing clients. He should strive to remain proficient in his practice and should accept employment only in matters which he is or intends to become competent to handle."

   <u>E-C 6-4</u>
   Having undertaken representation a lawyer should use proper care to safeguard the interests of his client.

   (AM Jur 2nd Desk Book Item #68A)

5. Florida Rules of Civil Procedure 1.100 <u>Pleadings and Motions</u>
   (B.) "An application to the court for an order shall be by motion which shall be made in writing unless made during a hearing or trial, shall state with particularity the grounds therefore and shall set forth the relief or order sought."

6. Federal Rules of Evidence
   RULE 102.   <u>Purpose and Construction</u>

   Purpose of Federal Rules of Evidence is to secure fairness in administration, elimination of unjustifiable expense and delay, and promotion of growth and development of the law of evidence to the end that truth may be ascertained and proceedings justly determined.

   Florida Rules Of Civil Procedure
   1.010   <u>Scope and Title of Rules</u>

   "These rules shall be construed to secure the just, speedy and inexpensive determination of every action".

7. Federal Rules of Evidence
   RULE 103.   <u>Rulings on Evidence</u>

   a. <u>Effect of erroneous ruling</u> — Error may not be predicated upon a ruling which admits or excludes evidence unless a substantial right of the party is affected . . . .
   d. <u>Plain error</u> — Nothing in this rule precludes taking notice of plain errors affecting substantial rights although they were not brought to the attention of the court.

   Federal Rules of Evidence
   RULE 105.   <u>Limited Admissibility</u>

   When evidence which is admissible as to one party or for one purpose but not admissible as to another party or for another purpose is admitted, the court, upon request, shall restrict the evidence to its proper scope and instruct the jury accordingly.

Florida Evidence Code, Chapter 90
90.107   Limited Admissibility

When evidence that is admissible as to one party or for one purpose, but inadmissible as to another party or for another purpose is admitted, the court, upon request, shall restrict such evidence to its proper scope and so inform the jury at the time it is admitted.

8. Federal Rules of Evidence
    RULE 401.   Definition of Relevant Evidence

"Relevant evidence" means any evidence having any tendency to make the existence of any fact that is of consequence to the determination of the action more probable or less probable than it would be without the evidence.

Federal Rules of Evidence
RULE 402.   Relevant Evidence Generally Admissible; Irrelevant Evidence Inadmissible

Relevant evidence is admissible except as otherwise provided.... Evidence which is not relevant is not admissible.

Florida Evidence Code, Chapter 90
90.401   Definition of Relevant Evidence

Relevant evidence is evidence tending to prove or disprove a material fact.

Florida Evidence Code, Chapter 90
90.402   Admissibility of relevant evidence

All relevant evidence is admissible, except as provided by law.

Florida Evidence Code, Chapter 90
90.403   Exclusion on grounds of prejudice or confusion

Relevant evidence is inadmissible if its probative value is substantially outweighed by the danger of unfair prejudice, confusion of issues, misleading the jury, or needless presentation of cumulative evidence. This section shall not be construed to mean that evidence of the existence of third-party benefits is inadmissible.

9. Federal Rules of Evidence
    RULE 601.   General Rule of Competency

Every person is competent to be a witness, except as otherwise provided in these rules. However, in a civil action ... as to which state law applies the rule of decision, the competency of a witness shall be determined in accordance with State law.

Florida Evidence Code, Chapter 90
90.601   General Rule of Competency

Every person is competent to be a witness, except as otherwise provided by statute.

10. Federal Rules of Evidence
     RULE 104.   Preliminary Questions

a. Questions of admissibility generally — Preliminary questions concerning the qualification of a person to be a witness, the existence of a privilege, or the of evidence shall be determined by the court, subject to the provisions of subdivision (b). In making its determination it is not bound by the rules of evidence except those with respect to privilege.

b. Relevancy conditioned on fact — When the relevancy of evidence depends upon the fulfillment of a condition of fact, the court shall admit it upon, or subject to, the introduction of evidence sufficient to support a finding of fulfillment of the condition.

e. Weight and credibility — This rule does not limit the right of a party to introduce before the jury evidence relevant to its weight of credibility.

Florida Evidence Code, Chapter 90
90.105   Preliminary Questions

(1) Except as provided in subsection (2), the court shall determine preliminary questions concerning the qualification of a person to be a witness, the existence of a privilege, or the admissibility of evidence.

11. Federal Rules of Evidence
     RULE 602.   Lack of personal knowledge

A witness may not testify to a matter unless evidence is introduced which is sufficient to support a finding that he has personal knowledge of the matter. Evidence to prove personal knowledge may be given by the witness himself.

12. Florida Evidence Code, Chapter 90
     90.608   Who may impeach

Any party, including the party calling the witness, may attack the credibility of a witness by:

(1) Introducing statements of the witness which are inconsistent with his present testimony.
(2) Showing that the witness is biased.
(3) Attacking the character of the witness in accordance with the provisions of Statute 90.609 or 90.610.
(4) Showing a defect of capacity, ability, or opportunity in the witness to observe, remember, or recount the matters about which he testified.
(5) Proof by other witnesses that material facts are not as testified to by the witness being impeached.

Federal Rules of Evidence
RULE 607.   Who May Impeach

The credibility of a witness may be attacked by any party including the party calling the witness.

13. Federal Rules of Evidence
     RULE 615.   Exclusion of Witnesses

At the request of a party, the court shall order witnesses excluded so that they cannot hear the testimony of other witnesses, and it may take the order of its own motion. This rule does not authorize exclusion of:

(1) a party who is a natural person; or
(2) officer ... of corporation; or
(3) a person whose presence is shown by a party to be essential to the presentation of the party's cause.

Florida Evidence Code, Chapter 90
90.616   Exclusion of Witnesses

(1) At the request of a party the court shall order, or upon its own motion the court may order, witnesses excluded from a proceeding so that they cannot hear the testimony of other witnesses except as provided in subsection (2).

(2) A witness may not be excluded if he is:

(a) A party who is a natural person.

(b) In a civil case, an officer or employee of a party that is not a natural person. The party's attorney shall designate the officer or employee who shall be the party's representative.

(c) A person whose presence is shown by the party's attorney to be essential to the presentation of the party's cause.

14. Typically:

Florida Rules of Civil Procedure

RULE 1.280   General Provisions Governing Discovery

(a) Discovery Methods. Parties may obtain discovery by one or more of the following methods: depositions upon oral examination or written questions; written interrogatories; production of documents or things or permission to enter upon land or other property for inspection and other purposes; physical and mental examinations; and requests for admission. Unless the court orders otherwise and under subdivision (c) of this rule, the frequency of uses of these methods is not limited, except as provided in rule 1.200 and rule 1.340

(b) Scope of Discovery. Unless otherwise limited by order of the court in accordance with these rules, the scope of discovery is as follows:

(1) In General. Parties may obtain discovery regarding any matter, not privileged, that is relevant to the subject matter of the pending action, whether it relates to the claim or defense of the party seeking discovery or the claim or defense of any other party, including the existence, description, nature, custody, condition, and location of any books, documents, or other tangible things and the identity and location of persons having knowledge of any discoverable matter. It is not ground for objection that the information sought will be inadmissible at the trial if the information sought appears reasonably calculated to lead to the discovery of admissible evidence.

Florida Rules of Civil Procedure

RULE 1.350   Production of Documents and Things and Entry upon Land for Inspection and Other Purposes

(a) Request; Scope. Any party may request any other party (1) to produce and permit the party making the request, or someone acting in the requesting party's behalf, to inspect and copy any designated documents, including writings, drawings, graphs, charts, photographs, phonorecords, and other data compilations from which information can be obtained, translated, if necessary, by the party to whom the request is directed through detection devices into reasonably usable form, that constitute or contain matters within the scope of rule 1,280(b) and that

are in the possession, custody, or control of the party to whom the request is directed.

Florida Rules of Civil Procedure

RULE 1.351   Production of Documents and Things without Deposition

(a) Request; Scope. A party may seek inspection and copying of any documents or things within the scope of rule 1.350(a) from a person who is not a party by issuance of a subpoena directing the production of the documents or things when the requesting party does not seek to depose the custodian or other person in possession of the documents or things.

(c) Subpoena. If no objection is made by a party under subdivision (b), the clerk shall issue a subpoena directing the production of the documents or things in accordance with the notice and deliver it to the party serving the notice. The subpoena shall require production of the documents or things specified in it. The subpoena may give the recipient an option to deliver or mail legible copies of the documents or things to the party serving the subpoena.

15. Typically:

Florida Rules of Civil Procedure

RULE 1.410   Subpoena

(a) Subpoena for Testimony before the Court.

(1) Every subpoena for testimony before the court shall be issued by the clerk under the seal of the court and, when requested, shall state the name of the court and the title of the action and shall command each person to whom it is directed to attend and give testimony at a time and place specified in it.

(2) On oral request of an attorney or party and without praecipe, the clerk shall issue a subpoena for testimony before the court or a subpoena for the production of documentary evidence before the court signed and sealed but otherwise in blank, both as to the title of the action and the name of the person to whom it is directed, and the subpoena shall be filled in before service by the attorney or party.

(b) For Production of Documentary Evidence. A subpoena may also command the person to whom it is directed to produce the books, papers, documents, or tangible things designated therein.

(d) Subpoena for Taking Depositions.

(1) Filing a notice to take a deposition as provided in rule 1.310(b) or 1.320(a) with a certificate of service on it showing service on all parties to the action constitutes an authorization for the issuance of subpoenas for the persons named or described in the notice by the clerk of the court in which the action is pending. The subpoena may command the person to whom it is directed to produce designated books, papers, documents, or tangible things that constitute or contain evidence relating to any of the matters within the scope of the examination permitted by rule 1.280(b).

(2) A person may be required to attend an examination only in the county wherein the person resides or is employed or transacts business in person or at such other convenient place as may be fixed by an order of court.

(e) Contempt. Failure by any person without adequate excuse to obey a subpoena served upon that person may be deemed a contempt of the court from which the subpoena issued.

16. Typically:

Florida Rules of Civil Procedure
RULE 1.390   Depositions of Expert Witnesses

(a) Definition. The term "expert witness" as used herein applies exclusively to a person duly and regularly engaged in the practice of a profession who holds a professional degree from a university or college and has had special professional training and experience, or one possessed of special knowledge or skill about the subject upon which called to testify.

(b) Procedure. The testimony of an expert or skilled witness may be taken at any time before the trial in accordance with the rules for taking depositions and may be used at trial, regardless of the place of residence if the witness or whether the witness is within the distance prescribed by rule 1.330(a)(3). No special form of notice need be given that the deposition will be used for trial.

(c) Fee. An expert or skilled witness whose deposition is taken shall be allowed a witness fee in such reasonable amount as the court may determine. The court shall also determine a reasonable time within which payment must be made, if the deponent and party cannot agree. All parties and the deponent shall be served with notice of any hearing to determine the fee. any reasonable fee paid to an expert or skilled witness may be taxed as costs.

(d) Applicability. Nothing in this rule shall prevent the taking of any deposition as otherwise provided by law.

Florida Rules of Civil Procedure
RULE 1.310.   Depositions Upon Oral Examination

(a) When Deposition May Be Taken. After commencement of the action any party may take the testimony of any person, including a party, by deposition upon oral examination.

(b) Notice; Method of Taking; Production at Deposition.

(1) A party desiring to take the deposition of any person upon oral examination shall give reasonable notice in writing to every other party to the action. The notice shall state the time and place for taking the deposition and the name and address of each person to be examined, if known, and, if the name is not known, a general description sufficient to identify the person or the particular class or group to which the person belongs. If a subpoena duces tecum is to be served on the person to be examined, the designation of the materials to be produced under the subpoena shall be attached to or included in the notice.

(c) Examination and Cross-Examination; Record of examination; Oath; Objections.

Examination and cross-examination of witnesses may proceed as permitted at the trial. The officer before whom the deposition is to be taken shall put the witness on oath and shall personally, or by someone acting under the officer's direction and in the officer's presence, record the testimony of the witness, except that when a deposition is being taken by telephone, the witness shall be sworn in by a person present with the witness who is qualified to administer an oath in that location. The testimony shall be taken stenographically or recorded by any other means ordered in accordance with subdivision (b)(4) of this rule. If requested by one of the parties, the testimony shall be transcribed at the initial cost of the requesting party and prompt notice of the request shall be given to all other parties.

(d) Motion to Terminate or Limit Examination.

At any time during the taking of the deposition, on motion of a party or of the deponent and upon a showing that the examination is being conducted in bad faith or in such manner as unreasonably to annoy, embarrass, or oppress the deponent or party, the court in which the action is pending or the circuit court where the deposition is being taken may order the office conducting the examination to cease forthwith from taking the deposition or may limit the scope and manner of the taking of the deposition under rule 1.280(c). If the order terminates the examination, it shall be resumed thereafter only upon the order of the court in which the action is pending. Upon demand of any party or the deponent, the taking of the deposition shall be suspended for the time necessary to make a motion for an order. The provisions of rule 1.380(a) apply to the award of expenses incurred in relation to the motion.

(e) Witness Review. If the testimony is transcribed, the transcript shall be furnished to the witness for examination and shall be read to or by the witness unless the examination and reading are waived by the witness and by the parties. Any changes in form or substance that the witness wants to make shall be listed in writing by the officer with a statement of the reasons given by the witness for making the changes. The changes shall be attached to the transcript. It shall then be signed by the witness unless the parties waiving the signing or the witness is ill, cannot be found, or refuses to sign. If the transcript is not signed by the witness within a reasonable time after it is furnished to the witness, the officer shall sign the transcript and state on the transcript the waiver, illness, absence of the witness, or refusal to sign with any reasons given therefore.

17. INSTRUCTIONS TO CLIENT OR WITNESS FOR DEPOSITION

1. Always be truthful in your answers.
2. Be polite and courteous to the opposing attorney despite any attempt to anger or intimidate you.
3. Do not be intimidated by the opposing attorney.

4. Do not guess. If you do not know the answer, say so.

5. Do not lose your temper, and above all, do not argue with or attempt to out-maneuver the opposing attorney.

6. Do not assume anything - testify only as to what you know to be fact.

7. Take your time, do not rush. Be sure you understand what is being asked of you.

8. Insist on clarification of the question if you do not understand it.

9. Do not volunteer information other than that which is specifically requested, unless your attorney has so instructed.

10. Listen for your attorney to warn you of a dangerous question. He will give you a previously agreed on coded cue.

11. Do not be afraid to ask to look at any relevant documents, notes or letters. If you need this assistance in remembering dates, amounts or other facts, ask to review the document referred to. It is better to do this than make a false statement or estimate.

12. Speak slowly and clearly. If you feel that you answered a question incorrectly, do not be afraid to clarify your answer before proceeding.

13. If the opposing attorney cuts off your answer, be sure to say that you feel that your answer was not complete. Your attorney will clarify the point if necessary.

14. If your attorney makes an objection, wait until the two attorneys have resolved that objection before beginning or continuing your answer.

15. Do not look to your attorney. Meet the opposing attorney eye-to-eye and answer his questions directly.

16. If you are asked if you have spoken with your attorney in preparation for the deposition, admit it readily.

17. Do not try to second-guess the opposing attorney or decide what sort of statement will "help" your case. Tell the truth as directly as you can.

18. If you are certain of a fact, do not be afraid to insist on your answer. Do not back down on questions, such as, "are you absolutely certain?"

19. Do not express opinions; testify as to facts. Be straight-forward and attentive. (Expert opinion excepted).

20. Do not nod your head yes or no; the court reporter cannot make a record of that gesture. Say on the record what you mean.

21. Watch what you say "off the record".

22. Do not chew gum or smoke while testifying.

23. Do not joke with the opposing attorney when testifying. Be firm, polite but serious.

24. Four answers cannot be misunderstood when the deposition is read months later. These are: "yes," "no," "I don't remember," and "I don't know".
The statement "I don't remember" doesn't imply that you won't remember in the future, but the statement "I don't know" implies that you never knew the answer to begin with.

18. Typically:
Florida Standard Jury Instructions
1.3   Deposition Testimony

"Members of the jury, the sworn testimony of [name], given before trial, will now be read to you. You are to consider and weigh this testimony as though the witness had testified here in person."

Florida Rules of Civil Procedure
RULE 1.330   Use of Depositions in Court Proceedings

(a) Use of Depositions. At the trial or upon the hearing of a motion or an interlocutory proceeding, any part or all of a deposition may be used against any party who was present or represented at the taking of the deposition or who had reasonable notice of it so far as admissible under the rules of evidence applied as though the witness were then present and testifying in accordance with any of the following provisions:

(1) Any deposition may be used by any party for the purpose of contradicting or impeaching the testimony of the deponent as a witness.

(3) The deposition of a witness, whether or not a party, may be used by any party for any purpose if the court finds …

(f) the witness is an expert or skilled witness.

19. Federal Rules of Evidence
RULE 602.   Lack of Personal Knowledge (Supra)

Federal Rules of Evidence
RULE 701.   Opinion Testimony by Lay Witnesses

If the witness is not testifying as an expert, the witness' testimony in the form of opinion or inference is limited to those opinions or inferences which are:

(a) rationally based on the perception of the witness, and (b) helpful to a clear understanding of the witness testimony or the determination of a fact in issue.

Florida Evidence Code, Chapter 90
90.701   Opinion Testimony of Lay Witnesses

If a witness is not testifying as an expert, his testimony about what he perceived may be in the form of inference and opinion when:

(1) The witness cannot readily, and with equal accuracy and adequacy, communicate what he has perceived to the trier of fact without testifying in terms of inferences or opinions and his use of inferences or opinions will not mislead the trier of fact to the prejudice of the objecting party; and

(2) The opinions and inferences do not require a special knowledge, skill, experience, or training.

Federal Rules of Evidence
RULE 702.   Testimony by Experts

If scientific, technical or other specialized knowledge will assist the trier of fact to understand the evidence or to determine a fact in issue, a witness qualified as an expert by knowledge, skill, experience, training or education, may testify thereto in the form of an opinion or otherwise.

Florida Evidence Code, Chapter 90
90.702   Testimony by Experts

If scientific, technical or other specialized knowledge will assist the trier of fact in understanding the evidence or in determining a fact in issue, a witness qualified as an expert by knowledge, skill, experience, training or education, may testify about it in the form of an opinion; however, the opinion is admissible only if it can be applied to evidence at trial.

20. Gwathmey v. United States, 215 Fed.Reptr. 2nd 148, 5th Circuit Court of Appeals (1954).

21. Federal Rules of Evidence
    RULE 706.   Court Appointed Experts

    (a) Appointment—the court may on its own motion or on the motion of any party enter an order to show cause why expert witnesses should not be appointed and may request the parties to submit nominations. A witness so appointed shall advise the parties of witness findings, if any, the witness deposition may be taken by any party; and the witness may be called upon to testify by the court or any party. The witness shall be subject to cross examination by each party, including a party calling the witness.
    (b) Compensation
    (c) Disclosure of Appointment.
    (d) Party Experts of Own Selection. Nothing in this rule limits the parties in calling expert witnesses of their own selection.

    Federal Rules of Evidence
    RULE 614.   Calling and Interrogation of Witnesses by Court

    (a) Calling by court
    (b) Interrogation by court - the court may interrogate witnesses, whether called by itself or by a party.
    (c) Objections

    Florida Evidence Code, Chapter 90
    90.615   Calling witnesses by the Court

    (1) The court may call witnesses whom all parties may cross-examine.
    (2) When required by the interests of justice, the court may interrogate witnesses, whether called by the court or by a party.

22. Typically, as in the Florida case, Edith Mills v. Redwing Carriers, 127 So.2d 453, 2nd Dist. Ct. Appeal. (1961), where the court also stated "when the opinion is nothing more that the speculation of an admitted non expert on the issues involved, it invades the province of the jury".

    Federal Rules of Evidence
    RULE 702.   Testimony by Experts (supra)

23. Federal Rules of Evidence
    RULE 607.   Who May Impeach

    The credibility of a witness may be attacked by any party including the party calling the witness.

Federal Rules of Evidence
RULE 611.   Mode and Order of Interrogation and Presentation

(a) Control by court—the court shall exercise reasonable control over the mode and order of interrogating witnesses and presenting evidence as to:
    (1) make the interrogation and presentment effective for the ascertainment of the truth;
    (2) avoid needless consumption of time; and
    (3) protect witnesses from harassment or undue embarrassment.
(b) Cross examination should be limited to the subject matter of the direct examination and matters affecting the credibility of the witness. The court may, in the exercise of discretion, permit inquiry into additional matters as if on direct examination.
(c) Leading questions

Florida Evidence Code, Chapter 90
90.706   Authoritativeness of literature for use in cross-examination

Statements of facts or opinions on a subject of science, art, or specialized knowledge contained in a published treatise, periodical, book, dissertation, pamphlet, or other writing may be used in cross examination of an expert witness if the expert witness recognizes the author of the treatise, periodical, book, dissertation, pamphlet or other writing to be authoritative, or, notwithstanding, nonrecognition by the expert witness, if the trial court finds the author or the treatise, periodical, book, dissertation, pamphlet, or other writing to be authoritative and relevant to the subject matter.

24. Robert Parker v. Miracle Strip Boat(Florida), 341 So2d 197, 1st D.C.A. 1977.

    The witness was an insurance adjuster whom the insurer was trying to qualify as an expert. The court said "although Mr. Purrington might have been qualified under certain circumstances, appellant's counsel failed to ask the proper questions which would have qualified him as an expert".

25. Nat Harrison Assoc. v. Ruth Byrd, a widow, 256 So2d 50, 4th D.C.A. (1971).

26. Federal Rules of Evidence
    RULE 703.   Basis of Opinion Testimony by Experts

    The facts or data in the particular case upon which an expert bases an opinion or inference may be those perceived by or made known to the expert at or before the hearing. If of a type reasonably relied upon by experts in the particular field in forming opinions or inferences upon the subject, the facts or data need not be admissible in evidence.

    Federal Rules of Evidence
    RULE 704.   Opinion on Ultimate Issue

    ... testimony in the form of an opinion or inference otherwise admissible is not objectionable because it embraces an ultimate issue to be decided by the jury.

Florida Evidence Code, Chapter 90
90.703   Opinion on Ultimate Issue

Testimony in the form of an opinion or inference otherwise admissible is not objectionable because it includes an ultimate issue to be decided by the trier of fact.

Florida Evidence Code, Chapter 90
90.704   Basis of Opinion Testimony by Experts

The facts or data upon which an expert bases an opinion or inference may be those perceived by, or made known to, him at or before the trial. If the facts or data are of a type reasonably relied upon by experts in the subject to support the opinion expressed, the facts or data need not be admissible in evidence.

Florida Evidence Code, Chapter 90
90.705   Disclosure of Facts or Data underlying Expert Opinion

(1) Unless otherwise required by the court, an expert may testify in terms of opinion or inference and give his reasons without prior disclosure of the underlying facts or data. On cross examination he shall be required to specify the facts or data.

(2) Prior to the witness giving his opinion, a party against whom the opinion or inference is offered may conduct a voir dire examination of the witness directed to the underlying facts or data for his opinion. If the party establishes a prima facie evidence that the expert does not have a sufficient basis for his opinion, the opinions and inferences of the expert are inadmissible unless the party offering the testimony establishes the underlying facts or data.

See also: Hialeah v. Weatherford, 466 So2d 1127, 3rd D.C.A.(1985).

27. Pettigrew v. Pettigrew, 586 So2d 508, 5th D.C.A. (1991)

Speculation and conjecture are inadmissible to prove value of property.

Walters v. State Road Dept., 239 So2d 878, 1st D.C.A. (1970)

In a land condemnation proceeding the only expert called by the landowner had his appraisal stricken as speculative and conjectural to prove value after the following cross examination:

Q: So, how much did you enhance this property in its better location, or how much did you decrease it to make it fit the subject property?

A: Rather than go into the ups and downs of how much for each one, I made an overall adjustment factor of 110 per cent which is simply combining an adjustment for date of sale, offset somewhat by adjustment for location.

Q: I'd like you to tell the jury how you got to that, you use an adjustment for date of sale and an adjustment for location, now, which percentage did you adjust to what to come out to 110 percent?

A: This is an overall adjustment estimate.

Q: How did you get to it? You had to adjust up to make a 1961 sale applicable to a 1968 situation, didn't you?

A: Yes, sir.

Q: But you had to adjust down in order to make Eastport Road—

A: Yes, sir.

Q: The Eastport Road location fit the subject property?

A: Yes, sir.

Q: All right, so how much did you go up on one and down on the other to make them come out to 110 percent?

A: I can't tell you.

Q: You just said 110 per cent out of the clear blue?

A: No, sir, I didn't.

Q: I would like for you to tell us how you did it.

A: I can sit down and work backwards for maybe twenty or thirty minutes. When I worked these things out originally, I work out the adjustment - they work out a hundred one, one point one two, and rather that put in a complicated composite adjustment I round them off.

Q: I am just asking for the formula, you don't want to tell the jury how you did it.

A: Well, I can't.

Q: That's true on these other adjustments that we used, you can't?

A: That's right.

Q: You arrived at some adjustment that you applied to as-called comparable and came out to today's value of this property, that's what happened, isn't it?

A: That's the method I used.

28. Honeywell, Inc. v. Trend Coin, 449 So2d 876, 3rd D.C.A. (1984)

Method of Evaluation used by appraiser should not have been excluded by court since its use was reasonable and exclusion of his testimony was reversible error.

Dade County v. Miami Herald Publishing, 285 So2d 671, 3rd D.C.A. (1973)

Where an established value is nonexistent, the process of valuation must comprehend not only one but all of the influencing factors going to make up the intrinsic value including future potential use. The weight to be accorded the expert testimony of the appraiser rests with the triers of fact, the jury.

Rochelle v. State Road Dept., 196 So2d 477, 2nd D.C.A. (1977)

Method of evaluation used by an appraiser-expert witness (in condemnation action) is not a matter relating to competency of his testimony to be ruled upon by trial judge, unless method used by witness is so totally inadequate or improper that adoption of method would require a departure from all common sense and reason or would require adoption of an entirely new and unauthenticated formula in field of appraising.

29. Typically:

Florida Standard Jury Instructions

2.1   <u>Introductory Instruction</u>

Members of the jury, I shall now instruct you on the law that you must follow in reaching your verdict[s]. It is your duty as jurors to decide the issues, and only those issues, that I submit for determination by your verdict. In reaching your verdict, you should consider and weigh the evidence, decide the disputed issues of fact, and apply the law on which I shall instruct you, to facts as you find them from the evidence.

The evidence in this case consists of the sworn testimony of the witnesses, all exhibits received in evidence, [and] all facts that may be admitted or agreed to by the parties [,and any fact of which the court has taken judicial notice (explain as necessary)].

In determining the facts, you may draw reasonable inferences from the evidence. You may make deductions and reach conclusions which reason and common sense lead you to draw from the facts shown by the evidence in this case. But you should not speculate on any matters outside the evidence.

Florida Standard Jury Instructions

2.2   <u>Believability of Witnesses</u>

a.   General Considerations.

In determining the believability of any witness and the weight to be given the testimony of any witness, you may properly consider the demeanor of the witness while testifying; the frankness or lack of frankness of the witness; the intelligence of the witness; any interest the witness may have in the outcome of the case; the means and opportunity the witness had to know the facts about which the witness testified; the ability of the witness to remember the matters about which the witness testified; and the reasonableness of the testimony of the witness, considered in the light of all the evidence in the case and in light of your own experience and common sense.

b.   Expert Witnesses

[You have heard opinion testimony [on certain technical subjects] from a [person][persons] referred to as [an] expert witness[es].] [Some of the testimony before you was in the form of opinions about certain technical subjects.]

You may accept such opinion testimony, reject it, or give it the weight you think it deserves, considering the knowledge, skill, experience, training or education of the witness; the reasons given by the witness for the opinions expressed and all the other evidence in the case.

Florida Standard Jury Instructions

7.1   <u>Prejudice and Sympathy</u>

Your verdict[s] must be based on the evidence that has been received and the law on which I have instructed you. In reaching your verdict[s], you are not to be swayed from the performance of your duty by prejudice, sympathy or any other sentiment for or against any party.

30. Typically:

Florida Standard Jury Instructions

6.1   <u>Personal injury and property damages: introduction</u>

If you find for the defendant[s] you will not consider the matter of damages. But, if you find for (claimant) you should award (claimant) an amount of money that the greater weight of the evidence shows will fairly and adequately compensate him for such [loss] [injury] [or] [damage], including any such damage as (claimant) is reasonably certain to [incur][experience] in the future. You shall consider the following elements: (Elements vary from case to case)

31. <u>Hannah v. Martin</u>, 49 So2d 585, Fla. Supreme Court (1950)

In other words, the damages awarded should be equal to and precisely commensurate with the injury sustained.

<u>Clearwater Assoc. v. Hicks Laundry</u>, 433 So2d 7, 2nd D.C.A. (1983)

Uncertainty as to precise amount of, or difficulty in proving damages does not preclude recovery if there is some reasonable basis in evidence for the amount awarded. Where damage cannot be precisely determined the trial judge is vested with reasonable discretion on making award of damages.

32. <u>Meerdink v. Housing Authority of West Palm Beach</u>, 7 So2d 788, Fla. Sup. Ct. (1942)

In an action for destruction by fire of a house filled with antiques and heirlooms the court said:

"The evidence as to value of the property lost is conflicting in some aspects and like the evidence as to what could have been saved, is largely opinion evidence but this in no sense discredits it or removes it from the province of the jury on which to predicate a verdict. It is shown that the house was an old building and constructed from better material than can now be secured but it was a home and had a value for that which was subject to evaluation. The personal property was shown to be china, pictures, furniture, a piano and other articles to adorn and equip the home many of which were antiques and heirlooms inherited by Mrs. Webster from parents and were shown to be of great value.

It is often impossible to place a current market value on such articles but the law does not contemplate that this be done with mathematical exactness. The law guarantees every person a remedy when he has been wronged. If the damage is to personal property as in this case, it may be impossible to show that all of it had a market price. In fact it may be very valuable so far as the owner is concerned but have no value as far as the public is concerned. It would be manifestly unfair to apply the test of market value in such cases.

When the wrong is shown it becomes the duty of court and jury to apply a test that will reasonably compensate the person wronged rather than one that makes it impossible to do so.

See also:

Allied Van Lines v. McKnab, 331 So2d 319, 2nd D.C.A. (1976)

An appellate court reversed a trial court award of damages for destruction of personal goods, saying:

"The remaining point relates to the value of the destroyed personal goods. The plaintiff testified as to the original cost of the items and further related that the value of the items at the time of their destruction was greater that the original purchase price. She further testified that the total value of the goods was $35,315, which was the exact amount of the final judgment." (original cost $35,315)

"We find it inconceivable that household goods, some of which were 20 years old and none of which were brand new, could increase in value from their original cost. This testimony as to the value of the destroyed items is not competent, substantial evidence which accords with logic and reason. In measuring plaintiff's damages, the proper measure of damages for loss of personal property is its market value on the date of the loss."

Loury v. Loury, 431 So2d 701 [Fla. App. 2nd Dist. 1983]

Former husband sued for failure to deliver certain items of personal property which court ordered be delivered to former wife.

"The trial court erred in awarding a money judgment against him. The proper measure of damages for loss of personal property is the market value on the day of the loss. Accordingly, the lower court erred in awarding a judgment based entirely on evidence concerning replacement cost."

33. Ft. Lauderdale Transfer & Rigging v. Callahan Motor Co., 446 So2d 138, 4th D.C.A. (1984)

"We agree with appellant's contention that appellee failed to adequately prove its claim for damages for the total loss of the machine. Appellee's evidence established only that the machine had a value of $35,000 before the loss. Appellee's expert testified that the machine had a market value and that it could be fixed. However, the expert failed to offer any opinion as to either the salvage value of the machine or its repaired value. The Restatement of Torts sets forth the measure of proof which we hold necessary to recover damages such as those claimed by appellee for the loss of the press brake machine:

Where a person is entitled to a judgment for harm to chattels not amounting to a total destruction in value, the damages include compensation for

(a) the difference between the value of the chattel [personal property] before the harm and the value after the harm or, at the plaintiff's election, the reasonable cost of repair or restoration where feasible, with due allowance for any difference between the original value and the value after repairs, and

(b) the loss of use.

34. Typically:

Florida Statute 475.610: Purpose to regulate real estate appraisers

Florida Statute 475.611: Definitions

"Appraisal foundation" or "foundation" means The Appraisal Foundation established on November 20, 1987, as a not for profit corporation under the laws of Illinois.

Uniform Standards of Professional Appraisal Practice means the most recent standards approved and adopted by the Appraisal Standards Board of The Appraisal Foundation.

Chapter 5

Valuation for Specific Purposes and Intended Uses

Fair Market Value

Fair market value as a hypothetical concept is three distinct words. **Fair** implies the large scope of what is ordinary, with no one having an advantage and with equality of intention. **Market** implies the large scope of supply and demand, a place for exchange, exchange rights and the exercising of rights, levels, opportunity and frequency in a forum. **Value** implies the large scope of understanding that these are estimates of value, not prices, that can be tracked by happening and frequency; value is an expression of use and utility; the quantification of value ultimately hinges on what others have similarly experienced with a property in a similar situation.

Fair Market Value is a specific hypothetical concept of value framed by the Federal Government for use in the context of tax liability assessment. It is the only value accepted by the Internal Revenue Service for such assessment, whether pertaining to estate tax, gift tax or income tax liability including deductions for charitable donations.

Fair Market Value is widely misunderstood and commonly confused with other types of value thought of as **fair** or **equitable**. A fundamental difference distinguishing Fair Market Value from these others, however, pertains to the notion of **ownership as the enjoyment of retained benefits**. Taxable estate properties sold within the closing of an estate are taxed on the actual amount realized from sale, as the government considers the sales price of a property the most probative evidence of its Fair Market Value. However, those taxable properties left unsold, and, hence, untested in the market, are taxed on their value held, or in other words, on their value unsold. This notion of different values for sold and unsold properties is rooted in the Federal Government's interpretation of the basic concept of property ownership as

a **bundle of rights** (Treasury Regulation Sec. 20.2031-8[b]) that includes not only the right to sell and enjoy the benefits of sales proceeds, but also the right not to sell and, hence, to hold a property and continue any and all benefits and enjoyments attendant to ownership. Fair Market Value was developed specifically to gauge and express this value of taxable properties for which all benefits and enjoyments attendant to ownership are retained.

Therefore, Fair Market Value is not intended to comment upon Marketable Cash Value (the net proceeds yielded from the sale of a property), Replacement Value or any other expression of value other than that defined by the Federal Government under Title 26, Chapter I, subchapter B, Part 20, in Treasury Regulation Sec. 20.2031-1[b]:

"The **Fair Market Value** [emphasis added] is the price at which the property would change hands between a willing buyer and a willing seller, neither being under any compulsion to buy or sell and both having reasonable knowledge of relevant facts."

The fair market value of a particular item of property included in the decedent's gross estate is not to be determined by a forced sale price. Nor is the fair market value of an item of property to be determined by the sale price of the item in a market other than that in which such item is most commonly sold to the public, taking into account the location of the item wherever appropriate. Thus, in the case of an item of property included in the decedent's gross estate which is generally obtained by the public in the retail market, the fair market value of such an item of property is the price at which the item or a comparable item would be sold at retail. For example, the fair market value of an automobile (an article generally obtained by the public in the retail market) included in the decedent's gross estate is the price for which an automobile of the same or approximately the same description, make, model, age, condition, etc., could be purchased by a member of the general public and not the price for which the particular automobile of the decedent would be purchased by a dealer in used automobiles.

Explicit in this definition is the appraiser's responsibility to determine the most active and relevant market in which to appraise each property. This determination is of central importance to the concept of Fair Market Value and deserves emphatic comment; the apposite value conclusion of any Fair Market Value appraisal turns upon it. Special knowledge of, and experience with, like properties and their markets are requisite to the determination of that specific market **in which such item is most commonly sold to the public.**

The criteria for determining this market are not satisfied necessarily or automatically by any particular marketplace. For example, we know that a public auction may qualify as a marketplace for both wholesale and retail market transactions (wholesale transactions being those in which properties are purchased for resale, and retail transactions are those in which properties are purchased by an ultimate consumer). Both markets, in their various layers or levels, may operate in the same marketplace, given the appropriate circumstances. And these circumstances are the outcome of a wide range of market factors including: the specific type, nature, quality and condition of the property; the prevailing nature or fashion of acquisition most typically attending like properties; and the time, place and advertising of the sale (among others). A well-advertised, well-catalogued public auction may be the suitable stage on which retail sales transactions may be said to occur when properties are purchased by their ultimate consumers, such as collectors, rather than by intermediary agents, such as dealers or interior designers, for resale to those ultimate consumers.

Conversely, it is just as possible to view specific sales transacted in retail stores and galleries as wholesale market transactions when they represent purchases for resale. Such may happen, for example, in the situation wherein the seller is deficient in that specialized expertise necessary to recognize and ultimately realize the full retail potential of a property. Or it may happen when a dealer purchases from another dealer, both being retail vendors, for resale to an ultimate consumer not available to the latter. Hence, formulae prove unreliable, and the all-important determination of Relevant Market remains the province of the qualified appraiser.

It is important to note that the courts recognize that the market i**n which such item is most commonly sold to the public** is not necessarily the primary market, and that the **public** is not limited to individual consumers (i.e., from the general public). Thus, in *Anselmo v. Commissioner of Internal Revenue*, 80 T.C. 872 (1983), *aff'd*, 757 F.2d 1208 (11th Cir. 1985), the Tax Court determined that the Fair Market Value of a large quantity of low quality, unmounted gems was not the price paid by individual consumers from the general public purchasing at retail jewelry stores—as such items are not most customarily sold in this manner—but rather the manufacturers or jewelers capable of preparing such items for sale to such buyers from such vendors. The court viewed the ultimate consumer of these stones to be a different party than the ultimate consumer of the jewelry items in which the stones would be later included.

In spite of the common perception of manufacturers and retail stores normally purchasing on the **wholesale** level (for resale to an ultimate consumer), these parties were observed by the court to be the last stage in the chain of distribution of a specific commodity (an unmounted stone of a certain quality dictating a certain commercial usage) that would be transformed thereafter into an entirely different commodity (a finished piece of jewelry with a different type of ultimate consumer). And therefore, as ultimate consumers of that particular commodity, these manufacturers, jewelers or retail jewelry stores would be making retail rather than wholesale purchases of such properties. In affirming the tax court position and decision, the appellate court cited an hypothetical example of determining the Fair Market Value of live cattle: "For example, the general buying public for live cattle would be comprised primarily of slaughterhouses rather than individual consumers. The fair market value of live cattle accordingly would be measured by the price paid at the livestock auction rather than at the supermarket." (*Anselmo v. Commissione*r, 757 F.2d 1208, 1214-15.)

Therefore, the **public** referred to in Treasury Regulation Sec. 20.2031-1 (b) is understood to mean only the most appropriate and customary consumer of such items, a consumer not limited to individuals from the general public purchasing on the primary market. (See *Sandler v. Commissioner*, 52 T.C.M. (CCH) 563, 566 (1986) for language specifically identifying the secondary market as a relevant market on which to determine fair market value [when such market is the most active marketplace for such items].)

Furthermore, the Federal Government considers any buyer's premium attached to a sale at public auction to be a component of the sales price (as is customarily recognized in the industry) and, therefore, part of the Fair Market Value of any property valued for estate tax, gift tax or income tax purposes. (See IRS Technical Advice Memorandum 9235005 [Code Sec. 2031] of May 27, 1992.)

In conclusion, Fair Market Value is a specific hypothetical concept of value limited to the function of tax liability assessment on properties held and not sold. It represents the amount that would be obtained (paid in full [including any buyer's premiums, taxes, etc.] by buyer) rather than retained (received, net, by seller) from sale in an arm's-length transaction between willing and informed parties in a relevant market.

Marketable Cash Value

Marketable Cash Value is most customarily understood to represent the anticipated net proceeds that would be yielded from the sale of a property in a relevant market and in an appropriate time frame. It is the cash amount that would be left **in hand** to the seller from a willing and unrestricted market transaction once all incurred costs of sale were deducted from the obtained sale price.

A helpful description of the type of market transaction in which Marketable Cash Value is said to operate can be found in the definition of Fair Market Value laid down by the Federal Government in Treasury Regulation Section 20.2031-1(b) under Title 26, Chapter I, subchapter B. (See definition in previous section.)

However, Marketable Cash Value is not synonymous or interchangeable with Fair Market Value. The latter is a specific hypothetical concept of value framed by the Federal Government for use in the particular context of tax liability assessment of estate-owned, gifted or donated properties remaining unsold and, hence, valued to reflect continued enjoyment of ownership benefits. The definition quoted previously from the Treasury Regulation is an extract from a much longer paragraph which goes on to specifically exclude any consideration of selling costs from the amount said to be the Fair Market Value of an assessed property. Therefore, although Marketable Cash Value and Fair Market Value may be said to share the same market transaction basis or climate (i.e., between a willing and informed seller and buyer in a relevant market, as contrasted with

a forced liquidation climate), the two value concepts differ sharply at that point where proceeds of sale are considered, Fair Market Value representing the gross proceeds and Marketable Cash Value the net proceeds of sale.

Net proceeds are those left (**in hand**) once any costs incurred in achieving the sale are subtracted from the gross sale amount. These costs may include (1) brokerage fees (such as those customarily charged by auction houses, galleries, dealers or other agents—whether calculated on a percentage basis or on a flat rate), (2) promotion costs (such as photography, publication in catalogs, advertisement or related costs customarily charged to the seller above and beyond the agreed fee), (3) handling costs (such as shipping, intermediary storage, insurance or related costs) and (4) preparation costs (such as cleaning, restoration, conservation, framing or related marketability enhancements).

But attention to the proceeds aspect of a sales transaction does not in itself satisfy the conditions requisite to Marketable Cash Value. Any discussion of this value concept necessarily hinges upon a careful consideration of two key conditions mentioned in the first paragraph of this value definition: **relevant market** and **appropriate time frame**.

Relevant market is here (and most customarily) understood to be that market in which such property is most commonly sold to its customary consumer public, keeping in mind the type, nature, quality and condition of the property (or quantity of properties). The criteria for determining this market are not satisfied necessarily or automatically by any particular marketplace. For example, we know that a public auction may qualify as a marketplace wherein either or both wholesale and retail market transactions may be said to occur. Since wholesale transactions may be defined as those in which properties are purchased for resale, and retail transactions as those in which properties are purchased by an ultimate consumer, either market may be said to operate in the same marketplace, given the appropriate circumstances. And these circumstances are the outcome of a wide range of market factors including (1) the specific type, nature, quality and condition of the property (or quantity of properties), (2) the prevailing nature or fashion of acquisition most typically attending like properties and (3) the time, place and advertising of the sale, among others. A well-advertised, well-catalogued public auction may be the suitable stage on which retail sales transactions may be said to occur when properties are purchased by their ultimate consumers, such as collectors, rather than by intermediary agents, such as dealers or interior designers, for resale to those ultimate consumers. Conversely, as discussed under Fair Market Value, it is just as possible to view specific sales transacted in retail stores and galleries as wholesale transactions when they represent purchases for resale. Such may happen, for example, in the situation wherein the seller is deficient in that specialized expertise necessary in recognizing and ultimately realizing the full retail potential of a property. Or it may happen when a dealer purchases from another dealer, both being retail vendors, for resale to an ultimate consumer not available to the latter. Hence, formulae prove unreliable, and the all-important determination of Relevant Market remains the province of the qualified appraiser.

Appropriate time frame most customarily is understood to be the market exposure time necessary for the orderly sale of a property in its relevant market. This period may encompass the time it takes to effectively advertise or otherwise promote the property to its customary consumer public. And it may include that time requisite to the preparation (cleaning, restoration, framing, etc.) of the property thought beneficial to the most effective marketing of such a property or to the related expenses of time considered typical to the orderly sale of like items. It is in this respect that Marketable Cash Value is most obviously distinguished from Forced Liquidation Value, as the latter operates in a climate wherein the time frame of sale is typically determined by criteria other than marketing advantages, the result of such **disorderly** sale being a necessary sacrifice of Relevant Market.

Marketable Cash Value is also not intended to comment upon the Replacement Value of a property. Typically neither the customary buying patterns of the seller nor the estimated reproduction costs of the property (aspects often associated with or relevant to the concept of Replacement Value) are considered relevant to the criteria in forming Marketable Cash Value.

In conclusion, Marketable Cash Value represents the anticipated net proceeds (or cash **in hand**) that would be yielded from the orderly sale of a property once all costs of sale were subtracted. It represents the amount not merely obtained (paid in full [including any buyer's premiums, taxes, etc.] by buyer) but retained (received, net, by seller) from sale.

Replacement Value

Replacement Value is a concept of value with particular relevance to insurance coverage and is most customarily understood to represent that amount of money required to replace a property with another of similar qualities within a reasonable length of time in an appropriate and relevant market.

Similar qualities are understood to include numerous characteristics of two basic types: physical and attributed. Physical characteristics include those such as medium, materials, subject, shape (or format), size, weight (when applicable), condition and overall appearance. Attributed characteristics include those such as authorship (individual or collective), culture, region, period or specific date, provenance, historical importance, prestige factors (such as conferred status associated with a particular vendor or a famous person) and measurable aesthetic quality or appearance. The extent to which such qualities are judged similar with regard to the comparison of a property with its replacement property depends upon the relative importance attached to these qualities in the market. For example, while an ancient earthenware funerary figure with some restoration may still serve as an acceptable replacement for a similar one without such restoration, it is quite likely that the same would not hold true in the case of a modern porcelain figure, wherein the market concern for material **integrity** often supersedes concern for historical significance. The difference in acceptability between two such replacements appears to have far less to do with specific issues of medium, age or function than simply with the prevalent attitudes, concerns and priorities of collectors as expressed in the market. And these attitudes need not be logical or easily rationalized. A crack to a small, delicate porcelain or cloisonné **cabinet** vase may have a far more devastating impact on the marketability of the vase than would a proportionately consistent crack to a large **floor** vase of the same material, age, design, maker and type. Hence, the final arbiter of **similar qualities** is inevitably the market.

But apart from these considerations of specific criteria which may decide the suitability of a particular replacement of property remains the more general and theoretical question of what is actually being insured. Most of the properties normally found described on special schedule insurance policies are by their very nature as artwork, or other **non-replaceables**, unique and, hence, irreplaceable. Even prints and sculptures pulled from the same matrixes and molds can be discernibly different from one another, as is often demonstrated in the market. No amount of insurance premiums can actually **insure** these objects in the sense of protecting them from physical harm or theft. Once gone, there is no

replacing them in the literal sense; there is only left the remedy of substituting for them similar objects of comparable value. That entity that can be said to be insured, therefore, is the value thought necessary to procure an acceptable substitution, thereby continuing the enjoyment and benefits inherent in the **bundle of rights** we call property ownership. Since the rights conferred in the ownership of a property normally include not only the right to enjoy the benefits of maintained ownership but also the right to sell and enjoy the proceeds of sale, it could be said that one insures not a specific tangible object but rather the valuable rights associated with that object.

Reasonable length of time is understood to be that period of time in which anyone as knowledgeable as the insured — and hence, anyone having no more special or privileged access to such properties than the insured — could be expected to replace a property with a similar one in a manner of efficiency and expedience most consistent with the customary buying habits of that party. For example, focused and fastidious buyers who normally spend more to purchase from specialized high-level retail vendors can normally expect to find acceptable replacements of lost properties from such vendors, and at such prices, with far greater expedience and assurance to which such higher prices typically privilege them. Similarly, buyers customarily active on lower levels of the market are not best served by paying insurance premiums based on these higher priced replacements, which are unrealistic to the manner in which these items would be most typically **replaced**. Ultimately, therefore, any discussion of **reasonable length of time** must involve a discussion of **appropriate and relevant market**.

Appropriate and relevant market, in the context of insurance coverage, is most customarily understood to be that market in which the insured most typically purchases like items. This market may be either the retail market in which a property is purchased by its ultimate consumer, or the wholesale market, in which a property is purchased for resale. However, it is an observable fact that there is usually more than one level to any one market, whether retail or wholesale. Therefore, since different consumers customarily buy on different levels of the market, as well as in different markets, strict attention to the prospective replacement cost of an insured property upon any one isolated market or market level without consideration of the insured's specific customary buying habits proves misleading.

As discussed above under **appropriate length of time**, there are buyers who customarily purchase from specialized high-level retail vendors. The higher-end prices normally associated with such vendors are typically justified in the minds of such buyers by certain benefits often seen to be conveyed with these purchases. Such benefits may include a more extensive warranty than might normally be available from vendors on lower market levels. They may also include any added **pedigree**, called **provenance**, which may be conferred with purchase from such a vendor, as well as any prestige value or status. Since there does indeed exist a commonly recognized status associated with certain vendors, and since that status is commonly thought to be conferred upon the purchased item as an enhancement of its value, as well possibly as an enhancement of status to the owner, it should be quite reasonable to expect that the same item may be worth more to a consumer when purchased at one vendor or marketplace than at another. An insured accustomed to the prestige value and other privileges conveyed to them with the purchase from such a vendor or marketplace may be seen as poorly served by the replacement of that item with one lacking these enhancement qualities or privileges. In such case the apposite Replacement Value should realistically be that which includes any and all additional costs necessary to replacing a lost property in the manner most typical to original purchase, including (1) costs incurred in purchasing from a specific dealer, gallery or auction house, (2) those incurred in the engagement of a consultant, interior designer or other commissioner and (3) those incurred in any transportation or installation of the property. To insure a buyer used to a lower market or market level on the basis of these upper-level costs is generally thought to be unrealistic and inappropriate.

In conclusion, Replacement Value is a concept of value with particular relevance to insurance coverage. It represents the amount of money required to replace a property with another of similar qualities within a reasonable length of time in an appropriate and relevant market.

Estimating Value for Orderly Liquidation

In the case of properties being appraised for liquidation, the concept of **value in exchange** is assumed. There are basically two types of liquidation, forced liquidation and orderly liquidation. When circumstances dictate that certain properties must be sold immediately without regard to relevant marketplace, this would be considered forced liquidation. Where no such limitations are imposed, the sale or liquidation is considered orderly, with orderly liquidation defined as the most probable price in terms of cash or other precisely revealed terms, for which the property would change hands under required and limiting conditions in an orderly manner, generally advertised, with reasonable time constraints, in an appropriate and relevant marketplace, with knowledgeable buyers.

There are various jurisdictional exceptions requiring specific limitations on the conditions of sale when estimating the fair market value of a property for a specific legal purpose. A notable example would be in the appraisal of certain categories of properties held by the United States Marshall's Service for sale. These properties consist of a variety of types from several sources including seized properties from enforcement agencies of the United States Treasury Department. Other examples of jurisdictional exceptions are those imposed by courts for types of cases or specific cases. In every appraisal assignment, the appraiser must identify the specific jurisdictional guidelines and limitations to be applied.

In appraising property for orderly liquidation, the appraiser has a greater need to describe the range of possible results from the liquidation options. If there is a possible gain to be realized by moving the property geographically because of a larger or more appreciative market, the appraiser must reveal the potential results of both moving and not moving to another locale. If there are gains to be made by advertising, sale previews, auction or priced sale, or other means of maximizing returns, the potential gain and why it can be expected must be explained. In all cases, the effect of time on the sale of the property must be addressed, including anticipated exposure time necessary to accomplish the sale.

The various potential results of the many possible alternatives create the need for the appraiser to review the options from which the client can make an economic decision. The more limitations imposed at the outset, the fewer paths to be explored. The fewer the restrictions placed on the **orderly liquidation**, the larger the range of options that exist.

Estimating Value for Equitable Distribution

In contrast to appraising property for sale, the concepts of **fair market value** and of **value in use** are of concern in property distribution appraisals. The need for arriving at estimates of value that reflect just compensation is often the result of the dissolution of a relationship that held property jointly, such as in divorce or partnership dissolutions. Another circumstance may include the division of estate properties among heirs. The under-lying tenet of the valuation is that it estimates the amount of money necessary to replace the utility or the enjoyments of property that is being divided. That amount must not be so high or so low that the option of keeping the property is any greater or lesser than replacing the property, making it fair for both the party retaining the property and the party taking compensation.

In estimating the value of normally depreciating property such as household manufactured furniture or utility property like appliances, it is necessary to identify the remaining life of the property and any factors that contribute to its depreciation. Since most properties depreciate at different rates, no set "formula" satisfies the needs of the appraisal problem. Most property is available in used condition; market comparisons are useful in estimating value. Market access is a primary factor in estimating fair market value or, alternatively, value in use, and the appraiser must be specific in identifying the choice of markets used and defending the decision to exclude the ones not used. Reliance on the consistency of fixed retail markets such as galleries or department stores, or replacement specialists like pattern matching services for china and silver may be appropriate.

State laws regarding the appropriate designation of values in instances of division of property vary; some regulate the use of the concept of fair market value, others actual cash value, others value in use, others net value, etc. The appraiser should ascertain the appropriate value definition for each assignment.

Net value is a term of jurisdictional exception that dictates, in certain states, the valuation of marital property for equitable distribution based on the "market value, if any, less the amount of any encumbrance serving to offset or reduce market value." *Alexander v. Alexander*, 68 N.C. App. 548, 551, 315 S.E.2d 772, 775 (1984). Encumbrances may include actual indebtedness on the property or normal and expected commissions or other costs necessarily paid in selling the property in its appropriate and relevant market.

In the final analysis for jurisdictions in which either fair market value or value in use are mandated in matters of equitable distribution, it is required that the appraiser identify all of the factors necessary for a fair compensation of value and utility. This includes research and analysis of the ability of the parties to participate in the marketplace, the normal behavior patterns of the populations of the various markets investigated, including buying habits, the precise utility of the subject properties, and any enhancements or impairments to value from the causes of appreciation or depreciation on value.

Hypothetical Appraisals

The function or intended use for which a personal property appraisal report is normally prepared includes insurance, donation, estate or probate, equitable distribution and liquidation. A hypothetical appraisal report may be prepared for any of these uses.

The purpose or type of value for which a personal property appraisal is prepared includes replacement, fair market, marketable cash, value in use, and liquidation value. A hypothetical appraisal report may be prepared in estimating any of these values.

In the preparation of a hypothetical appraisal report for any of the stated functions or types of value, an appraiser must understand the appropriate regulations governing such functions. When confronted with a requirement to prepare a hypothetical appraisal, the appraiser must conscientiously determine the following:

1. The circumstances requiring the hypothetical appraisal
2. The function the hypothetical appraisal will serve
3. The type of value appropriate for the particular function
4. The motive(s) for the hypothetical appraisal

When a hypothetical appraisal report is prepared, a definitive statement must be included which contains all relevant information concerning the reason it was necessary to prepare a hypothetical appraisal, a detailed explanation of the information made available and upon which the appraisal is based, as well as the sources of the information provided. A complete explanation of limiting and contingent conditions is an especially important element of the hypothetical appraisal report.

Hypothetical appraisals are addressed specifically by both the *Principles of Appraisal Practice and Code of Ethics* (*PAPCE*) of the American Society of Appraisers and by the Ethics Provision of the *Uniform Standards of Professional Appraisal Practice* (*USPAP*):

> If an appraisal is a hypothetical one, it is required that it be labeled as hypothetical, that the reason a hypothetical appraisal was made be stated, and that the assumed hypothetical conditions be set forth. (Par. 8.3, *PAPCE*).

> The development of an appraisal, review, or consulting service based on a hypothetical condition is unethical unless: 1) the use of the hypothesis is clearly disclosed; 2) the assumption of the hypothetical condition is clearly required for legal purposes, for purposes of reasonable analysis, or for purposes of comparison and would not be misleading, and 3) the report clearly describes the rationale for this assumption, the nature of the hypothetical condition, and its effect on the result of the appraisal, review, or consulting service.

(*USPAP*, 1994, Ethics Provision, Conduct Section Comment)

Estimating Value for Insurance Coverage

References to valuations for insurance purposes have been found in the United States and England since the seventeenth century. While appraisal methodology and standard practice have become increasingly sophisticated, it is well to keep in mind that few general insurance professionals today are truly knowledgeable about fine arts, antiques and collectibles, nor are they as yet fully trained to interpret personal property appraisal documents.

The burden often rests with the client to find a knowledgeable appraiser who understands insurance requirements and whose professional work can withstand the investigations of values which insurance companies may conduct prior to payment of a claim. However, it is not the role of the appraiser to determine for a client the type of insurance policy most desirable for their needs. That decision remains the responsibility of the client with advice from their insurance professional.

Therefore, a professional appraiser must generate an appraisal report that succeeds in answering the appraisal questions, describes the purpose of the assignment, identifies the intended use and defines the values, avoiding esoteric jargon methods employed. The report must lend itself to the scrutiny of third parties who may utilize it at any time in the future for potential insurance coverage-related purposes. Insurance appraisals will always have two other readers to be considered, the underwriter and the claims adjuster.

The underwriter reviews an application for a valuable articles policy or extended category limit. The underwriter is particularly concerned with the claims record of the policyholder and with whether the nature of the property and the value claimed seem appropriate for the location and circumstances in which it will be kept. Value is considered only as one element of risk, and the policyholder statement of value will be examined only if it is so excessive as to raise a warning of fraud.

The claims adjuster is called in after a substantial loss, when there are suspicious circumstances, or when there is disagreement regarding the company's settlement offer. An appraisal may be offered by the policyholder in support of his claim, as proof of existence and value. The adjuster will place importance on the quality of the appraiser's property description, which must have enough detail to be the basis of specification for replacement. Also, he will look at the reasonableness of the corresponding value in estimating his own value. Because adjusters are not responsible for proving value, formal training and credentials are not required, and, in fact, most of the adjuster's training is in the field. Through experience, he attempts to gain enough knowledge to negotiate convincingly with the consumer and to recognize suspicious circumstances.

Clearly, it is advantageous for an appraiser to be familiar with the policies and procedures governing the coverage which a client may purchase in order that the insured be provided with the best possible basis from which the client and his insurance agent will determine appropriate levels and types of insurance coverage. By doing so the appraiser will also play an important role in helping to establish a clear communication between the appraisal profession and the insurance industry through common definitions and language.

When Should a Property Be Appraised for Insurance?

Many times clients are unclear as to whether or not to include certain properties in the insurance appraisal. Criteria which have been suggested by various insurance professionals and appraisers include: (1) if the property exceeds $250 in value; (2) if the market is not commonly known, as with specialized collectibles; (3) if the characteristics central to a property's value might not be commonly recognized, such as exceptionally good condition, rare features, or superior design; (4) if the property is to be insured by floater, Inland Marine or Valuable Items Policy.

Policies

The most common policy available to consumers for insurance of their real and personal property is a package offered in a standard form, HO-3, used by companies across the country with their own titles but with little variation. This policy gives the homeowner replacement cost coverage of his dwelling against various risks. His personal property is covered for actual cash value against a list of named perils. Replacement cost coverage of personal property is usually available by endorsement. There is a specific limit on the insurance company's obligation to pay for personal property, set at a percentage of the value for which the dwelling is insured with additional limitations for various property categories. Blanket coverage, or extended limits, for any category is available by endorsement, with the payment of extra premium for such coverage. Extended limits apply to individual objects or to sets of jewelry, stamps, fine art, silver, guns, coins, furs, or collections, which will be listed and described with the appropriate value in the endorsement to the policy, known as **scheduling**.

The large insurance companies which specialize in the coverage of substantial personal assets, specifically collections of the fine and decorative arts, publish detailed policy statements defining terms of coverage by amount and type, as well as terms of payment for such **valuable articles coverage**. A study of such policies simply aids the appraiser in understanding the insurance company's professional stance.

Enrollment in a sophisticated risk management program which is available to those with substantial personal property assets will be instrumental in making the client aware of the need to document the property in writing with visual supplementation by photographs and/or videotape. Thus, an appraiser provides a viable and significant service to the client and to the insurance industry.

Insurance of personal property is available separately from typical homeowner's insurance coverage, through **Floaters** or **Inland Marine** policies. The insurance industry has marine roots through its historical insuring of the cargoes of ships; cargoes transported overland were designated as inland marine. This type of insurance is now extended to include the personal property of ordinary individuals, but the policies are still known as Floaters.

Floaters normally cover property for all risks (with specified exclusions) but may also be written for named perils; they may be written to pay **actual cash value**, **replacement value**, or **agreed value**. Each item or set of items insured on a Floater will be scheduled, i.e., listed along with its value. The policyholder is expected to have some documentation to support each listed claim of value, such as a receipt or an appraisal, which usually is attached to the policy.

Three categories of property are subject to special exceptions when insured by a floater: (1) Fine Arts, including fine art, antiques, decorative arts and collectibles, are usually covered only in the continental United States and Canada except by endorsement; (2) particularly fragile property such as glass is subject to a higher deductible; (3) when coins and stamps are insured an additional six perils are excluded such as damage from handling, loss in shipment or regular mail, and theft from an unattended automobile. Premium rates for various categories of properties may vary.

Insurance Value Terms

A crucial provision in all these policy variations for the consumer and the appraiser is the definition and method of calculation of the value insured. Only **Agreed Value** is what it seems. After a total loss, the insurance company will pay the value scheduled for the property. After a partial loss, the insurer will pay the documented cost of repair plus any reduction (diminution) of value due to the property's now being in restored rather than original condition; or, at its option, the insurer will pay the agreed value and retain the property. Agreed value is generally issued for highly valuable properties by selective insurance companies.

Actual Cash Value is commonly defined as replacement cost less depreciation. This insurance industry definition is intentionally elusive, to allow the claims adjuster some discretion in negotiating settlements. Actual cash value is more specifically defined as the price in terms of cash or other precisely revealed terms that would be necessary to replace a property with another of similar age, quality, origin, appearance, size and condition within a reasonable length of time in an appropriate and relevant market. This definition encompasses the concept of "as is" or "with or without restoration." It is the market value of a property, plus appreciation or less all forms of depreciation.

The insurance industry is currently in a period of transition regarding establishment of Actual Cash Value, as demonstrated by the following:

> An extension or clarification to this definition in many jurisdictions is the Broad Evidence Rule, which gives consideration to all aspects of value in addition to replacement cost less depreciation, factors such as market value and replacement cost may tend to establish the correct Actual Cash Value.

> The objective of the Broad Evidence Rule is to compensate for actual loss. Accordingly, it does not follow one specific rule but gives latitude in accomplishing its goal. A solid investigation of the facts, including a complete gathering of value information, is needed. It may be necessary to determine: (a) value to the owner; (b) original cost; (c) cost of replacement; (d) condition of the item, and (e) the use to which it is put, for example if an item is obsolete or no longer serves any practical use, it may not have any value (Aetna Rl02)

One technical area which may warrant further exploration by an appraiser involves the concept of depreciation and the application of the Age/Life formula for estimating it, as well as the extensive guidelines under which the insurance industry lists the Reasonable Life Expectancy for all manner of personal property for the use of claims adjusters.

Replacement Cost has been defined as the cost of property to replace damaged or destroyed property. Several issues can complicate the estimation of replacement cost. For example, there may be peripheral issues regarding what constitutes the replacement of property with "like kind and quality." Secondly, there may be a substantial difference in the cost of replacement to a policy-holder buying at retail and to a large insurance company buying at volume discount. The claims adjuster is urged to conduct his own price research. Thirdly, an adjustment called betterment is often applied to calculations of replacement value. The principle of insurance is to return the property of the policy holder to its condition prior to loss, neither worse nor better. In cases where repairs to a property make it more valuable than before the loss, the increase in value due to betterment may be deducted. In the case of antiques, fine art and other property whose markets place a premium on original condition, of course, repairs which are virtually undetectable may still reduce the value of the object rather than improve it, resulting in diminution of value rather than betterment.

The value sought in an appraisal for insurance coverage of personal property is replacement value. Replacement Value may be broken into three categories: Replacement Value — Comparable; Replacement Value — Cost New; and Replacement Value — Reproduction Cost. The professional appraiser is the qualified expert within his area of designation to make the determination of the correct and appropriate means of replacement for a particular property, whether it should be with a new article, either commonly available or reproduced to replicate the lost property or replacement with a comparable item in age, quality, condition and other factors to the lost property. In an appraisal report, this designation of the appropriate avenue of replacement is an important determinant in estimating the value at which a property should be insured.

In all cases of damage or loss, the claims adjuster will conduct his own research and calculations to arrive at the company's position in the settlement negotiations. If the claims adjuster is not familiar with the type of property in a claim and especially if no prior appraisal of the property is available, he will give the description and value to a vendor or dealer from whom he would get a replacement. The consultant may be asked to write an opinion on the validity of the description and value, with the understanding that he should be prepared to furnish a replacement for whatever value he recommends. If the property is fine art or antiques, for example, he is instructed to examine authenticity and conformance to the description. This consultant's opinion, which may include photographs, may take the form of a brief letter or a consulting opinion.

Formal Appraisal in Claim Settlement

An appraiser often is the expert on whom the claims adjuster relies. In cases of insurance coverage **other** than agreed value scheduling endorsements to policies for antiques, fine arts, jewelry, etc., the insurance company may not require a complete appraisal document as a requisite for scheduling the property. However, professional appraisal reports containing full explanations of the assignment, purpose, method, logic, evidence, limiting conditions, sources and appraiser's credentials can become a vital part of the most difficult stages of highly contested settlements. A credible professional appraisal will be very helpful to the policyholder in shortening negotiations with the claims adjuster and influencing their outcome in his favor.

If the policyholder does not find any of the claims adjuster's offers of settlement acceptable, most policies provide for formal appraisal and arbitration. In most cases the costs of the appraisal and of the arbitration are shared equally by the policyholder and the insurance company.

Conclusion

The challenge for appraisers is in the marketing of their services to the public and to the insurance industry. Education and membership in a recognized professional organization such as the American Society of Appraisers are the tools that the appraiser must possess if he is to be respected as a professional by both the insured and the insurer.

Estimating Value for Insurance Damage and Loss Claims

Appraisers are often called upon to determine values for damage and loss claims. They are usually contacted by an adjuster, whose responsibilities as an insurance representative include investigating personal property damage and making judgments for effecting settlements.

These adjusters normally work for individual insurance companies who handle homeowner policies, or for large marine or inland marine companies who handle transportation of items across land and sea, or for na-

tional or local moving companies. Attorneys also contact appraisers when policy owners sue insurance or moving companies over a settlement of claims. Additionally, a policy holder may call the appraiser on a direct basis to support his claim of value on damaged items for the insurance company.

Adjusters need assistance from qualified appraisers since the adjusters do not have the training to assess values of fine art, antiques, decorative arts, collectibles and appreciating residential contents.

Adjusters often ask the appraiser to go directly into the field. This occurs when the adjuster cannot get to the scene of the loss or the adjuster is so unfamiliar with the property in question that an appraiser is engaged to handle the loss for the insurance company.

Before beginning the assignment, the appraiser must be sure to understand the appraisal question and type of value required by the adjuster. In general, **Actual Cash Value** is defined as the market value of a property, plus appreciation or less all forms of depreciation and is normally established by an insurance adjuster based on insurance industry guidelines and depreciation guides. **Actual cash value** is being replaced through case law and state legislation by the **broad evidence rule**. Different states subscribe to different rules, as in California, where Actual Cash Value and Fair Market Value are cited as one and the same (*Jefferson Insurance Company of New York v. Superior Court of Alameda County*, 1970 475 P.2d 880). As another example, in the state of Pennsylvania the law gives actual cash value the meaning of replacement cost (*Judge v. Celina Mut. Ins. Co.* 1982 449 A.2d 658). Also, policy clauses present different statements and exclusions, as in the homeowners HO-3 form which promises to settle personal property losses "at actual cash value at the time of the loss but not more than the amount required to repair or replace."

The appraiser should approach the assignment basically in the same manner as any appraisal, i.e., examine and identify the damaged item. However, during the inspection, many more aspects need to be considered. Notes should be taken concerning an opinion of the condition of the item prior to damage. If the item has considerable age, the appraiser should note whether there is normal wear, or whether the piece has sustained previous damage and possible repair, restoration or replacement of parts.

If the item is crushed or broken, the appraiser has the task of making all determinations necessary from observations of the splinters, shards, or remnants presented. This can also be the case with items partially destroyed by fire. Even charred bits of wood can give clues as to the construction and age, and sometimes general shape or size. The appraiser must use all the information and evidence available to present a complete professional report.

Antique, fine and decorative art objects often have **inherent vice** or **the nature of the property**. The term inherent vice, according to The National Underwriter Co., 1991, is an older term and is now more normally referred to as **hidden or latent defect**. *Black's Law Dictionary* confirms this definition. This condition is an exception to common carrier liability. Special form CP 10 30 "excludes loss or damage due to wear and tear, rust, corrosion, fungus, decay, deterioration, or animal infestation" or "any quality in the property that causes it to damage or destroy itself." These exclusions also include settling, cracking, shrinking, or expansion, or any dampness or dryness of atmosphere, and changes in or extremes of temperature. (See *Plaza Equities Corp. v. Aetna Casualty and Surety Co.*, 372 F.Supp. 1325 (1974).)

Moving companies are particularly aware of these types of exclusions. For instance, a small antique table can be intact but extremely fragile. The table may be fine standing in a protected corner of a room, but when handled, packed, and shipped, it may sustain damage. In this case, the adjuster will ask the appraiser to determine how the table may have been damaged: Did it receive rough handling? Is there a mark to indicate that the object was struck hard? Or did the dry glue joints fail with the stressful move? This information is necessary so that the adjuster can determine the liability.

Extremes of temperature in a moving van or a storage facility may change or damage an item. Paintings on canvas are often affected by temperature extremes, as are wooden properties that can warp or shrink. Textiles and carpets can be damaged in storage by insect or animal destruction. Mildew and other bacteria can cause damage. Again, it is up to the appraiser to evaluate and thoroughly report so that the adjuster can determine liability.

Frequently a piece of porcelain or pottery has a very old and stained crack. The appraiser must note if the old crack was associated with the present damaged state. Did the item fail along the extension of the old crack? Did it receive a blow which caused the old crack to open as well as numerous other cracks or breaks? The appraiser distinguishes new damage from prior damage. New damage, particularly to wood, will be lighter in color, and the edges of a break or damage may be rough. Older damaged surfaces usually show evidence of age, wear, or discoloration.

The appraiser should examine the item in detail, making note of new damage to the piece and itemizing all damage, indicating, for example, the size of the chunk of wood that is missing, the length of the crack, and the position on the property of all damages. Notes should be made as to whether the pieces broken off have been retained, so that a restoration may be made. If original parts are lost, the value after restoration will be less with replaced parts than with the original parts restored.

Photography is particularly useful in appraising damaged items. It is recommended that a macro lens be used to obtain detailed photos of a damaged area or a mark, as well as the overall photo of the item. Photos are an excellent means by which to amplify the description for the adjuster and should be labeled.

Because insurance policies give the insuring company two options in case of damage, it may be requested for the appraiser to provide estimates of probable professional restoration costs for the property. If the restoration estimate is higher than the value of the item prior to damage, the adjuster needs this information promptly to make a settlement determination. The restoration estimate includes only repair of the damage and **not a betterment** of the property. It should be noted that the methods of loss settlement are not determined by the insured but rather are at the sole option of the insurance company.

In addition to standard report writing requirements, an appraisal report for insurance damage and loss claims should:
1. State the condition of the property prior to the new damage
2. Provide details of the new damage
3. State opinions:
   a) Can the property be repaired or restored?
   b) Can the appraiser provide a repair estimate?
   c) What is the effect of restoration or repair on the estimate of the value of the property prior to damage? If the item cannot be repaired, the loss is the full value in undamaged condition.
4. State the valuation equation.

Example:

VALUATION PRIOR TO DAMAGE:	$1000.00
PRESENT VALUATION:	0.00
DIMINUTION OF VALUE:	$1000.00

If there are numerous items on the report, one must be sure to do a separate valuation equation for each item.

Legal Guidelines for Appraisals Used to Substantiate Charitable Contribution Income Tax Deductions

© 1994 by Corinne L. Richardson, J.D., M.V.S.

1. Introduction

When Congress enacted the Tax Reform Act of 1986, its goal was to simplify the tax laws and place restrictions on deductions while lowering tax rates. With respect to charitable contribution deductions, Congress continued the extensive changes made in 1984 as well as its policy of permitting taxpayers to deduct charitable contributions subject to regulations of the Treasury Department. Congress also expressed its concern over tax abuses and reaffirmed penalties for overvaluation resulting in understatements of tax liability.

The scope of this chapter is limited to art object appraisals used to substantiate charitable contribution income tax deductions under the 1986 Tax Reform Act. Under Section B, Part II, of Form 8283, "art" as a type of donated property includes the following:

> paintings, sculptures, watercolors, prints, drawings, ceramics, antique furniture, decorative arts, textiles, carpets, silver, rare manuscripts, historical memorabilia, and other similar objects.

Other items such as stamp collections, real estate, coin collections, gems/jewelry, and books are listed under Form 8283 as different categories of property and not included in the scope of this chapter.

For substantiation of charitable contribution deductions of art objects, the Treasury Regulations recognize as acceptable only what those Regulations label and define as "appraisal summaries" and "qualified appraisals" by "qualified appraisers." For example, the Regulations define at length who is a "qualified appraiser."[1] If "qualified" under the Regulations, appraisers must verify the identity and condition of the property, and then state their assessment of the fair market value in the appropriate marketplace based on comparable sales or some other valuation method.

This identification and assessment of the fair market value concept along with other specifics of the appraisal prepared by the appraiser for a charitable contribution deduction of an art object may be subject to Internal Revenue Service audit and subsequent court decision.

Some appraisers today express reluctance to appraise personal property donated for charitable deduction tax purposes.[2] One reason may be the $1,000 penalty under Section 6701 of the Internal Revenue Code, which the Internal Revenue Service may impose if it finds that the appraiser has aided or assisted in the preparation or presentation of an appraisal which results in an understatement of tax liability. The appraiser may be subjected to this civil penalty even though there was no collusion. Unlike other penalties, however, the Internal Revenue Service bears the burden of proof that the penalty is "properly imposed."

Under Public Law 98-369 enacted in 1984, any appraiser who has been assessed a penalty under Section 6701(a) for aiding or assisting in the preparation or presentation of an appraisal resulting in an understatement of tax liability will be subject to disciplinary action. After the appraiser has received notice and an opportunity for a hearing, the Treasury Department (1) may bar the appraiser from appearing before the Internal Revenue Service or the Treasury Department for the purpose of offering opinion evidence on the value of property or other assets, and (2) may provide that appraisals by the appraiser shall have no probative effect in any administrative proceedings before the Internal Revenue Service or the Treasury Department.

The present law concerning charitable contribution deductions is Section 170 of the Internal Revenue Code.[3] The only applicable provision for income tax returns is subsection a(1) which provides:

> GENERAL RULE — There shall be allowed as a deduction any charitable contribution (as defined in Subsection (c)) payment of which is made within the taxable year. A charitable contribution shall be allowed as a deduction only if verified under *regulations* prescribed by the Secretary.[4]

Since the above section alone does not provide guidance for the appraiser, it is important for the appraiser who chooses to do an appraisal for tax purposes to be thoroughly familiar with the Treasury Department's Regulations and Procedures. (The relevant parts are in Appendix A (recordkeeping required); Appendix B (substantiation requirements); Appendices C, D, and E (qualified appraisals, the appraisal summary, and qualified appraisers); and Appendix F (Revenue Procedure 66-49)). The appraiser should obtain Form 8283 (Non Cash Charitable Contributions), Instructions for Form 8283, Internal Revenue Service Publications 526 (Charitable Contributions) and 561 (Determining the Value of Donated Property) from an Internal Revenue Service center.

However, knowledge of these written rules and regulations is not enough. The appraiser should have at least some basic acquaintance with the underlying legal principles and the manner in which the Internal Revenue Service and the courts deal with challenged income tax deductions.[5]

The court's decision concerning the fair market concept is dependent in each particular case on the evidence presented and the qualifications of the appraisers and quality of their testimony. To state it another way, in many cases, attorneys choose which evidence to present and rarely in any given case is every shred of evidence presented to the judge or jury. Therefore, the possibility always exists that in any given case had the attorney chosen to present other evidence that was available or to change the emphasis concerning the evidence presented, the result of the case could well have been different. Moreover, as stated by the court in a 1974 decision:

> We emphasize that our determination is based exclusively upon what the particular record herein shows — and also does not show — and that such determination is solely for the purposes of this case without in any way implying what it would be on the basis of another record containing different facts and different testimony.[6]

Thus, while studying the facts and evidence presented in one or several court decisions may be educational or helpful in one sense to an appraiser, he or she would be well advised to concentrate on an understanding of the legal principle or principles involved in *all* of the relevant court decisions. In fact, the legal principles contained in the court decisions form the basis of the fair market value concept. These principles are many and varied.

The scope of this chapter is restricted to a review of the Internal Revenue Service Forms, Treasury Regulations, Revenue Procedures and court decisions applicable to income tax deductions for charitable contributions of objects of art. Also included are a few cases from analogous subjects such as charitable contributions of gems, books, and other types of personal property.

This chapter does provide (1) an outline of the requirements of an appraisal summary under Form 8283 and of an appraisal by an appraiser who meets the qualifications of the Treasury Regulations (Appendices A through F) together with (2) the principles of law as expressed in tax and federal court cases that underlie the Internal Revenue Code provisions and regulations governing charitable contribution deductions of art objects. Examples of language contained in specific cases along with the holdings of the cases are used to give insight into the reasoning process of the judiciary.

Through an understanding of the requirements for an appraisal of an art object which is the subject of a charitable tax deduction and the full range of legal principles involved, the appraiser can make a checklist or worksheet of the relevant and material principles to consider in preparing appraisals in his or her appraisal specialty or designation. If, in applying the fair market value concept to the appraisal of a particular art object, the appraiser wants more information relating to one or more legal principles, he or she can locate the topic in the table of contents and through use of the footnotes, find the names of the applicable case decisions and in many instances read specific language of the decisions for further explanation of the legal principle.

This chapter is written for the appraiser, not the taxpayer or the taxpayer's attorney or accountant. The person who appraises art objects, knowing that the appraisal will be used to substantiate a deduction from the taxpayer's taxable income, should confine himself or herself to areas of the appraiser's own expertise, unless the appraiser is also a certified accountant or licensed attorney. The hard, practical reasons are potential liability of the appraiser for negligence or lack of competence and the possibility that heavy penalties may be imposed by the government under law.

II. Court Setting

A. Introduction

The appraiser needs to have a basic understanding of how disputes between the taxpayer and the government over the amount of the charitable contribution income tax deduction can be resolved, and if not settled between the parties, the process by which the taxpayer files suit in a court to resolve the conflict. This process is outlined under subsection A, *infra*.

Subsection B, *infra*, explains that, once the valuation dispute is taken to court by the taxpayer, (1) the amount that the government has determined in its deficiency notice as the value of the deduction is presumed by the court to be correct and (2) it is the taxpayer's burden to prove otherwise. Depending on which procedure the taxpayer chooses to follow (*i.e.*, in which court the taxpayer sues the government), the procedure as to who bears the initial burden of presenting evidence and the burden of proving their facts (before the other side has to do anything) differs from court to court.

Subsection C, *infra*, discusses the attitude of the courts about its determination of the fair market value concept and alerts the appraiser to the "reception" he or she can expect in court.

Subsection D, *infra*, again alerts the appraiser to expectations concerning his or her appearance in court as an expert witness. The court has great latitude to accept or reject expert testimony and does not have to support its rejection of testimony with reasons other than it finds the testimony to be unconvincing, inappropriate, or simply not of sufficient value in the opinion of the court for use in making its decision. None of these types of reasons are descriptive or helpful to the appraiser for future reference, except as a warning to the appraiser to be prepared for close scrutiny by a judge who already may think that the case should have been settled and resents being placed in the role as the decision maker.

B. The Appeals Process

After the taxpayer files Form 1040 together with Form 8283 (Noncash Charitable Contributions), the Internal Revenue Service may decide to audit the return. The Internal Revenue auditor will follow the procedure outlined in the Internal Revenue Manual. If the value set by the auditor differs from that of the taxpayer, they may agree on the amount that the taxpayer then claims as the charitable contribution deduction. In other words, the issue concerning the amount of the deduction may be settled between them. If not, the taxpayer may seek a second opinion from the auditor's supervisor. However, if this step does not result in settlement, the taxpayer has the option either (1) to file suit directly (see illustration) or (2) to take advantage of the last interim step available to the taxpayer before filing suit in court.[7] This last interim step is to file a protest with and have a hearing set before an Internal Revenue Service regional appeals officer. Some tax experts recommend taking this last interim step since appeals officers have more leeway to compromise cases and at this juncture about 50 percent of all tax cases are settled.

If the taxpayer and the Internal Revenue Service are still at an impasse, the taxpayer may proceed along the lines drawn below.

C. Presumptions and Burden of Proof of Parties Appearing Before the Court

As summarized in an article appearing in the St. Louis Bar Journal:

> The tax court rules provide generally that the burden of proof is on the taxpayer. This burden of overcoming the presumption of correctness that attaches to each deficiency determination is satisfied if a preponderance of evidence supports the taxpayer's position.

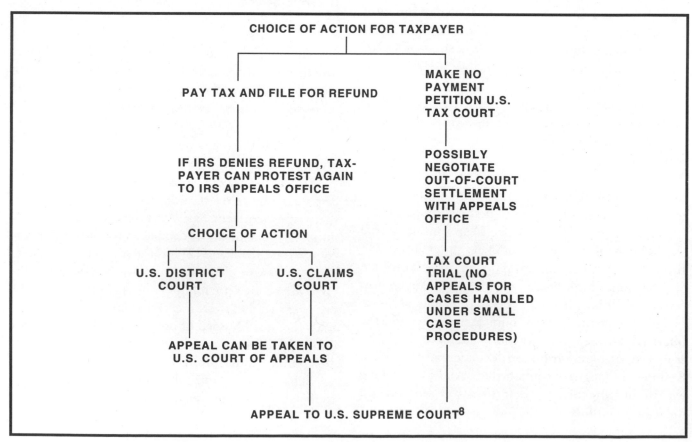

62

In the claims court and the district court, the taxpayer must sustain a double burden of proof, establishing by a preponderance of the evidence both (a) the error(s) in the government's tax determination(s) and (b) the correct amount of tax.

The allocation of the burden of proof may also differ among the three forums as to new issues raised by the government. In the tax court, the government bears the burden of proof as to any new matter. In the claims court or the district court, the burden of proof on a new issue may be on the government or on the taxpayer, depending on the nature and origin of the issue raised.[9]

If the taxpayer meets the burden of proof required, the issue of valuation becomes one of fact "to be resolved from consideration and weighing of all relevant evidence in the record."[10] The court then determines which side has presented the most credible evidence and rules in that side's favor or, taking all the evidence into consideration, places its own value on the property.[11]

D. Attitude of the Courts Toward Determination of Valuation Issues

Quite simply, the courts do not like to decide valuation cases. As stated by a court in a 1988 opinion,

The process of determining fair market value in the context of litigation is particularly unsatisfying. Each party typically produces expert witnesses who purport to discern the precise valuation formula that should be used in a particular case, and each expert testifies with apparent confidence as to exactly what is wrong with the other expert's approach. We previously have lamented as follows:

Too often in valuation disputes the parties have convinced themselves of the unalterable correctness of their positions and have consequently failed successfully to conclude settlement negotiations — a process clearly more conducive to the proper disposition of disputes such as this. The result is an overzealous effort, during the course of the ensuing litigation, to infuse a talismanic precision into an issue which should frankly be recognized as inherently imprecise and capable of resolution only by a Solomon-like pronouncement.*** [Messing v. Commissioner [Dec. 28,532], 48 T.C. 502, 512 (1967)].[12]

The courts repeatedly caution the parties that:

The Court may find the evidence of valuation by one of the parties sufficiently more convincing than that of the other party, so that the final result will produce a significant financial defeat for one or the other, rather than a middle-of-the-road compromise which we suspect each of the parties expects the Court to reach.[13]

Or, as stated by another court,

...What is more to the point is the fact that the parties herein have seemingly made a conscious effort to force us to assume a role which is certainly distasteful, if not unwise.[14]

Or, as one court laments,

...it is astounding that these parties would seek a court solution to such a fact situation, rather than arbitration by another expert.[15]

What this attitude of the court means for appraisers is that they must be prepared for close scrutiny of their opinions by trial judges. The reported cases are replete with negative observations and expressions of distrust about appraisers' testimony. Some courts have viewed various appraisers as biased,[16] inexact,[17] secretive,[18], not knowledgeable about the subject,[19] unreliable,[20] sloppy in research,[21] predisposed to place a high value on the object,[22] or even purposefully deceitful.[23] In one case, appraisers were referred to as experts but only with quotes around that word. About their testimony, that court said:

Although in certain respects, each witness' testimony was informative, we were left with the overall feeling of dissatisfaction and consequent frustration [to the conclusion that] the primary guidelines for the presentation of the case by both parties was that the less, rather than the more, the Court knew, the better.[24]

E. The Appraiser as an Expert Witness

Opinions of experts are admissible in court and relevant to any determination of value. However, "such evidence must be weighed in light of the qualifications of the witness and all other relevant evidence of value."[25] The court may reject expert testimony when in its opinion the testimony is not of probative value or "appropriate"[26] and even if the testimony is undisputed.[27]

In weighing the testimony of appraisers, the courts consider as important

their demonstrated qualifications to form an opinion, their relationship and prior dealings with petitioner [taxpayer], their selections of comparative sales, their familiarity and contact with the potential market for the contributed property, and, of course, their familiarity with the contributed material.[28]

They further consider

the 'expert' witnesses relative expertise as judged and observed by us, the time spent on and thoroughness of their appraisals, and their knowledge of the particular field both before and after research.[29]

On the relative merits of two appraisers, one court stated:

> We have said that although we will not reject expert evidence without objective reasons for doing so, one such reason is that the evidence provided by another expert is more persuasive.[30]

Even if recognized as an expert and therefore considered by some as "more persuasive," the appraiser still may not expect his or her opinion as to value to be accepted without question. As Mertens, *Law of Federal Income Taxation*, has said:

> A common fallacy in offering opinion evidence is to assume that the opinion is more important than the facts. To have any persuasive form, the opinion should be expressed by a person qualified in background, experience, intelligence, familiarity with the property, and with the valuation problem involved. *It should also refer to all the underlying facts upon which an intelligent judgment of valuation should be based.* The facts must corroborate the opinion; otherwise, the opinion will be discounted.[31]

In other words, an opinion of even the most qualified appraiser is only as meaningful as the facts that support it.

III. The Appraisal Summary In Form 8283 And The "Qualified Appraisal" Under Treasury Regulations and Revenue Procedures

Introduction

In order to provide basic information for the beginning appraiser, first this section clarifies the general application of Internal Revenue Service Form 8283.

Internal Revenue Service Form 8283, Noncash Charitable Contributions, must be attached to an individual income tax return if a noncash charitable contribution deduction exceeds $500.

Section A of Form 8283 is restricted to donations of items or groups of similar items with a fair market value of $5,000 or less. It will be noted that no expert or written appraisal is required under Section A, although, of course, one may be obtained. No signature is required of the taxpayer, the donee or an appraiser, but the blanks provided should be filled in by the taxpayer or another acting under the taxpayer's direction.

Section B, the Appraisal Summary portion of Form 8283, is to include "only items or groups of similar items which have a claimed value of $5,000 per item or group." The Appraisal Summary consists of four parts:

Part I, Donee Acknowledgment "to be completed by the charitable organization";

Part II, Information on Donated Property, including a description and "appraised fair market value," all of which is "to be completed by the taxpayer and/or appraiser";

Part III, Taxpayer-Donor Statement" to be completed for items listed in Section B, Part II, with appraised value of $500 or less per item"; and

Part IV, Certification of Appraiser, "to be completed by the appraiser of the donated property."

For completion of Section B, there must be a separate "qualified appraisal" and a separate Form 8283 for each item of property except for those items that are part of a group of similar items of property. The appraiser's certification in each case must be made by a "qualified appraiser."

The Internal Revenue Service's instructions for completion of Form 8283 are detailed and clear. The "qualified appraisal" by a "qualified appraiser" required by Treasury Regulation Section 1.170A-13(c)(3)(1988) (Appendix C) contains almost everything needed for completion of Section B.

However, problems may arise concerning who actually completes the individual parts of Section B and who interprets the various legal requirements imposed on the taxpayer and donee. First, if the appraiser agrees to fill out all of Part II (information on the donated property), the appraiser must rely, in part, on information supplied by the taxpayer, *i.e.*, the date and manner in which the property was acquired, the taxpayer's cost or adjusted basis of the property, and the overall physical condition of the property at the time of the gift. The appraiser, without notice to the contrary, must assume that this information did not change since the appraiser's last inspection of the property.

Second, many taxpayers and donees may expect the appraiser to fill out some or all of the other blanks for them. Again, if the appraiser chooses to comply with this request, the appraiser is relying on information about which the appraiser has no direct, personal knowledge.

Third, many taxpayers and donees may expect the appraiser to answer questions about the law including Internal Revenue Service procedures, publications, rulings, and regulations.

It may be difficult for the appraiser not to comply with at least some of the requests mentioned above. And there are valid reasons for agreeing. For example, if the appraiser does not complete Part II (and Part III if the appraiser prepared a "qualified appraisal" of the item), the taxpayer may misstate the answers to questions, later causing problems for both the taxpayer and the appraiser.

The author recommends that the appraiser develop a form suitable to the appraiser's specialty or designation and available to be given to the taxpayer requesting in writing such information as the initial cost of acquisition of the item by the taxpayer, whether the item has been authenticated and if a certificate of authentication exists and the like. Return of the form to the appraiser provides written documentation of specific information concerning the property, some of which only the taxpayer knows or has access. The appraiser can use the information provided to assist in the preparation of the appraisal and retain the form for later reference, if necessary.

A request for the appraiser to complete Part I for the donee's signature is beyond the scope of the appraiser's employment and role as contemplated by the Internal Revenue Service. If either the taxpayer or the donee asks for legal advice, the appraiser can decline since it is beyond the scope of his or her expertise. The appraiser can refer the taxpayer or donee to the Instructions for Form 8283 and Internal Revenue Service Publications 526 and 561.

Explanation of the seven major areas outlined in the following subsections A through G. Using the requirements under the Internal Revenue Code together with Treasury Regulations and Revenue Procedures, the author has narrowed the essential elements or areas of an appraisal summary and a "qualified appraisal" of a charitable contribution income tax deduction of an art object to seven major areas. Under each of these areas, the specific requirements of both the appraisal summary and "qualified appraisal" are outlined. Further, the author discusses in detail the underlying legal principles applicable to each of the seven major areas for the appraiser's use in preparing an art object appraisal for charitable contribution income tax deduction purposes. The seven major areas are: (A) interest conveyed; (B) qualifications of the appraiser (including the fee arrangement between the appraiser and the taxpayer); (C) description, history, and physical condition of the property; (D) purpose of the appraisal, identification of the donee, and date of contribution; (E) conclusion as to value (the fair market value concept: fair market value in the appropriate marketplace); (F) basis or methodology used to arrive at valuation; and (G) assumptions, qualifying conditions, and certification of the appraiser.

A. *Interest Conveyed*

Appraisal Summary — donation of property valued at more than $5,000. The interest conveyed does not have to be specified in Section B of the appraisal summary. This is in contrast to Part II of Section A of Form 8283 (covering items or groups of items having a claimed value of $5,000 or less) which the taxpayer must complete if less than the entire interest in the property is given or if restrictions are attached to the contribution.

However, any restrictions on the interest conveyed in property valued at more than $5,000 could be specified under Section B, Part II 3(a) description of the donated property, or, at least in that subsection, a notation that the "qualified appraisal" contains a description of the interest conveyed and limitations or restrictions, if any, on the property donated.

"Qualified Appraisal." As specified in Treasury Regulation Section 1.170A-13(c)(3) (1988), a "qualified appraisal" must include the terms of any agreement entered into by the donor which relates to the use, sale or other disposition of the contributed property.

Comments:

Restrictions of any kind should be negotiated between the donee and the taxpayer-donor, without involvement of the appraiser. It is important for the appraiser to be aware that, regardless of the value of the property donated, the legal effect of any restrictions should be determined by the taxpayer in consultation with an accountant or lawyer.

If only a partial or limited interest in the property is being donated, or if there are restrictions on the use of the property, the appraiser would be well advised to ask that it be described in writing by the taxpayer's accountant or lawyer. That description could be incorporated in the "qualified appraisal."

Where a restriction has been placed by the taxpayer on the donee's use of the property or sale of the item for a period of years after donation, this fact must be taken into consideration in determining fair market value.[32] A restriction such as salability of the property affects the present marketability of the property donated and is a factor of "more than negligible significance on value."[33]

B. *Identification and Qualifications of the Appraiser*

Appraisal Summary — donations of property valued at more than $5,000. The appraiser must complete Part III (Certification of Appraiser) of Form 8283 wherein he or she states that

I declare that I am not the donor, the donee, a party to the transaction in which the donor acquired the property, employed by or related to any of the foregoing persons, or a person whose relationship to any of the foregoing persons would cause a reasonable person to question my independence as an appraiser. Also, I declare that I hold myself out to the public as an appraiser and that because of my qualifications as described in the appraisal, I am qualified to make appraisals of the type of property being valued. I certify the appraisal fees were not based upon a percentage of the appraised property value. Furthermore, I understand that a false or fraudulent overstatement of the property value as described in the qualified appraisal or this appraisal summary may subject me to the civil penalty under section 6701(a) (aiding and abetting in the understatement or tax liability). I affirm that I have not been barred from presenting evidence or testimony by the Director of Practice.

"Qualified Appraisal." For the appraisal itself, a form similar to the one set out in Appendix G must be included as part of the appraisal.

C. Description and History of the Property

Appraisal Summary — donation of property valued at more than $5,000. Under Section B, Part II of Form 8283, the information concerning the donated property required to be completed by the taxpayer and/or appraiser is contained in the following subsections: 2 — designation of the type of property; 3 — (a) a description of the donated property, (b) the date the property was acquired by the taxpayer-donor, (c) how the property was acquired by taxpayer-donor, (d) the taxpayer-donor's cost or adjusted basis, and 4 — a brief summary of the overall physical condition of the property at the time of the donation. It is suggested that the taxpayer complete sections 3(b), (c) and (d) and that the appraiser complete sections 2, 3(a), and 4.

"Qualified Appraisal." Under the Treasury Regulation 1.170A-13(c)(1) (1988) (Appendix D), Revenue Procedure 69-49 (Appendix F), and court decisions, the "qualified appraisal" of art objects should include:

1. A complete description[34] of the art object "in sufficient detail for a person who is not generally familiar with the type of property to ascertain that the property that was appraised is the property that was (or will be) contributed."[35] Specifics include:
   a. Size,[36]
   b. Subject matter or title,[37]
   c. Medium,
   d. Name of the artist,
   e. Approximate date created,
   f. Condition of the property at the time of the donation,[38]
   g. Quality,[39] and
   h. Standing of the artist in his or her profession and in the particular school or time period involved.[40]
2. The cost, date, and manner of acquisition.[41]
3. A history of the item, including
   a. Proof of authenticity such as a certificate of authentication, if such exists,
   b. Provenance,[42] including
      1. Citations in literature,[43]
      2. Public exhibitions (a record of any exhibitions at which the particular art object has been displayed),[44] and
      3. Rarity of the item.[45]
   c. Historical association,[46] and
   d. Subsequent treatment by the donee.[47]
4. "For art with an aggregate value of $20,000 or more and donated after December 31, 1987, [the taxpayer] must attach a complete copy of the signed appraisal and include an 8 × 10 inch color photograph (or a color transparency, no smaller than 4 × 5 inches)."[48]

Comments:

(i) In addition, if possible, the condition at the time of acquisition should be described. This information could have a bearing on fair market value if any restoration or other changes to or in the property has been made.[49]

(ii) Concerning the tendency of taxpayers to donate works of art when it is difficult to establish the particular artist who created the work. William M. Speiller in a law review article wrote:

> Misattribution is a significant factor causing overvaluation, particularly in the case of older, unsigned works. If the donor believes that he has contributed a painting by an eighteenth century French master he will value his gift on the basis of prices obtained for works by that artist, though in fact he may be donating the work of an unknown artist whose paintings have only minimal commercial value. A person who wishes to dispose of a work of questionable attribution would be more likely to donate the work than sell it. Buyers would be more likely to check the authenticity of a work than the beneficiary of a gift, and if doubts arose the buyer would discount the purchase price. Consequently, the taxpayer who cannot prove the authenticity of a particular work may well profit more by donating than by sale.[50]

(iii) Authenticity can be a deciding factor for the courts in determining fair market value.[51] Or, the courts can determine fair market value after concluding that authenticity was undeterminable and that a knowing buyer and seller would take that fact into consideration. One court said:

> ... [We] refuse to decide the underlying question of authenticity; we believe there is sufficient question on this record to conclude that a serious depressant on market value would exist on the critical date.[52]

(iv) Reliance by an appraiser on descriptions of an art object which are furnished by a person who has an interest in the donation being made (such as an employee of the donee) "without the benefit of independent and reliable visual examination" may lead to rejection of the appraisal. On the other hand, photographs without visual inspection can be the basis of an appraisal if the photographs are shown to be a fair representation of the object.[53]

(v) For art valued at less than $20,000, it is recommended that the appraiser (1) provide a color photograph, (2) sign and date the back of the photograph, and (3) make at least four copies of the photograph, one for the taxpayer, one for his or her attorney, one for the Internal Revenue Service, and one for the appraiser's records.

The requirements outlined above for art objects are generally the same for appraisals of gems,[54] music,[55] literary material,[56] copyrights,[57] books,[58] lithographs,[59] and coins.[60]

D. Purpose of the Appraisal, Identification of the Donee, and Date of Contribution

Appraisal Summary — donations of property valued at more than $5,000. Under Form 8283, Section B, the donee organization itself fills out this part, giving required identifying information and acknowledging the date on which the property was received.

"Qualified Appraisal." A statement that the appraisal is prepared for income tax purposes, identification of the donee organization, and the date of contribution all must be made in the appraisal. The appraisal must have been made not earlier than 60 days prior to the date of contribution and not later than the filing date of the return claiming the deduction. The appraiser must give the exact date that the appraisal was made.[61]

E. Conclusion as to Value (the Fair Market Value Concept: Fair Market Value in the Appropriate Marketplace).

Appraisal Summary — donations of property valued at more than $5,000. Under Section B, Part II, 3(e), the taxpayer and/or the appraiser specifies the appraised fair market value of the property.

If any item(s) listed under Section B, Part II, has the appraised value of not more than $500 per item, the taxpayer is required to identify the item and verify that its appraised value is not more than $500.

"Qualified Appraisal." The conclusion as to fair market value on the date (or expected date) of the contribution must be made in a summary statement in the appraisal.

Fair market value is defined by Treasury Regulation 1.170 as:

> the price at which the property would change hands between a willing buyer and a willing seller, neither being under any compulsion to buy or sell and both having reasonable knowledge of relevant facts.[62]

This simple definition does not offer much guidance for the appraiser. It does not answer relevant questions. Who is a willing buyer? A willing seller? Where do the willing buyer and seller meet? Is the price at wholesale? At retail? When is a sale "under compulsion"? Is it at auction? Is list price "the price at which the property would change hands"? What is reasonable knowledge? And what are the relevant facts?

Because the answers to these and other questions are neither easy nor uniform, the author here discusses the various concepts that the appraiser should consider in determining fair market value in the appropriate marketplace of a particular item being appraised.

1. *The willing buyer:* in 1967, by case decision, the "willing buyer" was determined to be the "ultimate consumer," and not a dealer buying for resale.[63]

2. *The marketplace:* depending on the nature of the item for sale, the willing buyer and willing seller may meet at different markets.

a. *The usual marketplace.* Under the facts in most cases, the courts look to what a willing buyer would pay in an open, retail market. However, the willing buyer of a particular item may not be the individual consumer.

> ... For example, the general buying public for live cattle would be comprised primarily of slaughterhouses rather than individual consumers. The fair market value of live

cattle accordingly would be measured by the price paid at the livestock auction rather than at the supermarket.[64]

Thus, in the case of loose, unset gems, "the 'public' for low quality, unmounted gems … [is] the jewelry manufacturer and jewelry stores that created jewelry items, rather than the individual consumer."[65] For scholarly reprint books, the market in which they are ordinarily sold is that specific "retail marketplace, comprised largely of institutional buyers (libraries) and to a minor extent, of individuals seeking a specific scholarly text.[66]

b. The most active marketplace. Courts have construed these words in their common, everyday meaning. For example, in considering the value of a large number of lithographs, the court in a recent case looked to the source of purchase by the taxpayer and found:

> Lithographs may be purchased by individuals from galleries or from those dealers that sell each lithograph separately, but such are not the only sources for purchasing lithographs. Indeed, the facts of this case demonstrate that most of the lithographs of the types at issue were not purchased from such sources … [but from a sole distributor of the lithographs].[67]

In holding that the most active marketplace was the one where the taxpayers purchased the lithographs, the same court defined the word "retail" as meaning the price an ultimate consumer would pay in the most active marketplace.

> … The sales of the lithographs to the petitioners were as much sales to 'ultimate consumers' as the sales by art galleries and dealers to other individuals upon which the petitioners rely. It is common knowledge that a consumer can pay a whole range of retail prices for the same item depending on where he chooses to shop and how much investigating he does of the various sources of a particular item.… We do not construe the term *retail* as used in this context to mean that where a consumer has a choice of several sources for an item, only the most expensive source is a retail sale and all other sources are wholesale. Rather *the sale to the ultimate consumer is any sale to those persons who do not hold the item for subsequent resale … and the most appropriate marketplace for valuation purposes is the most active marketplace for the particular item involved.*[68]

In summary, this court noted three important facts: (1) the petitioners did not purchase the lithographs for resale, but for their own use or donation, (2) the taxpayer made bulk purchases, but received no special discount, and (3) the distributors from whom they bought the lithographs acted as art dealers and made substantial sales in the market of the lithographs. These facts lead the court to conclude that: "In the present case, the most active marketplace for (the lithographs) was the marketplace in which the petitioner purchased them."[69]

To understand the reasoning of court opinions determining "the most active marketplace," consider the facts of a 1991 case involving the value of ancient Hebrew Torah manuscript fragments purchased in 1972 for approximately $11,000 as an investment. The taxpayer, who was a knowledgeable antiquities collector, donated the fragments to Duke University in 1979 and 1980. He claimed a charitable contribution based on a $700,000 valuation by a professor in Hebrew studies. His appraiser advocated that "the most likely purchaser of the fragments would be an academic institution" since, in his opinion, the fragments had a "more scholarly than artistic value." The government agreed, but valued the collection at about $25,000. The tax court disregarded both appraisals as presenting "academic rather than commercial valuations." Because the taxpayer had bought the fragments as a collector for an investment, could have chosen to sell them to another collector, and, in fact, received two previous offers in 1978 to buy the fragments, the court concluded that "the most active marketplace for theoretical sale of the donated fragments would be the collectors' market." The court also disregarded the $1 million insurance value provided for the purpose of insuring the collection while in transit to the donee, Duke University, since the appraiser for insurance purposes had not even seen pictures of the fragments. The court then arrived at a value of $337,500, the exact figure of one of the two offers to buy the fragments from the taxpayer.[70]

c. Auction versus gallery as the marketplace. Art objects are sold primarily in two markets: in galleries that establish a retail price and at auction, which is usually considered to establish wholesale price, although such is not always the case. The choice by the appraiser of the appropriate market to determine value is particularly important when valuing art objects, such as paintings.

The leading court decisions are *Kaplan v. Commissioner,*[71] the holding of which was then distinguished in *McGuire v. Commissioner.*[72] The facts in both cases are almost identical: in both, the taxpayers gave items of sued personal property to the same hospital which then sold the properties at subsequent auction. In *Kaplan,* the Court found the value set by the auctioneer at the time of the donation and prior to the auction as "nothing more than a sham" and held that:

> While sales at auction are not always the best criterion of value, and certainly are not conclusive, we believe that in this

instance the actual value of the whole property is more nearly established by the auction sale than by any other testimony before us.[73]

The *McGuire* decision then held that the subsequent auction of the property was not fair market value, the Court stating that:

> … [P]rices obtained at forced sales at public auction sales, or sales on restricted markets are not always the best criterion of value, and are certainly not conclusive, particularly where there is evidence that the property would sell for more under different circumstances.… Here the auction sales were made in a limited market and in a manner and under conditions over which the petitioners had no control.… We do not think that an 'unrestricted' auction where the property is sold to the highest bidder with no minimum bid or number of bids being required, is necessarily indicative of the fair market value of the property, particularly where there is evidence that the property had an intrinsic value far in excess of the auction sales price and could have been sold under other circumstances at a considerably higher price.[74]

After these two decisions, three cases were decided that recognized that "auction prices are evidence of value in the art field."[75]

> Auctions form the visible vertebrae of the art market. Auctions provide the only public records of sales, and only auctions provide open, competitive bidding on a particular painting.… The museums make their insurance evaluations from auction catalogues. The dealers move prices up and down and serious collectors learn the value of their works according to sales at auction. Auctions establish prices.[76]

As to the difficulties of using auction sales as evidence of fair market value, Pamela J. Lajeunesse wrote in 1981 in a law review article that:

> But the establishment of fair market value is not accomplished simply by tracking auction sales and making allowance for dealer mark-up. The business of art is a much more complex-and-chaotic-system. Although art dealers participate in auctions, auction prices are not necessarily wholesale prices because a dealer may be bidding on behalf of a client. Collectors themselves often buy at auction rather than exclusively through a gallery, as had been the practice in the early part of this century. Furthermore, the art auction is hardly the perfect paradigm of the open marketplace. Secret bids, reserves, and "auction fever" distort the sales process and the participants do not all stand on equal footing or possess reasonable knowledge of the relevant facts.[77]

Courts recently have taken opposing views toward the use of auction prices as establishing fair market value of art objects. One court which determined the marketplace to be the art gallery reasoned as follows:

> … [Taxpayer's] expert … is the most reliable witness and presented entirely probative evidence as to the fair mar-

ket.… [His] extensive experience with both auction and gallery sale makes credible his testimony that auction prices are often lower than gallery prices.[78]

Compare, however, the holding of another recent case:

> Petitioners argue that the only relevant retail prices in this case are those obtained in what they characterize as the 'orderly private market' for the work of the specific artist, i.e., private treaty or gallery sales to art collectors or museums. Petitioners assert that prices obtained at public auction sales should be disregarded as they represent a 'disorderly market,' do not reflect real value and are wholesale prices, i.e., many purchases at such sales are by art dealers for resale. We are not persuaded by petitioners' arguments and agree with respondent that auction sale prices are relevant to the determination of fair market value in this case.[79]

Upon which line of cases is the appraiser to rely? The answer depends entirely upon the individual case. As one court concluded:

> … We emphasize that our determination is based exclusively upon what the particular record herein shows — and also does not show — and that such determination is solely for the purposes of this case without in any way implying what it would be on the basis of another record containing different facts and different testimony.[80]

In choosing between auction and retail market prices, one court states:

> … The controlling question is whether art auction sales represent sales to the ultimate consumer, not whether identical 'consumer' prices are also available to dealers. It is clear that a significant number of auction sales are to consumers and this Court has previously recognized the significance of such sales in determining the fair market value of art.… As with gallery sales, in evaluating contemporary auction sales, an assessment of the variations in numerous characteristics of the specific painting, including quality, size, subject matter and condition are necessary to determine if such sales are of comparable items. *Unless comparability exists, contemporary sales can provide no guidance in valuing a given work.*[81]

After analyzing the court decisions above, the author suggests that the appraiser first look for comparable sales, without regard to the marketplace where the comparables were sold. The next inquiry would be to ascertain the "climate" or circumstances surrounding the sale, e.g., whether it was a forced sale or a sale to a dealer buying for resale, etc. If the sale was for wholesale price, the problem then becomes one of calculating what is the mathematical relationship between that price and retail. Unfortunately, while some cases comment on the differences between the two values, none of the cases involve situations where a taxpayer successfully used a formula to translate wholesale into retail market value.

    d. Where the taxpayer acquired the item in the marketplace or cost as the ultimate determination of value. "Reliable evidence" of the fair market value of a contributed item is the cost of the item to the taxpayer.[82] Cost often influences the court's determination of fair market value when purchase of the item by taxpayer, even in an open market, took place close to the valuation date.[83]

Cost may not be fair market value as to the time of contribution if (1) the item was purchased at a substantial discount[84] or (2) the market changed in the intervening time between acquisition and donation. For example, in a 1988 case, the court held that the taxpayer was entitled to a deduction for an opal he donated to a university in an amount greater than that which he paid, but less than that which his appraiser valued the opal. The court rejected the government's contention that the deduction should be limited to the price that the taxpayer paid for the opal. Instead, the court accepted the testimony of one of taxpayer's appraisers that the donated opal was an exceptionally fine and unusual gem and that its value at the time of purchase vastly exceeded its actual purchase price. However, the court rejected this appraiser's testimony as to the opal's value at the time of contribution. The reason was that, although the court agreed as to the proper rate of inflation to apply to the purchase price to determine value at the time of contribution, the court decreased the resulting amount to reflect the fact that the appraisal of the opal did not take into consideration that, although the opal was purchased as part of a matching set, it was donated by itself.[85]

However, in other cases, the taxpayer has encountered difficulty in showing that the donated item was bought at a bargain price and that the taxpayer should not be held to the original cost of the item as the value of the donation. For example, in one case involving the contribution made in December of a jade desk set valued by the taxpayer at $22,500, he was held to the price of $55,000 which he paid for the desk set in March of the same year. The court reasoned that the taxpayer could offer no explanation as to why the seller sold the item for one-fourth of its alleged value.[86]

In the normal case, where the item was acquired in an arm's-length transaction between a willing buyer and seller, both knowledgeable of the facts, the taxpayer bears an almost insurmountable burden of showing that the market within a few months thereafter substantially appreciated. In one case, the taxpayer proved that later sales of "single prints from the same editions" that he donated for contribution were at prices similar to retail and in excess of what he had paid for his prints. After determining that these sales used for comparables were isolated sales "of single prints to dealers and non-dealers" and were "incidental and [did] not reflect the prices commonly paid" for the prints, the court then held that the cost of the prints was the proper valuation of the contribution.[87]

The decisive factor for the courts' decisions appears to be that, in most of the cases where the taxpayer is held to cost or government value, the courts suspect or conclude that the taxpayer purchased an item at "wholesale" with the intent to contribute it at "retail" and make "profit." That one factor would explain the courts' rulings in cases involving contributions of a substantial number of gems,[88] lithographs,[89] Indian artifacts,[90] African art objects,[91] and jewelry.[92]

In other words, while a taxpayer's obvious desire "to avoid or eliminate taxes by contributing … property to charities cannot be used as a basis for disallowing the deduction" altogether, this fact may well subconsciously influence a court's decision to limit the taxpayer's deduction to cost or government value.[93] If possible, the taxpayer should introduce evidence that some other reason at least contributed to the taxpayer's decision to donate the property to a charity. In one case which involved a substantial number of paintings donated by a taxpayer who was a private collector and made contributions "when he had little room left in his house or office for more paintings," the court took a more "lenient" view of the significance of cost as a factor, saying:

> Cost figures alone, however, do not establish fair market value. But they are a significant starting point to which relevant adjustments may be made.[94]

In that case the court, after considering other factors, assessed contribution value at slightly more than double the paintings' costs even though the time between the purchase of the paintings and contribution varied between one and three and a half years.

However, a word of caution: the courts have not always found that cost is the lowest fair market value of an item. In one recent case, the court valued a tourmaline at $1,390 when it had been purchased one year before donation for $3,300. The court commented that it was "neither surprising nor unusual that petitioners paid more than fair market value…. Knowledgeable dealers of gemstones would not be expected to give bargains."[95]

e. The flooded marketplace. When a large number of the same item or various items by the same artist are donated, the courts consider the depressant effect that simultaneous marketing of the entire amount of items could have on the market and on fair market value. Using the analogy to the "blockage rule" utilized in connection with the sale of a large number of securities, in a case involving a large number of sculptures, the court stated that:

> We think that a museum or individual collector of art objects would not completely ignore the resale value of a given item, although it obviously has far less significance than in the case of a dealer. Moreover, the 'retail market' claimed by respondent may well encompass the use of an auction method of disposal (to be distinguished from the usual forced-sale concept) for at least a part of the art objects; in such a situation the presence of a large number of pieces on the market at one time would be a most material factor.... [T]he amount which an *en bloc* purchaser for resale would pay and the aggregate of the separate 'one at a time' values to be obtained by a variety of dispositions in the 'retail market' would be the same.[96]

If a relatively small, but substantial, amount of a large purchase of an item of personal property by the taxpayer is donated, then, depending on the nature of the item and the exact qualities involved, the taxpayer is not held to a blockage discount, but to "the lower available market prices ... not bulk prices."[97] And where the number donated by the taxpayer represents only a small portion of the total amount, for example, of prints available within an edition "and an even smaller portion of the total work produced and outstanding by [the] artist," the court held in one case that:

> [A] blockage discount is not warranted.... The marginal increase in supply which would have resulted from a sale by petitioners would not have seriously affected the prices of these prints.[98]

Similarly, courts have declined to apply "blockage reasoning" where comparable sales do not exist if the donated items were sold as a collection, but comparable sales do exist as to individual items. In a 1989 case involving the largest collection of glass stereoscopic negatives, the court declined to determine, as the government advocated, the fair market value of the collection by estimating the price at which a comparable collection could be sold, in its entirety. The reason was that the five collections used by the government in its appraisal were not comparable to the collection at issue. The court, reluctantly, agreed with taxpayer that "a per unit method is preferable given the unique size and content of the collection." However, because the taxpayer's appraisers who used the per unit approach failed to show direct computational evidence of how they arrived at their values, the court found that the total valuation of all the fragments to be at the low end of the different values set by the taxpayer's appraisers.[99]

f. The limited marketplace. Neither a limited market[100] for an item nor the uniqueness of an item[101] is a barrier to valuation. Nor does either factor prevent the donated property from having substantial value.[102]

In cases involving a race car,[103] music manuscripts,[104] a 19 pound unfinished topaz crystal,[105] a mosaic table from the Vatican Studio,[106] a Han dynasty jar,[107] a 72-foot-high obeliscoid sculpture,[108] cartoons,[109] architectural illustrations,[110] a wooden, massive, cabinet-like object,[111] and aircraft,[112] the courts were asked to determine the marketplace for these unusual pieces. In one case, the taxpayer sought the services of Sotheby Parke Bernet to value a mosaic table purchased from the Vatican Studio before it closed.[113] This auction firm refused "because there were no adequate sales of comparable art pieces in the United States." However, in that case and others, appraisers have been able to place a value on an item despite the absence of a readily available marketplace.[114]

g. The undefined market,. Cohan v. Commissioner[115] is a 1930 case in which the taxpayers could not produce evidence to substantiate value. In that case, the Court held that the government could have made a determination of value based on "as close an approximation as it can, bearing heavily if it chooses upon the taxpayer whose inexactitude is of his own making."[116] Arguments used by taxpayers that their contributions are worth something, even if they cannot offer any proof as to value, is known as advancement of the *Cohan* rule.

Courts recently have refused to allow any deduction under similar circumstances where the taxpayer cannot substantiate value,[117] while others have, in addition, imposed a 5 percent penalty for negligence of the taxpayer.[118]

h. The market after contribution: subsequent sale of the item as establishing its prior market value. Some courts have specifically considered the use to which the donated property is put as relevant to a determination of value. The reasoning is that the fact that the donee cannot sell the donated items and chooses to warehouse them, or liquidates them at auction, or sells them at substantially lower prices than given in the taxpayer's appraisals leads some courts to disregard or discount the appraised values of the donated items.[119]

Other courts have determined fair market value using the price that the donated items brought in a subsequent sale.[120] However, the subsequent sale may be disregarded if it can be shown that the charity was forced to sell the item and the subsequent sale price did not establish fair market value at the time of contribution.[121] In one case, the court refused to rely on a sale of the donated painting two years after donation since the taxpayer's appraiser explained the reduction in value at the time of the subsequent sale.[122]

i. The international market. With the advent of advanced communication and computer systems, anyone can purchase almost anything in the world at any given time. These technological changes could affect the scope and extent of the appraiser's research. To date, a few cases have considered the open market as international.[123]

j. Appraised value as one fixed market value. While many courts find that fair market value at best is but an estimation of value,[124] one court supported the theory that at any given time, there is only one fixed, true market value.

> [The treasury regulations] contemplate a valuation process occurring in the context of an 'efficient' market where both buyers and sellers possess reasonable knowledge of the relevant facts and act in a rational manner. In such a market, an item may only have a single price at a given time. The commodities markets and the stock exchanges are examples of such efficient markets. Two separate trading prices for the same item will never exist (unless an error occurs) because the rational buyer will always trade at the lower price. Therefore, the selection of the relevant market at a given time for appraisal purposes is tantamount to selecting the price.[125]

But compare the language of a 1989 opinion wherein the court rejected the taxpayer's concept of fair market value as "the highest price at which an object would change hands between a willing seller and a willing buyer." The objects at issue were pre-Colombian art. The court stated:

> The argument really misses the mark. The market in this case is the retail sales market at art galleries dealing in pre-Colombian art. Value is the price a customer would pay the gallery for a piece of this type of art.… The range of prices arises out of the fact that, as both expert witnesses agree, galleries have no way of uniformly fixing the price for items which are comparable.… The range which the experts describe cover … the range of prices among various art galleries.… Every price in that range should reflect at least in theory the price which might be realized by an art gallery

> in a sale of a comparable item to a retail customer. Thus, again in theory, the entire range reflects retail sale prices. Thus, fair market value as defined by the [treasury] regulations is *on this record* not a single price but a range of prices.[126]

k. Summary. Having the background of these underlying principles of fair market value in the appropriate marketplace will enable the appraiser to identify issues that arise in the appraisal of an art object for charitable contribution income tax deduction purposes. While the foregoing material is complex, the author suggests that the appraiser first prepare a checklist of issues to consider in making an appraisal. Then, if warranted and for further information, the appraiser using the above outline of the material presented together with the footnote references can read the material and obtain any relevant cases from a law library.

F. Basis or Methodology Used to Arrive at Valuation

Appraisal Summary — donation of property valued at more than $5,000. Under Section B of Form 8283, the taxpayer is not required to state the method used to arrive at valuation.

"Qualified Appraisal." For objects of art, the Internal Revenue Service assumes that comparable sales will be the methodology used. The requirements under Treasury Regulation Section 1.170A-13(3)(ii)(J) and (K) (1988) are:

> The method of valuation used to determine the fair market value, such as the income approach, the market data approach, and the replacement-cost-less depreciation approach; and … the specific basis for the valuation, if any, such as specific comparable sales transactions.…

Under Revenue Procedure 66-49 (Appendix F), the procedure is more specific for art objects:

> (5) A statement of the factors upon which the appraisal was based, such as:
> (a) Sales of other works by the same artist particularly on or around the valuation date.
> (b) Quoted prices in dealers' catalogs of the artist's works or of other artists of comparable stature.
> (c) The economic state of the art market at or around the time of valuation, particularly with respect to the specific property.

Comments:

Appraisers in court-tried cases used different methods to arrive at value. These methods are:

1. *The square inch or "French Point System."* In two cases,[127] the appraisers used the square-inch rule:

[This system, also known as] 'the French Point System' ... according to [one appraiser] is employed by major galleries in the United States and Europe. Under this valuation technique, a value per square inch for an artist's work is determined through sales of other pieces by the artist.[128]

In that case involving the value of a local west-coast artist, the court held this system to be "unsubstantiated and unreliable." This method failed because the appraiser did not identify the sales figures used as a basis for his calculations, the "number of such sales on which the figure is based," and the "details as to whom such sales were made." The court also found that the "French Point System is not a widely used valuation technique, and is used only for 'celebrated artists,' artists who are well-known," not true in the case before the court.[129]

In another case involving the use of this same approach in valuing a Braque painting, the court rejected the method:

One [appraiser] used a 'square inch' method of valuing the painting — a method that does not appear to be commonly accepted as a basis for determining fair market value of paintings generally or of the works of Braque in particular.[130]

A similar approach to the "French Point System" has been advocated by taxpayers in cases involving the fair market value of gems. In a recent 1990 case where the value of a carved opal was at issue, the taxpayer's appraiser "analyzed the carved opal as a composite of cabochons" and presented the court with "the sum of their values, the break-up value as it were." The court rejected this approach and based its decision on other appraisals that valued the carved opal as a single piece.[131]

2. Future use of the donated item. Similar to a determination of the highest and best use of property, a method used to value real estate, is value based on the future use of the donated item. For example, in a case involving a 19-pound topaz crystal with a brown coloring, the taxpayer unsuccessfully argued that the value was $1.2 million, based on conversion of the color to blue through radiation and heat treatment (found by the court as "too remote and speculative") and future sale of the item at retail in jewelry stores after the crystal had been cut into small gemstones. The court assessed value at $750 which was the price the taxpayer paid for the crystal purchased six years prior to the first year of a three-year series of donations.[132]

In another case, speculation as to the future worth of a copyright was not considered by the court as a valid method to determine present value.[133]

However, in an interesting case involving the donation of a race car to the Motorsports Hall of Fame, the appraiser for the taxpayer based value on

information generally relied on in the business of appraising collectible cars, including race cars. His approach to appraising an antique or collector car was to use market or replacement value. His appraisal of Number 71 was also based on its restoration...; its historical significance as a record-setting race car ... and its high public exposure. His valuation was also influenced somewhat by the fact that the car was to be contributed to a museum where it would be viewed by at least 250,000 annually rather than to a collector.... In final analysis, he concluded that this Dodge Charger Daytona was a unique and irreplaceable car and a true historical monument to the sport of stock car racing.[134]

In other words, the appraiser, with whom the court agreed, placed a value on the future use of the car to be viewed on exhibition in a museum, a use which could be argued as the highest and best use of unique items such as rare works of art.

For comments on restrictions placed by the taxpayer-donor on the donee's future use of the property, see Section III-A, *supra.*

3. Reconstruction or replacement costs. In another unusual case involving the value of a 72-foot-tall sculpture entitled *Expanding Universe* created by Beniamino Bufano, the appraiser for the taxpayer utilized three separate methods to value the sculpture.

The methods considered the cost in 1979 to reconstruct a full scale replica of Expanding Universe, extrapolated the fair market value of Expanding Universe from the fair market value of Bufano's smaller art works, and considered the amounts that would be charged to create a 72-foot-tall statue by comparably famous California artists such as Bruce Beasley, Tom Martin Browne, Jerome Kirk, Fletcher Benton and Mark DiSuvero.

This amount [of $600,000] shows that the value determined was not simply averaged, but rather, were [sic] weighted. We find that the relative weighing apparently used by the report is in accord with weighing we would use to reflect our appreciation of how indicative each method was of fair market value of Expanding Universe. Considering the lack of data more indicative of fair market value, we feel that this approach was the best way to value Expanding Universe.[135]

This approach is an excellent example of the creative reasoning that an appraiser can use in appraising a unique item for which comparable sales or other data do not exist.[136]

However, note the language of a 1988 opinion wherein the court held that the original costs of production or what irreplaceable videotapes of Bolshoi Ballet performances would cost to produce at the time of the donation as "not relevant considerations" to a determination of fair market value:

> … There are works of art that cost very little to create for which a willing buyer would pay a great deal. On the other hand, a work of cultural significance could cost a substantial sum to produce but might not fetch anything approaching the cost of production.… Moreover, when [the taxpayer] claims that the films are "irreplaceable," i.e., not capable of reproduction, the cost of reproducing them … is simply not an appropriate measuring stick.[137]

Further, note the danger of attempting to use the cost of reproduction or replacement to establish fair market value where an active market exists with substantial comparable sale items. In one 1992 case, taxpayers unsuccessfully tried to rely solely on replacement cost of donated animal mounts. Replacement cost included average costs involved in the hunt to obtain specimens, e.g., safari costs, trophy fees, taxidermy, and shipping. In this case, the court found the testimony of the government's appraiser concerning comparable sales as convincing, particularly since the taxpayers did not present any evidence of comparable sales.[138]

4. *Insurance value.* The insurable value of an art object is the highest value within the range of fair market value.[139] Difficulties arise when the taxpayer insures an item for X dollars and then claims a higher figure for donation purposes,[140] or when the taxpayer tells the donee to insure the item for less than the taxpayer claims as the value of the donation.[141]

In recent cases, the courts have commented on the lack of information regarding whether an art object was insured.[142] In one case, the court stated:

> It seems wholly unlikely that a rare 18th century Kuba rug, with a valuation in excess of $10,000, would remain uninsured by petitioner, whose principal occupation during the taxable year in issue was that of investor. Yet, the record is silent on this point. The lack of any evidence as to such insurance, which would have had a stated value, is damaging to petitioner's case.[143]

5. *Grouping items together to determine value.* In one case involving the value of Indian artifacts of "varied quality and value," the court disregarded a method in which the appraiser "grouped artifacts according to tribal association." The court's reasoning was that this method failed to demonstrate the degree of particularity necessary to assess a determination of value of each item.[144]

6. *Appraiser's own judgment.* In cases where the appraiser used his or her "street knowledge,"[145] general experience as a collector and appraiser,[146] or subjective or emotional reaction to the art object,[147] the courts have rejected the appraiser's testimony and judgment as to value. Artistic merit is, however, a valid factor to consider in determining an art object's value.[148]

7. *List prices or offers to sell.* List prices are not actual sale prices and should not be used for comparable "sales." As such, list prices contained in catalogs are not evidence of value of charitable contributions of property unless there is also evidence that items listed actually sold at such prices. There must be actual market for items listed in order for list prices to be relevant. As one court noted:

> [T]he prices on the list, according to petitioner's own expert, were sometimes kept artificially high, out of 'honor and sympathy' for an artist whose work might not sell if it appeared is [sic] was declining in value.[149]

Note, however, that Revenue Procedure 66-49 (Appendix F) requires that information concerning quoted prices in dealers' catalogues of the artist's works or of other artists of similar or comparable stature be stated in a "qualified appraisal." The reason is that a list price would set the outer parameters of value.

8. *Comparable sales.* Prices obtained from sales of other similar items are the usual evidence given to substantiate value. Comparable sales need not be restricted to sales made during the year of the donation. In a 1991 case involving the value of Calder tapestries and a rare book, the court stated:

> In some cases, sales that occurred during years other than those in issue are helpful in determining fair market value because they can either show a trend or indicate the fair market value for the years in issue.… Subsequent events or facts may be used to corroborate an appraisal that is based on facts known as of the valuation date.… We also consider sales of comparable property occurring after the valuation date if there are no uncertain probabilities or contingencies which affect the value of the property.[150]

Certain general rules regarding this method of valuation can be gathered from the cases. First, comparability must be shown to exist; that is, the items whose sales are used as evidence of value of a particular donated item must be of a similar nature. For example, in one case, the appraiser sought to establish the value of a painting attributed to Tintoretto by using list prices of paintings by Rembrandt, Modigliani, Van Gogh, Manet, Monet, Picasso, Renoir, Toulouse-Lautrec and Velazquez. The court held that, since these artists were from different schools and periods, "the vast majority of listed sales [were] totally incomparable," and, unlike the painting in issue, as to listed sales by the appraiser of "true masterpieces" (such as Rembrandt's *Aristotle Contemplating the Bust of Homer*), the court said that it "would not begin to consider these paintings comparable."[151]

Secondly, and specifically, the appraiser should —

a. if possible, compare sales of items by the same artist[152] or of the same school;[153]

b. identify and describe each comparable in as much detail as the item which is the subject of the appraisal, including the physical condition of the comparable item, its size, medium, subject matter, date of execution, extent of restoration (if any), rarity, artistic quality,[154] and authenticity;[155]

c. explain why the items are comparable;[156]

d. give the dates of the comparable sales;[157]

e. identify the sources of the sales information;[158]

f. describe the art markets at the times of the comparable sales;[159] and

g. describe the circumstances surrounding the sales such as the "climate" at auction sales and any "other factors which may have influenced the particular sales prices."[160]

In one case, the court disregarded prices obtained in auction sales by Sotheby Parke Bernet in New York and Los Angeles because (1) the appraiser did not view the auctioned items prior to or at their sale and (2) while he considered auction catalogues to be accurate generally, he did concede that the information given there was "somewhat skimpy, ... sometimes inaccurate and that he would not make an important purchase solely on the basis of catalog information." The court further stated that "while comparable sales are evidence of value in the art field ... we are unconvinced that the method was properly utilized herein."[161] Therefore, the appraiser should assemble much more information about the works listed in an auction catalog than the prices stated therein, at least enough to be able to discern whether the item is truly comparable.[162]

9. *Summary.* In most cases the appraiser will use comparable sales as the method to determine the fair market value in the appropriate marketplace. However, for the unusual situation, the appraiser needs to be aware of other methods that may prove useful to the appraiser's determination, depending on the circumstances and the item being appraised.

G. Assumptions, Limiting Conditions and Appraiser's Certification

Every appraiser should be prepared to state the assumptions upon which the appraisal was based, the conditions under which the appraisal was prepared. The assumptions and limiting conditions need not be outlined in any particular order but the appraiser must include all of them.

A sample form of the appraiser's certification is given in Appendix G.

IV. Conclusion

In preparing an art object appraisal that will be used to substantiate a charitable contribution tax deduction, the appraiser cannot rely on a handful of court decisions to explain all of the legal and valuation principles involved. Rather, the appraiser needs to have an extensive and thorough background in the full range of legal and valuation principles involved in the preparation of such an appraisal. However, the appraiser cannot be expected to have the training and experience of an accountant or lawyer and still maintain full-time occupation as an appraiser. Just keeping abreast of the latest valuation theories is difficult in and of itself.

To be able to identify all of the legal issues involved in the preparation of an appraisal through the reading of court decisions would not only be time consuming but at times might create an overwhelming burden for the appraiser. Should the appraiser need more information regarding one or more of the legal principles discussed in this paper, the appraiser can read the applicable and relevant cases that are listed in the footnotes throughout this paper at any law library located in a main courthouse or law school. Reading a court decision is far preferable to reading a digest or someone else's synopsis of the decision.

In conclusion, the ideal background that the appraiser can obtain is through a formal, educational program where the fair market value concept along with the underlying legal and valuation principles is taught. With the increasing hurdles that the government seems determined to place in the path of the appraiser, education and experience provide the best training that the appraiser can have.

Appendix A©

Recordkeeping Requirements for Deductions for Charitable Contributions

- **Regulations**

[¶1.867A] § 1.170A-13. Recordkeeping and return requirements for deductions for charitable contributions. — (a) *Charitable contributions of money made in taxable years beginning after December 31, 1982* — (1) *In general.* If a taxpayer makes a charitable contribution of money in a taxable year beginning after December 31, 1982, the taxpayer shall maintain for each contribution one of the following:

(i) A canceled check.

(ii) A receipt from the donee charitable organization showing the name of the donee, the date of the contribution, and the amount of the contribution. A letter or other communication from the donee charitable organization acknowledging receipt of a contribution and showing the date and amount of the contribution constitutes a receipt for purposes of this paragraph (a).

(iii) In the absence of a canceled check or receipt from the donee charitable organization, other reliable written records showing the name of the donee, the date of the contribution, and the amount of the contribution.

(2) *Special rules* — (i) *Reliability of records.* The reliability of the written records described in paragraph (a)(1)(iii) of this section is to be determined on the basis of all of the facts and circumstances of a particular case. In all events, however, the burden shall be on the taxpayer to establish reliability. Factors indicating that the written records are reliable include, but are not limited to:

(A) The contemporaneous nature of the writing evidencing the contribution.

(B) The regularity of the taxpayer's recordkeeping procedures. For example, a contemporaneous diary entry stating the amount and date of the donations and the name of the donee charitable organization made by a taxpayer who regularly makes such diary entries would generally be considered reliable.

(C) In the case of a contribution of a small amount, the existence of any written or other evidence from, the donee charitable organization evidencing receipt of a donation that would not otherwise constitute a receipt under paragraph (a)(1)(ii) of this section (including an emblem, button, or other token traditionally associated with a charitable organization and regularly given by the organization to persons making cash donations).

(ii) *Information stated in income tax return.* The information required by paragraph (a)(1)(iii) of this section shall be stated in the taxpayer's income tax return if required by the return form or its instructions.

(3) *Taxpayer option to apply paragraph (d)(1) to pre-1985 contributions.* See paragraph (d)(1) of this section with regard to contributions of money made on or before December 31, 1984.

(b) *Charitable contributions of property other than money made in taxable years beginning after December 31, 1982* — (1) *In general.* Except in the case of certain charitable contributions of property made after December 31, 1984, to which paragraph (c) of this section applies, any taxpayer who makes a charitable contribution of property other than money in a taxable year beginning after December 31, 1982, shall maintain for each contribution a receipt from the donee showing the following information:

(i) The name of the donee.

(ii) The date and location of the contribution.

(iii) A description of the property in detail reasonably sufficient under the circumstances. Although the fair market value of the property is one of the circumstances to be taken into account in determining the amount of detail to be included on the receipt, such value need not be stated on the receipt. A letter or other written communication from the donee acknowledging receipt of the contribution, showing the date of the contribution, and containing the required description of the property contributed constitutes a receipt for purposes of this paragraph. A receipt is not required if the contribution is made in circumstances where it is impractical to obtain a receipt (*e.g.*, by depositing property at a charity's unattended drop site). In such cases, however, the taxpayer shall maintain reliable written records with respect to each item of donated property that include the information required by paragraph (b)(2)(ii) of this section.

(2) *Special rules*—(i) *Reliability of records.* The rules described in paragraph (a)(2)(i) of this section also apply to this paragraph (b) for determining the reliability of the written records described in paragraph (b)(1) of this section.

(ii) *Content of records.* The written records described in paragraph (b)(1) of this section shall include the following information and such information shall be stated in the taxpayer's income tax return if required by the return form or its instructions:

(A) The name and address of the donee organization to which the contribution was made.

(B) The date and location of the contribution.

(C) A description of the property in detail reasonable under the circumstances (including the value of the property), and, in the case of securities, the name of the issuer, the type of security, and whether or not such security is regularly traded on a stock exchange or in an over-the-counter market.

(D) The fair market value of the property at the time the contribution was made, the method utilized in determining the fair market value, and, if the valuation was determined by appraisal, a copy of the signed report of the appraiser.

(E) In the case of property to which section 170(e) applies, the cost or other basis, adjusted as provided by section 1016, the reduction by reason of section 170(e)(1) in the amount of the charitable contribution otherwise taken into account, and the manner in which such reduction was determined. A taxpayer who elects under paragraph (d)(2) of § 1.170A-8 to apply section 170(e)(1) to contributions and carryovers of 30 percent capital gain property shall maintain a written record indicating the years for which the election was made and showing the contributions in the current year and carryovers from preceding years to which it applies. For the definition of the term "30-percent capital gain property," see paragraph (d)(3) of § 1.170A-8.

(F) If less than the entire interest in the property is contributed during the taxable year, the total amount claimed as a deduction for the taxable year due to the contribution of the property, and the amount claimed as a deduction in any prior year or years for contributions of other interests in such property, the name and address of each organization to which any such contribution was made, the place where any such property which is tangible property is located or kept, and the name of any person, other than the organization to which the property giving rise to the deduction was contributed, having actual possession of the property.

(G) The terms of any agreement or understanding entered into by or on behalf of the taxpayer which relates to the use, sale, or other disposition of the property contributed, including, for example, the terms of any agreement or understanding which —

(1) Restricts temporarily or permanently the donee's right to use or dispose of the donated property.

(2) Reserves to, or confers upon, anyone (other than the donee organization or an organization participating with the donee organization in cooperative fund-raising) any right to the income from donated property or to the possession of the property, including the right to vote donated securities, to acquire the property by purchase or otherwise, or to designate the person having such income, possession, or right to acquire, or

(3) Earmarks donated property for a particular use.

(3) *Deductions in excess of $500 claimed for a charitable contribution of property other than money* — (i) *In general.* In addition to the information required under paragraph (b)(2)(ii) of this section, if a taxpayer makes a charitable contribution of property other than money in a taxable year beginning after December 31, 1982, and claims a deduction in excess of $500 in respect of the contribution of such item, the taxpayer shall maintain written records that include the following information with respect to such item of donated property, and shall state such information in his or her income tax return if required by the return form or its instructions:

(A) The manner of acquisition, as, for example, by purchase, gift, bequest, inheritance, or exchange, and the approximate date of acquisition of the property by the taxpayer or, if the property was created, produced, or manufactured by or for the taxpayer, the approximate date the property was substantially completed.

(B) The cost or other basis, adjusted as provided by section 1016, of property, other than publicly traded securities, held by the taxpayer for a period of less than 12 months (6 months for property contributed in taxable years beginning after December 31, 1982, and on or before June 6, 1988) immediately preceding the date on which the contribution was made and, when the information is available, of property, other than publicly traded securities, held for a period of 12 months or more (6 months or more for property contributed in taxable years beginning after December 31, 1982, and on or before June 6, 1988) preceding the date on which the contribution was made.

(ii) *Information on acquisition date or cost basis not available.* If the return form or its instructions require the taxpayer to provide information on either the acquisition date of the property or the cost basis as described in paragraph (b)(3)(i)(A) and (B), respectively, of this section, and the taxpayer has reasonable cause for not being able to provide such information, the taxpayer shall attach an explanatory statement to the return. If a taxpayer has reasonable cause for not being able to provide such information, the taxpayer shall not be disallowed a charitable contribution deduction under section 170 for failure to comply with paragraph (b)(3)(i)(A) and (B) of the section.

(4) *Taxpayer option to apply paragraph (d)(1) and (2) to pre-1985 contributions.* See paragraph (d)(1) and (2) of this section with regard to contributions of property made on or before December 31, 1984.

(c) *Deductions in excess of $5,000 for certain charitable contributions of property made after December 31, 1984* — (1) *General Rule* — (i) *In general.* This paragraph applies to any charitable contribution made after December 31, 1984, by an individual, closely held corporation, personal service corporation, partnership, or S corporation of an item of property (other than money and publicly traded securities to which § 1.170A-13(c)(7)(xi)(B) does not apply) if the amount claimed or reported as a deduction under section 170 with respect to such item exceeds $5,000. This paragraph also applies to charitable contributions by C corporations (as defined in section 1361(a)(2) of the Code) to the extent described in paragraph (c)(2)(ii) of this section. No deduction under section 170 shall be allowed with respect to

a charitable contribution to which this paragraph applies unless the substantiation requirements described in paragraph (c)(2) of this section are met. For purposes of this paragraph (c), the amount claimed or reported as a deduction for an item of property is the aggregate amount claimed or reported as a deduction for a charitable contribution under section 170 for such items of property and all similar items of property (as defined in paragraph (c)(7)(iii) of this section) by the same donor for the same taxable year (whether or not donated to the same donee).

(ii) *Special rule for property in which section 170(e)(3) or (4) applies.* For purposes of this paragraph (c), in computing the amount claimed or reported as a deduction for donated property to which section 170(e)(3) or (4) applies (pertaining to certain contributions of inventory and scientific equipment) there shall be taken into account only the amount claimed or reported as a deduction in excess of the amount which would have been taken into account for tax purposes by the donor as costs of goods sold if the donor had sold the contributed property to the donee. For example, assume that a donor makes a contribution from inventory of clothing for the care of the needy to which section 170(e)(3) applies. The cost of the property to the donor was $5,000, and pursuant to section 170(e)(3)(B), the donor claims a charitable contribution deduction of $8,000 with respect to the property. Therefore, $3,000 ($8,000-$5,000) is the amount taken into account for purposes of determining whether the $5,000 threshold of this paragraph (c)(1) is met.

Appendix B©

Substantiation Requirements

Treasury Regulation Section 1.170A-13 (1988).

(2) *Substantiation requirements* — (i) *In general.* Except as provided in paragraph (c)(2)(ii) of this section, a donor who claims or reports a deduction with respect to a charitable contribution to which this paragraph (c) applies must comply with the following three requirements:

(A) Obtain a qualified appraisal (as defined in paragraph (c)(3) of this section) for such property contributed. If the contributed property is a partial interest, the appraisal shall be of the partial interest.

(B) Attach a fully completed appraisal summary (as defined in paragraph (c)(4) of this section) to the tax return (or, in the case of a donor that is a partnership or S corporation, the information return) on which the deduction for the contribution is first claimed (or reported) by the donor.

(C) Maintain records containing the information required by paragraph (b)(2)(ii) of this section.

Appendix C©

Qualified Appraisal

Treasury Regulation Section 1.170A-13(c)(3) (1988)

(3) *Qualified appraisal* — (i) *In general.* For purposes of this paragraph (c), the term "qualified appraisal" means an appraisal document that —

(A) Relates to an appraisal that is made not earlier than 60 days prior to the date of contribution of the appraised property nor later than the date specified in paragraph (c)(3)(iv)(B) of this section;

(B) Is prepared, signed, and dated by a qualified appraiser (within the meaning of paragraph (c)(5) of this section);

(C) Includes the information required by paragraph (c)(3)(ii) of this section; and

(D) Does not involve an appraisal fee prohibited by paragraph (c)(6) of this section.

(ii) *Information included in qualified appraisal.* A qualified appraisal shall include the following information:

(A) A description of the property in sufficient detail for a person who is not generally familiar with the type of property to ascertain that the property that was appraised is the property that was (or will be) contributed;

(B) In the case of tangible property, the physical condition of the property;

(C) The date (or expected date) of contribution to the donee;

(D) The terms of any agreement or understanding entered into (or expected to be entered into) by or on behalf of the donor or donee that relates to the use, sale, or other disposition of the property contributed, including, for example, the terms of any agreement or understanding that —

(*1*) Restricts temporarily or permanently a donee's right to use or dispose of the donated property,

(*2*) Reserves to, or confers upon, anyone (other than a donee organization or an organization participating with a donee organization in cooperative fund-raising) any right to the income from the contributed property or to the possession of the property, including the right to vote donated securities, to acquire the property by purchase or otherwise, or to designate the person having such income, possession, or right to acquire, or

(*3*) Earmarks donated property for a particular use.

(E) The name, address, and (if a taxpayer identification number is otherwise required by section 6109 and the regulations thereunder) the identifying number of the qualified appraiser; and, if the qualified appraiser is acting in his or her capacity as a partner in a partnership, an employee of any person (whether an individual, corporation, or partnerships), or an independent contractor engaged by a person other than the donor, the name, address, and taxpayer identification number (if a number is otherwise required by section 6109 and the regulations thereunder) of the partnership or the person who employs or engages the qualified appraiser;

(F) The qualifications of the qualified appraiser who signs the appraisal, including the appraiser's background, experience, education, and membership, if any, in professional appraisal associations;

(G) A statement that the appraisal was prepared for income tax purposes;

(H) The date (or dates) on which the property was appraised;

(I) The appraised fair market value (within the meaning of § 1.170A-1(c)(2)) of the property on the date (or expected date) of contribution;

(J) The method of valuation used to determine the fair market value, such as the income approach, the market-data approach, and the replacement-cost-less-depreciation approach; and

(K) The specific basis for the valuation, such as specific comparable sales transactions or statistical sampling, including a justification for using sampling and an explanation of the sampling procedure employed.

(iii) *Effect of signature of the qualified appraiser.* Any appraiser who falsely or fraudulently overstates the value of the contributed property referred to in a qualified appraisal or appraisal summary (as defined in paragraph (c)(3) and (4), respectively, of this section) that the appraiser has signed may be subject to a civil penalty under section 6701 for aiding and abetting an understatement of tax liability and, moreover, may have appraisals disregarded pursuant to 31 U.S.C. § 330(c).

(iv) *Special rules* — (A) *Number of qualified appraisals.* For purposes of paragraph (c)(2)(i)(A) of this section, a separate qualified appraisal is required for each item of property that is not included in a group of similar items of property. See paragraph (c)(7)(iii) of this section for the definition of similar items of property. Only one qualified appraisal is required for a group of similar items of property contributed in the same taxable year of the donor, although a donor may obtain separate qualified appraisals for each item of property. A qualified appraisal prepared with respect to a group of similar items of property shall provide all the information required by paragraph (c)(3)(ii) of this section for each item of similar property, except that the appraiser may select any items whose aggregate value is appraised at $100 or less and provide a group description of such items.

(B) *Time of receipt of qualified appraisal.* The qualified appraisal must be received by the donor before the due date (including extensions) of the return on which a deduction is first claimed (or reported in the case of a donor that is a partnership or S corporation) under section 170 with respect to the donated property, or, in the case of a deduction first claimed (or reported) on an amended return, the date on which the return is filed.

(C) *Retention of qualified appraisal.* The donor must retain the qualified appraisal in the donor's records for so long as it may be relevant in the administration of any internal revenue law.

(D) *Appraisal disregarded pursuant to 31 U.S.C. § 330(c).* If an appraisal is disregarded pursuant to 31 U.S.C. § 330(c) it shall have no probative effect as to the value of the appraised property. Such appraisal will, however, otherwise constitute a "qualified appraisal" for purposes of this paragraph (c) if the appraisal summary includes the declaration described in paragraph (c)(4)(ii)(L)(2) and the taxpayer had no knowledge that such declaration was false as of the time described in paragraph (c)(4)(i)(B) of this section.

Appendix D©

Appraisal Summary

Treasury Regulation Section 1.170A-13(c)(3) (1988)

(4) *Appraisal Summary* — (i) *In general.* For purposes of this paragraph (c), except as provided in paragraph (c)(4)(iv)(A) of this section, the term "appraisal summary" means a summary of a qualified appraisal that—

(A) Is made on the form prescribed by the Internal Revenue Service;

(B) Is signed and dated (as described in paragraph (c)(4)(iii) of this section) by the donee (or presented to the donee for signature in cases described in paragraph (c)(4)(iv)(C)(2) of this section);

(C) Is signed and dated by the qualified appraiser (within the meaning of paragraph (c)(5) of this section) who prepared the qualified appraisal (within the meaning of paragraph (c)(3) of this section); and

(D) Includes the information required by paragraph (c)(4)(ii) of this section.

(ii) *Information included in an appraisal summary.* An appraisal summary shall include the following information:

(A) The name and taxpayer identification number of the donor (social security number if the donor is an individual or employer identification number if the donor is a partnership or corporation);

(B) A description of the property in sufficient detail for a person who is not generally familiar with the type of property to ascertain that the property that was appraised is the property that was contributed;

(C) In the case of tangible property, a brief summary of the overall physical condition of the property at the time of the contribution;

(D) The manner of acquisition (*e.g.*, purchase, exchange, gift, or bequest) and the date of acquisition of the property by the donor, or, if the property was created, produced, or manufactured by or for the donor, a statement to that effect and the approximate date the property was substantially completed;

(E) The cost or other basis of the property adjusted as provided by section 1016;

(F) The name, address, and taxpayer identification number of the donee;

(G) The date the donee received the property;

(H) For charitable contributions made after June 6, 1988, a statement explaining whether or not the charitable contribution was made by means of a bargain sale and the amount of any consideration received from the donee for the contribution;

(I) The name, address, and (if a taxpayer identification number is otherwise required by section 6109 and the regulations thereunder) the identifying number of the qualified appraiser who signs the appraisal summary and of other persons as required by paragraph (c)(3)(ii)(E) of this section;

(J) The appraised fair market value of the property on the date of contribution;

(K) The declaration by the appraiser described in paragraph (c)(5)(i) of this section;

(L) A declaration by the appraiser stating that —

(*1*) The fee charged for the appraisal is not of a type prohibited by paragraph (c)(6) of this section; and

(*2*) Appraisals prepared by the appraiser are not being disregarded pursuant to 31 U.S.C. § 330(c) on the date the appraisal summary is signed by the appraiser; and

(M) Such other information as may be specified by the form.

(iii) *Signature of the original donee.* The person who signs the appraisal summary for the donee shall be an official authorized to sign the tax or information returns of the donee, or a person specifically authorized to sign appraisal summaries by an official authorized to sign the tax or information returns of such donee. In the case of a donee that is a governmental unit, the person who signs the appraisal summary for such donee shall be the official authorized by such donee to sign appraisal summaries. The signature of the donee on the appraisal summary does not represent concurrence in the appraised value of the contributed property. Rather, it represents acknowledgment of receipt of the property described in the appraisal summary on the date specified in the appraisal summary and that the donee understands the information reporting requirements imposed by section 6050L and § 1.6050L-1. In general, § 1.6050L-1 requires the donee to file an information return with the Internal Revenue Service in the event the donee sells, exchanges, consumes, or otherwise disposes of the property (or any portion thereof) described in the appraisal summary within 2 years after the date of the donor's contribution of such property.

(iv) *Special rules* ... [relating to stock]

(B) *Number of appraisal summaries.* A separate appraisal summary for each item of property described in paragraph (c)(1) of this section must be attached to the donor's return. If, during the donor's taxable year, the donor contributes similar items of property described in paragraph (c)(1) of this section to more than one donee, the donor shall attach to the donor's return a separate appraisal summary for each donee. See paragraph (c)(7)(iii) of this section for the definition of similar items of property. If, however, during the donor's taxable year, a donor contributes similar items of property described in paragraph (c)(1) of this section to the same donee, the donor may attach to the donor's return a single appraisal summary with respect to all similar items of property contributed to the same donee. Such an appraisal summary shall provide all the information required by paragraph (c)(4)(ii) of this section for each item of property, except that the appraiser may select any items whose aggregate value is appraised at $100 or less and provide a group description for such items.

(C) *Manner of acquisition, cost basis and donee's signature.* (*1*) If a taxpayer has reasonable cause for being unable to provide the information required by paragraph (c)(4)(ii)(D) and (E) of this section (relating to the manner of acquisition and basis of the contributed property), an appropriate explanation should be attached to the appraisal summary. The taxpayer's deduction will not be disallowed simply because of the inability (for reasonable cause) to provide these items of information.

(2) In rare and unusual circumstances in which it is impossible for the taxpayer to obtain the signature of the donee on the appraisal summary as required by paragraph (c)(4)(i)(B) of this section, the taxpayer's deduction will not be disallowed for that reason provided that the taxpayer attaches a statement to the appraisal summary explaining, in detail, why it was not possible to obtain the donee's signature. For example, if the donee ceases to exist as an entity subsequent to the date of the contribution and prior to the date when the appraisal summary must be signed, and the donor acted reasonably in not obtaining the donee's signature at the time of the contribution, relief under this paragraph (c)(4)(iv)(C)(2) would generally be appropriate.

(D) *Information excluded from certain appraisal summaries*. The information required by paragraph (c)(4)(i)(C), paragraph (c)(4)(ii) (D), (E), (H) through (M), and paragraph (c) (4)(iv)(A)(3), and the average trading price referred to in paragraph (c)(4)(iv)(A)(4) of this section do not have to be included on the appraisal summary at the time it is signed by the donee or a copy is provided to the donee pursuant to paragraph (c)(4)(iv)(E) of this section.

(E) *Statement to be furnished by donors to donees.* Every donor who presents an appraisal summary to a donee for signature after June 6, 1988, in order to comply with paragraph (c)(4)(i)(B) of this section shall furnish a copy of the appraisal summary to such donee.

(F) *Appraisal summary required to be provided to partners and S corporation shareholders.* If the donor is a partnership or S corporation, the donor shall provide a copy of the appraisal summary to every partner or shareholder, respectively, who receives an allocation of a charitable contribution deduction under section 170 with respect to the property described in the appraisal summary.

(G) *Partners and S corporation shareholders.* A partner of a partnership or shareholder of an S corporation who receives an allocation of a deduction under section 170 for a charitable contribution of property to which this paragraph (c) applies must attach a copy of the partnership's or S corporation's appraisal summary to the tax return on which the deduction for the contribution is first claimed. If such appraisal summary is not attached, the partner's or shareholder's deduction shall not be allowed except as provided for in paragraph (c)(4)(iv)(H) of this section.

(H) *Failure to attach appraisal summary.* In the event that a donor fails to attach to the donor's return an appraisal summary as required by paragraph (c)(2)(i)(B) of this section, the Internal Revenue Service may request that the donor submit the appraisal summary within 90 days of the request. If such a request is made and the donor complies with the request within the 90-day period, the deduction under section 170 shall not be disallowed for failure to attach the appraisal summary, provided that the donor's failure to attach the appraisal summary was a good faith omission and the requirements of paragraph (c)(3) and (4) of this section are met (including the completion of the qualified appraisal prior to the date specified in paragraph (c)(3)(iv)(B) of this section).

Appendix E©

Qualified Appraiser

Treasury Regulation Section 1.170A-13(c)(3) (1988)

(5) *Qualified appraiser* — (i) *In general*. The term "qualified appraiser" means an individual (other than a person described in paragraph (c)(5)(iv) of this section) who includes on the appraisal summary (described in paragraph (c)(4) of this section), a declaration that —

(A) The individual either holds himself or herself out to the public as an appraiser or performs appraisals on a regular basis;

(B) Because of the appraiser's qualifications as described in the appraisal (pursuant to paragraph (c)(3)(ii)(F) of this section), the appraiser is qualified to make appraisals of the type of property being valued;

(C) The appraiser is not one of the persons described in paragraph (c)(5)(iv) of this section; and

(D) The appraiser understands that an intentionally false or fraudulent overstatement of the value of the property described in the qualified appraisal or appraisal summary may subject the appraiser to a civil penalty under section 6701 for aiding and abetting an understatement of tax liability, and, moreover, the appraiser may have appraisals disregarded pursuant to 31 U.S.C. § 330(c) (see paragraph (c)(3)(iii) of this section).

(ii) *Exception.* An individual is not a qualified appraiser with respect to a particular donation, even if the declaration specified in paragraph (c)(5)(i) of this section is provided in the appraisal summary, if the donor had knowledge of facts that would cause a reasonable person to expect the appraiser falsely to overstate the value of the donated property (*e.g.,* the donor and the appraiser make an agreement concerning the amount at which the property will be valued and the donor knows that such amount exceeds the fair market value of the property).

(iii) *Numbers of appraisers.* More than one appraiser may appraise the donated property. If more than one appraiser appraises the property, the donor does not have to use each appraiser's appraisal for purposes of substantiating the charitable contribution deduction pursuant to this paragraph (c). If the donor uses the appraisal of more than one appraiser, or if two or more appraisers contribute to a single appraisal, each appraiser shall comply with the requirements of this paragraph (c), including signing the qualified appraisal and appraisal summary as required by paragraphs (c)(3)(i)(B) and (c)(4)(i)(C) of this section, respectively.

(iv) *Qualified appraiser exclusions.* The following persons cannot be qualified appraiser with respect to particular property:

(A) The donor or the taxpayer who claims or reports a deduction under section 170 for the contribution of the property that is being appraised.

(B) A party to the transaction in which the donor acquired the property being appraised (*i.e.,* the person who sold, exchanged, or gave the property to the donor, or any person who acted as an agent for the transferor or for the donor with respect to such sale, exchange, or gift), unless the property is donated within 2 months of the date of acquisition and its ap-praised value does not exceed its acquisition price.

(C) The donee of the property.

(D) Any person employed by any of the foregoing persons (*e.g.,* if the donor acquired a painting from an art dealer, neither the art dealer nor persons employed by the dealer can be qualified appraisers with respect to that painting).

(E) Any person related to any of the foregoing persons under section 267(b), or with respect to appraisals made after June 6, 1988, married to a person who is in a relationship described in section 267(b) with any of the foregoing persons.

(F) An appraiser who is regularly used by any person described in paragraph (c)(5)(iv)(A), (B), or (C) of this section and who does not perform a majority of his or her appraisals made during his or her taxable year for other persons.

(6) *Appraisal fees* — (i) *In general.* Except as otherwise provided in paragraph (c)(6)(ii) of this section, no part of the fee arrangement for a qualified appraisal can be based, in effect, on a percentage (or set of percentages) of the appraised value of the property. If a fee arrangement for an appraisal is based in whole or in part on the amount of the appraised value of the property, if any, that is allowed as a deduction under section 170, after Internal Revenue Service examination or otherwise, it shall be treated as a fee based on a percentage of the appraised value of the property. For example, an appraiser's fee that is subject to reduction by the same percentage as the appraised value may be reduced by the Internal Revenue Service would be treated as a fee that violates this paragraph (c)(6).

(ii) *Exception.* Paragraph (c)(6)(i) of this section does not apply to a fee paid to a generally recognized association that regulates appraisers provided all of the following requirements are met:

(A) The association is not organized for profit and no part of the net earnings of the association inures to the benefit of any private shareholder or individual (these terms have the same meaning as in section 501(c)),

(B) The appraiser does not receive any compensation from the association or any other persons for making the appraisal, and

(C) The fee arrangement is not based in whole or in part on the amount of the appraised value of the donated property, if any, that is allowed as a deduction under section 170 after Internal Revenue Service examination or otherwise.

(7) *Meaning of terms.* For purposes of this paragraph (c) —

(i) *Closely held corporation.* The term "closely held corporation" means any corporation (other than S corporation) with respect to which the stock ownership requirement of paragraph (2) of section 542(a) of the Code is met.

(ii) *Personal service corporation.* The term "personal service corporation" means any corporation (other than an S corporation) which is a service organization (within the meaning of section 414(m)(3) of the Code).

(iii) *Similar items of property.* The phrase "similar items of property" means property of the same generic category or type, such as stamp collections (including philatelic supplies and books on stamp collecting), coin collections (including numismatic supplies and books on coin collecting), lithographs, paintings, photographs, books, nonpublicly traded stock, nonpublicly traded securities other than nonpublicly traded stock, land, buildings, clothing, jewelry, furniture, electronic equipment, household appliances, toys, everyday kitchenware, china, crystal, or silver. For example, if a donor claims on her return for the year deductions of $2,000 for books given by her to College A, $2,500 for books given by her to College B, and $900 for books given by her to College C, the $5,000 threshold of paragraph (c)(1) of this section is exceeded. Therefore, the donor must obtain a qualified appraisal for the books and attach to her return three appraisal summaries for the books donated to A, B, and C. For rules regarding the number of qualified appraisals and appraisal summaries required when similar items of property are contributed, see paragraphs (c)(3)(iv)(A) and (c)(4)(iv)(B), respectively, of this section.

(iv) *Donor.* The term "donor" means a person or entity (other than an organization described in section 170(c) to which the donated property was previously contributed) that makes a charitable contribution of property.

(v) *Donee.* The term "donee" means —

(A) Except as provided in paragraph (c)(7)(v)(B) and (C) of this section, an organization described in section 170(c) to which property is contributed.

(B) Except as provided in paragraph (c)(7)(v)(C) of this section, in the case of a charitable contribution of property placed in trust for the benefit of an organization described in section 170(c), the trust, or

(C) In the case of a charitable contribution of property placed in trust for the benefit of an organization described in section 170(c) made on or before June 6, 1988, the beneficiary that is an organization described in section 170(c), of if the trust has assumed the duties of a donee by signing the appraisal summary pursuant to paragraph (c)(4)(i)(B) of this section, the trust. In general, the term refers only to the original donee. However, with respect to paragraph (c)(3)(ii)(D), the last sentence of paragraph (c)(4)(iii), and paragraph (c)(5)(iv)(C) of this section, the term "donee" means the original donee and all successor donees in cases where the original donee transfers the contributed property to a successor donee after June 6k, 1988.

(vi) *Original donee.* The term "original donee" means the donee to or for which property is initially donated by a donor.

(vii) *Successor donee.* The term "successor donee" means any donee of property other than its original donee (*i.e.*, a transferee of property for less than fair market value from an original donee or another successor donee).

(viii) *Fair market value.* For the meaning of the term "fair market value," see section 1.170A-1(c)(2).

Appendix F©

Revenue Procedure 66-49, 1966-2 C.B. 1257

Section 1. Purpose

The purpose of this procedure is to provide information and guidelines for taxpayers, individual appraisers, and valuation groups relative to appraisals of contributed property for Federal income tax purposes. The procedures outlined are applicable to all types of noncash property for which an appraisal is required such as real property, tangible or intangible personal property, and securities. These procedures are also appropriate for unique properties such as art objects, literary manuscripts, antiques, etc., with respect to which the determination of value often is more difficult.

Section 2. Law and Regulations

.01 Numerous sections of the Internal Revenue Code of 1954, as amended, give rise to a determination of value for Federal tax purposes; however, the significant section for purposes of this Revenue Procedure is section 170, Charitable, Etc., Contributions and Gifts.

.02 Value is defined in section 1.170-1(c) of the Income Tax Regulations as follows:

"... The fair market value is the price at which the property would change hands between a willing buyer and a willing seller, neither being under any compulsion to buy or sell and both having reasonable knowledge of relevant facts...."

.03 This section further provides that:

"... If the contribution is made in property of a type which the taxpayer sells in the course of his business, the fair market value is the price which the taxpayer would have received if he had sold the contributed property in the lowest usual market in which he customarily sells, at the time and place of contribution (and in the case of contribution of goods in quantity, in the quantity contributed)...."

.04 As to the measure of proof in determining the fair market value, all factors bearing on value are relevant including, where pertinent, the cost, or selling price of the item, sales of comparable properties, cost or reproduction, opinion evidence and appraisals. Fair market value depends upon value in the market and not on intrinsic worth.

.05 The cost or actual selling price of an item within a reasonable time before or after the valuation date may be the best evidence of its fair market value. Before such information is taken into account, it must be ascertained that the transaction was at arm's length and that the parties were fully informed as to all relevant facts. Absent such evidence, even the sales price of the item in question will not be persuasive.

.06 Sales of similar properties are often given probative weight by the courts in establishing fair market value. The weight to be given such evidence will be affected by the degree of similarity to the property under appraisal and the proximity of the date of sale to the valuation date.

.07 With respect to reproductive cost as a measure of fair market value, it must be shown that there is a probative correlation between the cost of reproduction and fair market value. Frequently, reproductive cost will be in excess of the fair market value.

.08 Generally, the weight to be given to opinion evidence depends on its origin and the thoroughness with which it is supported by experience and fact. It is only where expert opinion is supported by facts having strong probative value, that the opinion testimony will in itself be given appropriate weight. The underlying facts must corroborate the opinion, otherwise such opinion will be discounted or disregarded.

.09 The weight to be accorded any appraisal made either at or after the valuation date will depend largely upon the competence and knowledge of the appraiser with respect to the property and the market for such property.

Section 3. Appraisal Format

.01 When it becomes necessary to secure an appraisal in order to determine the values of items for Federal income tax purposes, such appraisals should be obtained from qualified and reputable sources, and the appraisal report should accompany the return when it is filed. The more complete the information filed with a tax return the more unlikely it will be that the Internal Revenue Service will find it necessary to question items on it. Thus, when reporting a deduction for charitable contributions on an income tax return, it will facilitate the review and the acceptance of the returned values if any appraisals which have been secured are furnished.... The above-mentioned regulations prescribe that support of values claimed should be submitted and a properly prepared appraisal by a person qualified to make such an appraisal may well constitute the necessary substantiation. In this respect, it is not intended that all value determinations be supported by formal written appraisals as outlined in detail below. This is particularly applicable to minor items or [*sic*] property or where the value of the property is easily ascertainable by methods other than appraisal.

.02 In general, an appraisal report should contain at least the following.

    (1) A summary of the appraiser's qualifications.

    (2) A statement of the value and the appraiser's definition of the value he has obtained.

(3) The bases upon which the appraisal was made, including any restrictions, understandings, or covenants limiting the use or disposition of the property.

(4) The date as of which the property was valued.

(5) The signature of the appraiser and the date the appraisal was made.

.03 An example of the kind of data which should be contained in a typical appraisal is included below. This relates to the valuation of art objects, but a similar detailed breakdown can be outlined for any type of property. Appraisals of art objects, paintings in particular, should include:

[Note that the following breakdown is in addition to the preceding (1) through (5) under .02, above.]

(1) A complete description of the object, indicating the size, the subject matter, the medium, the name of the artist, approximate date created, the interest transferred, etc.

(2) The cost, date, and manner of acquisition.

(3) A history of the item including proof of authenticity such as a certificate of authentication if such exists.

(4) A photograph of a size and quality fully identifying the subject matter, preferably a 10" X 12" or larger print.

(5) A statement of the factors upon which the appraisal was based, such as:

(a) Sales of other works by the same artist particularly on or around the valuation date.

(b) Quoted prices in dealers' catalogs of the artist's works or of other artists of comparable stature.

(c) The economical state of the art market at or around the time of valuation, particularly with respect to the specific property.

(d) A record of any exhibitions at which the particular art object had been displayed.

(e) A statement as to the standing of the artist in his profession and in the particular school or time period.

.04 Although an appraisal report meets these requirements, the Internal Revenue Service is not relieved of the responsibility of reviewing appraisals to the extent deemed necessary.

Section 4. Review of Valuation Appraisals

.01 While the Service is responsible for reviewing appraisals, it is not responsible for making appraisals, the burden of supporting the fair market value listed on a return is the taxpayer's. The Internal Revenue Service cannot accord recognition to an appraiser or group of appraisers from the standpoint of unquestioned acceptance of their appraisals. Furthermore, the Service cannot approve valuations or appraisals prior to the actual filing of the tax return to which the appraisal pertains and cannot issue advance rulings approving or disapproving such appraisals.

.02 In determining the acceptability of the claimed value of the donated property, the Service may either accept the value claimed based on information or appraisals submitted with the return or make its own determination as to the fair market value. In either instance, the Service may find it necessary to:

(1) contact the taxpayer and ask for additional information,

(2) refer the valuation problem to a Service appraiser or valuation specialist,

(3) recommend that an independent appraiser be employed by the Service to appraise the asset in question. (This latter course is frequently used by the Service when objects requiring appraisers of highly specialized experience and knowledge are involved).

Appendix G

Certification of the Appraiser

Sample form

The appraiser certifies and agrees that:

1. The appraiser has no present or contemplated future interest in the property appraised; and neither the employment to make the appraisal, nor the compensation for it, is contingent upon the appraised value of the property.

2. The appraiser has no personal interest in or bias with respect to the subject matter of the Appraisal Report.

3. The appraiser has personally inspected the subject property. To the best of the appraiser's knowledge and belief, all statements and information in this Appraisal Report are true and correct, and the appraiser has not knowingly withheld any significant information.

4. All contingent and limiting conditions are contained in this Appraisal Report.

5. The Appraisal Report has been made in conformity with and is subject to the requirements of the Code of Professional Ethics and Standards of Professional Conduct of the American Society of Appraisers.

6. All conclusions and opinions set forth in the Appraisal Report were prepared by this appraiser. No change of any item in the Appraisal Report shall be made by anyone other than the appraiser, and the appraiser shall have no responsibility for any such unauthorized change.

7. Unless otherwise stated, the value given in the Appraisal Report represents the opinion of value as of the date (or expected date) of contribution which is _____ (date).

_____

(name of appraiser)

Dated at _____,
           (city)

_____ this _____
(state)

day of _____,

19_____

NOTARY PUBLIC STATEMENT IF DESIRED

Endnotes

1. See Appendix E.
2. The impact of the Art Advisory Panel review in all cases involving a $20,000 charitable contribution deduction and the 1984 and recent tax law changes have been aptly expressed in two articles appearing in the 1986 August and September issues of the Maine Antique Digest.

    Irwin Hersey, author of *I Will Not Be Doing Donation Appraisals* writes:

    … A likely scenario would see an appraiser valuing a piece of donated property for, say $10,000 and giving his reasons for this value. 'No way,' says the government. 'We checked with one dealer and he says he sold something just like this for only $2000, and that's all we are prepared to allow you.'

    Now, the burden of proof as to the property's value is entirely on the taxpayer and his appraiser to prove that the property is actually worth $10,000, since any appraisal is nothing more or less than an estimate of what the property might bring if it were to be sold. Since many pieces of personal property are unique items, the $10,000 figure is hypothetical, as is the government's $2,000. The hitch is that the taxpayer and his appraiser have to prove the $10,000. All the government has to do is question and suggest a lower value.

    If that $10,000 value cannot be proved, then the taxpayer and his appraiser may be in for real trouble, since the IRS can then arbitrarily accuse the appraiser of aiding and abetting the taxpayer in understating his tax liability and subject both of them to all sorts of penalties.…

5 The Appraiser, December 1985 at 5.

    To this article, Emyl Jenkins, ASA, replied by writing *Form 8283: To Sign or Not to Sign:*

    The basic information required on Form 8283 is that the appraiser correctly identify the specific object by preparing a full description of the object and that the appraiser be able to substantiate the appropriate fair market value of the piece. To do this, the appraiser must 1) correctly identify the object, 2) correctly acknowledge condition of the piece, and 3) state his assessment of the fair market value of the object based on *substantiated values of other comparable pieces in the appropriate marketplace.* To my way of thinking, these requirements are the basic requirements the professional appraiser should employ in every job he does.…

In the end, the bickering among appraisers over 'to sign or not to sign' is going to do more harm than good to the reputation of the appraisal community. Furthermore, it may cause ill-will towards us from well intentioned donors and honest donees. Put simply, if you do not feel qualified to do the job, or even if you just don't want to go to the trouble to do the thorough job required by the IRS, say so. The donor will be better off getting the right appraiser.

Meanwhile, however, appraisers have an opportunity to help collectors and museums preserve our material culture for future generations. We can hinder the process by being hung up on Form 8283 paranoia, or we can get on with doing our jobs.

5 The Appraiser, December 1985 at 3, 4.

3. The history of charitable contribution deductions began in 1894 with changes in the tax status of corporations. However, it was not until 1917 that "individuals were first permitted a deduction for contributions to qualified charities.… The deduction was extended to corporations in 1935. Most of the refinements and complexities of current law were added as anti-abuse measures by the Tax Reform Act of 1969." Wiedenback, *Charitable Contributions: A Policy Perspective*, 50 Mo. L. Rev., Winter 1985 at 85, 87.

4. Subsection (c) relates to the type of donees, a gift to whom would qualify as a charitable contribution. I.R.C. Sec. 170(c).

5. Tim L. Melevin, a senior tax accountant with Price-Waterhouse, wrote in 1982 that:

… It should also be noted that revenue procedures [contained in the publications of the Internal Revenue Service] represent the official interpretation of the law by the IRS, and, as such, they do not have the same authority as Treasury Regulations, court cases or the

Internal Revenue Code. Accordingly examination of the courts' interpretations and applications of the above criteria [the publications] will produce a more meaningful view of the legal reasoning.

Valuation of Charitable Contributions of Works of Art, 60 Taxes 756, 758 (October 1982).

6. Farber v. Commissioner, 33 T.C.M. (CCH) 673 (1974), *aff'd*, 37 A.F.T.R. 2d 76-346 (2d Cir. 1975).

7. Falk & Lawton, *Forum Selection in Federal Tax Litigation*, 33 St. Louis B.J., Summer, 1986 at 16.1; Lock, *IRS Audits and Appeals*, 33 St. Louis B.J., Summer, 1986 at 6, 8-14.

8. *What to do if you're audited*, U.S. News & World Report, April 27, 1987, at 67.

9. Lock, *IRS Audits and Appeals*, 33 St. Louis B.J., Summer, 1986 at 6, 8-14.

10. 10 Mertens, Law of Federal Taxation, sec 59.03 at p. 9 (1976).

11. *Id.*; Kuderna v. Commissioner, 24 T.C.M. (CCH) 749, 750 (1965); see also Section IV, *infra*.

12. Winokur v. Commissioner, 90 T.C. 733, 741 (1988); Messing v. Commissioner, 48 T.C. 502, 512 (1967), cited with approval in, Farber v. Commissioner, 33 T.C.M. (CCH) 673, 674 (1974), *aff'd*, 37 A.F.T.R. 2d 76-346 (2d Cir. 1975); Johnson v. Commissioner, 85 T.C. 469, 476 (1985); Estate of Smith v. Commissioner, 57 T.C. 650, 655 (1972) *aff'd on another issue*, 510 F.2d 479 (2d Cir. 1975), *cert. denied* 423 U.S. 827 (1975).

13. Johnson v. Commissioner, 85 T.C. 469, 476 (1985), citing Buffalo Tool & Die Mfg Co. vs. Commissioner, 74 T.C. 441, 452 (1980); *in accord* Koftinow v. Commissioner, 52 T.C.M. (CCH) 261, 262 (1986); Farber v. Commissioner, 33 T.C.M. (CCH) 673 (1974), *aff'd*, 37 A.F.T.R. 2d 76-346 (2d Cir. 1975).

14. Farber v. Commissioner, 33 T.C.M. (CCH) 673 (1974), *aff'd*, 37 A.F.T.R. 2d 76-346 (2d Cir. 1975), citing Mathias v. Commissioner, 50 T.C. 994, 998 (1968).

15. Ferrari v. Commissioner, 58 T.C.M. (CCH) 221, 224 (1989).

16. Frates v. Commissioner, 53 T.C.M. (CCH) 96 (1987); in Williams v. Commissioner, 54 T.C.M. (CCH) 1471 (1988), the Court found that even though the appraiser had extensive experience with valuation of Caddo Indian artifacts, his friendship with the individual from whom the taxpayer had acquired the artifacts and his role in their acquisition cast doubt on the integrity of his appraisal. The Court then gave no weight to his appraisal and accepted the IRS's appraised value.

17. In Farber v. Commissioner, 33 T.C.M. (CCH) 673 (1974), aff'd, 37 A.F.T.R. 2d 76-346 (2d Cir. 1975), the authenticity of a painting named "Susanna," attributed to Jacopo Robusti (known as Tintoretto) was in dispute. The painting was an oil on canvas, measuring 44 ¥ 36.6 inches. One of the taxpayer's appraisers compared "Susanna" to "Susanna and the Elders," a famous Tintoretto painting. The Court commented by saying that:

> In fact, one of petitioners 'experts' computed the size of the two figures [in the paintings] and found them to be identical, [and then in a footnote, stated:] His method for reaching this conclusion is somewhat in doubt. The following excerpt is from cross-examination:
>
> Respondent's counsel: Now, how do you know that the two figures have the same dimensions?
>
> Expert: Because I know the dimension of the — of the Vienna painting, which is a published figure, and I physically measured parts of the body in this one, and computed on a mathematical basis the —
>
> Q. But you did not —
>
> A. Exact size of the figure in Vienna, and it corresponds to this one.
>
> Q. You did not actually measure the size of the figure in the Vienna painting?
>
> A. I did by computation.
>
> Q. But not actual measurement?
>
> A. No I did not.
>
> 33 T.C.M. (CCH) at 674 n.1.

18. Id. 33 T.C.M. (CCH) at 675 wherein the Court stated "For various reasons, revealed by the record, we were unable to put much confidence into any witness' study of the painting or his conclusions" and footnoted this statement by:

> The witness, who was subjected to interrogatories, was less than forthcoming with respect to an article he had written on the subject painting. He refused to answer at whose request he had written the article, he did not know if it had been published, and he refused to state whether he had been paid for writing it. He also stated that he had 'never met Contessa Navarro,' although that person was also identified to him in the interrogatory as 'Mrs. Sid Farber.' The foregoing is to be contrasted with the stipulation of the parties that the article was written at the request of the petitioners and that they paid the witness for it.
>
> 33 T.C.M. (CCH) at 675.

19. In Neely v. Commissioner, 85 T.C. 934 (1985), the value of a large quantity of African art objects was at issue. In evaluating the testimony of Hommel, one of the petitioner-taxpayer's witnesses, the Court said:

> Hommel's definition of traditional African art is deficient, most conspicuously for its failure to include the actual use of the item within the cultural group as an element. Each of the other experts (including petitioners' expert, Willis) included actual use of the art as an essential element in defining traditional African art. We have found that most of the donated art is not traditional. Because of the questionable circumstances surrounding Hommel's fallacious assumption that all of the art is traditional, we reject the valuations determined by him.

85 T.C. at 946.

In Farber v. Commissioner, 33 T.C.M. (CCH) 673 (1974) *aff'd*, 37 A.F.T.R. 2d 76-346 (2d Cir. 1975), the Court stated that:

> ... the 'expert' witnesses gave the painting only the most cursory examination and ... none of them had even heard of the painting until 1973, when they were brought into the case, or, as regards the deposed witness, when petitioners exhibited the painting in Italy in 1964. There is no provenance of the work and apparently no mention of it in any art literature or catalogues.

33 T.C.M. (CCH) at 675.

Isbell v. Commissioner, 44 T.C.M. (CCH) 1143 (1982) involved a donation of a ceramic jar produced in China during the Han dynasty and given to the taxpayer's cousin by Madame Chiang Kai-shek. About one appraisal, the Court found:

> The Sanford/Young appraisal is also suspect. Nothing in the record indicates that Sanford or Young had any expertise in appraising Asian art objects. Additionally, the description given of the jar in their appraisal is inaccurate, suggesting that they were not fully aware of the nature of the piece they were appraising.

44 T.C.M. (CCH) at 1145.

In Shein v. Commissioner, 53 T.C.M. (CCH) 1292 (1987), the Court determined the fair market value of two paintings donated to a university and a government department. About petitioners' expert's opinion, the Court said:

> ... [H]e has only seen the works in question while visiting petitioners' house socially; he did not physically inspect the paintings when forming his professional opinion; he could not remember the names of dealers he called to obtain comparative prices; and, with respect to the Lane painting, his written report refers to a picture recently seen in a Boston gallery, but he could not recall the title, size or composition

of that painting, or even whether it was signed.

53 T.C.M. (CCH) at 1294.

Accord Silverman v. Commissioner, 27 T.C.M. (CCH) 1066, 1073 (1968) (appraiser was familiar with the work of only a few of the 28 artists involved); Harken v. Commissioner, 50 T.C.M. (CCH) 994, 1002 (1985) (experts were unaware of the artist and exhibitions of his paintings and not knowledgeable of the art market where petitioner-taxpayer resided and where the donee-museum was located); David v. Commissioner, 35 T.C.M. (CCH) 1436, 1439 (1976) (lack of expertise in popular music field left the Court in doubt as to the accuracy of appraisals).

20. In Biagiotti v. Commissioner, 52 T.C.M. (CCH) 588, 593 (1986), the appraiser's lack of both sales experience and formal training or study of pre-Colombian art (the items at issue) plus lack of specificity in the comparative sales used to establish value led the Court to reject an appraiser's opinion.

21. In Farber v. Commissioner, 33 T.C.M. (CCH) 673, 675 (1974), *aff'd*, 37 A.F.T.R. 2d 76-346 (2d 76-346 (2d Cir. 1975), two witnesses could not agree on the sale price of the same comparable that both were using as a basis for their opinion as to value; Ferrari v. Commissioner, 58 T.C.M. (CCH) 221, 224 (1989).

22. In Postner v. Commissioner, 35 T.C.M. (CCH) 943 (1976), the value of a painting by Antonio Zanchi was at issue; the opinion of one of petitioner-taxpayer's experts was discounted by the Court as follows:

> Respondent contends that Mr. Newhouse's testimony should be entitled to little weight, because in the letter he wrote to Mr. Milkovitch in December 1969 giving his evaluation of the painting, he incorrectly described the subject of the painting to be "The Good Samaritan." In the letter, that incorrect designation was crossed out, and "Death of Seneca" was substituted ... [This change] suggests that the letter was composed and typed before

Mr. Newhouse had completed his research, inasmuch as he testified that his research had led him to the conclusion that the subject matter of the painting was "Death of Seneca." Consequently, the $15,000 valuation given the painting in the letter suggests that Mr. Newhouse was predisposed to value the painting in such an amount.

35 T.C.M. (CCH) at 946.

23. Silverman v. Commissioner, 27 T.C.M. (CCH) 1066 (1968), the issue was the value of paintings donated over a five-year period. The Court commented on one appraiser's testimony:

We had ample opportunity to observe [the appraiser] and to draw inferences as to his reliability, taking into account also various letters in evidence which he had written. Although it was clear that he was knowledgeable in the field of art generally, we had no confidence in his valuations, which appeared to be highly inflated. He impressed us as a cynical person with flexible scruples. An example of his conduct which troubled us was the request that he made of some donees that they include in their letter of receipt a statement reading "We have had these paintings professionally appraised as follows" and then to set forth [his] appraisal of the items involved. Any such letter of acknowledgment would be highly misleading, in that it would raise a reasonable, but false, inference that the donee had obtained an independent appraisal.

27 T.C.M. (CCH) at 1073.

Pamela Lajeunesse in a law review article states:

The complexity of setting a realistic fair market value invites abuse in and of itself, but the temptations are increased by the interaction among dealers, collectors, critics and museums. Museum curators attempt to curry the favor of donors who possess substantial collections; dealers perform appraisals for collectors whom they may serve as clients and place values on works of artists whose work they may sell; the critics provide contemporaneous indicators of the quality of works sold, donated, and exhibited. This interdependence of roles has led to charges of cooperation in obtaining the highest possible valuations, if not outright collusion in procuring and accepting works with inflated values.

Tax Incentives for Support of the Arts: In Defense of Charitable Deduction, 85 Dick. L. Rev. 663, 674-675 (1981).

24. Farber v. Commissioner, 33 T.C.M. (CCH) 673, 674-675 (1974), *aff'd*, 37 A.F.T.R. 2d 76-346 (2d Cir. 1975).

25. Biagiotti v. Commissioner, 52 T.C.M. (CCH) 588, 593 (1986), citing Anderson v. Commissioner, 250 F. 2d 242, 249 (5th Cir. 1957), *cert. denied* 356 U.S. 950 (1958); Johnson v. Commissioner, 85 T.C. 469, 477 (1985).

26. Angell v. Commissioner, 52 T.C.M. (CCH) 939, 942 (1986), citing Helvering v. National Grocery Co., 304 U.S. 282, 295 (1938); Chiu v. Commissioner, 84 T.C. 722, 734 (1985). In Weil v. Commissioner, 26 T.C.M. (CCH) 388 (1967), the Court summarized the appraiser's testimony and its reasons for totally disregarding his testimony:

[The appraiser who was also an] art dealer since about 1930 ... was called as a witness by petitioner. He described the painting as an oil, about 24 inches by 29 1/2 inches in size (framed size 35 by 39 inches) which he had examined in petitioner's home in about November 1960 and which he had then appraised as 'reasonably worth $1,500, in today's market' but he could recall no further details of the picture.

[The appraiser] did not know much about Frederick Ede [the artist]. He did not know his nationality, the usual subjects of his paintings or of any gallery that had ever exhibited any of them or sold any of them, or of any sales whatsoever of any Ede painting. [He] could not describe the subject matter, the shape or color of the painting in question or the manner of its execution (impasto). He had no prospective buyer in mind when he made the appraisal but stated simply that having been asked to appraise it, and having been informed that his appraisal would be used to establish the amount of a charitable deduction, that he had examined the painting and concluded that it was a nice one, a "home run," with a fair market value of $1,500.

The record contains no evidence of the value of the Ede painting in question other than the opinion of [that appraiser] which is described above.

… [B]urden of proof is on petitioners to establish that the Frederick Ede painting in question had a fair market value at the date of gift in excess of $900. [The appraiser's] unfamiliarity with the painting, the artist and his other works allows us to assign no weight to his opinion and consequently the respondent's determination of a $900 value is sustained.

27. Goldman v. C.I.R., 46 T.C. 136 (1966), *aff'd* 388 F.2d 476, 478 (6th Cir. 1967), citing Dubin v. Commissioner, 52 T.C.M. (CCH) 456 (1986); Silverman v. Commissioner, 27 T.C.M. (CCH) 1066 (1968); Weil v. Commissioner, 26 T.C.M. (CCH) 388, 390 (1967).

28. Wiltshire v. Commissioner, 40 T.C.M. (CCH), 463, 494 (1980).

29. Jarre v. Commissioner, 64 T.C. 183, 188-189 (1975), cited with approval in David v. Commissioner, 35 T.C.M. (CCH) 1436, 1439 (1976).

30. Neely v. Commissioner, 85 T.C. 934, 946 (1985), citing Buffalo Tool & Die Mfg. Co. v. Commissioner, 74 T.C. 441, 452 (1980); Angell v. Commissioner, 52 T.C.M. (CCH) 939, 942 (1986) comparing the merits of two appraisers.

31. Mertens quoted in Reynolds v. Commissioner, 43 T.C.M. (CCH) 115, 116 n.2 (1981).

32. In Silverman v. Commissioner, 27 T.C.M. (CCH) 1066 (1968), the Court held that:

Another consideration affecting the fair market value of Silverman's donated paintings is the condition that he imposed whereby the donee agreed not to sell or dispose of the paintings for a three-year period. This restriction certainly had an adverse effect on fair market value. As we said in [the] Jacob J. Cooley [decision], "… property otherwise intrinsically more valuable which is encumbered by some restriction or condition limiting its marketability must be valued in the light of such limitation."

27 T.C.M. (CCH) at 1075.

33. *Id.; see* Transamerica Corp. v. U.S., 902 F.2d 1540 (Fed. Cr. 1990) (tax payer retained right to obtain exclusive access to safety film for commercial purposes in perpetuity).

34. Peterson v. Commissioner, 44 T.C.M. (CCH) 650, 651 (1982).

35. Treas. Reg. Sec. 1.170A-13(c)(3)(ii)(A) (1988).

36. Cukor v. Commissioner, 27 T.C.M. (CCH) 90, 95 (1968) (size of a Braque painting was a factor of "considerable importance").

37. *Id.*

38. Mills v. Commissioner, 62 T.C.M. (CCH) 1345, 1346 (1991) (Court lowered value of donated Corvair because taxpayer failed to show its condition at the time of donation, *e.g.*, the state of repair or disrepair of the exterior and interior of car, including the engine).

39. "Quality generally refers to the aesthetic impression of the object, as distinguished from historical value or literary associations, but in recent years scholars and curators have recognized that these attributes may be inseparable from the totality of the work." Lajeunesse, *Tax Incentives for Support of the Arts: In Defense of the Charitable Deduction*, 85 Dick. L. Rev. 663, 671 n. 46 (1981).

40. Rev. Proc. 66-49, 1966-2 C.B. 1257.

41. Cost can have a decided effect on the fair market value depending on the time span between the date of acquisition and date of contribution. See Section V-D, *infra*. Cost data is relevant and failure to furnish the information to the Internal Revenue Service can have a negative effect on the court's decision. *See* Silverman v. Commissioner, 27 T.C.M. (CCH) 1066, 1073 (1968).

42. "Provenance not only supports the authenticity of the work, Mathias v. Commissioner, 50 T.C. 994, 999 (1968) (provenance of taxpayer's painting by Gilbert Stuart differed from that of painting listed in authoritative compilation of Stuart's work), but it also enhances the value if the work was at one time part of an important collection or if it appeared in a major exhibition. *See* Crocker Nat'l Bank v. United States, 39 A.F.T.R. 2d (P-H) paras. 77-779 (C.D. Cal. 1976)." Lajeunesse, *Tax Incentives for Support of the Arts: In Defense of the Charitable Deduction*, 85 Dick. L. Rev. 663, 672 n. 51 (1981).

    As stated in Peters v. Commissioner, 36 T.C.M. (CCH) 552 (1977), *aff'd by unpublished opinion*, 601 F.2d 603 (9th Cir. 1979):

    > Provenance is the history of a work of art; it may describe, for example, how a given work was commissioned and who owned it throughout the years. Provenance is requested by reputable art appraisers, dealers, and auction houses. Provenance supports the authenticity of a work, thereby enhancing its value.
    > 36 T.C.M. (CCH) at 552.

43. *Cf.* Posner v. Commissioner, 35 T.C.M. (CCH) 943 (1976).

44. Furstenberg v. United States, 595 F.2d 603, 608 (Ct. Cl. 1979).

45. Rarity of the item can be a separate factor for consideration. *Id.* at 606; Hawkins v. Commissioner, 44 T.C.M. (CCH) 716, 718, 726 (1982) (mosaic table purchased from the Vatican Studio which was closing); Holtman v. Commissioner, 40 T.C.M. (CCH) 350 (1980).

    Another related factor is the death of an artist between the time of purchase and contribution.

Harken v. Commissioner, 50 T.C.M. (CCH) 994 (1985).

46. Gordon v. Commissioner, 35 T.C.M. (CCH) 1227 (1976) (painting); Hawkins v. Commissioner, 44 T.C.M. (CCH) 716 (1982) (mosaic table); Krauskopf v. Commissioner, 48 T.C.M. (CCH) 620 (1984) (race car); Mauldin v. Commissioner, 60 T.C. 751 (1973) (cartoons); Skala v. Commissioner, 49 T.C.M. (CCH) 419 (1985) (aircraft).

47. A depressant on value can be the poor treatment by the donee of the donation. In one case, storage of prints in a basement in a neglected condition led the Court to question the value of an artist's sketchbooks. Harken v. Commissioner, 50 T.C.M. (CCH) 994, 1003 (1985); Lio v. Commissioner, 85 T.C. 3292, 3299 (1985), *aff'd. sub. nom.* Orth v. Commissioner, 813 F.2d 837 (7th Cir. 1987) (lithographs were not insured, "accessioned to its permanent collection, or displayed" by the donee-museum; the Court held that "the use to which donated property is put is relevant in determining fair market value"); Rupke v. Commissioner, 32 T.C.M. (CCH) 1098 (1973) (after donation, the donee-college disassembled the wooden object given it and stored the object in the boiler room).

48. Form 8283.

49. The amount of restoration can be an issue. In Farber v. Commissioner, 33 T.C.M. (CCH) 673 (1974), *aff'd*, 37 A.F.T.R. 2d 76-346 (2d Cir. 1975), the Court said:

    > Not only were the 'expert' witnesses in conflict as to the authenticity of the painting but they were diametrically opposed on its condition. Faced with this irreconcilable situation, we watched one of respondent's witnesses conduct a black light examination in the darkened courtroom. Based on this examination, we found as a fact that there had been substantial amount of restoration to the painting.... Much of this was of poor quality. Although this amount of restoration may not be un-

usual for a painting this old, it is a factor to be considered in valuing the work. 33 T.C.M. (CCH) at 675.

See also Furstenberg v. United States, 595 F.2d 603, 607-608 (Ct. Cl. 1979) (distressing effect on value of poor restoration and the possibility of removal of the restoration [overpainting]); Krauskopf v. Commissioner, 48 T.C.M. (CCH) 620, 629 (1984).

50. Speiller, *The Favored Tax Treatment of Purchasers of Art*, 80 Colum. L. Rev. 214, 228-229 (1980).

51. Appraisers sometimes try to hedge concerning authenticity. For example, experts' statements such as "we have found no positive evidence that the item is not authentic" and "according to the … [results of laboratory tests and microscopic examination] the coin may be genuine" led one Court to conclude that the item was of questionable authenticity, and to take that fact into consideration in determining fair market value. Holtzman v. Commissioner, 40 T.C.M. (CCH) 350, 366 (1980).

In the following four cases, the court decided the question of authenticity: Dubin v. Commissioner, 52 T.C.M. (CCH) 456, 459 (1986); Monaghan v. Commissioner, 42 T.C.M. (CCH) 27, 29 (1981); Rupke v. Commissioner, 32 T.C.M. (CCH) 1098, 1100 (1973); Vander Hook v. Commissioner, 36 T.C.M. (CCH) 1394, 1396-1397 (1977).

In the following five cases, the court declined to decide the question of authenticity: Farber v. Commissioner, 33 T.C.M. (CCH) 673, 676 (1974), *aff'd*, 37 A.F.T.R. 2d 76-346 (2d Cir. 1975); Gordon v. Commissioner, 35 T.C.M. (CCH) 1227, 1228 (1976); Holtzman v. Commissioner, 40 T.C.M. (CCH) 350, 361, 366-368 (1980); Peters v. Commissioner, 36 T.C.M. (CCH) 552, 553 (1977), *aff'd by unpublished opinion*, 601 F.2d 603 (9th Cir. 1979); Mathias v. Commissioner, 50 T.C. 994, 998 (1968).

52. Farber v. Commissioner, 33 T.C.M. (CCH) 673, 676 (1974), *aff'd*, 37 A.F.T.R. 2d 76-346 (2d Cir. 1975).

53. Hawkins v. Commissioner, 44 T.C.M. (CCH) 716, 726 (1982), Johnson v. Commissioner, 85 T.C. 469 (1985); Lightman v. Commissioner, 50 T.C.M. (CCH) 266, 270 (1985). However, photographs cannot be the basis of an appraisal if authenticity, condition, and age of the object are factors. Obviously personal viewing under such circumstances is preferred. Sammons v. Commissioner, 51 T.C.M. (CCH) 1568, 1575 (1986), *aff'd*, 838 F.2d 330 (9th Cir. 1988). Photographs are used extensively by the Art Advisory Panel. Lightman v. Commissioner, 50 T.C.M. (CCH) 266 (1985); Johnson v. Commissioner, 85 T.C. 469 (1985).

54. Anselmo v. Commissioner, 80 T.C. 872 (1983), *aff'd*, 757 F.2d 1208 (11th Cir. 1985).

55. Jarre v. Commissioner, 64 T.C. 183, 188 (1975); David v. Commissioner, 35 T.C.M. (CCH) 1436, 1439 (1976).

56. Barrett v. Commissioner, 36 T.C.M. (CCH) 437 (1977).

57. Harken v. Commissioner, 50 T.C.M. (CCH) 994, 998, 1002 (1985).

58. Skripak v. Commissioner, 84 T.C. 285 (1985).

59. Lio v. Commissioner, 85 T.C. 56 (1985), *aff'd. sub nom.* Orth v. Commissioner, 813 F.2d 837 (7th Cir. 1987).

60. Holtzman v. Commissioner, 40 T.C.M. (CCH) 350 (1980).

61. Treas. Reg. Sec. 1.170A-13(c)(3)(A) (1988).

62. Treas. Reg. Sec. 1.170A-1 (1988); United States v. Cartwright, 411 U.S. 546 (1973).

63. Goldman v. C.I.R., 46 T.C. 136 (1966), *aff'd*, 388 F.2d 476, 478 (6th Cir. 1967) (fair market value of bound volumes of medical journals given to a hospital). In Koftinow v. Commissioner, 52 T.C.M. (CCH) 261, 262 (1986), the Court rejected the government's appraisal report because it valued a sculpture piece in "a market in which the purchasers buy to resell."

64. Anselmo v. Commissioner, 80 T.C. 872 (1983), *aff'd*, 757 F.2d 1208, 1214 (11th Cir. 1985).

65. *Id.* at 1215.

66. Skripak v. Commissioner, 84 T.C. 285 (1985).

67. Lio v. Commissioner, 85 T.C. 56 (1985), *aff'd sub nom.* Orth v. Commissioner, 813 F.2d 837 (7th Cir. 1987).

68. *Id.* (Emphasis added).

69. *Id.*, followed in Goldstein v. Commissioner, 89 T.C. 535, 545-546 (1987).

70. The "Torah" generally refers to the Five Books of Moses. Ashkar v. Commissioner, 61 T.C.M. (CCH) 1657, 1662 (1991).

71. 43 T.C. 663 (1965).

72. 44 T.C. 801 (1965).

73. 43 T.C. at 666.

74. 44 T.C. at 809-810.

75. Farber v. Commissioner, 33 T.C.M. (CCH) 673, 675 (1974), *aff'd,* 37 A.F.T.R. 2d 76-346 (2d Cir. 1975); Mathias v. Commissioner, 50 T.C. 994, 999 (1968); Estate of Smith v. Commissioner, 57 T.C. 650, 658 (1972), *aff'd on another issue* 510 F.2d 479 (2d Cir. 1975), *cert. denied,* 423 U.S. 827 (1975).

76. S. Burnham, The Art Crowd 53 (1973).

77. Lajeunesse, *Tax Incentives for Support of the Arts: In Defense of the Charitable Deduction,* 85 Dick. L. Rev. 663, 673-674 (1981).

78. Biagiotti v. Commissioner, 52 T.C.M. (CCH) 588, 593 (1986); *accord* Peterson v. Commissioner, 44 T.C.M. (CCH) 650, 654, 655 (1982) and Ferrari v. Commissioner, 58 T.C.M. (CCH) 221 (1989).

79. Lightman v. Commissioner, 50 T.C.M. (CCH) 266, 269 (1985).

80. Farber v. Commissioner, 33 T.C.M. (CCH) 673, 676 (1974), *aff'd,* 37 A.F.T.R. 2d 76-346 (2d Cir. 1975).

81. Lightman v. Commissioner, 50 T.C.M. (CCH) 266, 269 (1985) (emphasis added).

82. Dubin v. Commissioner, 52 T.C.M. (CCH) 456, 459 (1986); Chiu v. Commissioner, 84 T.C. 722, 734-735 (1985); Estate of Kaplin v. Commissioner, 748 F.2d 1109, 1111 (6th Cir. 1984); Straw v. Commissioner, 62 T.C.M. (CCH) 1057, 1058 (1991).

83. Hunter v. Commissioner, 51 T.C.M. (CCH) 1533, 1537 (1986); Estate of Kaplin v. Commissioner, 748 F.2d 1109; Chiu v. Commissioner, 84 T.C. 722, 734-735 (1985); Andrews v. Commissioner, 13 B.T.A. 651 (1928), *aff'd,* 38 F.2d 55 (2d Cir. 1930); Ferrell v. Commissioner, 53 T.C.M. (CCH) 209 (1987); In re DeLisser, 90-2 USTC 85,080, 95,081 (1990).

84. Hunter v. Commissioner, 51 T.C.M. (CCH) 1533, 1537 (1986); Wiltshire v. Commissioner, 40 T.C.M. (CCH) 493, 495 (1980); Rhoades v. Commissioner, 55 T.C.M. (CCH) 1159 (1988).

85. Rhodes v. Commissioner, 55 T.C.M. (CCH) 1159, 1161-1163 (1988).

86. Dubin v. Commissioner, 52 T.C.M. (CCH) 456 (1986).

87. Hunter v. Commissioner, 51 T.C.M. (CCH) 1533, 1537 (1986); Lio v. Commissioner, 85 T.C. 56 (1985), *aff'd. sub nom.* Orth v. Commissioner, 813 F.2d 837 (7th Cir. 1987).

88. Anselmo v. Commissioner, 80 T.C. 872 (1983), *aff'd,* 757 F.2d 1208 (11th Cir. 1985); Schachter v. Commissioner, 51 T.C.M. (CCH) 1428 (1986); Rev. Rul. 80-69, I.R.B. 1980-11.

89. Hunter v. Commissioner, 51 T.C.M. (CCH) 1533 (1986); Lio v. Commissioner, 85 T.C. 56 (1985), *aff'd. sub nom.* Orth v. Commissioner, 813 F.2d 837 (7th Cir. 1987); Lightman v. Commissioner, 50 T.C.M. (CCH) 266 (1985); Goldstein v. Commissioner, 89 T.C. 535 (1987).

90. Sammons v. Commissioner, 51 T.C.M. (CCH) 1568, 1575 (1986), *aff'd* 838 F.2d 330 (9th Cir. 1988).

91. Neely v. Commissioner, 85 T.C. 934 (1985).

92. Tripp v. Commissioner, 22 T.C.M. (CCH) 1225 (1963), *aff'd,* 337 F.2d 432 (7th Cir. 1964); Chou v. Commissioner, 58 T.C.M. (CCH) 1496, 1497 (1990).

93. See notes 96-101, *infra.*

94. Silverman v. Commissioner, 27 T.C.M. (CCH) 1066, 1074 (1968). In that case, other factors in favor of the taxpayer were the price concessions made by the seller to the taxpayer originally, the generally higher state of the market in the United States as opposed to France where the paintings were bought, and an increase generally in the value of paintings of two of the artists and the rejection of the sale prices obtained at a distressed sale of some of the paintings after the donation. In the government's favor was the failure of the

taxpayer to produce cost figures (the government did secure them from the customs records), the condition attached to the donation whereby the donee agreed not to sell or dispose of the paintings for a three-year period, and the fact that in assessing value of other paintings made to the taxpayer's children, the taxpayer used cost as fair market value.

95. Kerckhoff v. Commissioner, 53 T.C.M. (CCH) 1139, 1143 (1987).

96. Estate of Smith v. Commissioner, 57 T.C. 650 (1972), *aff'd on another issue*, 510 F.2d 479 (2d Cir. 1975), *cert. denied* 423 U.S. 827 (1975); *accord* Jarre v. Commissioner, 64 T.C. 183, 189-190 (1975) (music manuscripts).

97. Lightman v. Commissioner, 50 T.C.M. (CCH) 266, 270 (1985).

98. Hunter v. Commissioner, 51 T.C.M. (CCH) 1533, 1538 (1986); *accord* Anselmo v. Commissioner, 80 T.C. 872 (1983), *aff'd*, 757 F.2d 1208 (11th Cir. 1985).

99. Mast v. Commissioner, 56 T.C.M. (CCH) 1522, 1528-1530 (1989).

100. Krauskopf v. Commissioner, 48 T.C.M. (CCH) 620, 627 (1984); Dellinger v. Commissioner, 32 T.C. 1178, 1185 (1959); Publicker v. Commissioner, 206 F.2d 250, 254 (3rd Cir. 1953), *cert. denied* 346 U.S. 924 (1954).

101. Krauskopf v. Commissioner, 48 T.C.M. (CCH) 620, 627 (184); Cupler v. Commissioner, 64 T.C. 946 (1975).

102. Jarre v. Commissioner, 64 T.C. 183, 190 (1975).

103. Krauskopf v. Commissioner, 48 T.C.M. (CCH) 620 (1984).

104. David v. Commissioner, 35 T.C.M. (CCH) 1436 (1976); Jarre v. Commissioner, 64 T.C. 183 (1975).

105. Dubin v. Commissioner, 52 T.C.M. (CCH) 456 (1986).

106. Hawkins v. Commissioner, 44 T.C.M. (CCH) 716 (1982).

107. Isbell v. Commissioner, 44 T.C.M. (CCH) 1143 (1982).

108. Koftinow v. Commissioner, 52 T.C.M. (CCH) 261 (1986).

109. Mauldin v. Commissioner, 60 T.C. 751 (1973).

110. May v. Commissioner, 24 T.C.M. (CCH) 205 (1965).

111. Rupke v. Commissioner, 32 T.C.M. (CCH) 1098 (1973).

112. Krauskopf v. Commissioner, 48 T.C.M. (CCH) 620 (1984).

113. Hawkins v. Commissioner, 44 T.C.M. (CCH) 716, 724-725 (1982).

114. *Id* at 725-726.

115. 39 F.2d 540 (2d Cir. 1930); Zmuda v. Commissioner, 79 T.C. 714 (1982), *aff'd* 731 F.2d 1417 (9th Cir. 1984).

116. *Id* at 544; Bosworth v. Commissioner, 55 T.C.M. (CCH) 750 (1988); cf. Abbrecht v. Commissioner, 53 T.C.M. (CCH) 613 (1987).

117. Martin v. Commissioner, 11 T.C.M. (CCH) 946 (1952); Sylvester v. Commissioner, 37 T.C. 79 (1978).

118 Van Skiver v. Commissioner, 40 T.C.M. (CCH) 466 (1980); Breslin v. Commissioner, 7 T.C.M. (CCH) 818 (1948) (size of charitable contribution was reduced and a 5% negligence penalty was imposed).

119. Jennings v. Commissioner, 56 T.C.M. (CCH) 595, 600 (1988); see Lio v. Commissioner, 85 T.C. 56, 71 (1988), *aff'd sub nom.* Orth v. Commissioner, 813 F.2d 837 (7th Cir. 1987); Chiu v. Commissioner, 84 T.C. 722, 736 (1985); Skripak v. Commissioner, 84 T.C. 285, 322 (1985).

120. *Compare* Kaplan v. Commissioner, 43 T.C. 663 (1965) *with* McGuire v. Commissioner, 44 T.C. 801 (1965) *and* Isbell v. Commissioner, 44 T.C.M. (CCH) 1143 (1982); *see also* cases where comparable sales after donation were part of the evidence of value: Posner v. Commissioner, 35 T.C.M. (CCH) 943 (1976), and Hartwell v. Commissioner, 24 T.C.M. (CCH) 278, 284 (1965).

121. DeBie v. Commissioner, 56 T.C. 876 (1971).

122. Schapiro v. Commissioner, 27 T.C.M. (CCH) 205 (1968).

123. Posner v. Commissioner, 35 T.C.M. (CCH) 943 (1976); Gordon v. Commissioner, 35 T.C.M. (CCH) 1227 (1976); Reynolds v. Commissioner, 43 T.C.M. (CCH) 115, 116 (1981);

cf. Silverman v. Commissioner, 27 T.C.M. (CCH) 1066 (1968); *contra* Harken v. Commissioner, 50 T.C.M. (CCH) 994, 1002 (1985) (the Court stated that the experts should have considered the market where the taxpayer resided and the donee-museum was located); Jennings v. Commissioner, 56 T.C.M. (CCH) 585, 600 (1988).

124. In David v. Commissioner, 35 T.C.M. (CCH) 1436 (1976), the Court stated that:

> There are so many variables operating in the value equation that an appraisal of the property [music] donated by petitioner necessitates some estimation. We have kept this in mind in evaluating the appraisals offered into evidence and in arriving at our final conclusions as to value.

35 T.C.M. (CCH) at 1439.

Other cases expressly characterize valuation as an inherently imprecise process. Estate of Smith v. Commissioner, 57 T.C. 650, 655 (1972), *aff'd on another issue*, 510 F.2d 479 (2d Cir. 1975), *cert. denied* 423 U.S. 827 (1975); Messing v. Commissioner, 48 T.C. 502, 512 (1967); Hawkins v. Commissioner, 44 T.C.M. (CCH) 716, 725 (1982).

125. Anselmo v. Commissioner, 80 T.C. 872 (1983), *aff'd*, 757 F.2d 1208, 1213 (11th Cir. 1985).

126. Ferrari v. Commissioner, 58 T.C.M. (CCH) 221, 223 (1989). (Emphasis added.)

127. Harken v. Commissioner, 50 T.C.M. (CCH) 994 (1985); Cukor v. Commissioner, 27 T.C.M. (CCH) 90 (1968).

128. Harken v. Commissioner, 50 T.C.M. (CCH) 994, 997 (1985).

129. *Id.* at 1001-1002.

130. Cukor v. Commissioner, 27 T.C.M. (CCH) 90, 94 (1968).

131. Chou v. Commissioner, 58 T.C.M. (CCH) 1496, 1498-1500 (1990). *See also* Dubin v. Commissioner, 52 T.C.M. (CCH) 456 (1986).

132. Dubin v. Commissioner, 52 T.C.M. (CCH) 456 (1986).

133. Harken v. Commissioner, 50 T.C.M. (CCH) 994, 1000 (1985). *See also* Sanz v. Commissioner, 60 T.C.M. (CCH) 1160 (1990) (foreign language books for use in obscure teaching method found to have close to salvage value only).

134. Krauskopf v. Commissioner, 48 T.C.M. (CCH) 620, 628, 629 (1984). *See also* Skala v. Commissioner, 49 T.C.M. (CCH) 419 (1985).

135. Koftinow v. Commissioner, 52 T.C.M. (CCH) 261, 263 (1986).

136. *Cf.* Harken v. Commissioner, 50 T.C.M. (CCH) 994, 1003 (1985) (discussing problems that arise with valuing the works of an unknown artist).

137. Saltzman v. U.S., 750 F. Supp. 61, 66 (E.D.N.Y. 1988).

138. Epping v. Commissioner, 63 T.C.M. (CCH) 3012, 3014-3015 (1992), distinguishing Estate of Miller v. Commissioner, 62 T.C.M. (CCH) 998 (1991) where the court concluded that replacement costs were probative since the government's appraiser admitted he was unaware of comparable sales for a majority of items in the collection of numerous animal trophies.

139. Babcock, Appraisal Principles and Procedures 153-154 (1980); Blagbrough, *The Valuation of Paintings Appraisals in the U.S.A.*, Commentary on Personal Property Appraisal, Monograph No. 7 at 48 (1980).

140. Lio v. Commissioner, 85 T.C. 56 (1985), *aff'd sub nom.* Orth v. Commissioner, 813 F.2d 837 (7 Cir. 1987); Angel v. Commissioner, 52 T.C.M. (CCH) 939, 944 (1986) (taxpayer unsuccessfully tried to convince the Court that he deliberately insured the art works for less than their fair market value in order to reduce his insurance premiums); Chou v. Commissioner, 58 T.C.M. (CCH) 1496, 1497 (1990).

141. In Angell v. Commissioner, 52 T.C.M. (CCH) 939, 944 (1986), the taxpayer told the donee to insure the artworks for less than one-third of the claimed contribution value. Based on this fact, the Court found that "he knew that the appraisals and the amounts he claimed as charitable contributions were inflated." *But see* Lightman v. Commissioner, 50 T.C.M. (CCH) 266, 270 (1985), wherein the Court discounted the fact

that the taxpayer had determined the amount of insurance for the donee as the same as claimed for the deduction.

142. Farber v. Commissioner, 33 T.C.M. (CCH) 673, 674 (1974), *aff'd*, 37 A.F.T.R. 2d 76-346 (2d Cir. 1975). *Cf.* Furstenberg v. United States, 595 F.2d 603, 612 (Ct. Cl. 1979).

143. Wiltshire v. Commissioner, 40 T.C.M. (CCH) 493, 495 (1980).

144. Johnson v. Commissioner, 85 T.C. 469, 478-479 (1985).

145. Angell v. Commissioner, 52 T.C.M. (CCH) 939, 942 (1986).

146. Biagiotti v. Commissioner, 52 T.C.M. (CCH) 588, 591, 593 (1986); Harken v. Commissioner, 50 T.C.M. (CCH) 994, 999-1000 (1985); *but see* Peterson v. Commissioner, 44 T.C.M. (CCH) 650, 653 (1982).

147. Cukor v. Commissioner, 27 T.C.M. (CCH) 90, 94-95 (1968).

148. Harken v. Commissioner, 50 T.C.M. (CCH) 994, 999 (1985); Gordon v. Commissioner, 35 T.C.M. (CCH) 1227, 1228 (1976).

149. Hunter v. Commissioner, 51 T.C.M. (CCH) 1533, 1537 (1986); *accord* Reynolds v. Commissioner, 43 T.C.M. (CCH) 115, 116 (1981); *cf.* Furstenberg v. United States, 595 F.2d 603, 607 (Ct. Cl. 1979) (efforts to sell the particular painting in question by the taxpayer before the donation were unsuccessful); Malone v. Commissioner, 53 T.C.M. (CCH) 1144 (1987); Taylor v. U.S., 782 F. Supp. 1207, 1213-1214 (S.D. Ohio 1991).

150. Isaacs v. Commissioner, 62 T.C.M. (CCH) 828, 831 (1991); Williford v. Commissioner, 64 T.C.M. (CCH) 422 (1992).

151. Farber v. Commissioner, 33 T.C.M. (CCH) 673, 675 (1974), *aff'd*, 37 A.F.T.R. 2d 76-346 (2d Cir. 1975); *see also* Peterson v. Commissioner, 44 T.C.M. (CCH) 650, 651 (1982).

152. Furstenberg v. United States, 595 F.2d 603, 609 (Ct. Cl. 1979).

153. Farber v. Commissioner, 33 T.C.M. (CCH) 673, 675 (1974), *aff'd.* 37 A.F.T.R. 2d 76-346 (2d Cir. 1975); Biagiotti v. Commissioner, 52 T.C.M. (CCH) 588 (1986).

154. *Id.*; Lightman v. Commissioner, 50 T.C.M. (CCH) 266, 269 (1985); Cukor v. Commissioner, 27 T.C.M. (CCH) 90, 95 (1968).

155. Farber v. Commissioner, 33 T.C.M. (CCH) 673, 675 (1974), *aff'd*, 37 A.F.T.R. 2d 76-346 (2d Cir. 1975).

156. David v. Commissioner, 35 T.C.M. (CCH) 1436, 1440 (1976); *see* Wehausen v. Commissioner, 56 T.C.M. (CCH) 299, 301 (1988) (back issue periodicals held not to be comparable to second-hand periodicals, the donated items).

157. Farber v. Commissioner, 33 T.C.M. (CCH) 673, 675 (1974), *aff'd*, 37 A.F.T.R. 2d 76-346 (2d Cir. 1975); Harken v. Commissioner, 50 T.C.M. (CCH) 994, 997 (1985).

158. Biagiotti v. Commissioner, 52 T.C.M. (CCH) 588, 590 (1986).

159. Furstenberg v. United States, 595 F.2d 603, 607 (Ct. Cl. 1979).

160. Farber v. Commissioner, 33 T.C.M. (CCH) 673, 675 (1974), *aff'd*, 37 A.F.T.R. 2d 76-346 (2d Cir. 1975).

161. Peterson v. Commissioner, 44 T.C.M. (CCH) 650, 653 (1982).

162. *Cf.* Holtzman v. Commissioner, 40 T.C.M. (CCH) 350 (1980).

Chapter 6

Documenting Opinions: Research and Analysis

Modern professional appraisal practice requires supported opinions of value. The basis of the support is thorough research and competent analysis using accepted methodology.

Research

Research is the core of appraisals. The evidence disclosed by research is the primary means by which the client, the courts, and third parties will weigh the credibility of an appraisal.

The key to good research is clearly identified goals and a solid work plan. Museums, universities, and public libraries have rich resources for investigating the identity, importance and origins of a property.

Usually one proceeds from general sources to increasingly specific ones; for example, in researching an unfamiliar artist, craftsman or property, one might begin with a general encyclopedia entry sure to encompass the subject, and use its bibliography to take the next step, rather than search specialized books for mention of your specific subject.

There are many indices for certain areas of research which will direct the appraiser to dictionaries and periodicals, which in turn will lead to the specialized literature with a minimum of wrong turns. Those indices available on computer or microfiche, as many library catalogs now are, may be even quicker to use than those in print.

There are two excellent guides to research in art history and connoisseurship which are recommended for more specific information. One is written by David Beasley, the chief research librarian at the New York Public Library; the other, by Lois Swan Jones, includes a substantial annotated bibliography of the fine and decorative arts, as well as a research planning guide. The full citations to these references are in the bibliography at the end of this section.

Most museum libraries have resources for market information — from published indices of auction sales and dealer asking prices, to in-depth collections of auction catalogs. It would be difficult for an appraiser to demonstrate due diligence in the research aspect of an appraisal if such extensive resources have not been consulted.

The research an appraiser can accomplish in libraries is only one aspect of total research. Identifying a property and estimating its age and origin are processes of comparison, with the object appraised being compared to examples whose authenticity is generally acknowledged; printed sources relating to the type of property being appraised, an exhibition or a sale catalog of the property being appraised or a closely comparable one are requisite sources. When an appraiser does not have adequate specialized training and experience to make a knowledgeable comparison, then the necessary comparison might be made by a curator, academic or other person who does possess that specialized knowledge. But the decision to rely upon or reject such comparisons remains the appraiser's.

Sources must be corroborated, checking one source against another for consensus. The further the source is from primary observation, the more corroboration is required. Consider, for example, how misleading auction catalog photographs can be, either unflattering due to the printer's limits or harsh lighting or flattering in concealing flaws. In such cases, auction house personnel are often helpful and thorough in providing condition reports.

Dealers, auctioneers and collectors may be sources of properties for comparison, and these sources are often of consequence for appraisal materials. Of course, it is only natural that dealers and collectors are enthusiastic about the positive attributes of their possessions and that auctioneers try to sell by presenting their properties in the best possible perspective. Dealers and auctioneers may have to keep confidential the source of their properties, and seldom will they identify a buyer. Similarly, an appraiser usually must keep the identity of the client in confidence. It is an appraiser's obligation to weigh the evidence and opinions received from these sources, appreciating their enthusiasm, respecting their responsibilities, and then objectively analyzing their responses.

Many of these people may have important insights about the sales you are analyzing and about trends and recent events in the market. They will share information readily with a professional appraiser who is well prepared and has done adequate preparatory research.

Relevant sales can be identified quickly through electronic indices, as well. One index of art sold at auction is available over the telephone and at least two are available online, computer to computer. For example, records of sales of decorative art properties at auction have been indexed by category of property as well as the name of the maker in the online services that are currently becoming available utilizing CD-ROM capacities of micro computers (See Chap. 8, Electronics Sources, for a more complete discussion of these resources). Relevant sales can also be identified through numerous auction catalogs and published price guides.

How much research is enough? The answer will vary with its credibility and relevance to the appraisal question. The criterion to be met is the standard of **Substantial Evidence**. As defined by *Black's Law Dictionary*, the standard of Substantial Evidence is "such evidence as a reasonable mind might accept as adequate to support a conclusion." Requisite in such a conclusion would be absence of bias, relationship, emotional involvement or pecuniary interest.

In times of stress, such as divorce and division of estates, clients may focus their disagreements on issues and objects which, in perspective, don't merit attention. At such times, an appraiser may be well-advised to continue research and apply analytical tools far beyond the usual sense of "reasonable." When a property presents serious questions of identification, authentication or valuation, extra effort beyond "reasonable" may be necessary to produce a professional answer.

Normally a "reasonable mind" would expect that the scale of effort would be in proportion to the importance and the value of the property or valuation issue. The principles, procedures and responsibilities of the appraiser remain the same regardless of the magnitude of the value conclusion. The professional appraiser will be thinking ahead and will be prepared and capable of justifying methods and results if questions are raised. The *Uniform Standards of Professional Appraisal Practice* specifically mandate this capability.

All the sources consulted in reaching a value conclusion should be recorded as a demonstration of the thoroughness of the research conducted, to establish its credibility, to permit the reader to follow the logic of the argument and to substantiate the conclusion. This recorded information has the benefit to the appraiser of serving as an aid in subsequent research on similar properties.

Analysis

To understand the meaning of analysis, it is essential to organize the collected data into a meaningful pattern. An analysis of a sampling which describes a pattern from a whole population is known as a **Market Model**.

For example, in order to weigh the probability that trends observed in a market will be repeated, it is important to understand the size of the market. In a market with a large number of active buyers and sellers who are diverse in social and economic backgrounds, rapid fluctuations in the market become less likely. Similarly, the larger the number of sales made in a year, the more stable prices will tend to be.

When a few participants are responsible for a high proportion of sales, a market is said to have a high **Concentration Ratio**. It will be stabilized by these players while they are active, but can be destabilized quickly if one fails or retires. An example of this can be found in 1990, when the world economic crisis caused many buyers to withdraw from the art market.

To explain the meaning of the individual sales which will be cited, one must describe the most common methods of marketing and the structure of the market. Do most sales occur at auction or privately? Are the leading prices, the ones whose influence can be seen across the market, set at auction, or by dealers? Are services, such as expert advice, delivery or installation, warranties or the social status associated with certain transactions important characteristics of value?

Most markets for personal property have a well-defined structure with distinct levels; similar properties will command a different price at each level. The levels in a market for new manufactured goods are commonly termed manufacturer, distributor or representative, wholesaler, and retailer, with different prices for the same item at each level. The market for new goods is quite distinct from that for used goods, and each has its level.

For items with antique or collectible value, the differences in value among levels may be dramatic. A property can move from a jobber or picker to an auction house, to a dealer, and ultimately to a collector. Each person has access to and is comfortable in a different market level.

It is critical for an appraiser to analyze which market level is relevant for each appraisal assignment, and then to determine which market level is represented by each of the comparable sales used. Dealers typically sell in two market levels, to other dealers and to collectors. Discounts are common, so it is important to distinguish asking prices from actual sale prices.

At auction, however, more careful and complicated analysis is required. Auction house personnel usually cannot name buyers, but they may be willing to characterize the buyer as collector or trade, American or European, Eastern or Western. Auction pre-sale estimates are less indicative of results than dealer asking prices; it usually can be assumed that a property that did not sell failed to reach its reserve, which would have been no higher than the low pre-sale estimate. The names of regular buyers are often mentioned in newspaper reviews of auctions, such as those published in *Art & Antiques*, *Antiques Weekly*, *Art & Auction*, *The Art Newspaper* and *Maine Antiques Digest*, among others.

The relevance of an inconsistent price realized should not be overlooked but rather should be investigated. Such a seeming aberration may indicate the market level in which the property was sold, or it may indicate that there were problems with the property that were not apparent nor mentioned in the catalog. For example, repairs may not be mentioned or may be described with a summary phrase which belies their importance to collectors. Uncertainty regarding authenticity, even rumors circulating before the sale, may drastically reduce the price achieved.

If sales of comparable properties are inadequate to make a strong argument for value, construction of a strong market model may allow consideration of additional sales that would otherwise seem too remote to be considered. When there are too few comparable properties on the market, a market model can buttress an argument that another type of property which does sell frequently would be an equally desirable substitute, and

therefore a parallel comparable for valuation. When no comparable property has sold recently, the changes in the market since the last sale may be described by analogy to the changes in the market for another type of property, by establishing models showing that the markets are comparable.

There are five basic criteria for comparing models of two markets and for assessing the credibility of any market model:

1. the property considered is all in the same collector category
2. the same characteristics of value have been considered
3. all the evidence considered is from the relevant market level
4. adjustment needed for the passage of time is considered
5. the sampling considered is adequantly representative.

It is possible to make adjustments if one of these criteria cannot be met, but to preserve credibility the adjustment should be justified.

There are several simple mathematical techniques, called Measures of Central Tendency, which are available to assess how well a sample represents the whole population. These **Measures of Central Tendency** comprise:

Mode: the observation which appears most frequently

Range: the difference between the largest observation and the smallest

Median: the middle value when observations are ranked, usually from the least to the greatest

Mean: the statistical average of the observations.

To make the meanings of these definitions clear, apply them to a small group of observations: $20,000, $23,500, $19,500, $22,000, $20,000, $23,000. The observations are most easily analyzed if they are first ranked, that is, arranged in order from least to greatest:

$19,500
$20,000
$20,000
$22,000
$23,000
$23,500

Only one observation occurs twice, $20,000, and therefore it is the mode. The range (the difference between least and greatest observation) is $23,500 less $19,500 or $4,000. The median is the middle value. Since there is an even number of observations, there is no middle observation; the median is therefore midway between the two central observations, as follows: $22,000 less $20,000 / 2 = $21,000. The mean is the sum of observations divided by the number of observations; i.e., $128,000 / 6 = $21,333. To summarize:

Mode   = $20,000
Range   = $ 4,000
Median = $21,000
Mean   = $21,333

Considering these four measures together, it can be seen how well the center of these observations represents all of them. The mean and median are close (within 1-1/2%), indicating a strong center. The mode is off center, but not by far. In addition, the range is fairly small (20% of the lowest observation), demonstrating that the spread of the observations is moderate. Taken together, these measures indicate that the mean and median are indicative of the whole population.

Much more sophisticated statistical methods are available to indicate not only the center of a group of observations but also the degree of confidence with which the center represents the whole. There are statistical techniques for discerning trends within a group of observations, such as price trends in a market and the probability that a trend will continue. A college-level statistics course is recommended to those who wish to attain a deeper understanding of these useful techniques.

Statistical analysis looks impressive, but often appraisers of personal property don't have a sufficient number of observations within a reasonable range to illustrate statistical significance. The larger the number of observations; i.e., the more comparable sales cited, the more credible any conclusion drawn from them will be. However, in many cases there simply are not enough available observations to make analysis any more statistically relevant than the simple measures of central tendency.

Three Approaches To Value

The three approaches to value involve comparison of properties which have sold, or which are producing income, or which have been created, to the property being appraised. To draw an indication of value from the comparisons, one needs tools for interpreting the differences. The three fundamental approaches to value are the Cost Approach, the Income Approach and the Market Comparison Approach. (See Chapter 3).

All three approaches involve research of actual market events, including actual costs charged, actual leases signed or actual sales. Each provides different informa-tion and a different perspective on the market. Thus, each balances and checks the others. While one approach is usually more relevant than the other two to a particular assignment, the other two can be important support to the argument for value. The more relevant approach simply is given more weight than the other two.

All three approaches are based on the **Principle of Substitution** (See Chapter 3), which posits that no reasonable buyer would pay more for the property being appraised than the cost of an equivalent substitute. This may be the cost of having a substitute property made, the cost of leasing a substitute property, or the price for which another property can be purchased. Key issues are the features that make the substitute equivalent and the market level in which a substitute can be found.

The Income Approach is also a direct expression of the **Principle of Anticipation**, which holds that value is created by anticipation of future benefits. From the point of view of the Cost and Market Comparison Approaches, the future benefits anticipated are the use and enjoyment of the property. The benefits considered in the Income Approach may be more tangible, such as future sale or steady stream of income.

The *Uniform Standards of Professional Appraisal Practice* [USPAP] mandate consideration of all three approaches to value. Specifically, *USPAP* Standards Rule 7-1 states:

In developing a personal property appraisal, an appraiser must be aware of, understand, and correctly employ those recognized methods and techniques that are necessary to produce a credible appraisal.

USPAP Standards Rules 7-3 and 7-3[g] state that:

In developing a personal property appraisal, an appraiser must observe the following specific guidelines: [g] consider the cost, income and sales comparison approaches and their degree of applicability in the valuation of personal property.

Sometimes that consideration may consist of a simple explanation of why one approach is not relevant to the assignment at hand, or why the data available for one or more approaches are not meaningful.

The Cost Approach

A corporation needs to insure the centerpiece of its headquarters building, a painting depicting the history of the company's operations and celebrating the heroism of its workers. The painting is 12 feet high, 160 feet long, and shows 197 life-size figures. The artist was one of America's most famous artists and its most popular muralist when the building was erected. The painting is mounted on the walls of an oval lobby. An appraiser has been retained to estimate the painting's replacement value.

The market place is going to yield insufficient comparable paintings ready to hang should the subject be lost to a disaster of some sort. More importantly, consider the function of the subject painting and imagine what existing paintings would satisfactorily fulfill the original's role to the owner and the site. If this painting were damaged, every effort would be made to restore it. But, if it should be beyond repair, there is no possibility of asking the original artist to paint another, since the artist died years ago. A copyist could be hired to duplicate it. However, the substitute would not be the same as the original painting. But the use of this approach would be appropriate in estimating the value of the role fulfilled by the painting to the corporation.

The Cost Approach is an essential tool in valuing three types of property:

1. immovable property
2. unique property
3. property for which no market exists

Replacing or restoring function forms the central issue in many appraisal assignments where the Cost Approach is essential. An appraiser must look beyond the property itself and identify the need that the property fulfills for a client. When doing insurance appraisals the Cost Approach is often utilized.

Replacement or Reproduction

The **Principle of Substitution** implies that a substitute object of equivalent function and desirability is available. Could an acceptable replacement be purchased in a reasonable length of time, with reasonable effort? Are there features of the property so unique and so central to its use or desirability that a substitute could be obtained only by reproducing it? The paths of research leading to replacement cost and reproduction cost are divergent and often point to very different conclusions. The two are so distinct in appraisal that the end of each path requires its own name and definition.

Reproduction Cost is defined as the total cost to reproduce a replica of a subject property at current costs. Reproduced property would be constructed by a qualified artist or craftsman, in design and with materials consistent with the described piece of property being replaced.

Replacement Cost New is defined as the cost to replace a property with an equivalent or substitute which is new, using materials, techniques and standards which satisfy the description or use of the replaced property; the present cost of replacing the property with one having the same quality and utility.

Note that while the property in both cases is new, there is much greater latitude in the requirements for Replacement Cost New and a much better chance of finding an acceptable substitute. Even when no substitute exists, making it necessary to create one, the definition of Replacement Cost New would permit elimination of features which had proven undesirable in contemporary use. The details of many types of personal property overshadow all else and virtually dictate use of Reproduction Cost as the means to achieve equivalent desirability.

The appraisal assignment and its context determine the criteria for making a substitute property acceptable. Appraisers can provide the research and analysis which help decide the suitability of the replacement by clearly identifying the function(s) being replaced. Both Reproduction and Replacement Costs indicate **Replacement Value** (See Chapter 3).

Common sense would indicate that adding the cost of a property's parts would yield the cost of the whole. It is necessary to realize, however, that the value of the whole may be greater than, lesser than, or equal to the sum of the parts. The **Principal of Contribution** (See Chapter 3) underlies the Cost Approach to value and asserts that the cost of a part or feature may be quite different from its value once incorporated in a whole property.

Both paths of Cost Approach research, reproduction and replacement new, seek the cost of a new property. The definition of **Replacement Value** calls for property of "similar age and condition." If the property is not brand new or reveals wear or other less than new characteristics, some adjustment of the Cost Approach for depreciation must be made. **Depreciation** is loss from the upper limit of value not restored by current maintenance, due to all factors causing ultimate retirement of the property. There are four factors contributing to depreciation:

1. Physical: impairment of condition
2. Functional: the difference in function, capability or production rate between the subject and new property
3. External: loss in value due to influences external to the property, such as changes in supply and demand, in the regulatory and legislative environment

4. Technological: loss in value because subject is superseded by a comparable property with superior function (See Discounts Applied to Value)

Current costs are not the only ones useful to an appraiser. **Historical cost** is the actual, first cost of the property at the time it was first placed in service. **Original cost** is the actual cost to the current owner.

While Historical Cost and Original Cost help place the property in a value context, they must be translated into a figure appropriate to the valuation date and expressed in **Current Dollars,** the unadjusted value of money at any point in time. In Current Dollars, as of the date of valuation, a Current Dollar in 1968 was worth much more in terms of exchange for goods and services, than a Current Dollar is now, the effect called inflation.

The U. S. Department of Commerce publishes tables for translation of Current Dollars into **Constant Dollars,** dollars which have been adjusted for the change in their purchasing power over time. One year is chosen as a base, and the dollars of all other years are expressed as a ratio of the base year dollar. For example, with 1982 as the base year, the dollar in 1986 could purchase .846 as much and the dollar in 1976 could purchase 1.757 as much. The measure of equivalence used is the **Consumer Price Index**, the total cost of purchasing a large and varied "market basket" of consumer goods, compared to the total cost in other years and expressed as a ratio.

Government and industry calculate many other index numbers for more specific areas of the economy. An **Index Number** measures the relative cost of purchasing a representative "market basket" of that category of property, expressed as a ratio of the cost in a base year. R. S. Means, for example, publishes a series of index numbers for costs in interior construction and decorating which can be very useful to appraisers of residential contents.

Index numbers must be used with caution. Care and thoroughness in gathering the data govern their accuracy. More importantly, the appraiser must weigh how well they express trends in the particular market and for the particular property under consideration. Such precise ratios can inspire a confidence which may not be warranted. A small error in the ratio will be magnified dramatically in its application.

The Income Approach

A great array of personal property generates income. Museum shops have led the way, pursuing applications for designs in their collection — wallpapers reproduced on scarves; famous paintings on neckties; anything and everything on note cards and calendars; reproduction paintings with impasto in period-style frames; sculptures in stone, bronze or epoxy; jewelry; pottery and objects de vertu. These items are selling beyond the museum walls through mail order catalogs, and even through shopping malls with "branch" museum stores, and a chain which sells only museum-made items.

The merchandise sold collaterally at museum exhibitions has become a source of income for both originating and host institutions. Museums like Winterthur and the Metropolitan, even local historical societies, license rights to manufacturers of "authorized" reproductions. Some museums lease works of art for home and office decoration.

Individuals may also realize income from their collections. A dealer plans to make money when he resells his inventory. Collectors have the same aspirations. Some collectors and dealers participate in reproduction projects, usually with the artist. A surprisingly large number of dealers and collectors have leased properties, even completely furnished households, to movie and theater companies.

All these ways of generating income with personal property can be converted into present worth — a specific value on a specific date — using the Income Approach to valuation. Future income can be an important benefit, if the money comes in as planned. But because the income is anticipated, the valuation may require discounting for risk.

The income can be realized in one of two ways: as a **Reversion,** a lump sum to be paid in the future, or as a **Stream of Income,** repeated payments in the future. A stream of regular payments at regular intervals is called an **Annuity.**

Careful scrutiny of the feasibility of income being paid as planned is the key to Income Approach. Comparison with actual events provides the best gauge of this. If the property has been generating income already, then its **Record of Performance** will be a good indicator of reliability. If it has produced income regularly and reliably, then five years is the common period for examination.

One must be alert to the possibility that conditions will change, and that the next five years will not be just like the past five. There may be periods of time without income, which are called **Vacancy.** Also, by the end of the period being projected, depreciation may become a factor in estimating any resale value the property has retained.

It is generally **Net Income** — Gross Income less Expenses — which is valued. Therefore, one must look for conditions which might change not only income but expenses. This projection of future performance relies on a series of assumptions derived from the record of past performance. These assumptions must be clearly stated.

The feasibility of projected performance is gauged also by comparison to similar properties generating income. Their records of performance are compared to the subject property's, to check the relevance of the assumptions made. Just as the Principle of Substitution suggests that a prudent buyer would shop for the best price, so a prudent investor in income property would consider alternative investments and their performance. If the subject property does not yet have a record of performance, then the record of performance for comparable properties could serve as the basis for projections.

Simply stated, all projections must be based on one of three basic assumptions:

1. net income will improve
2. net income will not change
3. net income will decline

There must be evidence derived from analysis of records of performance to support the chosen assumption. Charts commonly demonstrate both income and expenses for every period of the projection (usually weekly, monthly or annually).

Another assumption basic to any projection is the rate at which the effect of time will be calculated. The effect of general economic conditions, which has been inflation for many years, would demand a minimum rate so that the value of the investment does not erode.

Treasury bonds, which are guaranteed by the U. S. Government, are considered a safe investment. The rate paid of these bonds for a period being projected is termed the "safe rate." Since no projected income could be as reliable as the income from Treasury bonds, an astute investor would demand a premium over the safe rate for the greater risk. There are many methods for calculating the premium for risk. The simplest is to calculate the rate actually being paid by comparable properties.

Having made these two assumptions — projection of net income and rate — one uses printed tables or calculator programs appropriate to the period being projected and finds a factor for calculating the present worth of the future income.

The formula for a **Reversion** is

Present Value = Future Value x Factor

Since a reversion is a lump sum paid one time, the future value would be the price for which the object will sell or be resold. This equation answers the question, what is an object worth now if I can forecast what it will sell for in the future?

This equation can also tell a dealer what price to set on a property to make a profit. First, the dealer would decide how long it will be before the sale takes place (the period) and what rate of gross profit is desired. The table for the desired rate will list a factor for the period. The basic rules of algebra permit anything to be done to an equation, as long as the same thing is done to both sides. The goal is to isolate the answer desired on one side. If both sides are divided by the Factor, then the formula becomes:

Present Value /Factor = Future Value

or, substituting:

Purchase Price /Factor = Future Sale Price

Since the factor is tied to both the period and the rate, this formula can be used after the sale to calculate the rate of return. If both sides are divided by the Future Value, then the formula becomes:

Present Value/Future Value = Factor

or

Purchase Price/Sale Price = Factor

The factor thus calculated will be listed for the period which has elapsed between purchase and sale in the table for the rate of return achieved.

Lease, licensing and reproduction agreements usually specify payment of the income over time. If the payments are regular, constant in current dollars and paid every month, for example, then the income is an annuity. The formula for an **Annuity** is:

Present Value = Total Net Income /Period x Factor

A financial calculator can calculate monthly present value. Also monthly tables can provide these calculation factors. Any series of payments can be treated as present value reversions.

Another assumption is involved in this formula: not only are the period and the rate assumed but also the income to be received. If a movie company leased an object for three months at $50 per week, with no deductions for expenses, then the total net income would be ($50 x 4 x 3 = $600). Since the period is three months, then one need only specify the rate to calculate the present value of the lease agreement. Note that this simple example includes no vacancy or out of use time; any period without income would reduce the Total Net Income. If the movie company decided it didn't need the object for four weeks in the middle of the period, for example, creating a four week Vacancy, the total net income would be $50 x 8 weeks (instead of 12) = $400.

If recalculated, the present value of the lease would be reduced accordingly.

The rate of return achieved by a property with a record of performance can be calculated with the same formula, by isolating the Factor. Multiply both sides of the equation by the Period, and divide both sides by Total Net Income, and the formula becomes:

Present Value x Period / Total Net Income = Factor

The factor thus calculated will be listed with the appropriate period in the table for the rate of return achieved. Keep in mind that the Present Value is the value at the beginning of the period of performance, which in many cases may be the original cost. This method applied to comparable properties with a well-established record of performance is the best argument to support the choice of a rate of return, since it is based on facts.

What would the lease be worth if the movie company wanted to rent the object next year? The annuity formula would yield the Present Value at the beginning of the period, next year. To calculate the value of the lease now, first calculate its Present Value at the beginning of the period, next year, and then treat that Present Value as a Reversion, as if it were a lump sum payable next year. The Present Value of this Reversion is the procured result.

There is another formula for calculating Present Value when the payments are not regular. In fact, the formulae discussed here are only the two most commonly used by appraisers of personal property. There are four more which are discussed in various texts on the appraisal of income-producing property.

A great many items of personal property are income producers, and even more have the potential. For appraisal of the work of a living artist who publishes reproductions rather than selling originals, an indicator of the value may be the Income Approach. For appraisal of any object which is producing income, whether through leases, licenses or reproductions, the Income Approach must be developed and considered. Even if the object only has the potential for income, but its potential is feasible, the Income Approach should be considered and compared to the two other approaches.

The Market Comparison Approach

Shoppers going from store to store in search of a better value are using the Market Comparison Approach. By comparing features, evaluating service, and choosing their favorite retailer or antique gallery, they are defining their criteria and deciding which purchase will give them the greatest utility and satisfaction. They weigh the balance of asking price and satisfaction and normally select what they consider to be the best value for their dollars.

The **Market Comparison Approach** estimates value by comparison with properties sold in the relevant market, with adjustments made for all differences which affect value, such as differences in characteristics of value and in time. This is shopping in reverse, after the fact. Each property sold is compared to the property to be appraised, and an amount is added to or subtracted from the price achieved for every difference, with the sum yielding an indication of value.

The Market Comparison Approach is most reliable with manufactured objects, when the items sold are identical to the one being appraised. The only adjustments needed would be for any intangible differences such as warranty and service, for any change in value since the sale was made ("time" in the definition), and for any differences between the circumstances of the sale and the circumstances of the appraisal.

The amount of any adjustment is no more a matter of guesswork or "educated estimate" than any other part of the appraisal process. The **Principle of Contribution** tells us that the value of a component part of a property is the amount it contributes to the value of the whole or the amount by which its absence detracts from the value of the whole. We can measure the value of a component part of a sale by comparing two similar objects, assuming that any difference in the price achieved is attributable to the difference between them.

For example, research discloses that two identical Staffordshire vases were sold by two dealers in the same city, one charging $200 more than the other. The higher price was realized by a long-established gallery which warrants the authenticity of its inventory; the other vase was sold by a new gallery whose statements regarding authenticity are limited and vague. Knowing that new or fake Staffordshire pottery on the market is a concern to collectors, we can attribute the difference in price to the difference in one component part of the sale, the warranty offered. In comparing other sales of Staffordshire vases to the appraisal assignment, an adjustment of $200 for warranty is indicated.

It becomes more difficult with unique objects, when every sale must be adjusted for differences in characteristics as well. These adjustments can be more difficult to substantiate and the more of them, the weaker the argument for value. Some objects seem so unique that nothing like them has sold, and the appraiser would then consider the Cost or Income Approaches and accept or reject those approaches. If rejected, reliance on the **Principle of Substitution, which states that** the market place value of a replacement property indicated by the value of an equally desirable substitute property.

The key lies in the phrase "equally desirable." Equally desirable to whom? Desirability is assessed in certain cases to the client but always to the collectors and dealers who constitute a market. Instead of focusing on the characteristics of the property, it may be helpful to focus on how the property is regarded by its collectors and consider what other properties are equally desirable to the same market.

The value of a property is said to be what someone is willing to pay for it; but that describes only one transaction, which may not be rational and may not be repeatable. What a number of people would be willing and able to pay for a property on the date of valuation is value to an appraiser. This requires analysis of how the people able to buy make their decisions. What are their criteria? What characteristics of the property make a difference in the price they are willing to pay?

Every able buyer has a wide choice of ways to spend money. Several of the choices available may give the same utility and satisfaction. For example, some collectors find as much satisfaction in a Rookwood vase as in a Stickley chair; others need somewhere to sit, and Shaker will do as well as Stickley. Such individual preferences may seem arbitrary and difficult to predict, but they result in a decision and action. In a large number of actions (**a market**) consistent trends will be discernible.

There are many collector categories. Within each collector category, one property will be considered better than another; i.e., awarded a higher ranking. Collectors in many categories have developed formal grading systems, such as the one used for coins. Within any particular category, there will be specific criteria for ranking. The connoisseur considers **Elements of Quality**, which are primarily **questions of aesthetic judgment, independent of economics and fashion.**

In the market place, buyers consider **Characteristics of Value**, which are **primarily questions of fact and have an objective relationship to the market place.** The effect of a characteristic of value can be measured objectively by analyzing actual sales to see how the market responded.

It seems that there is a market for almost anything, and thus the Market Comparison Approach is a mainstay of personal property appraisal. The smaller the market, the more vulnerable it is to large fluctuations, and the more important the two other approaches to analyzing value become. When the object is personalized or so unique it has no apparent market, or when the assignment requires a different perspective on value than that of the market, the Market Comparison Approach may not be applicable at all.

The "market" is not a coherent organism with a strong will and one mind but is a great many individuals acting on their own preferences according to their own criteria. Through their actions, trends become discernible; the probability of these trends continuing will vary with their consistency and the number of actions (sales) realized over time.

Individuals do not act in a vacuum, but rather in an economic and social context. There are many influences on their ability and willingness to buy or sell. Their criteria for price decisions may be shared and a collector category thus created. The circumstances of their actions — whether they buy from reputable dealers or flea markets, whether they sell at auction or yard sales — are formed by the expectations and norms of their community.

In the sense that every sale is an agreement between two people, buyer and seller; that their actions are shaped by social and economic forces as well as their own preferences; and that a market is the accumulated sum of many sales by individuals, then value is a social agreement regarding a property. Nowhere is this social process more apparent than at auction, where many individuals interested in a property will assemble and express their opinions of value as bids, debating back and forth until at least two people agree what to pay. However, the seasoned appraiser knows that not all auctions are "arm's length" sales, nor are properties necessarily consigned by "willing sellers." The market in personal properties is made of several sectors; see Debra D. Homer, "Fine Art Appraisers: The Art, the Craft, and the Legal Design," *Columbia Journal of Art and the Law*, Vol. 8, 1984, pp. 457-511.

To understand what the most probable agreement would be, an appraiser must analyze both the motives which led to individual sales and the social and economic forces which shaped them. It is possible to make adjustments for observable differences between a property sold and the property being appraised and to quantify that adjustment logically, with evidence. It is possible to make adjustments for intangible components of a sale, such as warranty or time — indeed, for any characteristic of value. But to know which characteristics of value are significant and what effect their presence or absence has, an appraiser must understand the society or collector group which would agree on the value of the particular subject property.

Bibliography:

Alico, John, ed. *Appraising Machinery and Equipment.* New York: McGraw Hill / American Society of Appraisers, 1989.

Beasley, David. *How To Use A Research Library.* New York: Oxford Press, 1988.

Betts, Richard M. and Ely, Silas J. *Basic Real Estate Appraisal.* Washington, DC: American Society of Appraisers, 1990.

Black, Henry C. *Black's Law Dictionary.* 5th ed. St. Paul, MN: West Publishing Co., 1979.

Jones, Lois Swan. *Art Information Research Methods and Resources,* 3rd ed. Dubuque, IA: Kendall Hunt, 1990.

Lipsay et al. *Economics.* New York: Harper & Row, 1990.

Smith, Charles W. *Auctions, the Social Construction of Value.* Berkeley, CA: University of California, 1989.

Spurgin, Sally DeWitt. *The Power to Persuade.* Englewood Cliffs, NJ: Prentice Hall, 1985.

Discounts Applied To Value

Depreciation

Depreciation is a loss in value of property. The causes of any loss may come from a variety of sources both intrinsic and extrinsic to the property itself. **Depreciation** is a loss from the upper limit of value due to any cause contributing to the ultimate retirement of the property.

The four principle causes of depreciation are impairments to condition, and three forms of obsolescence: functional, economic and technological. These four factors act separately or in concert to impair the ability of a property to fully meet its identified function.

Condition is the physical description of the property as to its completeness for performing an identified role. Impairments could be any form of damage or loss of components, wear and tear, or inappropriate or unacceptable repairs.

Functional Obsolescence is the difference between the subject property's ability to produce the intended result and the ability of a new replacement to produce the same result. This differs from technological obsolescence, below, in that the subject and replacement are of comparable design and category.

Economic Obsolescence is external impairments on a property's ability to meet a function. Examples are changes in optimum use, legislative enactment's restricting use, and changes in supply and demand relationships.

Technological Obsolescence is change in the ability to create a new substitute for a property's function with modern methods or materials. An example of technological obsolescence would be the difference between the capacities of a phonograph machine and a compact disc player to reproduce musical tones. By the same token it could be the difference between a modern stereo system's ability to play records and that of a hand-cranked gramophone of the early twentieth century.

The first step in estimating depreciation is necessarily determining the precise utility of the property and the appraisal question. Where a property can be perceived to have alternative functions, the function addressed in the appraisal context must be expressed in order to make any argument for a depreciation to be valid. Consider, for example, an historic pair of antique vases in a public collection. Three potential functions of the vases can be identified: as collectible antiques with potential in the market place for appreciation in value; as a devise for holding floral arrangements or other decoration; and as an educational device demonstrating an aspect of history or culture. Another function of each vase individually would be to support the pair's symmetry. The appraisal context will determine the function to be considered leading to appropriate methodology for estimating loss due to an impairment such as damage and repair.

Depreciation can be estimated by any of the three traditional approaches to value, **cost, income** or **market comparison.** The cost approach is especially appropriate when function can be fully restored with the purchase or fabrication of a replacement. It is less appropriate when the property function is defined as a collectible, and the collectors in the category have an adverse response to repairs or replacements. In the latter case, the property may convert to a new category with different criteria. By way of example, while the serious collector of Hummel porcelain figurines would not be willing to purchase a repaired work, another collector seeking to accomplish a decorative motif may pay a different price for the same work as an appropriate piece of bricabrac. In the event of the second buyer paying a lower price than that of the first buyer's potential offer for an example in original condition, the appraiser has a basis for estimating depreciation through a market comparison approach.

The income approach is most effective when the causes of depreciation are external, such as economic obsolescence. Present value formulae can be helpful in estimating a loss of value due to impaired marketability resulting from market cycles, jurisdictional restrictions on sales, taxes and tariffs. Other reasons for impaired marketability might be potential losses of collector appetite for a property that has been over exposed or has a negative association with some event or person. In these cases, the assumption that the original value will be restored after a period of time must be supported fully in order to accurately estimate a loss in value.

Blockage

Blockage is essentially a form of depreciation resulting from a number of similar properties being offered that is too large for the normal market to absorb as of a specific date. The concept is rooted in estate taxation where the courts have allowed a discount from the total fair market value of a homogenous group of properties that would need to be sold over a period of time to realize their maximum potential return. The term comes from the first cases where discounts were applied to the value of large "blocks" of stock (sold *en bloc*). In recent years, cases involving artists' estate holdings of unsold works, most notably the estates of David Smith and Georgia O'Keeffe, have allowed similar discounts. It is necessary to differentiate between blockage discount and fair market value. In order to apply a discount for blockage, fair market value must first be estimated and supported.

Past estimates of blockage discounts for personal property in artists' estates have been made as "Solomon-like" decisions (c.f. Chapter 7, Legal Precedents). With more frequent and varied application of the concept in recent years, attempts to apply more satisfying methodology have come about. A leading approach is to apply a fully researched and analyzed present value formula to the property, adjusting for the amount of time that would be required for the market place to absorb the property normally.

In any attempt to estimate a blockage discount it is incumbent on the appraiser to fully research and analyze each component of the process including past performance or absorption rate; the homogeneity of the property, especially if it could be divided into smaller categories with different market reactions; and the appropriateness of the discount rate being applied to the formulae.

There are three important concepts of Blockage Discount and Present Worth:

1) Like Fair Market Value, "Blockage" and "Present Worth" are concepts; blockage is a concept of value within time. Blockage is a discount applied to a sum of value where a quantity of very similar properties would impact a market at one date. If such a quantity would have an adverse effect on the market a discount which considers a reasonable estimate of time for the market to absorb the quantity is applied. Blockage is not a set formula.

2) Present Worth is also a concept of value within time. A discount applied to the sum of value based on the anticipated absorption in a regular market. Present Worth is not a set formula.

3) Blockage and Present Worth concepts descend to the appraisal of personal property from the experience of the valuation of stocks and securities *en bloc*.

The following six court cases deal with the concept of blockage.

Edward A. Gallun, 33 T.C.M. (CCH) 1316 (1974), typifies the various issues that are considered in the valuation of a large quantity of shares of common stock.

Estate of David Smith, 57 T.C.M. 650 (1972), was the first application of the concept of blockage to the valuation questions for works of fine art, specifically that the marketing of all of the sculptures owned by the Smith Estate would have depressed the values of the individual sculptures.

The Court agrees with the argument of the executor, "The impact of ... simultaneous availability of an extremely large number of items of the same general category is a significant circumstance which should be taken into account." In this connection, the so-called blockage rule utilized in connection with the sale of a large number of securities furnishes a useful analogy. - 57 T.C.M. (CCH) 658.

Court disagrees with executor's value conclusion, the difference between the government's valuation and the executor's was split.

In re Rothko, 84 Misc. 2d 830 (NY Sur. Ct. 1975), demonstrates that the concept of "blockage" is not the same as "averaging." Averaging a large number of similar properties must be shown to have a reasonable basis for such computation.

Estate of Georgia T. O'Keeffe, docket no. 181344-90, T.C.M. (CCH) 1992-210, shows the inadequacy of applying arbitrary percentage discounts and of confusing blockage with averaging.

James L. Rose and Judy S. Rose., 88 T.C. No. 18. Docket No. 25635-83 2-5-87, concept of "present worth" was used by the government's expert. Valuations were discredited because, among other things, they failed to take into consideration the ability of a market to absorb a large quantity of similar properties.

Shuman et al. v. United States, Civ. No. H-85-1672 (SD Texas), concept of present worth used by the government's expert to demonstrate that the value of a large quantity of similar properties must be valued in the context of a relationship with the numbers of individual items and the reasonable rate at which the items can be absorbed.

In conclusion, the concepts of "Blockage-Discount" and "Present Worth" both require the appraiser to track past market experience and project future market experience.

Bibliography

Note: The following books as well as a catalogue of courses can be obtained through the American Society of Appraisers, Education Department. [703]478-2228.

The Blockage Discount and Present Worth, handbook from a Multidisciplinary Eduction Seminar presented by the International Personal Property Committee of the American Society of Appraisers, June 30, 1993, Seattle, Washington.

Betts, R. and S. Ely. *Basic Real Estate Appraisal*. John Wiley & Sons, 1986.

Fishman, J. and S. Pratt. *Guide to Business Valuations*. Practitioners Publishing Co., 1991.

Friedman, J. and N. Ordway. *Income Property Appraisal and Analysis*. Prentice-Hall / American Society of Appraisers, 1988.

Pratt, S. *Valuing a Business; The Analysis and Appraisal of Closely Held Companies*, Dow Jones-Irwin, 1989.

Revenue Ruling 59-60 An Alternative to Blockage in the Valuation of Artists' Estates

©1994 by Terrence M. Melia, CPA

Introduction

In the *Estate of Georgia T. O'Keeffe v. Commissioner of Internal Revenue* 63 T.C.M. (CCH) 2699, the Tax Court was called upon to determine the blockage discount applicable to the works of art created by an artist that were includible in her estate. After a lengthy trial, where, in the opinion of the Court, the conclusions of the experts of both the petitioner and respondent "as to the appropriate blockage discount suffers from substantial defects and is patently unreliable," the Tax Court arrived at a decision that "split the difference." While the opinion left little in the way of an objective formula for estate planners and appraisers to utilize in future artist estate valuations, it did discuss certain theoretical valuation considerations that estate planners and appraisers should consider.

Two other artists valuation cases have been brought before the court. In the *Estate of David Smith v. Commissioner of Internal Revenue* 57 T.C. 650, the Tax Court was similarly asked to determine the appropriate blockage discount. However, in reaching its conclusion, the Smith Court provided no methodology for its blockage determination and applied one discount to the entire appraisal of the individual pieces. The decision also disallowed the impact of sales commissions as a consideration in the valuation process. The *O'Keeffe* Court in its examination of the *Smith* case for guidance states that "nothing in the opinion, however, explains the conclusion of value by application of a particular percentage to the total."

In Louisa J. Calder v. Commissioner 85 T.C. 713, the Court was asked to render an opinion as to the appropriate blockage discount applicable to a gift of art by an artist's widow. In making its determination, the *Calder* Court utilized actual post-gift sales data to determine the liquidation period then calculated the present value of the income stream utilizing an agreed upon average retail value and annuity tables. Thus the court in *Calder* states that it utilized "a somewhat more sophisticated manner than the usual method of applying a single percentage discount to the retail value of the items." However, in *O'Keeffe* the court rejected this approach due to limited availability of data regarding post death sales by the petitioner and the fact that "only a small percentage of value has actually been liquidated in that manner."

Each of the aforementioned cases focuses its valuation on the collection of art work. While this may have been appropriate in *Calder,* the courts in both *O'Keeffe* and *Smith* could have focused on the valuation of the artist's proprietorship. Expanding the valuation process from that of the artist collection to that of the artists proprietorship should provide estate planners and appraisers with the objective business valuation techniques for which the court in *O'Keeffe* was searching.

Our focus then will be the development of a theoretical construction of authorities to permit the expansion of the valuation process from solely the artist's collection of artwork to a broader concept of business proprietorship which would include by definition the artist's works.

Facts

Georgia O'Keeffe began painting in 1914. When she died on March 6, 1986, at the age of 98, her career as an artist encompassed more than 70 years. From the 1920's until 1946, the distribution of O'Keeffe's works was controlled by her husband, Alfred Stieglitz, through his gallery in New York. After his death, O'Keeffe's works were marketed through several dealers. From the mid-1970's until her death, the distribution of her works, as well as many other aspects of her career, was guided by Juan Hamilton. During this later period, her sales became fewer and many times contained post-sale disposition limitations on the purchaser.

During her career it was estimated that she had produced between 1,100 and 1,200 substantial works. At the time of her death, approximately 400 works or groups of works remained in her possession. The quality of the remaining works ranged from top-quality major works, to smaller and lesser works of medium quality, to studio leftovers or failures of weak quality or atypical works; and, finally, to unfinished works and slight sketches. The values of the individual pieces of art ranged from less than $20,000 to over $1,000,000. While a few of her greatest works remained at her death, the majority of the works remaining would be classified as middle-range.

The individual value of each O'Keeffe work on hand at her death was determined by the appraisal of Mr. E. V. Thaw. The total value of the individual works determined b), Mr. Thaw approximated $72,000.000. Additionally, Mr. Thaw, determined that a 75 percent blockage discount should be applied to the sum of the individual works. While the appraisal categorized the works by medium, no differentiation in the application of the blockage discount by medium was made. In arriving at the blockage discount Mr. Thaw relied on his own experience in the art market and did not undertake a financial analysis. Thus the value of the O'Keeffe works of art included in her estate tax return filed with the Internal Revenue Service totaled approximately $18,000,000.

The appraisal made by Mr. Thaw was subsequently examined by the Art Advisory Panel (AAP) of the Internal Revenue Service (IRS). The AAP's report proposed the following changes to the Thaw appraisal:

- An adjustment to a portion of the individual artworks' appraised values; a determination that the bequeathed art should be excluded from the application of a blockage discount;
- A segmented approach in the application of the blockage discount based upon appraised values; and,
- The application of differing blockage discounts to each segment.

The differences in the individual appraised values contained in the AAP appraisal and the Thaw appraisal were ultimately resolved and agreed to by the parties. This was accomplished in face-to-face meetings between Mr. E. V. Thaw and Ms. Karen Carolan of the AAP. Thus the *O'Keeffe* Court was asked to only determine the appropriate blockage discount.

Opinions of the Experts

Expert witnesses at the trial testifying on behalf of the petitioner included:
- Mr. E. V. Thaw, an art dealer, collector, consultant and expert witness in the *Smith* case and former AAP member;
- Mr. James Maroney, a dealer of early American modernist art; and former AAP member; and
- Mr. Anthony M. Lamport, an investment advisor and advisor to venture investors.

Expert witnesses at the trial testifying on behalf of the respondent included:
- Mr. Warren Adelson, a dealer of American art and member of the AAP; and,
- Mr. Larry Walther, Ph.D. an associate professor of financial accounting topics.

The art experts for the petitioner testified as to the market for O'Keeffe's works, analyzing the annual auction market sales as well as sales by the artist, the state of the art market during the period surrounding her death and their opinions with respect to the future of the art market in general and O'Keeffe's in particular. Specific testimony included:

• The opinion that the art market in 1986 was at or near its peak,

• Traditional factors establishing value in the art market are rarity, quality, size, subject matter, medium and condition.

• The O'Keeffe works in the estate constituted at least a 10 year supply, excluding a residual of lesser student works.

• Given the market for O'Keeffe's, the estate's portion would approximate $4 to $5 million per year.

• Thaw and Rose advised that they would not have advised a seller of the works in the estate to sell them in bulk at the 75 percent discounted value.

The respondent's art expert testified that:

• The artwork should be categorized as "Bequested Art" and "Remaining Art" with zero blockage discount assigned to "Bequested Art."

• "Remaining Artwork" should be categorized by price with only a 10 percent discount assigned to work with a value over $200,000 since those pieces could be sold "within a few years."

• The remainder of the "Remaining Artwork," those with a value of less than $200,000, should have a blockage discount of 37 percent since it would "take years, perhaps a decade, to dispose of."

Analysis of the Opinion

The Court rendered an opinion that a blockage discount of 25 percent should be applied to half the works; 75 percent to the remainder, resulting in a evaluation of $36,400,000 or a 50 percent blockage discount. In arriving at this "split-the-difference" result the O'Keeffe Court was frustrated by the testimony of the experts for both the petitioner and respondent. The Court stated that "although each of the experts was qualified to express an opinion on the subject matter on which he or she was called to testify, each of them suffered from the same tendency to ignore relevant facts inconsistent with the position of the party employing the expert and to exaggerate facts consistent with the view espoused."

In spite of the result, the O'Keeffe decision contains important conclusions that estate planners and appraisers working with artists and their estates can utilize.

• In finding consistent with The Estate of Mary Frances Smith v. United States of America, 658 F2d 999, the O'Keeffe Court found that the respondent's position that bequeathed work should be excluded from blockage was incorrect as a matter of law. Accordingly, the prop-erty to be valued is the property that passes ignoring the legatee after death.

• The artwork, if it has significant variation, should be segmented to take such variation into account. These segments can then be addressed individually by the appraiser in the analysis of the market for each segment. While the experts in O'Keeffe may have done this mentally as a matter of practice after years of experience in the art world, the Court without the benefit of such experience, was troubled by lack of objective analysis collaborating such testimony.

• A present value analysis with respect to the work of the artist is an appropriate valuation technique. This is consistent with Calder, however the O'Keeffe Court utilized an analysis of "works that are salable within a relatively short period of time at approximately their individual values and works that can be marketed over a long period of years with substantial effort. The consensus of the experts was that the better works could be sold within 7 years, and a sale of the bulk of the estate would take more than 10 years.

• The application of future expenses in determining value is relevant. While not resolving the commission dispute of Smith, the O'Keeffe Court stated "that the works could not be sold simultaneously, on the date of death and that carrying costs would be incurred." The Internal Revenue Service argued that the Smith Court's finding which held that any reduction in value "based upon the gross sales price reduced. . .to take into account commissions. . .is precluded by decided cases." The Smith Court found that "the measure of value is what could be received on, not what is retained from, a hypothetical sale." Thus artist's estates must only look to IRC Section 2053. This section provides for an estate tax deduction for funeral and administration expenses allowed by the laws of jurisdiction under which the estate is administered.

Issues

To avoid "split the difference" decisions as was rendered in O'Keeffe and to avoid "Solomon-like pronouncements" as was rendered in Smith, artist estate valuation issues involving blockage discounts and the impact of carrying costs on value must be presented utilizing accepted business appraisal techniques. While the O'Keeffe Court's decision provides some useful valuation principles, it still rendered its decision as to "the fair market value of O'Keeffe works in the estate at the date of death." Similarly, in Smith the "critical issue in this case is the determination of the fair market value of the sculptures at the time of Smith's death." Thus the focus of both decisions is the value of the collections of the artists' works. However, if the courts in these cases had been called upon to render a decision relating to the value of the artist's respective proprietorship interest, would generally recognize business appraisal techniques sustained a different value? What authority exists for valuation of a deceased artists proprietorship? Can differences in the approaches utilized to value a collection of an artist's work, as opposed to his proprietorship interest, be supported and documented? These issues must next be addressed.

Discussion

IRC Section 2031(a) provides that the value of the gross estate of the decedent shall be determined by including the value at the time of his death all property real or personal, tangible or intangible, wherever situated. Estate tax regulation 20.2031-1(b) provides that the value of the property included in decedent's gross estate is its fair market value. That regulation defines fair market value as the price at which the property, would change hands between a willing buyer and willing seller, neither being under any compulsion to buy or to sell and both having reasonable knowledge of relevant facts. Estate tax regulation 20.2031-1(b) further provides that the value of items of property which were held by the decedent for sale in the course of a business generally should be reflected in the value of the business.

Estate tax regulation 20.2031-3 provides that the fair market value of any interest of a decedent in a business, whether a partnership or a proprietorship, is the net amount which a willing purchaser would pay for the interest to a willing seller, neither being under any compulsion to buy or to sell and both having reasonable knowledge of relevant facts. Facts to be considered in the determination of net value include:

- Appraisal of all the assets of the business both tangible and intangible;
- The demonstrated earnings capacity of the business; and
- Certain factors utilized in determining non-public corporate stock including economic outlook for the industry and "other relevant factors."

As stated in *Bright* "the property to be valued is the property which is actually transferred." Thus if the property that is transferred can be characterized as an interest in a proprietorship, the artist's work should be reflected in the value of the proprietorship as items held for sale in the course of the business. The proprietorship should then be valued giving due consideration to the relevant factors and valuation approaches proscribed in Rev. Rul. 59-60, 1959-1 C.B. 237. The principles of Rev. Rul. 59-60 were made applicable to business interests of any type by Rev. Rul. 65-192, 1965-2 C.B. 259.

Whether the decedent's artwork was held for sale in the course of a business and; therefore, includible in determining the value of the proprietorship under Estate tax regulation 20.2031-1(b) is determined by examining the facts of each case. In determining the existence of a proprietorship estate planners and appraisers may wish to consider IRC Section 6166(b). This section determines the portion of the estate tax for which deferred payments can be made when a closely held business is included in a decedent's estate. This section considers an "Interest in a closely held business" to include an interest as a proprietor in a trade or business carried on as a proprietorship. Rev. Rul. 75-366, 1975-2 C.B. 472, provides that in the case of a sole proprietorship, Section 6166 was intended to apply only with respect to a business such as a manufacturing, mercantile or service enterprise as distinguished from the management of investments assets. While other definitions are available for consideration, meeting this definition should enable the estate planner and appraiser to conclude that the asset subject to the appraisal is the proprietorship.

In the *O'Keeffe* case, the facts would indicate that the proprietorship had ceased. The facts indicating this include:

- Few works created for a significant period prior to death;
- Specific identification of more than 30 percent by value of her works as charitable bequests;
- Few sales by the artist in the years prior to death; and
- Methods of selling and post-sale constraints placed upon the buyer.

In the *Smith* case, however, the facts would indicate that the proprietorship did exist at the time of death; and, therefore, the artwork should have been included therein as property held for sale in the business as required by Estate tax regulation 20.2031-1(b). Facts indicating that a proprietorship existed in the *Smith* case include:

- The level of the artist's creative activity in the period preceding death;
- The gallery consignment agreement that authorized the gallery and others "to offer for sale all items of your work owned by you;"

• The consignment agreement requirement that the delivery of "each such item of your work to us at such location as we shall indicate"; and

• The fact that the consignment agreement was "binding upon and inure to the benefit of your and our respective executors, administrators, successors and assigns."

While the record would indicate evidence of a proprietorship in *Smith* with the relevant appraisal implications, it does not indicate any consideration of this fact in the *Smith* Court's decision. This failure could have had an impact on the *Smith* Court in reaching its decision to disallow the consignment commissions as a reduction of the individual fair market values of each work.

As previously mentioned, Rev. Rules 59-60, 65-192 and Estate Tax Regulation 20.2031-3 provide the principles to be followed in the valuation of a proprietorship or other closely held enterprise. Due to the uniqueness of each artist and each of their works, an earnings approach may be less appropriate to the valuation of the proprietorship than an asset valuation. This approach to valuation utilizes the value of the underlying assets of the enterprise as the primary factor in the valuation process. Rev. Rul. 59-60 provides that when using this approach, the fair market value of the assets should be determined and that consideration should be given to the enterprises operating costs.

An analysis of two asset valuation cases provides insight into how the Tax Court has applied this approach when called upon to value an entity containing property held for sale in the course of its business. In *Jack D. and Louise G. Carr v. Commissioner* 49 T.C.M. (CCH) 507, the Court examined the valuation process utilized to determine individual asset values. In determining the value of each asset, the Court permitted the deduction of a $5,000 per asset payment due on the sale of each asset. In *Estate of Clarence J. Grootemaat v Commissioner*, T.C. Memo 1979-49, when considering selling expenses as a component of the valuation the Court stated that "in determining the value of land, a prospective buyer looks to the rate of return . . . on his capital invested in the property through sales of the real estate after all of the expenses of development and disposition."

Thus, both *Carr* and *Grootemaat* give consideration to selling expenses in determining the individual asset value when utilizing the net asset value approach to value an enterprise. Similarly, Rev. Proc. 77-12, 1977-1 C.B.

569, provides procedures for determining the fair market value of inventory. The Rev. Proc. provides that "consideration should be given to ... the expenses that would be incurred in such disposition for example, all costs of disposition ... sales commissions...."

The Rev. Proc. was issued by the IRS to clarify liquidation valuation issues involving inventory. A like finding was reached in *Vernon R. and Jessie F. Berg v. United States of America*, 58-2 USTC 9937. In determining the value of inventory received in the liquidation of a corporation, the *Berg* Court concluded that "the proper method of determining fair market value of the inventory ... is to value said inventory at the price for which it could be sold ... less the necessary costs of disposition."

Thus, after the analysis of the cases noted above and the approach followed therein in determining the value of property held for sale, the only rational for the *Smith* Court's decision could be its failure to consider that the artwork was part of a proprietorship to be valued in accordance with Estate tax regulations 20.2031-1(b) and 20.2031-3. An examination of the authorities in *Smith* confirms this. In reaching its conclusion to exclude consignment commissions, the *Smith* Court relied upon two previously decided cases, *Rose Publicker v. Commissioner of Internal Revenue*, 53-2 USTC 10,912 and *Estate of Frank Miller Gould v. Commissioner*, 14 T.C. 414. Both cases involved the transfer, by gift and inheritance respectively, of jewelry for personal use. The decision held that the federal excise tax was to be considered in the determination of the fair market value of such property.

Additionally, the *Carr* Court examined the applicability of an "absorption discount." In determining the appropriateness of a "market absorption discount" the Court stated "that a discount of this nature is necessary in order to reflect the absence of time within which to make an orderly disposition of property. It is apparent that all of the lots owned ... if valued as a whole, would have a different value than if the value of the individual lots were totaled."

In considering a "market absorption discount" the *Grootemaat* Court stated "that if valued as a whole, it would have a different value than in the values of the individual parcels were totaled."

The similarity of the *Carr and Grootemaat* cases findings on the appropriateness of "market absorption discounts" to the appropriateness of blockage discounts in *Smith* and *O'Keeffe* is evident by comparing the *O'Keeffe* Court's discussion of the need for such a discount in its statement that "the fair market value of the aggregate ... therefore ... was substantially less than the total of the fair market values of each individual work. The overall approach of these business valuation cases are applicable anytime an artist's proprietorship is the property that is the subject of the valuation.

Conclusion

Each artist's estate represents a unique situation, the proper approach to valuation must be developed, taking into account all the facts unique to that situation. Estate planners and appraisers should property determine the assets to be valued, whether it is an art collection or a business proprietorship. In all cases where a proprietorship is the subject of the valuation, a qualified business appraiser should assist a qualified fine arts appraiser in determining the fair market value of the property held for sale.

In the cases where the property that passes is a collection of the artist's works, the art should be examined for segmentation in order that sound business assumptions can be documented. Most importantly, the Court will want to have objective evidence of the principles and procedures utilized in the determination.

Chapter 7

Information Management, Sources and Control

Appraisal Research Methods and Models

Efficient and diligent library research is of paramount importance to the appraiser's practice. In order to accomplish this task the appraiser must have a working knowledge of the basic library access systems, as well as a knowledge of how they are linked to other information systems and sources.

In order to efficiently locate and retrieve material from a library and other sources, inventory and access systems for various types of holdings have been devised. These systems require a classification and catalog scheme as well as some form of vocabulary control so that the patron can find material in a systematic rather than random manner. Each system has at least two major functions, 1) to create the basic access systems to a subject based classification scheme and a vocabulary controlled catalog and 2) to provide systematic access to additional materials created by scholars and commercial companies which are not included in the librarian-created classification and cataloging systems.

Material in a library is usually grouped by type (books, journals, microform, archival material, photographs, government documents, etc.) and by subject (history, economics, fine art, decorative art, etc.).

Classification Systems for Books

The two most commonly used classification systems are the Dewey Decimal and the Library of Congress classification systems, each created around the turn of the century. Both systems are subject/discipline based and were initially designed to facilitate systematic browsing of full texts in the stacks; consequently, volumes treating the same or similar subjects are positioned next to one another. Under these systems each book is given a code which designates its subject and location in the stacks.

The Dewey Decimal Classification (DDC) system is based on a numerical system from 000s for general works (including subject bibliographies) to 900s for history (*Example 1)*, and is primarily utilized by small to mid-size public and regional libraries. Under the Dewey system, the three beginning numbers state the general topic of the work followed by a decimal point and another set of numbers, each one denoting a specific aspect of the primary subject. The 016s are reserved for subject bibliographies; a further extension of that number corresponds to the subject of the particular bibliography. For example, a bibliography on drawing under the Dewey system would be classified as 016.741 (016 for bibliography and 741 for drawing). The point is that both the Dewey and the Library of Congress classification systems give special emphasis to subject bibliographies by designating a special class rather than placing them with monographs on the subject. However, the Dewey and Library of Congress schemes place bibliographies at opposite ends of their class schemes.

Letters are used to represent specific subject areas under the Library of Congress Classification (LCC) scheme *(Example 2)*, increasing the number of basic topics to 21 letters as compared to the ten numbers of the Dewey Decimal scheme. Due to the increased topics and broader scope, the LCC is favored by larger research libraries.

Two important elements of the Library of Congress classification scheme are the A and Z classes: They are unlike the B through V classes which constitute material by particular subject or discipline. The A class serves as a kind of "table of contents" to what follows in other classes; it is "for works too general or comprehensive to be classed with a particular subject."[1] It contains sources that provide introductions, general overviews and starting points for research on any subject but not in-depth

Second Summary*
The 100 Divisions

000	**Generalities**	360	Social problems & services	680	Manufacture for specific uses
010	Bibliography	370	Education	690	Buildings
020	Library & information sciences	380	Commerce (Trade)	**700**	**The arts**
030	General encyclopedic works	390	Customs, etiquette, folklore	710	Civic & landscape art
040		**400**	**Language**	720	Architecture
050	General serial publications	401	Linguistics	730	Plastic arts Sculpture
060	General organizations & museology	420	English & Anglo-Saxon	740	Drawing, decorative & minor arts
070	Journalism, publishing, newspapers		languages	750	Painting & paintings
080	General collections	430	Germanic languages German	760	Graphic arts Prints
090	Manuscripts and book rarities	440	Romance languages French	770	Photography & photographs
100	**Philosophy & related disciplines**	450	Italian, Romanian, Rhaeto-	780	Music
110	Metaphysics		Romanic	790	Recreational & performing arts
120	Epistemology, causation, humankind	460	Spanish & Portuguese languages	**800**	**Literature (Belles-lettres)**
130	Paranormal phenomena & arts	470	Italic languages Latin	810	American literature in English
140	Specific philosophical viewpoints	480	Hellenic Classical Greek	820	English & Anglo-Saxon literatures
150	Psychology	490	Other languages	830	Literatures of Germanic languages
160	Logic	**500**	**Pure sciences**	840	Literatures of Romance languages
170	Ethics (Moral philosophy)	510	Mathematics	850	Italian, Romanian, Rhaeto-Romanic
180	Ancient, medieval, Oriental	520	Astronomy & allied sciences	860	Spanish & Portuguese literatures
190	Modern Western philosophy	530	Physics	870	Italic literatures Latin
200	**Religion**	540	Chemistry & allied sciences	880	Hellenic literatures Greek
210	Natural religion	550	Sciences of earth & other worlds	890	Literatures of other languages
220	Bible	560	Paleontology	**900**	**General geography & history**
230	Christian theology	570	Life sciences	910	General geography Travel
240	Christian moral & devotional	580	Botanical sciences	920	General biography & genealogy
250	Local church & religious orders	590	Zoological sciences	930	General history of ancient world
260	Social & ecclesiastical theology	**600**	**Technology (Applied sciences)**	940	General history of Europe
270	History & geography of church	610	Medical sciences	950	General history of Asia
280	Christian denominations & sects	620	Engineering & allied operations	960	General history of Africa
290	Other & comparative religions	630	Agriculture & related technolo-	970	General history of North America
300	**Social sciences**		gies	980	General history of South America
310	Statistics	640	Home economics & family	990	General history of other areas
320	Political science		living		
330	Economics	650	Management & auxiliary services		
340	Law	660	Chemical & related technologies		
350	Public administration	670	Manufactures		

*Consult schedules for complete and exact headings

Example 1: Dewey, Melvil. *The Dewey Classification and Relative Index.* Albany, N.Y.: Forest Press, 1979. Volume 1, page 472.

literature found in the B through V classes. It holds general encyclopedias, dictionaries, indices, fact books, almanacs and directories, as well as general indices to newspapers.

The function of the Z class is to assemble bibliographic listings of works on all aspects of a particular subject when the works that are listed in the bibliography may themselves be widely scattered throughout B to V classes, may not be in the class sequence (non-book formats), or may not be the library.

They are placed at the very end of the classification system so that they may be made readily available in one easily accessible section of the library, not scattered throughout the stacks with the monographs. The Z class published bibliographies work like a kind of index to the material available on a particular subject, rather like an index to a multi-volume work such as an encyclopedia.

Card Catalogs

A card catalog primarily lists a library's book holdings. Serial (journals and periodicals) titles are usually listed but not individual articles or names of authors within them. Each card catalog entry categorizes the book by subject and designates its location in the stacks through a call number. Each card will include where applicable the name of the author or corporate entry, title of the work, date of publication, call number, number of pages, inclusion of bibliography or illustrations, whether the book is part of a series, name of the translator, foreign title, as well as subject headings and tracings or cross references.

As a rule every book held by the library will be represented by several cards filed at designated places in the card catalog. Each card will present basically an

LIBRARY OF CONGRESS CLASSIFICATION SCHEDULES

For sale by the Cataloging Distribution Service, Library of Congress, Building 159, Navy Yard Annex, Washington, D.C. 20541, to which inquiries on current availability and price should be addressed.

A	General Works
B-BJ	Philosophy, Psychology
BL-BX	Religion
C	Auxiliary Sciences of History
D	History: General and Old World (Eastern Hemisphere)
E-F	History: America (Western Hemisphere)
G	Geography. Maps. Anthropology. Recreation
H	Social Sciences
J	Political Science
K	Law (General)
KD	Law of the United Kingdom and Ireland
KE	Law of Canada
KF	Law of the United States
L	Education
M	Music
N	Fine Arts
P-PA	General Philology and Linguistics. Classical Languages and Literatures
PA Supplement	Byzantine and Modern Greek Literature. Medieval and Modern Latin Literature
PB-PH	Modern European Languages
PG	Russian Literature
PJ-PM	Languages and Literatures of Asia, Africa, Oceania, American Indian Languages. Artificial Languages
P-PM Supplement	Index to Languages and Dialects
PN, PR, PS, PZ	General Literature. English and American Literature. Fiction in English. Juvenile Belles Lettres
PQ Part 1	French Literature
PQ Part 2	Italian, Spanish, and Portuguese Literatures
PT Part 1	German Literature
PT Part 2	Dutch and Scandinavian Literatures
Q	Science
R	Medicine
S	Agriculture
T	Technology
U	Military Science
V	Naval Science
Z	Bibliography. Library Science

Example 2: *LC Classification Outline*. 4th ed. Washington, 1978.

identical description of the book; the only difference will be in the top line, which determines where the card will be filed: one card will be filed under the name of the author; one under the title of the work; and one or more will appear under subject headings assigned to correspond to the contents of the book.

The Library of Congress prepares cards for the card catalog of the books it receives, these cards are made available to other institutions for a fee. Usually a library or commercial company will purchase these cards instead of re-cataloging a book. Another source for record retrieval available to participating libraries is the OCLC system. A participating library can check to see if another institution has already catalogued a specific book and use the citation to generate needed records. These forms of card and record generation have assisted in forming a more standardized card catalog system nationwide as well as a vocabulary control system, since the subject headings for the card catalog are selected from the *Library of Congress Subject Headings* (see below). Although Library of Congress catalogers and other catalogers are not experts in all subjects and disagreements may occur, in general the cards are accepted by most institutions.

Often a card will include **tracings**. Each tracing or cross-reference designates other sources of information, and by noting these tracings, the user can locate further information on a chosen subject. It is important to note that in many cases these tracings are not carried over to a library's online catalog system due to cost.

Library of Congress Subject Headings

The *Library of Congress Subject Headings* (LCSH) indicate the specific subject headings used by the Library of Congress and are composed of four large volumes commonly referred to as "the red books." The major function of the LCSH is to create a basic access system to the classification scheme and the vocabulary controlled catalog in order to bring together in systematic and convenient groups the literature of the world, regardless of language. Thus, materials on the same subject that are grouped in only one subject in the stacks can be listed within several subject categories in the library's catalog and can be located and retrieved together *(Example 3)*.

It is important for the researcher to note the wide variety of uses of the LCSH, particularly as a thesaurus type research tool and vocabulary control model for numerous books, indices (including periodical indices), journals, computer databases, government documents, catalogs of special collections, institutions and commercial companies, in particular those that produce indices. Therefore, the LCSHs provide access to search numerous forms of recorded information in an efficient, predictable and systematic way. Reference to the LCSH at the outset of a research project permits location of the most commonly used terms and reveals more avenues of reference, resulting in efficient and time-saving research. The LCSH books are self-explanatory and include a section on directions for use. Particularly useful is the cross-reference system indicated below; if followed, it will reveal multiple access points (symbols).

BT	Broader Topic
NT	Narrower Topic
RT	Related Topic
SA	See also
UF	Used For
(May Subd Geog)	May be subdivided by place and class numbers

Decorative art
  USE   Decoration and ornament
Decorative arts *(May Subd Geog)*
       Here are entered comprehensive works on
       the various art forms having some
       utilitarian as well as decorative purpose,
       including furniture, woodwork, silverware,
       glassware, ceramics, textiles, the decoration
       of buildings, etc.
  UF   Applied arts
       Art industries and trade
       Arts, Applied
       Arts, Decorative
       Arts, Minor
       Minor arts
  BT   Art
  RT   Folk art
  NT   Antiques
       Architect-designed decorative arts
       Art metal-work
       Art objects
       Bamboo work

Calligraphy
Carving (Decorative arts)
Costume
Decoration and ornament
Decoupage
Enamel and enameling
Figurines
Furniture
Glass art
Jewelry
Kewpie art
Lacquer and lacquering
Leather work
Mosaics
Needlework
Porcelain
Pottery
Rosemaling
Tapestry
Textile fabrics
Woodwork

Example 3: *Library of Congress Subject Headings.* 14th ed. Volume 1. Cataloguing Distribution Service. Washington, D.C., 1991.

A brief list of reference tools adapting or using the LSCHs directly follows:

Art Index
Bibliographic Index
Business Index
Business Periodicals Index
Catholic Periodical and Literature Index
Education Index
Essay & General Literature Index
Humanities Index
Industrial Arts Index
Index to Legal Periodicals
Index to U. S. Government Periodicals
InfoTrac
Legal Resource Index
Reader's Guide to Periodical Literature
Magazine Index
Monthly Catalog of U. S. Government Publications
National Newspaper Index
Nineteenth Century Readers Guide
Social Science Index
P. A. I. S. (Public Affairs Information Service)
P. A. I. S. (Public Affairs Information Service) International
Social Science Index
Social Sciences & Humanities Index
All WILSONLINE Indexes and Abstracts & information access indices

Bibliographies

Published bibliographies and indices are the traditional means of gaining detailed access to non-book materials and the holdings of other libraries worldwide. They reveal the existence and contents of journal and periodical articles, government documents, microforms, special collections, and other non-book formats (including computer databases, vertical files, archives, maps, prints, photographs, etc.) that are not shelved in the regular book stacks .

Bibliographic online databases have added a new and important avenue of access to bibliographies, but an online computer search costs money and computer time can be expensive. Therefore, when using these types of searches the researcher should determine exactly what is being sought and have clear and concise queries formulated. Most importantly, the user should become familiar with use of the particular database and its strengths and weaknesses. Many public libraries currently have commercial online services available for a fee, and the librarians usually are familiar with the bibliographic databases and will assist or run searches.

Locating Materials in Other Libraries

A local library and/or online bibliographic database is the best place to start in order to discover what is available on a specific subject, to search holdings of other libraries and special collections, and to request an interlibrary loan. Literature on a particular subject can be identified through the following sources: 1) footnotes and 2) bibliographies in the books located in the card catalog and/or online catalog, 3) the classification scheme, 4) journal indices, 5) subject bibliographies and 6) databases. There are several other good sources for identifying books in an area of interest (these sources do not provide access to special collections, microform collections and government documents and other non-book formats); the most notable include: *Book Review Digest* which has a subject index, *Subject Guide to Books in Print,* the *Cumulative Book Index,* the *BPR Annual Cumulative,* and the *Library of Congress Catalogs: Subject Catalog,* now contained as part of the microfiche *National Union Catalog.*

Determining Who Owns a Copy — Union Lists

A union list records the holdings of more than one library. It is a location device that enables a researcher to determine which libraries actually own a copy of a needed source.

The two basic sources for locating copies of books are the *National Union Catalog* and the *Online Computer Library Center* (OCLC). The *National Union Catalog* (NUC) has two parts, a 754 volume pre-1956 retrospective set and a current, ongoing set that keeps the record up to date, as well as a microform set. The *National Union Catalog Pre-1956* set is an exhaustive listing of everything published worldwide in the Roman, Greek and Gaelic alphabets from the invention of printing through 1955. It is the largest list of books ever compiled, listing seven to nine million items. Over 1,000 research libraries throughout North America reported to the NUC project, with most libraries reporting only what they considered rare or unusual. Exceptions were, the Library of Congress, New York Public Library, University of Chicago, Harvard, Yale and the John Crear Library, which cataloged their complete collections. Since most institutions did not report their entire collections, it is possible that many own copies of the fairly common publications.

NUC is especially valuable to a researcher because it not only cites owners of a copy of a particular book but allows for determination of rarity or desirability of a publication by noting how many institutions own a copy. Anonymous works are arranged by title and all other works are arranged by author. The NUC list includes books; local, state, and federal government documents; foreign government publications; atlases; maps; music scores and printed material; microforms; some manuscripts; some serials and conference proceedings; and annual publications. There are many entries in other languages such as Arabic, Cyrillic, Hebrew, and the various Oriental and Indic languages. Each entry is usually a reproduction of a full card catalog entry including the tracings (subject headings), with the locations listed at the bottom of the entry. The most frequently used symbols are printed on the inside cover of each volume (*Example 4*).

NUC is basically the competitor of OCLC computer system, however, each contains information that is not in the other. OCLC usually provides more locations for each reported item and is more frequently updated. On the other hand the NUC covers many libraries not on the OCLC system, spanning all the libraries in the OCLC, RLIN (*Research Libraries Information Network*), WLN (*Washington Library Network*), and UTLAS (links Canadian libraries) systems.

The *Union List of Serials* and its supplement *New Serial Titles* provide broader coverage of the location of serials and journals than the NUC. A number of specialized union lists also cover journals in particular regions or on particular subjects or formats, as well as union lists of serials of other countries, most of which can be identified with the help of a reference librarian.

Interlibrary Loan Service

Many works can be obtained through the interlibrary loan service. In order to obtain material the book must be located and a loan request filled out. The general information required on the interlibrary loan form includes the full name of the author, title, publishing information and a verification reference such as a NUC or OCLC citation specifying the location of the book. The completed request is then sent to the lending library. It usually takes two to three weeks to receive the books requested. Recently this service has become more restricted due to library budget constraints.

Government Documents

Most researchers are not aware of the range, variety and depth of material published by the federal government or that copies of federal documents are widely available throughout the U. S. at approximately 1,400 regional or selective library depositories, with a list of these depositories available at most public libraries.[2]

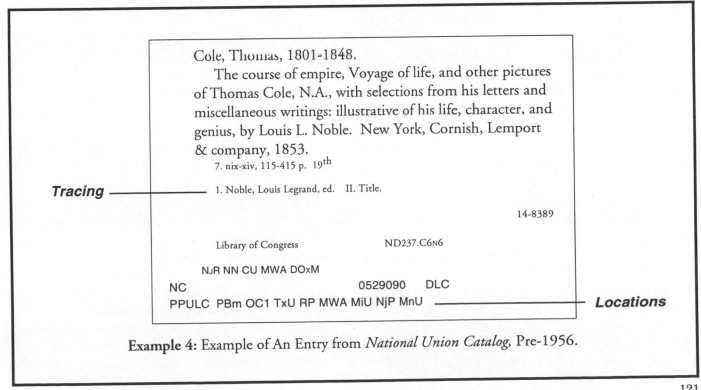

Example 4: Example of An Entry from *National Union Catalog*, Pre-1956.

This lack of awareness is primarily due to the following factors: the government does not advertise these publications, government documents are shelved separately in libraries; most librarians have little experience with access to, or the content of and potential use of these documents, and these materials are not covered in most indices or catalogs and are not sold in book stores.

There are two types of government document collections: regional depositories and selective depositories. Regional depositories are required by law to receive and permanently retain copies of all federal documents available through the depository program. Selective depositories can choose which categories of publications they wish to acquire and are not required to keep all the documents received. For instance, law school libraries usually are selective depositories confining their selection to law-related materials.

To locate regional or other depositories for federal, state, or local documents as well as the United Nations or other international and foreign documents in the United States, refer to *Directory of Government Documents Collections and Libraries* (CIS, revised irregularly). Its arrangement is first by state, then city; and it is particularly good for subject collections.

An extensive list of recently published government documents, some of which pertain to personal property, is listed in the review section of *Art Documentation,* the *Bulletin of the Art Libraries Society of North America* (ARLIS), published quarterly.

Systematic research in government documents requires the use of a combination of publications since each of the principal references has certain limitations. A good source listing these publications as well as other guides to government documents is *A Guide to Research Methods* by Thomas Mann. Following is a brief list of principal references: 1) *Monthly Catalog of U.S. Government Publications* referred to as the MOCat, is the basic index to government documents. It is intended to be a complete list, with cumulated annual indices to all federal publications; 2) As previously mentioned, a cumulative approach to local, state and federal documents through corporate author or agency name is provided in the *National Union Catalog Pre-1956* volumes 606-624; 3) Several other indices and catalogs for historical approaches are discussed in *Introduction to United States Public Documents,* 3rd edition, (Libraries Unlimited, 1983) by Joe Morehead; 4) The most comprehensive index to all congressional publications since 1970, including hearings, committee reports and House and Senate reports is the *CIS Index* (Washington: Congressional Information Service, Inc., 1970+; published monthly with annual five year cumulations). These reports often provide a kind of overview that is seldom available in any other form because Congress traditionally assembles top experts and the most interested parties on all sides of an issue to testify. These reports can often be particularly insightful and often include extensive documentary appended material.[3]

Searching Computer Generated Information Systems

There are four basic kinds of online computer searches: location searches, bibliographic searches, full text searches and library catalog searches. Most of these computer searches are available only through commercial services except for the online library catalog.

Location Searches such as OCLC and RLIN serve as book or journal location devices; they can tell which libraries in the country own a copy of the work being sought. OCLC can be searched by author or title, but it cannot be searched by subject. RLIN has wider searching capabilities. It can be searched by name, title, subject phrase or subject words and Boolean logic and with its subject access to millions of records is extraordinarily useful for getting quick leads on available materials in sources of familiar scholarly territory. Most libraries use either OCLC or RLIN, and each is available privately for a fee.

Bibliographic Online Database Searches are specialized searches through commercial systems such as Dialog, SDC, or BRS. They produce printouts of bibliographic citations on any subject, often with abstracts. Other online databases include the Library of Congress online catalogs *LC MARC* and *REMARC,* which can be searched via *Internet.*

Full Text Searches are available only through commercial companies; they can retrieve whole articles, reports, or tabular data rather than just citations to them.

Online Library Card Catalog Searches are searches using online catalogs of a particular library, providing bibliographic citations to some materials held by the institution. They contain computer records in machine-readable form of a portion of a library's collection. It is expensive for a library to enter all their holdings into an online system, and usually start-up and cut-off dates are determined for the online and card catalog files. Additionally, most of the following holdings will not be entered into either catalog: individual chapters of books, journal and magazine articles; newspaper articles; review articles; research reports; U. S. government documents; manuscripts and maps; microforms; photographs; print and document collections; posters; motion pictures; sound recordings; sheet music; vertical files; and archival materials. Since no one source lists all of a library's holdings, it is advisable to ask the librarian specifically what information is not included in the online catalog and card catalogs and how these other sources can be located.

There are more than one type of online catalog system utilized by libraries; instructions are fairly simple and usually are located next to each computer station. Searching is by author, title, subject, and can sometimes be refined to include Boolean logic, which is the method of using the words AND, OR and NOT to refine a search. AND links two ideas; OR expands a search, meaning that either of the two or more words and or phrases selected are acceptable; NOT narrows or limits a search, signifying that if a particular term or phrase is included in the search query, the computer will ignore that specific citation.

Advantages and Disadvantages of Computer Searching

The advantages of computer searches are that they allow keyword access to records otherwise available only through subject headings and that they allow for post-coordinate Boolean combinations of two or more different subjects that have not previously been cross-referenced in a vocabulary controlled subject heading. Beyond that, it is important to be aware that online searches do not provide access to **all** information; in fact, they have distinct disadvantages as well as advantages. Their ability to combine subjects can sometimes be matched or superseded by other, more conventional approaches. In brief, computer searches are a very powerful resource for researchers, but they are one resource among many and are by no means always are the best resource for particular inquiries.

In general, computer generated databases will be more current than printed forms, but most probably will not cover information that was recorded before the inception of a particular database. Therefore, it is best to check the earliest date and type of coverage for each particular database, CD-ROM and printed form, because often a combination of types will need to be searched. Generally speaking if there is a need to locate material that is 10 to 15 years old or older, that information may not be available from computer sources.

Locating Computer Information Systems

Following is a listing of some of the principal database directories cited in *Library Research Methods* by Thomas Mann.

1) *Database Directory* (Knowledge Industry Publications and the American Society for Information Sciences; irregular), covers 1800 files with an index by subject; 2) *Computer-readable Databases: A Directory and Data Sourcebook* (Knowledge Industry Publications, for the American Society for Information Sciences; biennial) covers 700 databases, with subject index; 3) *Online Bibliographic Databases: A Directory and Sourcebook* (Gale Research; revised irregularly), covers about 180 files; 4) *Encyclopedia of Information Systems and Services* (Gale Research; revised irregularly), describes about 1500 databases, including gateway(s) to which most libraries subscribe.[4]

Types of Research Models

Research models have been developed in order to organize access to recorded knowledge in a systematic and predictable way. To implement a model or plan a research approach it is important that one learn the "framework" of library research and the method of applying it to projects within a discipline. Research materials need to be looked at functionally, and an understanding of how they fit together and why they look the way they do is necessary. If the researcher only understands one way of using and searching books and research materials, he will be lost when faced with a question outside of his area of expertise and will not be able to efficiently determine where to enter the research system in order to obtain the required information.

Each type of model has the tendency to conceal as well as reveal information and to limit the range of questions that can be asked. Thus, it is crucial to define each study and formulate all queries. There are a number of different models available by which one can attempt to understand and structure the "avenues of access." However, some model or plan is necessary; otherwise one will get lost in the maze of available information.

Because knowledge of the most commonly used research models will help the researcher plan an overall approach and because a combination of models is usually the most efficient and diligent approach to a research question, the following models will be discussed: 1) the subject or discipline model, 2) types of literature model, 3) library science model, 4) published bibliographies and indices based model, 5) computer workstation and 6) methods of searching model.

Subject/Discipline Model

The subject or discipline model is based on the fact that each discipline has specialized lists of research materials which are essential to its study and which form the foundation to its working bibliography. It is one of the most popular models and has distinct advantages, particularly in its depth of access, since it typically includes sources of primary interest that would be difficult to locate through other models. However, there are limitations to this model. The most apparent limitation is that it has the tendency to become outdated; but more important is the shortcoming that it does not convey the principles of searching that can be used in any situation or discipline. Consequently, it does not give the researcher the power to locate and predict the existence of other sources because it does not reveal works of interest that frequently appear outside of a discipline.

Type of Literature Model

The type of literature model is based on the fact that there are certain types of literature that can reasonably and predictably be expected to exist in all subject areas. It is primarily a method for categorizing reference sources, not monographs. The advantage of this model is that it enables the researcher to see beyond a specific list of recommended sources to the predictable similarities among reference sources. If a researcher has the foreknowledge of the range of types of literature and an understanding of the kinds of questions that each type is best at answering, he will be able to move with confidence from any subject discipline.

Some of the same disadvantages apply to both the subject discipline model and the type of literature model. The primary disadvantage of each is that lists of sources arranged by subject or by type of literature do not convey "principles" of searching that can be used in any situation. Nor can either predict the existence of other sources that would answer a question when the sources on a given list are insufficient. Additionally, each is often conceived as a book of lists.

A selected list of some of the different types of literature follow, most of which are self-explanatory[5]:

Almanacs
Atlases
Bibliographies
Catalogs
Auction catalogs[6]
Trade (dealer) catalogs
Exhibition catalogs
Chronologies
Computer databases
Dictionaries
Encyclopedias
Festschriften [7]
Handbooks and manuals
Guides to literature
Indexes and abstracts
Patents, periodical union lists
Newsletters
Review articles/criticism
Treatises
Union lists for books
Yearbooks
Serials
Periodicals/journals/magazines
Government documents
Biographical sources
Conference proceedings
Archival resources/materials
Visual aids[8]
Pictorial archives
Photographs
Prints
Slide collections
Microform collections
Microfiche and microfilm

Traditional Library of Science Model

The traditional library of science model is based on knowledge of the Library of Congress classification scheme, the vocabulary controlled catalog, published bibliographies and indices and the *Library of Congress Subject Headings* (LCSH). The main advantages of this model are that the four schemes are closely linked and complement each other and that the LCSH is used in many other types of literature, references, and formats. Once the researcher has a thorough understanding of these systems he should be able to locate most information in an efficient and predictable manner. The main limitation to this model is that the classification scheme is designed primarily for books and neglects non-book formats such as journal articles, unclassified research reports, newspapers, microforms, government documents, photographs and prints, as well as sound recordings, online databases and CD-ROMs, manuscripts, motion pictures, maps, etc.

Computer Workstation Model

The computer workstation model relies primarily on commercial bibliographic computer systems and retrieval services. These services generally offer over 300 different databases. Each database is a file of information, usually of bibliographic citations to journal articles or research reports in a particular subject area, stored in machine-readable form. There is considerable overlap in files among the three major vendors: 1) Dialog Information Services, 2) System Development Corporation (SDC) which offers a service known as Orbit, and 3) Bibliographic Retrieval Services (BRS). The broadest range is provided by Dialog.

The advantage of a computer search is that it enables the user to quickly scan thousands of citations in any subject area at one time. The user in most cases then can generate a printed bibliography, and in some cases abstracts of articles are available. Because computer time can be expensive, one should be aware that many databases are exactly the same as the conventional printed index. Therefore it is advisable to check with a reference librarian to find out if the database needed is also available in other forms and if there are any differences in the hard copy as compared to the database or CD-ROM. Often there are only insignificant differences between the database and the printed form of the index. The most common differences are 1) online databases are usually more current, and 2) all other information included is relatively recent, whereas printed forms are available in earlier issues.

Methods of Searching Model

The methods of searching model is a conceptual model based on types of searches rather than solely generating needed information based on a subject/discipline, types of literature, traditional library science or the computer workstation model. Some of the advantages of this model include: 1) each of the ways of searching is applicable in any subject area, 2) searches are not confined to any one language, and 3) each type of search complements and balances the others. This model, designed by Thomas Mann, is based on eight different methods of searching knowledge records, and in order to be effective usually all eight ways of searching need to be utilized. These eight methods include: 1) controlled vocabulary searches in printed sources; 2) keyword searches in manual printed sources; 3) citation searches in printed sources; 4) searches through published bibliographies (including sets of footnotes in relevant subject documents; 5) searches through people sources; 6) computer searches, which can be done by subject heading, classification number, key word, or citation, but which add the possibility of post coordinate Boolean combinations while often limiting coverage; (7) related record searching (available only through three particular CD-ROM databases); (8) systematic browsing, especially of full-text sources arranged in predictable subject groupings.[9]

Footnote chasing locates previous sources to those earlier writings cited by the author of the work in hand. Citation searching locates subsequent articles, those written after the date of the work in hand and which cite it as a footnote. If a researcher already has a good source, he can use it for citation searching to generate a list of more recent literature that refers to the initial source. Related record searching enables one to search sideways in time (articles published within the same year) to find related articles published simultaneously. This type of search is available only on the CD-ROM versions of the following citation indices: 1) *Social Science Citation Index,* 2) *Arts & Humanities Citation Index,* and 3) *Science Citation Index.* Keyword searching allows the searcher to locate only a particular word or phrase; it is a limited form of access because it does not cross reference, search synonyms or related topics. In summary, footnote searching allows one to go back in time from the work in hand; citation searching allows one to go forward in time from the work in hand; related record searching allows one to search within the same time period as the work in hand; and keyword searching limits the search to a particular word or phrase.

Defining the Study

A necessary first step in any research project is distinguishing what is important from what is not. Once the necessary issues have been extracted and it has been determined exactly what is being sought, the next step is to decide what type of questions must be answered. Are they reference questions or research questions? Reference questions are those seeking specific factual data; they have specific answers. For instance, these answers can usually be located in "fact" books, such as almanacs, chronologies, biographical encyclopedias and sales indices. For this type of question the types of literature model is the most effective and these books are usually located in the 000s class in Dewey scheme and the A class in the Library of Congress scheme. A research question is an open ended inquiry that does not have a simple "correct" answer. The methods model is the most effective for most research questions.

Once the questions have been broken down and the specific goals have been determined, an approach can be selected and the various systems can be exploited. This means knowing where to effectively enter the research system, which can save the researcher grief, time and money.

Since individual judgments and practices differ, the researcher must decide what research process makes sense and which system works best for the particular subject and circumstances. But in order to decide on an approach to any research question the following points have been prescribed by Thomas Mann. They should be considered in any working model. A research model or approach should have the capabilities to perform the following functions: 1) has the power to predict the existence of likely sources; 2) is a systematic means to retrieve all sources outside a resource list or "subject" discipline list; 3) promotes cross-disciplinary research and does not concentrate on a particular type of literature/data (book or non-book formats); 4) allows for multiple access points and depth of access through cross references and tracings; 5) informs the researcher of types of literature available to search in a particular field; 6) is adaptable to all subjects and levels of research.

Time Management

Time management is a specific part of the research process. The researcher should plan how much time to allocate to each part of the research process and should set goals to make the whole process easier. If the questions have been defined, allowing a time budget to be set, then the research will be both efficient and effective and the results will be improved. Often a combination of models will need to be utilized to produce the desired results.

One of the things not generally considered at the outset of research but which should be stressed is how to judge when the research process should be stopped. The researcher is ultimately responsible for making the judgment as to when the research process can successfully be stopped. Devising "stop rules" is an important element. The following "stop" determinants are suggested as logical criteria for ending a search: 1) when the same information is being retrieved in each publication without the addition of new information; 2) when enough sources have been read to determine the consensus of opinion and knowledge on the subject; 3) when the effort of the search is a greater investment than the

yielded result. The practiced researcher in a specific area gains a sense of completeness and can judge wisely when a research task is complete.

The truly creative act is not locating materials but reading and synthesizing them. After the research process the following points should be considered when assembling a report: 1) remember that not everything published is correct; 2) gather and study as many of the facts as possible and then try to ascertain which are correct and reliable; 3) find someone who has previously done the work; in other words, determine who is the expert and what are considered definitive sources; 4) check and verify information; 5) do not plagiarize; 6) distinguish between primary data, secondary data and tertiary data. Primary data is first hand information, such as eyewitness accounts, letters and diaries, personal interviews and original works such as drawings. Secondary data is indirectly derived information which is provided by authors who have examined the subject and have come to certain conclusions concerning it. These persons have studied the primary data but have not experienced the event, created the work, nor been the writers of letters or diaries. Tertiary data/literature consists of reference works such as dictionaries, encyclopedias, handbooks, indices, etc.; they are usually assembled from numerous secondary and tertiary data, seldom from primary data.

Endnotes

1. *LC Classification Outline.* 4th ed. (Library of Congress, 1978): 1.

2. The local library was checked for the government publication listing government depositories. It was found that this publication was not listed in the online catalog. A 1984 copy of the pamphlet was located in the vertical files. This pamphlet only lists the depositories; it does not contain any information on government depositories themselves and it does not differentiate between regional and selective depositories.

3. Mann, Thomas. *Library Research Models, A Guide to Classification, Cataloguing and Computers.* (New York: Oxford University Press, 1993), 143-145.

4. Mann, Thomas. *A Guide to Library Research Methods* (New York: Oxford University Press, 1987), 101.

5. For definitions of the types of literature listed below refer to *Library Research Models, A Guide to Classification, Cataloguing and Computers* by Thomas Mann, (New York: Oxford University Press, 1993), 59-62. See also by Thomas Mann, *A Guide to Research*

Methods, (New York: Oxford University Press, 1987), 155-157. For further reference see Lois Swan Jones *Art Research Methods and Resources, A Guide to Finding Art Information*, 2nd. ed.), 15-36.

6. A thorough union list essentially does not exist for auction catalogs. The closest list would be SCIPIO which is part of the RLIN database. For a comprehensive article discussing sources of auction sales information see, "The Cutting Edge: New Auction Sources and Computer Projects" by Caroline Backlund, in *Art Documentation, the Bulletin of the Art Libraries Society of North America*. (Washington, D.C.: National Gallery of Art, Winter 1990), 175-178.

7. *Festschriften* is a collection of essays written in honor of a well-known person or institution. For most works, the individual essays in each volume is indexed separately in an ongoing publication called *Essay and General Literature index* (H.W. Wilson, 1900-) which provides and author subject approach and the subject terms it assigns are generally the same list as the LCSH used by the card catalog. There is a separate volume works indexed 1900-1969. *Festschriften* can be located through DIALOG and LC MARC.

8. For information regarding the range and types of microforms available, see *Art Research Methods and Resources, A Guide to Finding Art Information*, 2nd. ed. by Lois Swan Jones. See pp. 22 and 194 for exhibition catalogs on microfiche.

9. Mann, Thomas. *Library Research Models, A Guide to Classification, Cataloguing and Computers*. (New York, Oxford University Press, 1993), 156-157.

Selected Bibliography

Backlund, Caroline, "The Cutting Edge: New Auction Sources and Computer Projects." *Art Documentation, the Bulletin of the Art Libraries Society of North America*, Winter (1990): 175-178. Washington, D.C.: National Gallery of Art.

Jones, Lois Swan. *Art Research Methods and Resources, A Guide to Finding Art Information*. 2nd ed. Dubuque, Iowa: Kendall/Hunt Publications, 1984.

Mann, Thomas. *A Guide to Library Research Methods*. New York: Oxford University Press, 1987.

Mann, Thomas. *Library Research Models , A Guide to Classification, Cataloguing and Computers*. New York: Oxford University Press, 1993.

Patrick, Stephen and Patrick Allan. "Legal Resources in Art: A Bibliographic Strategy." *Art References Services Quarterly*. Vol. 1, No. 1, (1993): 63-83.

Ross, Barbara and Amanda Bowen. "Breaking Old Boundaries: Developing a Bibliography for the New Art History." *Art References Services Quarterly*. Vol. 1, No. 2, (1993): 37-51.

Electronic Information Resources for the Personal Property Appraiser

NOTE: The rapidly changing character of the computer and peripherals market requires that services, features, costs and contacts be researched for applicability and currency before determining which products best fit an individual's needs. The following information is not designed to be an inclusive listing, nor does mention of a specific product or service constitute an endorsement by the American Society of Appraisers.

From the beginning of recorded history, research on any subject was done manually, visually and mentally skimming through volumes of written information, and gathering together relevant material. When the researcher felt that sufficient data had been assembled, the evaluation process began. In the 1960's, the first computer-accessed databases for the general public appeared on the market, containing huge amounts of bibliographical and statistical data that could be searched for specific information with immediate results. The arrival of this new technology was to change forever the way in which information is gathered. The following discourse will investigate many of the databases and other electronic information resources available on the market today that may be utilized by the personal property appraiser.

As the profession of personal property appraising evolves and matures, the need for better access to information is imperative. Most professionals in the field have assembled large personal libraries. These professionals have also become very familiar with accessing both public and private libraries where knowledge of valuable indices, catalogues, periodicals, and the intricacies of interlibrary loan systems is fundamental. Being adept at research is essential to a personal property appraiser's business but the Electronic Information Age is here, and the professional appraiser is not going to be allowed to continue doing business in the traditional way.

According to Michael J. McCarthy, author of *Mastering the Information Age*, there is now too much information available with no time to process it all. It's not simply a matter of inefficient use of one's time. More new information has become available in the last 30 years than in all of the previous 5,000. Fifty thousand books and ten thousand periodicals are published every year in the United States alone. One issue of the *New York Times* (substitute *Maine Antique Digest*) contains more information than the average person of the sixteenth century would have confronted in his entire lifetime. This overwhelming explosion of accessible information is comparable in magnitude to that of the invention of the printing press.

In applying due diligence, and considering the massive amounts of data available on any given subject, the question is how to gather together all relevant information and then how to isolate only the information that is significant to the valuation question. The appraiser of today must develop the ability to research, access, and retrieve information from a worldwide community of sources. The vehicle to these sources is the computer.

Electronic Information

Anyone using the public library system today is aware of many changes happening there. Many metropolitan public libraries now have computer terminal stations that may be used by the general public in lieu of searching the card catalog. University libraries often have large databanks such as *Dialog* and *WILSONLINE* available to their students. The profession of "Librarian" is growing into an instructional position in the process of electronic as well as manual research, rather than simply as a provider of information.

Electronic information includes the sum of many library collections that are worldwide in scope. Research is not limited to the resources of one's local library. Electronic research is not a replacement for manual research, but is a more sophisticated tool for the mechanical parts of the research process. When electronic research and manual research are compared, the importance of knowing how to access both types of information gathering is apparent. The preliminary amassing of all relevant data is where electronic information is so valuable. As much as 80% of the time given to a research project can be spent in searching out and locating specific information, while the remaining 20% is spent in classifying, organizing, and evaluating what has been located. It is inefficient use of time to drive to the public library, thumb through several issues of *Reader's Guide* and *Art Index*, stand in line to use a microform reader, or wait for the use of a copier. These tasks can be accomplished without leaving the office through telephone wires connected to a computer. In many cases bibliographic citations, abstracts and even full text from periodicals can be printed out on the office printer.

In five years, there will be twice as much knowledge available in the humanities field as there is today. Staying current will require new skills in selective research. Before the development of automated systems of storage and retrieval, the search process could take hours or days. This can now be accomplished in minutes through the use of online databases which, by their very nature, are more comprehensive and up-to-date than printed sources.

Types of Computers

There are three types of computers. A main frame computer is a permanently installed, massive storage system. This is the type of computer used by Dialog Information Services, providers of biographical and statistical information from hundreds of databases to clients worldwide. A mini-computer is smaller, moveable by two individuals, and may be used by the local department store, for example, to process its daily accounts. The focus of this discussion is the micro-computer, portable by one individual, and capable of handling the needs of the average personal property appraiser. The micro-computer contains a memory and can process, organize and modify information. It can store and retrieve data instantly, and can "talk" to other computers.

The standard language through which computers exchange information is a series of on/off switches. Each letter of the alphabet and symbol of punctuation has an eight digit binary code which is understood by other computers. The sketch on the next page shows how this process works when one computer is "talking" to another computer.

Databases

A database is a large collection of information related to a specific topic in a machine-readable format. It is comparable to a "reference book" that has been placed on a computer disk, but with one important difference. This "book" can locate specific information with a few simple keystrokes on the computer keyboard. It ignores all irrelevant data therein, and brings to the computer screen all pertinent references being requested immediately. Once the required information has been located, all time and energy can be given to interpretation and evaluation of the found materials. There are approximately five thousand databases presently on the market, covering almost every conceivable subject, with an estimated three new databases appearing every day.

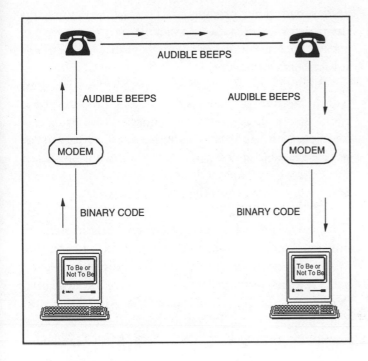

AUDIBLE BEEPS

AUDIBLE BEEPS   AUDIBLE BEEPS

MODEM   MODEM

BINARY CODE   BINARY CODE

To Be or Not To Be   To Be or Not To Be

What Can Databases Do?

Online databases have many benefits, their biggest being the time factor previously mentioned. Other benefits include:

• **The ability to get results with only partial information.** Sculptor "Daro ??ood" was found immediately in WILSONLINE's online database, *Art Index*.. A simple search produced all information on any artist with the unusual first name "Daro".

• **Obscure information is more easily found online..** Daro Flood, Arizona (1954-) was not listed in the usual places (*Who's Who, Benezit*, etc.) He was, however, interviewed in *Southwest Art Magazine* in 1984. Acknowledgment of this was immediately forthcoming from the WILSONLINE database search. Manual searching of the printed copies of *Art Index* would have been a long and difficult task, not to mention the possibility of no results if printed copies had not been searched back through 1984.

• **Online database information is never misplaced, out on loan, or stolen..** Unless there is a serious disruption in telephone service, the information is always available. It never deteriorates and can be shared simultaneously.

• **Most data online is updated frequently.** There is no lost time for manual printing and distribution. *Art Index* is updated twice a week online, every three months in the printed version. Some newspapers are updated daily.

• **Database and databank services have online support systems as well as toll-free numbers.** Assistance can be reached verbally to help with the search process.

• **Information in other languages has been translated.** Databanks, such as *Questel*, translate languages as difficult as Sanskrit and Mandarin into English and French.

• **Related information is suggested through the use of descriptor or key words.** Searching for information on "brilliant cut glass" in the *America: History and Life* database led to other valuable information indexed under "brilliant period glass," "cut glass," "Corning," and "table glass," all descriptor terms included in citations found under "brilliant cut glass."

What Can't Databases Do?

As exciting as this new form of data retrieval appears to be, there are some difficulties to be addressed. A significant problem is a psychological resistance to learning new ways of investigative research. Just as the coming of the printing press promised knowledge for every man, if he knew how to read and could pay for new books, electronic information promises a wealth of knowledge if one can learn how to "read" it and can pay for it.

Because computerized information is a new technology, there are inconsistencies and differences between suppliers that must be faced. A commonalty in usage of all electronic information systems is slowly beginning to develop. Until recently, each database vendor chose to program his system according to his own needs and knowing how to search one database did not automatically mean that every other database could be searched in the same way. Just as major computer manufactures have pulled computer hardware into reasonable compatibility, so too have databanks. They provide multi-database service to the public through the development of a common system.

The search process chosen can also influence results. As with all new skills, a vocabulary must be learned. If the researcher is not familiar with the use of a computer or the databases being searched, the results can be very poor. Not being able to type is a hindrance, and people with a subconscious distrust of mechanical devices may find this new technology difficult.

By far the most significant problem, however, is the cost of electronic data. Each database vendor must be paid for his services; databanks must be reimbursed for the brokering activities they provide, and telephone tolls are an integral part of the cost. Many databanks provide a toll-free number, but there is a surcharge added to the bill for this convenience.

Finally, because this technology is relatively new, start-up costs for the vendor are very high. Several useful databases have disappeared from the marketplace. The cost for their development and upkeep is more than database users are willing to pay. For example, *Art Link*, *Artlist*, *FaxThom*, and *Australian Art Index* are some that were recently disbanded. It is expected that databases with limited clientele will have difficulty staying online until the cost of producing a database decreases.

Types of Databases

Databases are offered in four formats: full text, bibliographic, statistical and directory.

Full text databases are citations taken verbatim from the printed source. *American Heritage* is an example of a full text database.

Bibliographic databases constitute most of the available databases in the humanities field at the present time. Bibliographic indices contain all the information normally found in a card catalog entry, as well as indexing terms (sometimes called descriptors or keywords) which refer to other possible search terms. Short summaries, or abstracts, are often included as well. *Arts and Humanities Search* is a bibliographic database indexing to over 1,300 leading arts and humanities journals

Statistical databases are useful to the personal property appraiser for the valuation part of reports. A statistical database such as *ArtQuest*, offered by Art Sales Index, Ltd., provides auction results of over 600,000 works of art since 1970.

Directory databases are full text of printed directories. *Marquis' Who's Who* is considered a directory database.

Databanks

Subscribing to each individual database of interest would be too cumbersome and expensive. Large databanks, sometimes called "information utilities" offer a wide selection of databases. The major databanks of interest to the appraiser are: Dialog Information Services, BRS (Bibliographic Research Services), WILSONLINE, RLIN (The Research Library Information Network), OCLC (Online Computer Library Center), and Questel.

Dialog Information Service, Inc., is by far the largest with approximately 450 databases. To help their users become proficient with the system, Dialog offers inexpensive training workshops held throughout the country and abroad. They provide free access time online and their customer assistance is available twenty-four hours a day. Dialog continues to grow with over 220,000 subscribers worldwide.

Bibliographic Research Services (BRS) has less than half the number of Dialog's databases. BRS offers some of the databases that are most requested on Dialog at a lower cost. BRS also offers BRS After Dark, an easy to use service available after 6 p.m., with significant savings in cost. Dialog's comparable after hours service is called Knowledge Index and offers savings as well.

WILSONLINE, a product of the H.W. Wilson Company, is a well known name in library reference indices. *Reader's Guide to Periodical Literature* , *Art Index, Biography Index*, etc., are the starting point for many research projects. WILSONLINE is less expensive than Dialog or BRS (excluding BRS After Dark and Knowledge Index). All WILSONLINE databases have recently been added to BRS, BRS After Dark, and OCLC.

The Research Libraries Information Network (RLIN), owned and operated by the Research Libraries Group is an online system that provides access to more than 100 research libraries, historical societies, museums, and archival repositories worldwide. Representing materials in more than 350 languages, RLIN is a database for serious researchers, and also describes works cataloged by the Library of Congress, Government Printing Office, and the British National Bibliography Library.

The Library of Congress Information System has recently become available to the researcher through computer terminals located in the James Madison Memorial Building in Washington, D.C. and through RLIN. This information system includes SCORPIO (Subject Content-oriented Retriever for Processing Information Online), which contains five types of files: all books cataloged by the Library of Congress (LCC) since 1968; selected periodical articles since 1976; federal legislation since 1973; copyright registrations since 1978; and a listing of organizations doing research or providing information to the public. For people who are not in the Washington D.C. area or do not have online connections with RLIN, LCC's MARC Search Service is a fee based program whose library staff provides bibliographic listings in printed form or on magnetic tape upon request.

Questel is a French databank service, with worldwide information databases. Questel's *Francis* is an arts and humanities index. *Francis* includes books, periodi-

OCLC's *ERIC* system, a list of state, regional, national and international libraries containing the required materials may be obtained by the researcher, who is then able to seek them out from the nearest facility.

All six databanks have an initial set-up fee and/or charge a usage fee based on the amount of time connected to the service. A fifteen minute search of approximately five topics, using a database like WILSONLINE's *Biography Index* of 2,700 periodicals, could result in ten or more usable bibliographic citations. These citations are commonly known as "hits." While the average connect time is normally less than fifteen minutes, other costs such as telecommunication charges, display charges, subscription fees, and account maintenance fees can be added to the usage fee and the cost escalates.

Proximity Searches

Dialindex, a database on Dialog contains only index files from other databases on the system. By beginning with Dialindex, the user can see which databases contain information on the topic he is seeking. This saves him the cost of entering a database only to produce zero hits for his efforts. Dialindex indicates how many times the search term is offered in any given database. Just as citation descriptors in a card catalog help suggest other paths for finding information on a subject, so too does Dialindex help the searcher find pertinent information in areas he might not ordinarily pursue. Again, the immediacy of the responses is what makes electronic searches so valuable.

Clipping Services

Most of the larger vendors provide a clipping service. Subscribers can request that all current newspaper and magazine articles on a specific topic be saved and sent to them either by telecommunications or by mail. In this way, the user is automatically aware of the latest information on his subject as it becomes available.

Gateways

Another way to search electronically is through "umbrella" information companies who carry a potpourri of general interest services such as entertainment and games, weather, sports, shopping and travel divisions, as well as research information. Called gateways, these mega-information systems provide access to many databanks.

CompuServe offers IQUEST with databanks *Dialog, BRS, WILSONLINE, NewsNet,* and *Orbit* (a scientific and technical databank). The researcher need not be a subscriber to each databank individually. IQUEST has been configured to help guide the casual user through the process with little pain. In addition to online database time charges, a fee of nine dollars per search is charged for this brokerage. Support is available around the clock. If problems arise while online, the user can type "SOS" and a customer service representative will come online and assist. CompuServe has a nominal start-up fee and is a viable way to learn the basics of electronic research.

Library Access

State and university libraries have begun to provide their patrons with online systems for locating library materials. Once the researcher has identified the materials needed, the library's computerized card catalog can be accessed from an office terminal. The ability to call up libraries with online card catalog searching systems makes it possible to browse through a library's collection without going through stacks or manually flipping through card catalogs. One can immediately check to see if the materials being sought are part of the collection or are on order, where they are physically located, and whether or not they circulate. Information on whether the materials have been loaned out, removed from circulation for repairs, etc., can be obtained without burdening the reference librarian or waiting on hold while someone does the searching. Armed with the necessary information, the researcher can then decide on a plan of action for obtaining what is needed. If the works are part of the library's collection but unavailable for loan, the next step may be to request photocopies. Photocopies may be obtained from a database vendor or through the library's interlibrary loan service. Just as in database systems, computerized card catalogs are adept at finding materials with only partial information. Other benefits are immediate access, simultaneous sharing with other searchers, and descriptor terms suggesting other possible avenues of finding desired information.

Many large public and university libraries also provide access to Dialog, OCLC, RLIN, etc., either free of charge or for a small pass-on fee.

Document Delivery

Newspaper and magazine articles can be located at the local library or requested through interlibrary loan. All databanks and gateways have online document ordering services and articles may be ordered immediately during the database search or by telephone at a later date. Dialog, for example, allows the user to choose from eighty suppliers: UMI Article Clearinghouse provides full text document delivery on 10,000 popular, scholarly, and technical journals, magazines, newspapers and government documents; Servicing EasyNet, OCLC, Dialog, and BRS, UMI will send the requested information by fax or by same day, overnight, or first class mail; UMI will photocopy and bind over 100,000 out-of-print books.

Electronic Bulletin Boards

Computer bulletin board systems (BBSs) are available in every local calling area in the United States. Most are run as a hobby by people called "SysOps", who donate their time and equipment to provide a forum for the exchange of ideas and public domain software. Anyone with the necessary equipment can send and receive free messages. Bulletin boards are an excellent way to develop expertise in the mechanics of electronic communications and can provide valuable services to their subscribers. Some bulletin boards are restricted to membership and may also be money making enterprises. CompuServe's National Bulletin Board, for example, offers a place to post wanted, for sale and classified listings for purchase, trade or barter nationwide. A listing of local bulletin boards can usually be found at the public library or through local computer clubs.

Electronic Mail

While facsimile machines are becoming quite popular for the immediate transmission of printed materials, it is possible to send and receive documents through electronic mail services offered by gateway companies and nationwide bulletin boards. This service, called E-Mail, will connect two computer terminals at different locations. Messages or entire documents may be logged in and retrieved at the convenience of the receiver. E-Mail can also connect a terminal with a fax machine, or send a subscriber's transmission through a system much like Western Union's process of sending telegrams. E-Mail is an extremely fast, efficient, and low cost way to send messages or data.

Sales Data Sources

Of particular importance to the personal property appraiser is the fact that auction and gallery sales information is provided by a growing number of sales data services.

ArtQuest, a product of Art Sales Index, Ltd., of England has been known for many years as a primary source for online art sales information. ArtQuest con-

tains sales results on 600,000 works of art by 100,000 artists, sold at auction throughout the world since 1970. Complete details of each picture or piece of sculpture, the artist's name, dates, and nationality are given. Analysis of sales prices showing the highest, lowest and average prices, as well as total sale and price trends are posted there. This database can handle uncertain spellings, is up-dated weekly, and contains a register of stolen pictures. ArtQuest is online twenty four hours a day, seven days a week.

Art Sales Index also offers information to people without computer terminals. ASI's Enquiry Service handles requests for information by fax or telephone.

SCIPIO (Sales Catalog Index Project Input Online) is produced by Research Libraries Group, Inc., of California. Available through RLIN, SCIPIO is a union list of approximately 95,000 auction catalogs dating from the year 1599. The information has been taken from catalog covers only. Updated daily, these records of fine and decorative arts pieces sold in Europe and the United States contain the date and place of the sale, a listing of the items in the sale, and where the sales catalog can be located. SCIPIO also includes announcements of upcoming auction sales throughout Europe and the United States. Photocopies can be requested from RLIN or through interlibrary loan services.

Artfact, a new CD-ROM product developed with the personal property appraiser in mind is a compilation of 475,000 recent auction records from large and small auction houses throughout the United States and Europe. This database reports everything from Impressionist watercolors to baseball cards, art glass to fine English furniture. All data from the sales catalog listing is included, as well as sales results and whether or not the piece was withdrawn. More than 3,000 images are on this database, and it is updated quarterly. ArtFact includes Falk's *Dictionary of American Artists' Monograms and Signatures* and Maloney's *Directory of Antiques and Collectible Resources*.

Other databases and information services of interest to the personal property appraiser are listed below. There are an expanding number of fine and decorative arts sales databases such as *Centrox, ADEC, ArtQuest*, etc., that have been developed in the last few years. It remains to be seen which ones will survive and grow.

Equipment

A micro-computer, communications software, modem and telephone line work in concert to access electronic resource systems. A micro-computer's main com-

this database, and it is updated quarterly. ArtFact includes Falk's *Dictionary of American Artists' Monograms and Signatures* and Maloney's *Directory of Antiques and Collectible Resources.*

Other databases and information services of interest to the personal property appraiser are listed below. There are an expanding number of fine and decorative arts sales databases such as *Centrox, ADEC, ArtQuest*, etc., that have been developed in the last few years. It remains to be seen which ones will survive and grow.

Equipment

A micro-computer, communications software, modem and telephone line work in concert to access electronic resource systems. A micro-computer's main component is the CPU or Central Processing Unit which understands and facilitates the user's commands. The keyboard is the instrument through which he issues these commands. The monitor displays input from the user, or from any other computer terminal to which it has been linked. The printer's job is to print out what has transpired during the transmission. These mechanical devices are called the "hardware".

Another piece of hardware, the modem, is attached to the CPU via an RS-232 cable. The modem converts the computer's transmission of binary code into audible sounds that are then sent over telephone wires. The computer at the other end is connected to a modem that converts these audible sounds back to binary code which the receiving computer can understand. As the conversation develops, both the researcher's transmission and the responding information system's transmission are displayed on the researcher's monitor. The printer can produce a paper record of the transmission, either during the transmission or after the conversation is terminated.

MS-DOS compatible computers are considered the standard in the computer industry. All information sources will interact with IBM-compatible equipment. Some electronic information services, such as CompuServe can accommodate Apple, Zenith, Commodore, or just about any system on the market. To have unlimited search capability, however, it is wise to avoid non-standard hardware without expansion capabilities.

Modems are available in a variety of speeds, known as baud rates. The speed at which the conversation takes place, can be as slow as 300 bits (binary digits) per second to as high as 14,400 bits per second. The 300 speed units are now obsolete. Most electronic information services demand a baud rate of from 1200 to 9600 bits per second. The faster the baud rate, the faster the transmission, the less time spent online. 9600 speed modems cost approximately twice as much as 2400 speed, but will pay for themselves in reduced telephone connect charges over time.

Parameters necessary for the successful transmission of information such as data bits, interactive modes, full or half duplex, parity, and so forth are difficult to understand. It is not necessary to know what these settings mean—only that both computers must be set to the same protocols.

Unless the researcher is willing to devote some time to the set-up of his telecommunications system, it is best to purchase all necessary equipment from a local computer supply center, where professional technicians can install the system and be available later for training and support.

Software is a generic term for any computer program. Communications software programs tell the hardware exactly how to proceed. They set up a basis for interaction between the micro-computer and the modem and keep a list of regularly called information services. They automatically dial up and log on each service and keep a record of the communications after sign-off. Available software programs may handle only telecommunications or can be multi-faceted, combining word processing, reports, filing, and accounting as well as communications. All levels of usage are available from simple to sophisticated. The software industry is an explosion of new products. Changes and improvements are happening so fast that a program is often outdated on the day it is purchased.

CD ROM

No discussion of electronic information resources and retrieval systems would be complete without mention of CD-ROMs. Based on audio compact disk technology, a single CD-ROM (Compact Disk-Read Only Memory) can store up to 620 megabytes of information. In layman's terms, that's equivalent to more than 300,000 typewritten pages. Its storage capacity is awesome, but its search and retrieval power is its real advantage. All 9,000 pages of *Grollier's Electronic Encyclopedia* can be placed on one CD-ROM disk and searched for a specific term. In seconds, a list of all the articles in which the term is mentioned is produced. CD-ROM can mix images, text and sound records all on one disk. It can read and reproduce photographs, drawings, charts and paintings. Databases such as *ArtFact, Art Index* and *Gordon's Print Price Annual* are available on CD-ROM disk. Public libraries are investing in the hardware needed to use this new technology because they are practically indestructible and can be used over and over again by the professional researcher and novice alike. The disks are updated frequently, and, unlike tapping into a database, once the initial investment for hardware is made, there is no additional usage charge. Originally, CD-ROMs were only cost effective for large academic libraries, but today this technology is well within the reach of the average appraiser.

The Internet

The Internet is a network of networks which allows its members to search the collections of other member libraries around the world. This enables a student at Emory University in Georgia to search the Liverpool University's online catalog in England. Originally available only to universities, government agencies and business, Internet is now available to the individual user through "providers" such as DELPHI for a fee. Internet is a behemoth of information services used by over one million people. The Internet provides everything from file transfer, E-Mail, and discussion groups, access to databanks (such as Dialog, BRS, RLIN, etc.), remote card catalog searches, and electronic journals and books. One of the services available via the Internet is *Carl UnCover*, a periodical index database and article delivery service for over 14,000 English language titles. Approximately 4,000 citations are added each day. Almost every article cited in *UnCover* can be ordered online and delivered by fax machine within 24 hours.

Miscellany

There are other computerized resources not directly accessible through micro-computers, but which are nonetheless worthwhile to the personal property appraiser.

The National Museum of American Art at The Smithsonian in Washington, D.C., has developed two comprehensive databases: American paintings executed before 1914, including oils, watercolors and pastels by artists born or working in the United States; and the sculpture database which covers pieces from the colonial settlement era up to the present.

Yale's *Index of British Art* concentrates on collections in the United States. With a reported 50,000 images on file, this library's staff will search their database, and, if a photograph of the artwork in question is sent to them, will try to match it with their photo archives.

The Future

Handwriting and speech recognition, flat color screens and handheld devices that respond to spoken commands, are just a few of the many plans of the computer industry. Scanners are reaching increased levels of competency. This technology, based on the bar code scanning system, is a useful tool for gathering information with a quick sweep of the hand or a pass across a written page. Scanners "read" the loops, bars and stems of printed words on a page, and identify them as individual letters, words and sentences. This information can then be saved and stored in the micro-computer without re-typing the information on the keyboard. Once scanners become portable, the next step could be to use them for all note taking.

Conclusion

The appraiser's research plan must be organized, succinct, and cost effective. "Due Diligence" is not just wishful thinking, but a client's right that must be taken very seriously by the professional appraiser. To conduct a thorough search, a comprehensive way to process huge amounts of information must be found so that conclusions are complete and defensible. Electronic information resources are in-place and capable of handling massive amounts of data very quickly. Because this new technology is still in its infancy, development costs are a serious problem. The feasibility and desirability of this new research tool, however, may outweigh such hindrances as the cost factor. Electronic research is here to stay. It is just a matter of time before the youthful glitches and delivery cost have been addressed and resolved.

Resources:

Gateways

A T & T's EasyLink
400 Interpace Parkway
Parsippany, NJ 07854
(800) 242-6005

CompuServe's IQUEST
P. O. Box 20212
Columbus, OH 43220
(800) 848-8990

INTERNET
Available through university libraries or companies such as:

DELPHI
General Videotex Corporation
Boston, MA or Kansas City, MO
(800) 695-4005

Databanks

BRS (Including BRS After Dark)
8000 Westpark Drive
McLean, VA 22102
(800) 955-0906

Dialog Information Services
3460 Hillview Avenue
Palo Alto, CA 93404
(800) 334-2564

OCLC's EPIC
6565 Franz Road
Dublin, Ohio 43017-3395
(614) 764-6000

Questel, Inc.
2300 Clarendon Blvd., Suite 1111
Arlington, VA 22201
(800) 424-9600

The RLIN Information Center
Research Libraries Group, Inc.
1200 Villa Street
Mountain View, CA 94041-1100
(800) 537-7546

WILSONLINE
The J. W. Wilson Company
Attention: Electronic Services
950 University Avenue
Bronx, NY 10452
(800) 367-6770

Arts and Humanities Databases

America: History & Life - available on Dialog
U.S. & Canadian history and current affairs.

Art Index - available on WILSONLINE/BRS/OCLC
Same as printed edition; also available on CD-ROM.

Arts & Humanities Search - available on Dialog/OCLC
Same as *Arts & Humanities Citation Index*; 1,185 International journals.

Art Bibliographies Modern - available on Dialog
Same as printed version.

Bibliographic Index - available on WILSONLINE/BRS
2,700 sources of biographic information.

Biography Index - available on WILSONLINE/BRS/OCLC
Same as printed version; also available on CD-ROM.

Biography Master Index - available on Dialog
Gale's biographical index of over three million people.

Book Review Digest - available on WILSONLINE/BRS
Approximately 6,000 books reviewed each year.

Book Review Index - available on Dialog
Two million citations of books; 500 periodicals and newspapers.

Books in Print - available on BRS/Dialog/OCLC
In print, out of print, forthcoming, and paperbound; also available on CD-ROM.

Dissertation Abstracts Online - available on BRS/Dialog
Every American dissertation since 1861.

Eighteenth Century Short Title Catalog - available on RLIN

Publications on the arts from Great Britain, 1701-1800.

ERIC - available on BRS/Dialog/OCLC
Same as *Resources in Education & Current Index to Journals in Education.*

Francis - available on Questel
Paris-based arts and humanities index of worldwide publications.

Grants - available on Dialog
Public & private grants in more than ninety academic disciplines.

Historical Abstracts - available on Dialog
Same as printed edition.

Humanities Index - available on WILSONLINE/BRS/OCLC
Same as printed edition; also available on CD-ROM.

ICONOS - available on Questel
Bibliographic index of photographic materials.

LC MARC - available on Dialog
Complete bibliographic records of all books catalogued since 1968.

Magazine Index - available on BRS/Dialog
Index of 500 publications; also available on CD-ROM.

Marquis' *Who's Who* - available on Dialog
Same as *Who's Who in American Art.*

Newspaper Abstracts - available on Dialog/OCLC
Major regional, national and International newspapers.

National Newspaper Index - available on BRS/Dialog

NY Times, Wall Street Journal, Christian Science Monitor, Washington Post, and the *L.A. Times* indexed.

Online Union Catalog - available on OCLC
Twenty three million bibliographic records and where they are housed

Reader's Guide to Abstracts - available on WILSONLINE/ BRS/OCLC
Same as printed edition.

Reader's Guide to Periodicals WILSONLINE/BRS/OCLC
Same as printed edition; edition; also available on CD-ROM.

Religion Index - available on BRS/Dialog
Two hundred journals indexed on religious subjects.

RILA - available on Dialog/RLIN
(Repertoire international de la literature de l'art)
same as printed edition.

SCIPIO - available on RLIN
Bibliographic records for art sales catalogs owned by eight art libraries.

Sociological Abstracts - available on BRS/Dialog/OCLC
Sixteen hundred journals indexed.

Art-Related Electronic Resources

ADEC-ONLINE Art Price Annual
Immagini, Inc.
47 Indian Hills
Bedford, NY 10506
(914) 234-0197

Sales results from fine arts auctions from 1989 to the present online, updated every two weeks; past andfuture sales with estimates and works not sold.

ADEC on CD-ROM
Gordon & Lawrence Art Reference
1840 8th Street South
Naples, FL 33940
(800) 726-2665

Same as above

ArtFact, Inc.
1130 Ten Rod Road Suite E104
N. Kingston, RI 02852
(401) 295-5656

CD-ROM listing of 450,000 auction records and 3,000 color images from 35 auction houses in the U.S. & abroad; decorative arts, fine arts & antiques.

Art Information Center
280 Broadway, Suite 412
New York, NY 10007
(212) 227-0282

65,000 contemporary artists are catalogued with exhibit and gallery information. Database not online; telephone access.

ArtQuest Sales Index, Ltd.
1 Thames Street
Weybridge, Surrey England
KT13 8JG
011-44-932-856426

More than one million art records online of art auction sales results from twenty countries; paintings, drawings, sculpture and other three-dimensional works and miniatures.

Bookmaster III
TAX Software Innovations
3285 Route 88
Newark, NJ 14513
(800) 869-5414

Floppy disk with listings of out-of-print & collectible books with prices

Centrox Corporation
145 East 57th Street
New York, NY 10022
(212) 319-4800

Online image database of global art market; 90,000 artists, 600,000 lots from 310 auction rooms.

Gordon's Print Price Annual
Gordon & Lawrence Art Reference
1840 8th Street South
Naples, FL 33940

CD-ROM version covers years 1985-1993. Complements its Price Sales information within 24 hours of auction; worldwide print shop inventories.

National Gallery of Canada
Elgin Street
Ottawa, Canada K1A 0M8
(613) 990-1985

Computerized indexing of Canadian art. Accessible by telephone, not on line. Free of charge.

Silver Update
1030 South Federal Highway
Suite 118
Delray Beach, FL 33483
(410) 750-3282

Listings of current production sterling and silverplated flatware and hollowware.

Smithsonian Institution
Inventories of American Paintings & Sculpture
National Museum of American Art
Washington, D.C. 20560
(202) 357-2941 (art)
or
(202) 786-2384 (sculpture)

Computerized index of pre-1877 art in the U.S. and Canada. Also, national inventory of publicly and privately owned sculptures by American Artists. Not online; accessible by telephone, free of charge.

Telepraisal, Inc.
P. O. Box 20686
New York, NY 10009
(800) 645-6002

Sales data from major national and international auctions of fine art and sculpture. Includes prints and low-end sales and gallery information. Reached by telephone; not online.

Chapter 8

Resource Directories

Introduction

An appraiser's most valuable skills, and those most complementary to the application of both general valuation theory and subject-specific knowledge, are creativity and diversity. These skills best come into play during the research aspect of a challenging or multi-part assignment, in analyzing the components of the project, identifying the key questions, and then applying a variety of traditional and non-traditional resources to answer them.

One need not have access to a major art or academic library in order to exercise due diligence and perform a thorough job of researching an object or topic; it simply takes more resourcefulness and more time. This resource directory was designed to do just that: to aid any appraiser in making the best use of the sources available for the field. Those sources, of course, are not limited to the printed word but can encompass associations, institutions, organizations, and key individuals.

A resource directory designed to serve the needs of all appraisers, from the novice to the seasoned professional, and from the generalist to the specialist, not to mention those in affiliated fields, could potentially cover literally hundreds of pages and thousands of citations. It would take volumes, not chapters, to cover all possible territory, from general research practice and theory to points of law, from the basics of process and style to advanced connoisseurship, from general to subject-specific works, in addition to hundreds of regional studies. In defining the parameters of this section, the spirit of the term "directory" has been emphasized. As a resource directory, this is a list of starting points, a map and a guidebook providing directions to the type of reference that, properly accessed and applied, will yield the necessary information. As a survey of types, rather than a comprehensive catalog, this directory is a means rather than an end.

Ideally, this directory will assist the appraiser in determining and defining the appraisal question, in identifying the needed information, and in focusing on the appropriate sources for that information. It is also designed to highlight examples of resources in one field that may inspire the appraiser to search for similar resources in another. In format, it is an attempt to follow the reasoning processes and the research methods applied by the personal property appraiser, in working from the general to the specific in terms of both subject and resources.

For specific fine and decorative arts, some basic resources have been cited. From there, remember the old lesson of learning to read a book back to front: bibliographies can be a trove of subject-specific citations. In order to avoid duplication of previously compiled lists, comprehensive sources, such as appropriate research guides and specialized bibliographies, are cited whenever possible. To introduce the appraiser to sources that may not be commonly considered when conducting specialized research projects, many references to directories and encyclopedias that are not directly arts or valuation related have been included. Not only are such volumes more apt to be readily available through the average public library, but they often contain the key to a source that may be one of the few available for a particular appraisal situation.

The material included here is divided generally by field, and then further by the appropriate question, following the old journalistic litany (who, what, when, where, why, how). In some cases, these questions will overlap, and the categories have been appropriately combined in those situations. Specialties have been under emphasized in order to make this a tool most useful to the largest number of appraisers. Any one specialty would easily justify its own resource directory, but some few citations have been briefly included in order to again provide a general idea of the type of research tool that may be available. No one can have boundless knowledge of all areas of personal property, but one can develop the ability necessary to locate the required information or expertise. And, perhaps most importantly, note the difference between information and knowledge: having access to one does not guarantee proficiency in the other.

Appraisal Practice and Theory — Resources and Materials

Appraisal and Valuation Resource Manuals. Washington, D.C.: American Society of Appraisers, 1955+.

Babcock, Henry A. *Appraisal Principles and Procedures.* Washington, D.C.: American Society of Appraisers, 1968.
> Basic textbook includes definitions and methodology in areas ranging from the meaning of property to the application of appraisal principles.

Bibliography of Appraisal Literature. Washington, D.C.: American Society of Appraisers, 1974.
> Resources for appraisals in all fields, including personal property.

Foreman, Robert L. *Communicating the Appraisal: A Guide to Report Writing.* Chicago: American Institute of Real Estate Appraisers, 1982.

Insurance Valuations: Definitions, Derivations and Appraisals. Monograph #4. Washington, D.C.: American Society of Appraisers, 1971.
> Topics covered include reproduction vs. replacement costs, depreciation, fine art and personal property insurance.

Miller, Anna. *Gems and Jewelry Appraising: Techniques of Professional Practice.* New York: Van Nostrand Reinhold, 1988.
> Although aimed at the jewelry appraiser, many of the basic appraisal principles and theories discussed here, along with guidelines for general business practice, are applicable to general personal property appraisal.

Personal Property Journal. Washington, D.C.: American Society of Appraisers. Vol. 1, no. 1+. Quarterly.
> The only periodical to deal solely and specifically with issues of personal property and gems and jewelry appraisal, the *Journal* features articles on methodology, education, connoisseurship, legal issues, resources and more.

Professional Appraisal Services Directory. Washington, D.C: American Society of Appraisers. Annual.
> Listing of membership by discipline, with special section on classified specialties. Separate membership directories for each discipline are also issued. Good source for locating expertise in specialized areas.

Valuation. Washington, D.C.: American Society of Appraisers, Vol. 1, no. 1+. Semi-annual.
> The ASA's official publication covers material on all aspects of appraisal technique, theory and methodology in general, as well as articles on discipline-specific topics, reflecting the multi-disciplinary character of the organization itself.

General Source Lists

Libraries and Research Centers — Directories

American Library Directory: A Classified List of Libraries in the United States and Canada with Personnel and Statistical Data. New York: R.R. Bowker. 1908+.
> Includes information on special collections and areas of interest for individual libraries.

American Association for State and Local History. *Directory of Historical Agencies in North America.* Nashville: AASLH, 1986.
> Directory features local historical societies, preservationist groups, etc., all of which are excellent resources for regional information on arts-related topics.

ARLIS/NA Directory. Tucson, AZ: ARLIS/NA. Annual.
> Directory of members in the Art Library Society of North America, this provides collection-specific information useful in identifying potential sources of data on given art-related topics.

D'Aleo, Richard. *Fed. Find: A Guide to Finding Government Information.* Springfield, VA: ICUC Press, 1982.

Directory of Archives and Manuscript Repositories in the United States. 2nd ed. Phoenix, AZ: Oryx, 1988.
> Description of specific collections.

Directory of Art Libraries in Europe or Libraries with Important Art Holdings, including the United Kingdom: A Second Preliminary List. Paris: IFLA Art Libraries Section, 1981.

Directory of Special Libraries and Information Centers in the U.S. and Canada. 8th ed. Detroit: Gale Research, 1988. 2 vols.

Eichholz, Alice, ed. *Ancestry's Red Book: American State, County and Town Sources.* Salt Lake City, UT: Ancestry Publishing, 1992.
> Designed primarily for genealogists, this volume contains regional institution information useful to all researchers.

Gale Directory of Databases. Detroit: Gale Research Inc., 1993+.
> Lists and describes both online and CD-ROM products, among others, in a variety of disciplines and interest areas.

Hoffberg, Judith and Stanley W. Hess, eds. *Directory of Art Libraries and Visual Resource Collections in North America.* New York: Neal-Schuman, 1978.

Information Industry Directory. 11th ed. Detroit: Gale Research, 1991+.
> Cites organizations that provide information to business and industry.

Markower, Joel, ed. *The American History Sourcebook.* New York: Prentice-Hall, 1988.

Guide to museums, libraries, historical societies, collections and sources of information on all aspects of U.S. history and culture. Geographically arranged, with subject and name indices, and unusually detailed entries on each institution.

National Inventory of Documentary Sources in the United States. Alexandria, VA: 1983+.

Three sections cover collections in the National Archives, Smithsonian, Presidential Libraries, Library of Congress, state archives, libraries and historical societies, and others.

National Library of Canada. *Research Collections in Canadian Libraries*. Ottawa: Information Canada, 1972.

Steele, Colin. *Major Libraries of the World: A Selective Guide*. New York: Bowker, 1976.

Starer, Daniel. *Who Knows What — The Essential Business Resource Book*. New York: Holt, 1992.

Where and how to find a maven for nearly every imaginable business-related topic.

Viaux, Jacqueline. *IFLA Directory of Art Libraries*. New York: Garland, 1985.

Washington Information Directory. Washington, D.C.: Congressional Quarterly, Inc. 1976+. Annual.

Address book of public and private institutions, associations and departments affiliated with, and/or of interest to, the federal government.

World of Learning. London: Allen and Unwin, 1947+. Annual.

Lists colleges, universities and other educational institutions internationally; useful for identifying the location of regional collections.

Libraries — Catalogs and Union Lists

Architectural Trade Catalogs from the Avery Library, Columbia University, on microfiche. New York: Clearwater Pub. Co., 1988.

Commercial catalog collection includes section on furnishings.

British Library, Reference Division, Rare Book Collections. *British Union Catalog of Books Printed Before 1801; Directory of British and Irish Libraries*. London: British Library, 1976.

Canadiana. Ottawa, Canada: National Library of Canada, 1951+.

Concentrates on materials with Canadian focus. Cumulative indices available.

Catalogue general des livres imprimes: auteurs, collectivites-auteurs, anonymes 1960-1964. Paris: Bibliotheque Nationale, 1965-67. 12 vols.

Author catalog of the Bibliotheque Nationale.

Catalog of the Yale Collection of Western Americana. Boston: G.K. Hall, 1961. 4 vols.

Dictionary Catalogue of the Library of the Provincial Archives of British Columbia: Victoria. Boston: G.K. Hall, 1971. 8 volumes.

Institution founded c. 1893; this volume lists its collections.

Kamincow, Marion J. *A Complement to Genealogies in the Library of Congress: A Bibliography*. Baltimore, MD: Magna Carta Book Co., 1981.

Useful tool in researching familial connections with material culture.

General Catalogue of Printed Books to 1955. London: Trustees of British Museum, 1956-65.

Catalog of the British Library, formerly the British Museum Library, and a depository library.

Library of Congress Catalogs. Washington, D.C.: Library of Congress.

Includes the comprehensive *National Union Catalog*, listing hundreds of thousands of citations, the *National Union Catalog of Manuscript Collections*, and *Newspapers in Microfilm*.

McKistry, E. Roger. *Trade Catalogues at Winterthur: A Guide to the Literature of Merchandising, 1750 to 1980*. New York and London: Garland Publishing, 1984.

Mainly American catalogues arranged in thirty categories with emphasis on house furnishings and goods, indexed by subject, date and place of publication and annotated to identify firms' ages and product lines. Features outstanding bibliography; each catalogue cited is available on microfiche.

New York Public Library. *Dictionary Catalog of the History of the Americas Collection*. Boston: G.K. Hall, 1961. 28 volumes.

Romaine, Lawrence B. *A Guide to American Trade Catalogs, 1744-1900*. New York: R.R. Bowker Co., 1960.

Provides current depository location of catalogs, listed by category, company name or date, and covering topics ranging from furniture and glass to agricultural material; includes bibliography and index.

Trade Catalogues in the Victoria and Albert Museum 1762-1939. London: Mindata, 1986.

18th-20th century British and European catalogs.

Trade Catalogs from the Hagley Museum and Library. Microfilm. Frederick, MD: UPA Academic Editions, 1989.

Features transportation-related subjects.

Victoria and Albert Museum: Liberty's Catalogs: Fashion, Design, Furnishings 1881-1949. London: Mindata, 1985.

The Winterthur Museum Libraries Collection of Printed Books and Periodicals. Wilmington, DE: Scholarly Resources, 1974. 9 vols.

Works printed between 1600 and 1840 with emphasis on the decorative arts. Volume 9 lists rare books and auction catalogs.

Museums and Collections — Directories

Abse, Joan. *Art Galleries of Britain and Ireland: A Guide to Their Collections*. London: Robson, 1985.

American Association of Museums. *The Official Museum Directory*. Washington, D.C.: AAM, 1971+. Biennial.
Invaluable handbook, with detailed descriptions of collections accessed by excellent indices to category of collection, among other subjects.

Arnold, Bruce. *Art Atlas of Britain and Ireland*. London: Viking in association with the National Trust, 1988.
Directory of private art collections, museums and galleries.

Canadian Museums Association. *The Official Directory of Canadian Museums and Related Institutions*. Ottawa: CMA, 1968+.
Published every three years.

Cartwright, W. Aubrey. *Guide to Art Museums in the United States*. New York: Duell, Sloan and Pierce. 1958+. Annual.

Duncombe, Brenda. *Art Museums of Southeast Asia with Travel Notes*. Sydney, NSW: Crafts Council of Australia, 1988.

Germaine, Max. *Artists and Galleries of Australia and New Zealand*. Sydney: Lansdowne Editions, 1979.
Includes artist biographies and gallery directories.

German Africa Society, comps. and eds. *Museums in Africa: A Directory*. New York: Africana Pub. Corp., 1970.

Guide to the Smithsonian Archives. Washington, D.C.: Smithsonian Institution Press, 1978.

Handbuch der Museen: Handbook of Museums. Munchen: Saur, 1981. Directory of Central European museums.

Historic Houses, Castles and Gardens in Great Britain and Ireland. East Grinstead: British Leisure Publications, 1965+.

Historic Site Surveys/Historic Furnishings Reports. Washington, D.C.: National Park Service. (Titles, dates and places of publication varies.)
U.S. Government publications document historic properties around the country. Very detailed inventories of household furnishings, art and decorative works, with exhaustive research tracing their historic and cultural significance to that particular site. Past publications included a volume on Eleanor Roosevelt's Valkill Farm furniture workshop, established in the 1940s, one of the few sources available for detailed information on those pieces.

Howarth, Shirley Reiff, ed. *ARTnews International Directory of Corporate Art Collections*. New York: ARTnews, 1988.

Jackson, Virginia, ed. *Art Museums of the World*. Westport, CT: Greenwood, 1987. 2 vols.
Features selected bibliography of museum publications.

Krantz, Les, ed. *American Art Galleries: the Illustrated Guide to their Art and Artists*. New York: Facts on File, 1985.

Lent, Max. *Photography Galleries and Selected Museums: A Survey and International Directory*. Venice, CA: Garlic Press, 1978.

McLanathan, Richard. *World Art in American Museums*. Garden City, NY: Anchor Press, 1983.
Guidebook to U.S. and Canadian museums.

Museums and Galleries in Great Britain and Ireland. Dunstable: Bedfordshire: ABC Historic Publications, 1989+.

Museums of the World: Museen der Welt. 4th ed. New York: New York: K.G. Saur, 1986.

Narkiewicz, Beverly and Lincoln S. Bates. *Uncommon and Unheralded Museums*. New York: Hippocrene Books, 1991.
State by state survey of unusual and significant museum collections, from the C.A.S.E. Museum of Russian Contemporary Art in Exile to the World o' Tools Museum. Name and subject indices.

National Register of Historic Places. Washington, D.C.: National Park Service, 1969+.
Register of historic properties throughout the country; useful in tracing affiliated museums and collections.

Ragghianti, Carlos Ludovico and Henry A. LaFarge, eds. *Newsweek: Great Museums of the World Series*. New York: Newsweek, 1967-1982.
Covers a worldwide variety, with focus on the collections, and featuring institutions from the Boston Museum to the Uffizi.

Robi, Ernest H. *Picture Sources 4: Collections of Prints and Photographs in the U.S. and Canada*. New York: Special Libraries Association, 1983.
Introduction to methodology of picture research, along with indices to sources and collections.

Rosen, Barbara. *World Museums Guide*. London: Threshold Books Ltd., 1973.

World of Art Libraries: Galleries Series. London: Thames and Hudson, 1964-73.
Detailed listing of specific collections, including the National Archives, Art Institute of Chicago, the Tate Gallery.

Associations and Organizations — Directories

American Art Directory. New York: R.R. Bowker, 1952+. Annual.

Covers institutions, galleries, museums and related resources in the U.S., Canada and Latin America.

Bedell, Kenneth. *Yearbook of American and Canadian Churches*. Nashville, TN: Abingdon Press. Annual.

Lists contacts for church/religious archives and depositories for church history materials.

Encyclopedia of Associations. Detroit: Gale Research. Annual.

Includes both U.S. and international volumes, listing a myriad of associations in all areas. Sections dealing with hobbies, education and business are of particular interest to the personal property appraiser. Also useful in identifying publications issued by the various organizational bodies, from periodicals to membership directories.

Huellmantel, Michael, ed. *Business Organizations, Agencies and Publications Directory*. 7th ed. Detroit: Gale Research, 1993.

Guide to organizations, agencies and publications concerned with U.S. and international business, trade and industry. Good source for manufacturing and industrial organizations, departments of trade and commerce, etc., all of which may yield information useful in tracking down personal property resource material.

International Directory of Arts: Internationales Kunst-Addressbuch. Frankfurt-am-Main: Verlag Muller G.M.B.H. 2 vols. Biennial.

Includes current data on museums, galleries, educational institutions, associations, collectors, dealers, artists, auction houses, publications and more, much of which can be difficult to locate on an international basis.

Marlow, Cynthia Ann and Robert Thomas, eds. *Directory of Directories*. 5th ed. Detroit, MI: Gale Research, 1987.

Lists approximately 9600 business and industrial directories, professional and scientific rosters, and myriad lists and guides of all kinds, all useful in networking.

North American Online Directory. New York: R.R. Bowker, 1985+.

Lists a variety of products and services, including machine-readable databases, bibliographical services, etc.

The World of Learning. Detroit: Gale Research, 1947+. 2 vols. Annual.

Directory of universities, art and architecture schools, society and research institutions, libraries, archives, museums.

World Trade Centers Association World Business Directory. Detroit, MI: Gale Research, 1992+.

Useful for tracking sources for international manufacturers.

Worldwide Chamber of Commerce Directory. Loveland, CO: n.p., 1993. Annual.

Potentially useful in locating information on regional specialty industries, general tourist information, etc.

Periodicals, Newspapers, Serials — Directories

The Art Press: Two Centuries of Art Magazines. London: Art Book, 1976.

British Union-Catalogue of Periodicals: Incorporating World List of Scientific Periodicals: New Periodical Titles 1960-1968. London: Butterworth, 1970.

Lists collections in selected British libraries.

Catalogue Collectif des periodiques du debut du XVII siecle a 1939. Paris: Bibliotheque Nationale, 1967-81. 5 vols.

Serials lists of major French libraries.

Irregular Serials and Annuals: An International Directory. New York: R.R. Bowker, 1967+. Irregular.

Complements *Ulrich's International Periodicals Directory*.

Jones, Linda Marilyn. *Preliminary Checklist of Pre-1901 Canadian Serials*. Ottawa: Canadian Institute for Historical Microreproductions, 1986. 3 vols.

Katz, William Armstrong. *Magazines for Libraries for the General Reader and School: Junior College, College and Public Libraries*. 5th ed. New York: R.R. Bowker, 1986.

Annotated entries include serials in art, architecture, interior decoration, archaeology with notes regarding indexing status for a given title, inclusion of book reviews, type of article included, etc.

Klos, Sheila M. and Christine M. Smith, eds. *Historical Bibliography of Art Museum Serials from the United States and Canada*. Tucson, AZ: ARLIS/NA, 1987.

Larson, Carolyn S., ed. *Art Serials: A Union List of Art Periodicals and Serials in Research Libraries in the Washington D.C. Metropolitan Area*. Washington D.C.: Washington Art Library Resources Committee, 1981.

McKenzie, Karen and Mary F. Williamson, eds. *The Art and Pictorial Press in Canada: Two Centuries of Art Magazines*. Toronto: Art Gallery of Ontario, 1979.

Oxbridge Directory of Newsletters. New York: Oxbridge Communications, 1979+. Annual.

Useful in identifying specialty publications and the special-interest groups which produce them throughout the U.S. and Canada.

Roberts, Helene E. *American Art Periodicals of the Nineteenth Century*. Rochester, NY: Rochester University, 1964.

The Subject Index to Periodicals. London: Library Association, 1915-1961.

Indexes over 285 English periodicals by subject and author. Superseded by *The British Humanities Index*.

Ulrich's International Periodicals Directory: A Classified Guide to Current Periodicals, Foreign and Domestic. New York: R.R. Bowker, 1932+.

Listings of in-print serials divided into general categories including "Art", "Art Galleries and Museums", etc. Includes date of first publication, indexing status, cessations; indices to international organization publications, new serials, titles.

Union List of Serials in Libraries of the United States and Canada. 3rd ed. New York: H.W. Wilson, 1965. 5 vols.

Provides dates of introduction and cessation, superseding titles, title changes, owning libraries. *New Series Titles* supplements this set.

Periodicals, Newspapers, Serials — Indices

Access: Supplementary Index to Periodicals. Evanston, IL: J.G. Burke. Annual.

Focuses on popular titles not covered by *Readers Guide*.

America: History and Life. Santa Barbara, CA: ABC-Clio. Vol. 1, 1964+.

Abstracts of articles from over 2000 U.S. and Canadian serials, monographs and dissertations.

Arts and Humanities Citations Index. Philadelphia: Institute for Scientific Information. Volume 1, 1979+.

Covers 1300 arts and humanities-related journals, in addition to appropriate material from 5000 other periodicals. Arranged alphabetically by author or artist name; specific titles of artworks are listed.

Avery Obituary Index to Architects and Artists. 2nd ed. Boston: G.K. Hall, 1980.

Covers approximately 17,000 individuals from the 19th and 20th centuries, with date and source citations. Copies of the original article can be requested from Avery Library's clipping file.

Biography Index: A Cumulative Index to Biographical Material in Books and Magazines. New York: H.W. Wilson. Vol. 1, Jan. 1946-June 1949+.

Currently published quarterly with yearly cumulative volume, this covers 2000 serials and collected biographical sources. Indices by surnames and professions: of interest here are painters, sculptors, designers, art collectors, art historians, artists, etc. Replaces biographical entries listed in other pre-1946 Wilson publications.

Biography and Genealogy Master Index. 2nd ed. Detroit: Gale Research, 1980. 8 vols.

Entries for over 2 million individuals, drawn from a variety of reference materials, including the *Who's Who* series.

British Humanities Index. London: Library Association. Vol. 1, 1962+.

Published quarterly, with yearly cumulation, superseding *The Subject Guide to Periodicals* (c. 1915-1961) and indexing 360 English serials including the *London Times Literary Supplement*.

Cushing, Helen Grant and Adah V. Morris, eds. *Nineteenth-Century Reader's Guide to Periodical Literature 1890-1899, With Supplementary Indexing 1900-1922.* New York: H.W. Wilson, 1944.

Design and Applied Arts Index. Gurnleys, Burnwash, Etchingham, East Sussex: Design Documentation, 1987+.

Humanities Index. New York: H.W. Wilson. Vol. 28, April 1974-March 1975+.

Author-subject index of serials covering archaeology, film, history, etc.

Index to Personal Names in the National Union Catalog of Manuscript Collection 1959-1984. Alexandria, VA: Chadwyck-Healey, 1988. 2 vols.

International Index to Periodicals. New York: H.W. Wilson, 1951+. Annual.

Cites publications in the arts and sciences.

Magazine Index Database. Foster City, CA: Information Access Company.

Subject and keyword indices to hundreds of serials in several arts-related subject areas, including *Art in America, Art Journal, Art News, Art Forum, Arts Magazine,* as well as general interest and news magazines. Available through both online and CD-ROM systems.

Marquis' Who's Who Publications: Index to All Books. Chicago: Marquis Who's Who, 1974.

Indexes the ten Marquis biographical dictionaries.

National Union Catalog of Manuscript Collections. Alexandria, VA: Chadwyck-Healey, 1988.

NUC provides description of contents and location of collection; particularly useful in finding artist and patron papers and architectural drawings. Use in conjunction with *Index to Personal Names in the National Union Catalog of Manuscript Collections 1959-1984.* (Alexandria, VA: Chadwyck-Healey, 1988.)

New York Times Index. New York: New York Times. Vol. 1, Sept. 1851-1862 to Vol. 15, 1912; 1913+.

Essential source for locating articles; subject index.

New York Times Obituary Index. New York: New York Times. Vol. 1, 1858-1968, 1970. Vol. 2, 1968-1970, 1980.

Cites date of death, date and location of obituary.

Poole, William Frederick and William I. Fletcher, comps. *Poole's Index to Periodical Literature.* 3rd ed. Reprint ed. Gloucester, MA: Peter Smith, 1957. 1 vol., 5 supplements.

Indexes approximately 250 periodicals c. 1802-1881, with supplements up to 1906. Article titles not listed; use *Transfer Vectors for Poole's Index to Periodical Literature* (Vinton A. Dearing, comp., Los Angeles: Pison Press, 1967) and *Cumulative Author Index for Poole's Index to Periodical Literature*

1802-1906 (C. Edward Wall, ed., Ann Arbor, MI: Pieran, 1971).

Reader's Guide to Periodical Literature: An Author and Subject Index. New York: H.W. Wilson. Vol. 1, 1900-1904+.
Indexes magazines covering a wide variety of topics by author and subject: *American Artist, Ceramics Monthly, Craft Horizons*, as well as nearly 200 general interest titles.

Subject-matter Index of Patents for Inventions Issued by the U.S. Patent Office from 1790-1873, Inclusive. 3 vols.
Lists every patent issued by inventor, invention and subject.

Publishers and Publications — Directories

In addition to the directories listed below, the value of maintaining collections of publishers' and book dealers' catalogs cannot be overemphasized in locating specific titles and compiling bibliographies for a particular property or field.

American Reference Books Annual. Littleton, CO: Libraries Unlimited. Annual.

Books in Print. New York: R.R. Bowker.
Annual Series, listing in-print U.S. publications, includes index volumes by author, title and (particularly useful) subject, along with a publishers' directory.

Canadian Books in Print. Toronto: University of Toronto, 1987+.

Catalog of Museum Publications and Media. Detroit: Gale, 1980+.
Directory and index of publications and media from museums throughout the U.S. and Canada.

Cumulative Book Index: A Word List of Books in the English Language. New York: H.W. Wilson. First issue, 1928+.
Interfiles author, title and subject headings.

Hanrahan, John, ed. *Literary Market Place: The Directory of American Book Publishing.* New York: Bowker, 1940+. Annual.

Les Livres Disponibles. Paris: Cercle de la Librairie. Biennial.
French equivalent of *Books in Print*, with author, title and subject volumes.

Monthly Catalog of United States Government Publications. Washington, D.C.: United States Government Printing Office, 1951+.
Indexes U.S. Government documents.

Montney, Charles B., ed. *Directories in Print: An Annotated Guide to Over 14,000 Directories Published Worldwide.* 10th ed. Detroit, MI: Gale Research, 1993.

Wasserman, Paul. *Museum Media.* Detroit: Gale Research, 1973.
Indexes publications issued by U.S. and Canadian museums (art, historical and other) by title and keyword.

Whitaker's Books in Print. London: J. Whitaker and Sons. 4 vols. Annual.
Formerly *British Books in Print*.

World Museum Publications. New York: R.R. Bowker, 1982.
Directory of publications of art and cultural museums.

Almanacs and Encyclopedias — General

Freitag, Wolfgang M., ed. *Encyclopedie des arts decoratifs et industriels modernes au xxieme siecle.* New York: Garland, 1977.
Reproduction of the official 1925 Paris exhibition catalog, featuring full-page illustrations.

Malraux, Andre and George Salles, general eds. *Arts of Mankind.* New York: G. Braziller, Odyssey Press and Golden Press, 1961-1973.
Extensive series covers subject areas ranging from Sumer to the South Pacific, with well-illustrated volumes offering glossaries, maps, chronological tables and detailed bibliographies.

Rees, Abraham. *Cyclopedia; or Universal Dictionary of Arts, Sciences and Literature.* n.p.: S.F. Bradford, 1810.
Landmark encyclopedia was the first to place primary emphasis on technological subjects; of particular interest is his section on timepieces.

Statistical Abstract of the U.S. Washington, D.C.: U.S. Government Printing Office, 1878+.
Appraisers will find cumulative and comparative tables on Consumer Price Indices and foreign exchange rates useful.

U.S. Patent and Trademark Office. *Official Gazette.* Washington, D.C.: Dept. of Commerce, Patent and Trademark Office. Serial.
Essential tool for researching U.S. patents.

World Book Encyclopedia. Chicago: Field Enterprises, 1917+.
Basic encyclopedias are still invaluable aids for capsule histories, identifying materials and personalities, questions of geography and location, and a plethora of additional data presented in a straightforward manner.

Dictionaries and Encyclopedias— Language and Terminology

Acronyms, Initialisms and Abbreviations Dictionary. Detroit: Gale Research, 1980.
Useful in translating and identifying unknown identification marks.

DeSola, Ralph. *Abbreviations Dictionary.* New York: Elsevier, 1986.

Fisher, David and Reginald Bragonier, Jr. *What's What: A Visual Glossary of the Physical World.* Rev. ed. Maplewood, NJ: Hammond, 1991.
Pictorial dictionary analyzes and names an exhaustive assortment of properties, component by component, from computers to musical instruments to firearms and suits of armor.

Girard, Denis, ed. *Cassell's French Dictionary.* New York: MacMillan, 1977.
One volume in an extensive series of foreign language dictionaries, including German, Italian, Latin, Dutch and others. Numerous other publishers (Harrap, Lagenscheidt, etc.) offer equally useful editions; such dictionaries are an integral part of the personal property appraisal library.

Oxford English Dictionary. 2nd ed. New York: Oxford University, 1989.
THE unabridged dictionary, in 12 volumes; the one to access when tracking an elusive term.

Pei, Mario, ed. *Liberal Arts Dictionary in English, French, German, and Spanish.* New York: Philosophical Library, 1952.
Goes beyond the usefulness of most polyglot dictionaries in its concentration on arts-related terms.

Room. Adrian. *Dictionary of Translated Names and Titles.* London: Routledge and Kegan Paul, 1986.
Provides conventional translations of over 4,000 names and titles of all types, including literary and artistic works, personal and place names, in English, French, German, Italian, Spanish and Russian.

Dictionaries and Encyclopedias — Symbols and Trademarks

Baker, Eric. *Trademarks and Symbols of the 1920s and 1930s.* San Francisco: Chronicle Books, 1985.

_____. *Trademarks and Symbols of the 1940s and 1950s.* San Francisco: Chronicle Books, 1985.

Barach, Arnold. *Famous American Trademarks.* Washington, D.C.: Public Affairs Press, 1971.
Helpful in both dating properties and in identifying character relationships.

Barraclough, E.M.C. and W.G. Crampton. *Flags of the World.* London: Warner, 1978.
Applicable in tracing marked properties to a geographic origin. Historical overview of flag design and development. Useful chart for dating U.S. flag by number of stars.

Cirlot, Juan Eduardo. *A Dictionary of Symbols.* Jack Sage, trans. 2nd ed. London: Rutledge and Kegan Paul, 1971.
Focuses on broad topics, excluding narratives.

Fox-Davies, Arthur Charles. *Complete Guide to Heraldry.* London: Nelson, 1950.
Basic reference for coats of arms, family crests, etc.

Hall, James. *Dictionary of Subjects and Symbols in Art.* 2nd ed., rev. New York: Harper and Row, 1979.
Covers themes and symbols in European art, from classical Greece to modern times. Includes bibliography of iconographical materials.

Kamekura, Yasuku. *Trademarks and Symbols of the World.* New York: Reinhold, 1965.

Trademark Register of the United States. Washington, D.C.: Patent Searching Service, 1968+.

Dictionaries and Encyclopedias — Who

Almanac of Famous People. Detroit: Gale, 1989+.
Good tool for quick biographical information on personalities.

Balteau, J. et al. *Dictionnaire de biographie francaise.* Paris: Letouzey et Ane, 1933-1993.

Delaney, John J. *Dictionary of Saints.* New York: Doubleday, 1980.
Useful in identifying attributes and iconographies.

Dictionary of Canadian Biography. Toronto: University of Toronto Press, 1966+.

Dizionario biografico degli italiani. Roma: Instituto della Enciclopedia italiana, 1960+.

Gurney, Gene. *Kingdoms of Asia, The Middle East and Africa: An Illustrated Encyclopedia of Ruling Monarchs from Ancient Times to the Present.* New York: Crown, 1986.

_____. *Kingdoms of Europe.* New York: Crown, 1982.
Excellent sources for identifying royal personages and associated symbols.

Hopkins, Joseph. *Dictionary of American Biography.* New York: Scribner's, 1977.

Hymanson, Albert M. *Dictionary of Universal Biography of All Ages and All Peoples.* 2nd ed. London: Routledge and K. Paul, 1962.

Neue Deutsche Biographie. Berlin: Duncker and Humblot, 1953+.

O'Donoghue, Freeman. *Catalog of Engraved British Portraits Preserved in the Department of Prints and Drawings in the British Museum.* London: By the Trustees, 1908-1925.

Placzek, Adolf. *MacMillan Encyclopedia of Architects.* New York: MacMillan, 1982. 4 vols.
Covers nearly 2500 architects, designers and firms from ancient Egypt to those born prior to 1931, providing general commentary on works, dates, locations. Particularly useful to personal property appraisers in researching architect-designed furnishings.

Roeder, Helen. *Saints and Their Attributes.* Chicago: Regnery, 1955.
Includes a guide to localities and patronage.

Stephen, Leslie, Sir. *Dictionary of National Biography.* London: Oxford University Press, 1922.

Webster's New Biographical Dictionary. Springfield, MA: Merriam-Webster, 1988.
 Capsule biographies of significant deceased figures, celebrated and notorious, international in scope.

Dictionaries and Encyclopedias — What

Benet's Reader's Encyclopedia. 3rd ed. New York: Harper and Row, 1987.
 Sourcebook for capsule reviews of classics and hints on literary allusions, characters, etc.

Brewer, E. Cobham. *Brewer's Dictionary of Phrase and Fable.* 14th ed. New York: Harper and Row, 1989.

Guirand, Felix, ed. *New Larouse Encyclopedia of Mythology.* Trans. by Richard Aldington and Delano Ames. Rev. ed. New York: G.P. Putnam's Sons, 1968.

Hammond, N.G.L. *Oxford Classical Dictionary.* 2nd ed. Oxford: Clarendon, 1970.

McKenzie, John L. *Dictionary of the Bible.* New York: MacMillan, 1965.
 Includes synopses of the books of the Bible, persons, themes and geographic sites.

Mythology of the World. Reprints. New York: P. Bedrick, 1983+.
 Series covers a variety of places and eras, from *North American Indian Mythology* to *European Mythology.*

New Catholic Encyclopedia. New York: McGraw-Hill, 1967.
 Fifteen-volume set provides information on culture and dogma.

Oxford Companion to Classical Literature. New York: Oxford University Press, 1989.
 Part of a series that includes volumes on American, English, Canadian, Australian, Welsh, and Children's literature, all useful in identifying literary allusions in fine and decorative arts.

Dictionaries and Encyclopedias — When

Haydn, Joseph. *Haydns' Dictionary of Dates Relating to All Ages and Nations.* 13th ed. London: Edward Moxon, 1868.

Kane, Joseph. *Famous First Facts: A Record of First Happenings, Discoveries and Inventions in American History.* 4th ed. New York: H.W. Wilson, 1981.

Dictionaries and Encyclopedias — Where

Abate, Frank S. *Omni Gazetteer of the United States of America.* Detroit, MI: Omnigraphics, 1991.
 Exhaustively detailed, multi-volume reference to place names past and present.

Atlas Series. New York: Facts on File.

Various volumes cover cultural and historical topics from Ancient Egypt to the Judaic world.

City Directories of the United States in Microform. Woodbridge, CT: Research Publications.
 Reproductions of actual city directories, from the earliest known examples (pre-1860) to 1935; earlier section based upon Dorothea Spear's *Bibliography of American Directories through 1860* (Worcester, MA: American Antiquarian Society, 1961.)

Kinder, Hermann and Werner Hilgemann. *The Anchor Atlas of World History.* Ernest A. Menze, trans. New York: Anchor, 1974.
 Two volumes with maps and outlines cover world history from the Stone Age to the American Bicentennial.

Sanborn Maps. Pelham, NY: Sanborn Map Co.
 Maps with street-by-street information for commercial, industrial and residential properties in 12,000 U.S., Canadian and Mexican towns and cities. Useful in tracing ownership or previous residences.

Shepherd, William R. *Shepherd's Historical Atlas.* New York: Barnes and Noble, 1980.

Times Atlas of the World. 9th ed. New York: Times Books, 1992.

U.S. Library of Congress. *Historic American Buildings Survey.* New York: distrib. by Chadwyck-Healey, 1980s.
 Surveys of properties in all states; available on microfiche.

Webster's New Geographical Dictionary. Springfield, MA: Merriam-Webster, 1988.
 Indispensible guide in identifying place names.

WPA Handbooks for the States. [Various subtitles]. New York: Viking, 1939.
 This Depression-Era project produced dozens of guides that remain some of the best sources of information on the history and culture of the individual states.

Dictionaries and Encyclopedias — How

Dunley, Dorothy H. and others. *Museum Registration Methods.* Rev. ed. Washington: American Association of Museums, 1979.
 Useful in establishing proper nomenclature.

Bibliographies — General

American Diaries: An Annotated Bibliography of American Diaries and Journals. Detroit: Gale Research, 1983.
 Two volumes (1492-1844 and 1845-1980) provide references to primary source material on individuals.

Art Reference Services Quarterly. Binghamton, NY: Haworth Press, 1993.

Publishes a variety of imprints, including *Art and Archaeology Technical Abstracts, Design and Applied Arts Index, Art Research* and *Architecture Research*.

Besterman, Theodore. *World Bibliography of Bibliographies and of Bibliographical Catalogues, Calendars, Abstracts, Digests, Indexes and the Like.* 4th ed., rev. and enl. Lausanne: Societas Bibliographica, 1965.

Bibliography of Museum and Art Gallery Publications and Audio-Visual Aids in Great Britain and Ireland. Teaneck, NJ: Somerset House, 1977+.

Books of the Fairs: Materials about World's Fairs 1834-1916 in the Smithsonian Institution Libraries. Chicago: American Libraries Association, 1991.
Useful guide to special collections.

Brownstone, David. *Twentieth Century Culture: A Dictionary of the Arts and Literature of Our Time.* New York: Prentice-Hall, 1991.

Franck, Marga and Ann Massie Case, eds. *Bibliographic Index: A Cumulative Bibliography of Bibliographies.* New York: H.W. Wilson, vol. 1, 1937-1942+.
Indexes bibliographies published in books, periodicals, pamphlets.

Hitchcock, Henry Russell. *American Architectural Books: A List of Books, Portfolios, and Pamphlets on Architecture and Related Subjects Published in America before 1895.* Minneapolis, MN: University of Minnesota, 1962.
References house pattern books, builders' guides, etc. Many of the books listed have been reprinted on microfilm as *American Architectural Books* (Woodbridge, CT: Research Publications).

Lesitner, Otto. *International Bibliography of Festschriften.* Osnabruck, Germany: Biblio Verlag, 1976.
Festschriften, collections of scholarly essays honoring an individual or institution, are listed here by name subject, but not by title. Appended section lists German and English translations of terms.

MLA International Bibliography of Books and Articles on the Modern Languages and Literature. New York: Modern Language Association. Vol. 1, 1919+.
Surveys approximately 3000, including *Festschriften*. (Entitled *American Bibliography 1919-1935*).

Sourcebooks

Kovel, Ralph and Terry Kovel. *Kovel's Collector's Sourcebook.* New York: Crown, 1983.
Sources of buyers and dealers, suppliers and vendors of antiques-related materials.

Maloney, David J., Jr. *Collector's Information Clearinghouse Antiques and Collectibles Resource Directory.* Radnor, PA: Wallace-Homestead, 1992.

Sourcebook with exhaustive resources, by category of property, for dealers, collectors, clubs, periodicals, auction houses, services, and more.

Thomas Register of American Manufacturers and Thomas Register Catalog File. New York: Thomas Publishing. Annual, 1905+.
Indexes manufacturers of every conceivable product by name of company and by general product line, with trade names index. *Catalog File* reprints sales catalogs in bound volumes.

Law and Government — Subjects and Sources

American Jurisprudence 2nd. Table of Statutes, Rules and Regulations Cited. 2nd ed. Rochester, NY: Lawyers' Cooperative Pub. Co., 1993+. Quarterly.

Black, Henry Campbell. *Black's Law Dictionary.* 5th ed. St. Paul, MN: West Publishing Co., 1979.
Indispensible guide to terms, meanings and pronunciations, in largely understandable language.

BlueBook: A Uniform System of Citation. 15th ed. Cambridge, MA: Harvard Law Review Association, 1991.
Key to unlocking legal citation formats. Particularly useful in pursuing case law research.

Cohen, Morris. *How to Find the Law.* 8th ed. St. Paul: West Publishing, 1983.
Useful guide to pinpointing a legal source or citation.

DuBoff, Leonard. *Art Law.* St. Paul, MN: West Publishing, 1984.
Case law and succinct commentary on all aspects of art law, from authentication to insurance to artist's legal rights and responsibilities to questions of copyright.

Federal Register. Washington, D.C.: Office of the Federal Register, National Archives and Records Service, General Services Administration. Vol. 1, No. 1, 1936+.
The official source for rules and regulations issued by the various regulations issued by federal government agencies, bureaus, and departments.

Feldman, Franklin and Stephen E. Weil. *Art Law: Rights and Liabilities of Creators and Collectors.* Boston: Little Brown, 1986. 2 vols. Supplement, 1988.
Collection of essays discusses such points of law as reproduction rights, purchase and sale of art, tax considerations, rights of ownership, etc., with case law citations, legal forms, etc.

Hodges, Scott. *Legal Rights in the Art and Collector's World.* Dobbs Ferry, NY: Oceana, 1986.

Merryman, John Henry and Albert E. Elsen. *Law, Ethics and the Visual Arts.* 2nd ed. Philadelphia: University of Pennsylvania, 1987. 2 vols.
Topics covered include collectors, museums, stolen art and artistic freedom.

Milrad, Aaron and Ella Agnew. *The Art World: Law, Business and Practice in Canada.* Toronto: Merritt, 1980.

Shepard's Acts and Cases by Popular Names: Federal and State. Colorado Springs, CO: Shepards/McGraw Hill. 1968+. Semi-annual.
Compilation and identification of cases by popular names, with constitutional or statutory references.

United States Code. Washington D.C.: United States Government Printing Office. Serial.
Includes the IRS regulations and tax codes, as well as U.S. Customs regulations, etc.

United States Government Manual. Washington, D.C.: Office of the Federal Register. Annual.
Directory to all governmental departments and agencies, with contact names and numbers, and descriptions of functions.

Approaches to Research

Techniques, Strategies, and Sources

Beasley, David R. *How to Use a Research Library.* New York: Oxford University Press, 1988.
Guidelines for basic approaches to a reference question or a research topic.

Bronner, Simon J. *American Folk Art: A Guide to Sources.* New York: Garland, 1984.
Collection of essays on various topics in the scholarship of folk art, each followed by an annotated bibliography.

Bunting, Christine, ed. *Reference Tools for Fine Arts Visual Resources Collections.* Art Libraries Society/ North America. Occasional Papers. Tucson, AZ: ARLIS/NA.

Dissertation Abstracts International: Abstracts of Dissertations. Available on Microfilm or as Xerographic Reproductions. Ann Arbor, MI: University Microfilms, Vol. 1 (1938+).
Includes abstracts of dissertations from 285 universities, issued monthly with author index. Indexing by key words lists all dissertations with that word in the title. Order numbers are assigned to those documents which are available; others may be ordered directly from the university. Invaluable tool in locating obscure research material for lend or purchase. *Comprehensive Dissertation Index, 1861-1972* and the *Comprehensive Dissertation Index Supplement* provide more complete indexing to the materials. (Volume 31 of the Index covers communication and the arts; Vols. 33-37 list authors.)

Evans, Hilary, et al. *The Picture Researcher's Handbook: An International Guide to Picture Sources and How to Use Them.* 3rd ed. Wokingham, Berkshire: Van Nostrand Reinhold, 1986.
Useful in introducing sources that might not be considered as typical fine- or decorative-arts research sites, such as trade unions or church archives. Indexes subjects, geographic sites, and other specialized sources, but note that most galleries and museums are not included.

Jones, Lois Swan. *Art Information: Research, Methods and Resources.* 3rd ed. Dubuque, IA: Kendall-Hunt, 1990.
Thorough introduction to available materials and how to apply them to a research question. Annotated bibliographies on all arts-related topics, from general methodology and tools to specific fine- and decorative-arts resources. Exhaustive in scope.

Kleinbauer, W. Eugene and Thomas Slavens. *Research Guide to the History of Western Art.* Chicago: American Library Association, 1982.

Library of Congress Subject Headings. 12th ed. Washington, D.C.: Library of Congress, 1989.
Useful in determining subject headings or topics to search for specific information.

Ludman, Joan and Lauris Mason. *Fine Print References: A Selected Bibliography of Print-Related Literature.* Millwood, NY: Kraus International, 1982.
Covers citations from 2500 internationally published books and catalogs.

Muehsam, Gerd. *Guide to Basic Information Sources in the Visual Arts.* Santa Barbara, CA: Jeffrey Norton Publishers/ABC Clio, 1978.

Pacey, Philip, ed. *Art Library Manual: A Guide to Resources and Practice.* New York: R.R. Bowker, 1977.

Schlereth, Thomas J. *Material Culture: A Research Guide.* Lawrence, KS: University Press of Kansas, 1985.
A series of essays includes material on American decorative arts and household furnishings, a guide to general research resources and more, with bibliographies.

Sheehy, Eugene P., ed. *Guide to Reference Books.* 10th ed. Chicago: American Library Association, 1986.
Includes basic references pertinent to any type of research, along with bibliographies tied to general themes such as the humanities, histories and area studies. A good introduction to locating material in any area.

Writing — Style Books and Methods

Barnet, Sylvan. *A Short Guide to Writing About Art.* 3rd ed. Glenview, IL: Scott, Foresman, 1989.

The Chicago Manual of Style for Authors, Editors and Copywriters. 13th ed. rev. and expanded. Chicago: University of Chicago, 1982.
Includes sections on manuscript preparation, footnote and bibliography styles, etc.

Goldman, Bernard. *Reading and Writing in the Arts: A Handbook.* Rev. ed. Detroit: Wayne State University Press, 1978.
Suggested readings as an overview to the field.

Sayre, Henry M. *Writing About Art.* Englewood Cliffs, NJ: Prentice-Hall, 1989.

Turabian, Kate L. *A Manual for Writers of Term Papers, Theses, and Dissertations*. 5th ed., rev. and expanded. Chicago: University of Chicago, 1987.
Much of this material is taken from *The Chicago Manual of Style* but is arranged in a more quick-reference manner, with easy access to sample bibliographies, etc.

Decorative Arts — General

Primary Reference Sources — Associations and Libraries

American Association for State and Local History. 172 2nd Ave. N., Ste. 202, Nashville, TN 37201.
Clearinghouse and coordinator for preservation projects, material and social history programs and activities, as well as publisher of related material.

American Craft Council Library and Museum. 72 Spring St., New York, NY 10012.
Has also published numerous bibliographies focusing on various media: clay, enamel, metal, wood.

American Life Foundation and Study Institute. Box 349, Watkins Glen, NY 148910349.
Furthers knowledge of decorative arts and architecture through publications and educational programs; maintains historic Century House.

Bibliotheque Forney. Hotel des Archeveques de Sens, 1, rue du Figuier, F-75004 Paris.
Contains references to fine, graphic and decorative arts, with outstanding collection of 19th and 20th century drawings of furniture and fabrics and large collection of French posters c. 1880-1985.

Cooper Hewitt Museum — Doris and Henry Dreyfuss Study Center. Smithsonian Institution, 2 East 91st St., New York, NY 10028.
One of the country's premier collections of American decorative arts and design, with extensive research collections.

Decorative Arts Society. Society of Architectural Historians. 1232 Pine St., Philadelphia, PA 19107.
Promotes the preservation of structures of historic and/or aesthetic significance. Publishes the *Decorative Arts Newsletter*, which includes notices of museum acquisitions and exhibitions, book reviews, articles.

Decorative Arts Trust. 106 Bainbridge, Philadelphia, PA 19147.
Curators, collectors and dealers interested in all aspects of the decorative arts; maintains national speakers' registry, provides information on sources for conservation, repair and identification.

Henry Francis du Pont Winterthur Museum. Rt. 52, Winterthur, DE 19735.
Outstanding decorative and cultural arts museum containing items from the 17th century to c. 1840, from interior architecture and furniture to ceramics, glass and Oriental carpets. Conducts extensive research in decorative arts, American material culture, and conservation, with attendant sponsor-

ship of fellowships, research grants and various educational programs. Reference library (70,000+ volumes) also includes microforms, manuscripts, periodicals and photographs relating to American arts and their English, European and Oriental origins. Extensive publications program includes the quarterly *Winterthur Portfolio*, with articles on American material culture, both regional and national.

National Art Library, Victoria and Albert Museum.. South Kensington, London, SW7 2RL, England.
Complements the outstanding V&A collections, with material on fine and applied arts.

National Trust for Historic Preservation. 1785 Massachusetts Ave. NW, Washington, D.C. 20036.
Clearinghouse for information on state, local and federal projects; numerous publications.

Society for the Preservation of New England Antiquities. 141 Cambridge St., Boston, MA 02114.
Seeks to preserve and conserve historic properties and decorative arts collections. Archives contain 1.5 million items related to the decorative arts and architecture, photographs, clippings, all with regional emphasis.

Victorian Society in America. 219 S. 6th, Philadelphia, PA 19106.
Seeks to foster an appreciation and understanding of 19th century America and the attendant things Victorian. Sponsors lectures, exhibits and tours.

Bibliographies

Ames, Kenneth L. and Gerald W.R. Ward, eds. *Decorative Arts and Household Furnishings in America, 1650-1920. An Annotated Bibliography*. Winterthur, DE: The Henry Francis du Pont Winterthur Museum, 1989.
Useful collection of chapter/essays on decorative, fine and applied arts and architecture and attendant recommended materials in each area, compiled by scholars in those fields. Particularly valuable for its relative currency.

de Winter, Patrick. *European Decorative Arts, 1400-1600: An Annotated Bibliography*. G.K. Hall Arts Bibliographies Series. Boston: G.K. Hall, 1988.

Ehresmann, Donald L. *Applied and Decorative Arts: A Bibliographic Guide to Basic Reference Books, Histories and Handbooks*. Englewood, CO: Libraries Unlimited, 1993.
Annotated entries cover a wealth of objects, from furniture to ivory, arms to textiles, jewelry to toys.

Franklin, Linda Campbell. *Antiques and Collectibles: A Bibliography of Works in English, 16th Century to 1976*. Metuchen, NJ: Scarecrow Press, 1978.
Briefly annotated entries on works related to antiques, decorative arts and collectibles, including theses, dissertations, exhibition catalogs, offprints and monographs. Arranged by author within subject categories. The sheer number of entries

— 10,000+ — makes this a significant, albeit currently somewhat outdated, guide to a overwhelming amount of material.

Kemplon, Richard. *Art Nouveau: An Annotated Bibliography*. Los Angeles: Hennessey & Ingalls, 1977.
Discusses all art forms, including some material c. 1903-1910.

Lackschewitz, Gertrud. *Interior Design and Decoration: A Bibliography Compiled for the American Institute of Decorators*. New York: New York Public Library, 1961.

Sokol, David M., ed. *American Decorative Arts and Old World Influences: A Guide to Information Sources. Art and Architecture Information Guide Series*. Detroit: Gale Research, 1980.
Bibliography of American decorative arts, c. seventeenth century to the present, with emphasis on post-1940 materials such as books, catalogs, and articles; brief annotations make this a usable, basic tool.

Tappert, Tara. *Decorative Arts: A Bibliography*. London: American Trust for the British Library, 1985.
Includes citations for works, c. 1880-1950, on American decorative arts.

Treanor, Betty McKee and John Garstka, eds. *IDEC Comprehensive Bibliography for Interior Design*. Richmond, VA: Interior Design Educators Council, 1984.

Vance, Mary A. *Interior Design and Decoration: A Bibliography of Books*. Monticello, IL: Vance Bibliographies, 1980.

Indices/Catalogs to Collections

Catalogue d'articles de periodiques: Arts decoratifs et beauxarts. [*Catalog of Periodical Articles: Decorative and Fine Arts*.] Boston: G.K. Hall, 1972.
Four-volume subject index to 1300+ articles from French and other serials.

Catalogue matieres: Arts-decoratifs, beaux-arts, metiers, techniques. Paris: Societe des Amis de la Bibliotheque Forney, 1970. *Supplement*, 1979.
Four-volume topical catalog.

Catalog of The Avery Memorial Architectural Library. 2nd ed. Boston: G.K. Hall, 1968. 19 vols. *First Supplement*, 1973. Four vols. *Second Supplement*, 1975. Four vols. *Third Supplement*, 1977. Three vols. *Fourth Supplement*, 1980. Three vols.
References materials on sculpture, mosaic, stained glass, tapestries, furniture design and ornament held in the Columbia University research facility.

Guide to the Index of Early Southern Artists and Artisans. New York: Clearwater Press, 1985.

The Index of Early Southern Artists and Artisans is a major reference to the fine and decorative arts of the American South, held at the *Museum of Early Southern Decorative Arts* in Winston-Salem, NC. Listing over 60,000 artisans working in 125 different trades prior to 1821, with material gleaned from newspapers, directories, private papers and court records, the Index may be accessed with the *Guide* by name or geographic location. (The Index itself is also arranged for access by trade, craft, tool, region, time period.) Excellent examples of both a comprehensive museum catalog and an extensive regional collection.

Index of American Design. New York: Chadwyck-Healey, 1979.
Depression-era Federal Art Project attempted to create a comprehensive visual survey of decorative, folk and popular art made in America pre-1900, the original drawings of which are in the National Gallery. This set, on microfiche, is assembled into ten divisions, including furniture and decorative accessories, ceramics and glass, firearms, domestic utensils, wood carvings and weathervanes, etc., creating a picture collection of those artist renderings. A printed *Catalog* indexes by renderer, owner, craftsman, designer, manufacturer and subject.

International Art & Antiques Yearbook: A Worldwide Dealers' and Collectors' Guide to the Art and Antiques Trade. London: National Magazine. Annual.
Lists art dealers, auctioneers, salesrooms and related service agencies, associations, serials and international antiques fairs, with specialist indices for each country.

Mace, Angel. *Royal Institute of British Architects: A Guide to Its Archives and History*. London: Mansell, 1986.
RIBA biography file includes material on 10,000+ architects and architectural historians and a file of periodical illustrations of works by RIBA members since 1900. Useful for references to architect-designed interiors and furnishings.

Minter-Dowd, Christine. *Finders' Guide to Decorative Arts in the Smithsonian Institution*. Washington, D.C.: Smithsonian Institution Press, 1984.
Invaluable handbook to the collections of the myriad divisions within the Institution, including the *Archives of American Art*, the *Cooper-Hewitt*, the *Freer Gallery of Art*, the *National Museum of African Art*, the *National Museum of American Art* (including the *Renwick Gallery*), the *National Museum of American History* (with all of its attendant divisions), the *Smithsonian Institution Furnishings Collection.*. Each entry includes a catalog of the collection, finding aids and an annotated bibliography of selected publications. Particularly useful in giving a detailed overview of the contents of individual collections.

Rink, Evald. *Technical Americana: A Checklist of Technical Publications Printed Before 1831*. Millwood, NY: Kraus International, 1981.
Lists period sources for surveys of, or manuals to, a variety of crafts and commerce.

Romaine, Lawrence B. *A Guide to American Trade Catalogs 1744-1900*. New York: R.R. Bowker, 1960.
Useful as both bibliography and collecting guide to this subject area.

Science and Technology Department Staff, Carnegie Library of Pittsburgh. *Index to Handicraft Books, 1974-1984*. Pittsburgh, PA: University of Pittsburgh Press, 1986.

Directories

Palder, Edward L. *Catalog of Catalogs III: The Complete Mail Order Directory*. Rockville, MD: Woodbine House, 1993.
Over 12,000 listings for business offering a variety of goods, from used books to collectible glassware to musical instruments. Invaluable for building the catalog collections essential to most appraisal libraries.

Periodicals

Antique Collector: An Authority in the Field of Fine and Applied Art and Antiques. 72 Broadwick St., London W1V 2BP England.
Articles on furniture, ceramics, metals, art, with lists of sales, exhibitions, etc.

Antique Trader Weekly. Box 1050, 100 Bryant St., Dubuque, IA 52004.
Classified ads and feature articles on a wide array of antique and collectible items, emphasizing the latter.

Collectrix: Books About Antiques and Collectibles. 200 N. Village Ave., Ste. 4C, Rockville Centre, NY 11570-2341.
Annotated reviews and previews.

Who — Biography, Marks

Bolton, Charles Knowles. *Bolton's American Armory: A Record of the Coats of Arms which Have Been in Use within the Present Bounds of the United States*. Reprint. Baltimore: Heraldic Book Co., 1964.
Originally published in 1927, this is still the single best source for identifying both important American coats of arms and the objects on which they were found (i.e. metalware, ceramics, etc.)

Bridenbaugh, Carl. *The Colonial Craftsman.*. Reprint. Chicago: University of Chicago Press, 1961.
Despite its shortcomings in socio-historical interpretation, this is a useful index to contemporary references (newspaper ads, diaries, etc.) re: artisans of the period.

The Guide to Arts and Crafts Workshops. Coral Gables, FL: Shaw Associates, 1990+. Serial.

Jervis, Simon. *The Facts on File Dictionary of Design and Designers*. New York: Facts on File, 1984.

Macdonald-Taylor, Margaret, comp. and ed. *A Dictionary of Marks: Metalwork, Furniture, Ceramics*. Rev. ed. London: Connoisseur, 1976.

Naylor, Colin, ed. *Contemporary Designers*. 2nd ed. Chicago: St. James Press, 1990.

Sprigg, June. *Shaker Design*. Exhibition catalog. New York: Whitney Museum of American Art, 1986.
Includes extensive index of artisans.

What — Identification of Form, Style, Material; Dictionaries

Anscombe, Isabelle. *Arts & Crafts Style*. New York: Rizzoli, 1991.
Covers the movement in the U.S. and Great Britain.

Bayer, Patricia. *Art Deco Source Book*. Oxford: Phaidon, 1988.

Bernasconi, John R. *The Collectors' Glossary of Antiques and Fine Arts*. 3rd ed. London: Estates Gazette, 1971.

Bingham, Don and Joan. *Tuttle Dictionary of Antiques and Collectibles Terms*. Rutland, VT: Charles Tuttle, 1992.
Useful pocket guide gives an added dimension to the usual decorative arts glossary by the inclusion of popular terms such as "Steiff" and "Fiesta Ware". Includes list of U.S. patent numbers and dates.

Boger, Louise Ade and H. Batterson Boger, eds. *The Dictionary of Antiques and the Decorative Arts: A Book of Reference for Glass, Furniture, Ceramics, Silver, Periods, Styles, Technical Terms, etc*. 2nd ed., enl. New York: Charles Scribner's Sons, 1967.

Bridgeman, Harriet and Elizabeth Drury. *Encyclopedia of Victoriana*. New York: MacMillan, 1975.

Buffet-Challie, Laurence. *The Art Nouveau Style*. New York: Rizzoli, 1982.

Davidson, Marshall B., ed. *The American Heritage History of Colonial Antiques*. New York: American Heritage Publishing Co., 1967.
Part of a series which also included volumes *From the American Revolution to the Civil War* and *From the Civil War to World War I*, this volume is well-illustrated, but provides little support for further research.

DiNoto, Andrea, ed. *The Encyclopedia of Collectibles*. Alexandria, VA: Time-Life, 1978. 16 volumes.
Covers the full spectrum of collectible objects, from advertising items to World War memorabilia. Brief but info-packed entries may include glossaries, marks, lists of associated museums, organizations and books, timelines, etc. Good example of a multi-volume survey of a general field.

Dizik, A. Allen. *Encyclopedia of Interior Design and Decoration*. Burbank, CA: Stratford House Pub. Co., 1976.

Duncan, Alastair, ed. *The Encyclopedia of Art Deco*. New York: E.P. Dutton, 1988.

Evans, Joan. *Pattern: A Study of Ornament in Western Europe from 1180 to 1900*. Reprint. New York: Da Capo Press, 1976.
Studies the development of motifs and themes in decorative arts and the conditions that influence folk and peasant art, as well as fine art.

Fleming, John and Hugh Honour. *The Penguin Dictionary of Decorative Arts*. New ed. New York: Viking, 1989.
Covers technical terms, materials, biographies and factory histories, marks.

Gilchrist, Brenda, gen. ed. *The Smithsonian Illustrated Library of Antiques*. Washington, D.C.: Smithsonian Institution, 1980.
Good example of a multi-volume survey of a given museum collection, in this case, the Cooper-Hewitt. Covering a variety of subjects, including clocks, prints, furniture and miniatures, well-chosen examples are enhanced by a subject glossary, bibliography and list of other significant collections.

Hardy, William, et al. *Encyclopedia of Decorative Styles, 1850-1935*. Oxford: Phaidon, 1978.

Kelley, Austin P. *The Anatomy of Antiques*. New York: Viking Press, 1974.
Excellent visual analysis of a variety of decorative arts objects, providing detailed glossaries of component parts for each.

Kovel, Ralph and Terry. *Know Your Antiques: How to Recognize and Evaluate Any Antique — Large or Small — Like an Expert*. 3rd ed. New York: Crown, 1981.
Detailed collecting hints on a wide variety of properties, including clues to age, information on processes, subject bibliographies. Companion volume in similar format: *Know Your Collectibles.*

Miller, Judith and Martin, eds. *Miller's World Encyclopedia of Antiques*. New York: Viking, 1989.
Well-illustrated general survey.

Osborne, Harold, ed. *The Oxford Companion to the Decorative Arts*. London: Oxford University Press, 1975.

Pegler, Martin. *The Dictionary of Interior Design*. New York: Crown, 1966.

Phipps, Frances. *The Collector's Complete Dictionary of American Antiques*. Garden City, NY: Doubleday, 1974.

Pile, John F. *Dictionary of Twentieth Century Design*. New York: Facts on File, 1990.

Quimby, Ian M.G. and Polly Anne Earl, eds. *Technological Innovation and the Decorative Arts*. Winterthur Conference Report 1973. Charlottesville: University Press of Virginia, 1974.
Series of essays explore the relationship between decorative arts and the technological innovations that affected or effected their production. Topics covered include metalware and electrolysis, pressed glass, Belter furniture and furniture-making machinery, printed textiles.

Ramsey, L.G.G., ed. *The Complete Color Encyclopedia of Antiques*. 2nd ed. New York: Hawthorn, 1975.
Covers all decorative arts, including pottery and porcelain, books and bookbinding, metal work, much more.

Random House Collector's Encyclopedia: Victoriana to Art Deco. New York: Random House, 1974.
Artisans, designers, terms and techniques discussed in a one-volume survey of a period c. 1851-1939.

Sears, Roebuck and Company. *The 1902 Edition of the Sears, Roebuck Catalogue*. New York: Crown, 1970.
Reprint provides primary source material for decorative arts and social history research; only one of a myriad of similar catalog reprints available.

Selz, Peter Howard. *Art Nouveau: Art and Design at the Turn of the Century*. Rev. ed. New York: Museum of Modern Art, 1975.
General survey of the movement and the period.

Wate, Dora and Maureen Stafford. *An Illustrated Dictionary of Ornament*. New York: St. Martin's Press, 1974.
Useful for tracing design/motif origins.

Wilson, Jose and Arthur Leaman. *Decorating Defined: A Dictionary of Decoration and Design*. New York: Simon and Schuster, 1970.

When

Edwards, Ralph and L.G.G. Ramsey, eds. *The Connoisseur's Complete Period Guides to the Houses, Decoration, Furnishing, and Chattels of the Classic Periods*. New York: Bonanza, 1968.
Six volumes cover the Tudor (1500-1603) through Early Victorian (1830-1860) periods, covering architecture as well as fine and decorative arts.

Fehrman, Cherie. *Postwar Interior Design, 1945-1960*. New York: Van Nostrand Reinhold, 1987.
Includes material on architect-designed furniture.

Garner, Philippe. *Contemporary Decorative Arts from 1940 to the Present*. New York: Facts on File, 1980.

Gere, Charlotte. *Nineteenth Century Decoration: The Art of the Interior*. New York: Abrams, 1989.

Grow, Lawrence. *American Victorian: A Style and Source Book*. New York: Harper and Row, 1984.

Mayhew, Edgar de N. and Minor Myers, Jr. *A Documentary History of American Interiors from the Colonial Era to 1915*. New York: Charles Scribner's Sons, 1980.
Survey goes beyond simple illustrations to provide furnishing diagrams, documentary references on such topics as fabrics and furnishing costs, homes of various classes, museums and historical societies with significant collections of American furniture and more. Comprehensive.

Naylor, Gillian. *The Arts and Crafts Movement: A Study of Its Sources, Ideals and Influence on Design Theory*. London: Studio Vista, 1971.

Seale, William. *The Tasteful Interlude: American Interiors through the Camera's Eye, 1860-1917*. 2nd ed., rev. and enl. Nashville: American Association for State and Local History, 1981.
A photographic record of private homes, from the wealthy to the working class, including Shakers, miners, ranchers. Introductory text discusses revival styles and the Arts and Crafts movement.

Thornton, Peter. *Authentic Decor: The Domestic Interior 16201920*. New York: Viking, 1984.
Exhaustively detailed text and contemporary images provide the "how" of placement and use of furnishings in England, Europe and the U.S.

Tracy, Berry B. and William H. Gerdts. *Classical America 1815-1845*. Exhibition catalog. Newark, NJ: Newark Museum, 1963.
Survey of furniture, silver, textiles, stoves, clocks and more in the classical style, with additional text on European sources and American outgrowths of that style.

Where

Bishop, Robert and Patricia Coblentz. *American Decorative Arts: 360 Years of Creative Design*. New York: Abrams, 1982.
Lavishly illustrated survey of objects c. 1620-1980. Extensive bibliography and index.

Calloway, Stephen. *Twentieth Century Decoration*. New York: Rizzoli, 1988.

Clark, Robert Judson. *The Arts and Crafts Movement in America, 1876-1916*. Exhibition catalog. Princeton, NJ: Princeton University Press, 1972.

Cooper, Wendy. *In Praise of America: American Decorative Arts 1617-1830. Fifty Years of Discovery Since the 1929 Girl Scouts Loan Exhibition*. New York: Alfred A. Knopf, 1980.
A retrospective examination of the landmark exhibition and the directions scholarship has taken since then in a series of essays that cover such topics as regionalism and the study of production outside major style centers.

Design in America: The Cranbrook Vision, 1925-1950. Exhibition catalog. New York: Abrams, 1983.
Documents modern American design as reflected in the collections and work of the Cranbrook community, including the work of the students and faculty of the Cranbrook Academy.

Duncan, Alastair. *Treasures of the American Arts and Crafts Movement*. New York: Abrams, 1988.

Groer, Leon de. *Decorative Arts in Europe, 1790-1850*. New York: Rizzoli, 1986.

Kardon, Janet, ed. *The Ideal Home: The History of Twentieth Century American Craft 1900-1920*. New York: Abrams, 1993.
Inaugural volume in a projected multivolume library to be issued by the American Craft Museum, this studies the effects of the American Arts and Crafts Movement in the domestic interior. Along with a catalog of objects and discussions of social and cultural implications, the outstanding feature is a resource section with artisan biographies, lists of manufacturers, exhibitions, societies, periodicals, small presses. Bibliography.

Savage, George. *French Decorative Art, 1638-1793*. New York: Praeger, 1969.

Schlee, Ernst. *German Folk Art*. Tokyo: Kodansha, 1980.
Survey of a country's decorative art forms, with regional variations, is also useful in tracing design influences that may appear in other countries.

Stoudt, John Joseph. *Early Pennsylvania Arts and Crafts*. New York: Bonanza Books, 1964.
Study of regional decorative arts, from the classical Philadelphia furniture designs to Pennsylvania Dutch *fraktur*.

Strange, Thomas Arthur. *French Interiors, Furniture, Decoration, Woodwork and Allied Arts*. New York: Bonanza Books, 1968.
Historical guide, c. 1650-1850.

Tschudi-Madsen, Stephan. *Sources of Art Nouveau*. New York: de Capo Press, 1976.

How

Drury, Elizabeth, ed. *Antiques: Traditional Techniques of the Master Craftsmen, Furniture, Glass, Ceramics, Gold, Silver, and Much More*. Garden City, NY: Doubleday, 1986.

Andre, Jean-Michel. *The Restorer's Handbook of Ceramics and Glass*. Jean Andre, trans. New York: Van Nostrand Reinhold, 1976.

Why

Bishop, Robert and William C. Ketchum, Jr., series consultants. *The Knopf Collectors' Guides to American Antiques*. New York: Alfred Knopf.

Volumes in this series cover metalware, glass, ceramics, furniture, textiles, dolls in a quick-reference format that emphasizes value points. Excellent, well-illustrated, quick surveys that go beyond superficial identification. Price guides; appendices of supplemental info (i.e. marks); bibliographies.

Bly, John, ed. *The Confident Collector: How to Recognize an Authentic Antique*. New York: Prentice-Hall, 1986. [Originally published as *Is It Genuine?*]

Points of authenticity and quality are discussed.

Smith, Charles W. *Auctions: The Social Construction of Value*. Berkeley: University of California, 1990.

Examines the hows and whys of the auction market.

Yates, Raymond Francis. *Antique Fakes and Their Detection*. New York: Harper & Brothers, 1950.

Detection of decorative arts fakes: furniture, glass, ceramics, pewter, paintings, etc. Useful points in questioning and testing authenticity.

How Much

Annuaire des cotes international/International Art Price Annual. Paris: ADEC-Production, 1988+. Annual.

Antique Market Report. 650 Westdale Dr., Wichita, KS 67209.

Reports results from various auction houses.

Antique Review. Ohio Antique Review, P.O. Box 538, Worthington, OH 43085.

Covers the midwest/Ohio region: shows, auctions, market reports, topics of both local and national interest.

Antiques and the Arts Weekly. Newtown Bee, Newton, CT 06470.

La gazette de l'hotel Drouot. Bethesda, MD: UPA, 1891+. Annual. Microfilm.

Important documentary source of information on sales of art and antiques from one of the major French auction houses. This microfilm format, with detailed descriptions and illustrations, is available from 1891 to the present.

The Lyle Official Antiques Review. New York: Perigree. Annual.

International auction reports, crediting the selling firm; photograph of each property.

Maine Antiques Digest: The Marketplace for Americana. P.O. Box 1429, Waldoboro, ME 04572.

Reports of sales and auctions, with extensive commentary and reports of prices realized; regional name belies the national scope of material covered. Backfiles available from University Microfilms Inc.

Marion, John L. *Sotheby's International Price Guide*. New York: Vendome Press. Annual.

Compilation of auction results in a single illustrated volume. This distillation of sales results should serve as a reminder that most major (and many minor) auction houses offer illustrated catalogs and prices realized lists by subscription. Carefully interpreted by the informed appraiser, these provide some of the best market data available and comprise the foundation of many appraisal libraries.

Miller, Judith and Martin, comps. and eds. *Miller's International Antiques Price Guide*. New York: Viking. Annual.

Photos with extensive descriptions and price "ranges".

Price Guide Series. Woodbridge, England: Antique Collector's Club.

A variety of subject titles, from furniture and ceramics to jewelry and bronzes, make this a good example of a series of volumes that combine solid text and research with market reports in varying degress of currency.

Rinker, Harry L. *Warman's Americana & Collectibles*. Radnor, PA: Wallace-Homestead. Annual.

Provides a market guide to those items that are often overlooked in general price guides. Companion series, *Warman's Antiques and Their Prices*, along with multiple special volumes on topics ranging from Continental ceramics to garden furnishings, creates a broad spectrum of reports on collectible properties. These should, like all price guides, be interpreted with caution and in as informed a manner re: sale situations, condition, etc., as possible. Added bonuses are references to organizations and publications at the beginning of each entry.

Ceramics

Primary Reference Sources

American Art Pottery Association. 125 E. Rose, St. Louis, MO 63119.

Membership includes collectors and dealers, designed to increase awareness of and appreciation for art pottery. Publishes *Journal of the American Art Pottery Association* bimonthly; sponsors conference with seminar.

English Ceramic Circle. 115 Church St., Marylebone, London NW88HA, England.

Multi-national membership concentrates on scholarship and collecting of English pottery, porcelain, and enamels of the 17th-19th centuries.

George R. Gardiner Museum of Ceramic Art. 111 Queen's Park, Toronto, Ontario M5S 2C7 (416) 593-9300.

North America's only ceramics museum holds a collection of over 2000 pieces, constituting one of the world's best collections of European porcelain.

Wedgwood International Seminar. 12526 Martindale Rd., Houston, TX 77048.

Collectors and scholars of 18th-20th century Wedgwood. Publishes lectures presented at seminars. (This is just one of many organizations which concentrates on the study and collecting of a particular ceramic type; see the *Encyclopedia of Associations* for more examples.)

Bibliographies

Branner, John Casper. *A Bibliography of Clays and the Ceramic Arts*. Columbus, OH: American Ceramic Society, 1906.
Includes several useful primary sources, many of them from fairly obscure publications; no subject index.

Campbell, James, ed. *Pottery and Ceramics. Art and Architecture Information Guide Series*. Detroit: Gale Research, 1978.

Heilpern, Gisela, comp. *Josiah Wedgwood, Eighteenth Century English Potter: A Bibliography. Bibliographic Contributions No. 3*. Carbondale: Southern Illinois University, 1967.
Indicative of the role Wedgwood played not only in his company's history but in the general history of English ceramics. Drawn from his own papers, as well as outside sources; several American collections are featured.

LaGrange, Marie J. *Pottery and Porcelain: An Annotated Bibliography*. Indianapolis: Indiana State University, 1938.

Oppelt, Norman T. *Southwestern Pottery: An Annotated Bibliography and List of Types and Wares*. 2nd ed. Metuchen, NJ: Scarecrow Press, 1988.
Emphasizes Native American pottery of the area in a regionally-oriented bibliography.

Strong, Susan R. *History of American Ceramics: An Annotated Bibliography*. Metuchen, NJ: Scarecrow Press, 1983.
Extremely useful volume covers a wide range of subjects (history, technology, regional and local potteries, art pottery, modern ceramics) in a wide range of formats (books, including single pertinent chapters from same, exhibition catalogs). Indices by title, author, subject.

Weidner, Ruth Irwin, comp. *American Ceramics Before 1930: A Bibliography*. Westport, CT: Greenwood Press, 1982.
Nearly 3000 entries organized by publication type (book, pamphlet, periodical, catalog); no annotations.

Weinrich, Peter H. *A Bibliographic Guide to Books on Ceramics/Guide bibliographique des ouvrages sur la ceramique*. Ottawa: Canadian Crafts Council, 1976.
Emphasizes books on English ceramics.

Indices

Ceramics Monthly. Box 12448, 1609 Northwest Blvd., Columbus, OH 43212.
Indexed publication targeted towards potters, ceramic artists, schools, craft centers, galleries, collectors and others with an interest in ceramics.

Who

Barber, Edwin Atlee. *Marks of American Potters*. Philadelphia: Patterson and White, 1904.
Reproduces 1000 marks, with illustrations.

Chaffers, William. *Marks and Monograms on European and Oriental Pottery and Porcelain*. 15th rev. ed. London: William Reeves, 1965.
Classic work on the subject, with lengthy text interspersed with mark facsimiles. For quick reference, *Collector's Handbook of Marks and Monograms on Pottery and Porcelain* by Chaffers (Los Angeles: Borden Publ., n.d.) reproduces the marks only, arranged by country, with an index to company names.

Cummins, Virginia Raymond. *Rookwood Pottery Potpourri*. Silver Spring, MD: Leonard and Coleman, 1980.
Provides biographies of the artisans who created this significant American art pottery line.

Danckert, Ludwig. *Directory of European Porcelain: Marks, Makers and Factories*. 4th ed. Rita Kipling, trans. London: N.A.G. Press, 1981.
Useful complement to other books of European ceramic marks in filling in gaps in documentation.

Dauterman, Carl Christian. *Sevres Porcelain: Makers and Marks of the Eighteenth Century*. New York: Metropolitan Museum, 1986.

Godden, Geoffrey. *Encyclopedia of British Porcelain Manufacturers*. London: Barrie and Jenkins, 1988.
Well-documented volume by a major researcher of English ceramics.

— . *Illustrated Encyclopedia of British Pottery and Porcelain Marks*. New York: Crown, 1966.
Arranged by firm name, this also provides indices to monograms, signs and devices used in marks.

Haslam, Malcolm. *Marks and Monograms of the Modern Movement, 1875-1930*. New York: Scribner, 1977.
Includes artists, designers, retailers and manufacturers; "modern" is here defined as the period from the Aesthetic Movement to Art Deco and Style Moderne.

Honey, William Bowyer. *English Ceramic Art from the End of the Middle Ages to About 1815: A Dictionary of Factories, Artists, Technical Terms, etc.* 2nd ed. London: Faber and Faber, 1963.
Facsimile signatures, marks, along with biographies and a useful bibliography.

Kovel, Ralph and Terry Kovel. *Kovel's New Dictionary of Marks: Pottery and Porcelain*. New York: Crown, 1986.
Covers American, European and Oriental marks, 1850 to the present. Useful appendices on dating systems used by specific factories and the genealogy of various companies.

Lehner, Lois. *Lehner's Encyclopedia of U.S. Marks on Pottery, Porcelain and Clay.* Paducah, KY: Collector Books, 1988.
Very well-researched with a fine bibliography, this covers the utilitarian wares as well as fine china and art pottery.

Mankowitz, Wolf and Reginald G. Haggar. *The Concise Encyclopedia of European Pottery and Porcelain.* New York: Praeger, 1968.
General overview, with list of pottery and porcelain transfer pattern engravers.

Rontgen, Robert E. *Marks on German, Bohemian, and Austrian Porcelain, 1710 to present.* Exton, PA: Schiffer, 1981.
With extensive bibliography, this is a useful tool for researching material from a limited region.

What

Barber, Edwin Atlee. *The Ceramic Collectors' Glossary.* New York: For the [Walpole] Society, 1914.

Berling, K., ed. *Meissen China: An Illustrated History.* Reprint. New York: Dover, 1972.
Festschrift commemorating the company's 200th anniversary, with a series of essays on the technical and commercial aspects of the company.

Boger, Louise Ada. *The Dictionary of World Pottery and Porcelain.* New York: Charles Scribner's, 1971.
Covers the gamut, geographically, as well as by product and artisan; line drawings only. Lengthy bibliography and notes. Good general source for terms.

Cameron, Elizabeth. *Encyclopedia of Pottery and Porcelain, 1800-1960.* New York: Facts on File, 1986.

Charles, Bernard. *Pottery and Porcelain: A Dictionary of Terms.* Newton Abbot, England: David and Charles, 1974.

Coysh, A.W. and R.K. Henrywood. *The Dictionary of Blue and White Printed Pottery, 1780-1880.* Vols. 1 and 2. Woodbridge, Suffolk: Antique Collectors Club, 1989.
Listings, by pattern name, inventory much of the popular blue and white transfer printed ware. Discussion of design sources and potters' marks; bibliography.

Cushion, John P. *Pottery and Porcelain Tablewares.* New York: William Morrow, 1976.
First publication solely devoted to tableware analyzes and identifies manufacturers by the blank's shape; cups, tankards, pitchers, teapots, plates are all reproduced in line drawings and named. In this system, marks, while key clues, are considered secondary.

Dodd, Arthur Edward. *Dictionary of Ceramics: Pottery, Glass, Vitreous Enamels, Refractories, Clay Building Materials.* New York: Philosophical Library, 1964.
Glossary includes technical and specialized terms.

Evans, Paul. *Art Pottery of the United States: An Encyclopedia of Producers and Their Marks.* New York: Scribner's, 1974.
Useful geographic listing of potteries; comprehensive.

Fournier, Robert. *Illustrated Dictionary of Pottery Form.* New York: Van Nostrand Reinhold, 1981.

_____. *Illustrated Dictionary of Practical Pottery.* Rev. ed. New York: Van Nostrand Reinhold, 1977.
Good companion to the author's above-cited work.

Haggar, Reginald G. *The Concise Encyclopedia of Continental Pottery and Porcelain.* New York: Hawthorn, 1960.

Jacobson, Gertrude Tatnall. *Haviland China: A Pattern Identification Guide.* Des Moines, IA: Wallace-Homestead, 1979.
Two-volume set catalogs the myriad patterns and blanks of Haviland china; includes color chart.

Karmason, Marilyn and Joan Stacke. *Majolica: A Complete History and Illustrated Survey.* New York: Abrams, 1989.
The first major study of majolica examines its properties, forms and producers, from England and the Continent to the U.S. Good bibliography and museum list.

Klamkin, Marian. *American Patriotic and Political China.* New York: Scribner's, 1983.
Useful in identifying and dating commemorative pieces.

Kovel, Ralph and Terry. *Kovels' American Art Pottery: The Collector's Guide to Makers, Marks and Factory Histories.* New York: Crown, 1993.
Listings of over 200 potteries, well-illustrated, with company terminology; includes a special section on tile companies. Individual factory bibliographies provided.

LaGrange, Marie J. *Staffordshire Romantic Transfer Patterns: Cup Plates and Early Victorian China.* Jeffersontown, KY: Fountain House East, 1978-1986.
History and identification of the products of the Staffordshire area.

Reilly, Robin. *Dictionary of Wedgwood.* Woodbridge: Antique Collectors Club, 1980.
Listings include types and forms, artisans, processes of the wares produced by the largest pottery and porcelain group of the Western world. Appendices of marks.

Rontgen, Robert E. *The Book of Meissen.* Exton, PA: Schiffer, 1984.
Thorough history, from founding to the present, with patterns, marks, forms, imitations. Many primary sources used, including old trade catalogs and design books.

Savage, George and Harold Newman. *Illustrated Dictionary of Ceramics.* London: Thames and Hudson, 1985.

Another volume in the publisher's decorative arts series, this is a useful guide to examples from antiquity to the present. Additional section on European factories and marks by John Cushion.

When

Axel, Jan. *Porcelain: Traditions and New Visions*. New York: Watson-Guptill, 1981.
Study of 20th centuries forms.

Lewenstein, Eileen and Emmanuel Cooper. *New Ceramics*. New York: Van Nostrand Reinhold, 1974.
Country-by-country survey of studio pottery, from Britain to Yugoslavia, illustrated by examples of specific studio potters' works.

Lipski, Louis. *Dated English Delftware: Tin-Glazed Earthenware, 1600-1800*. London: Sotheby Publications, 1984.

Meister, Peter Wilhelm and Horst Reber. *European Porcelain of the 18th Century*. Ithaca, NY: Cornell University Press, 1980.
Covers all aspects, from production and design influences to iconographic themes. Lists of patrons and collections; lengthy bibliography.

Savage, George. *18th Century German Porcelain*. London: Spring Books, 1958.
Text covers studies form specific companies, as well as from specific regions.

Where

Atterbury, Paul, ed. *English Pottery and Porcelain: An Historical Survey*. New York: Universe Books, 1978.
Fifty years of thoroughly-researched material culled from *Magazine Antiques*.

Clark, Garth. *American Ceramics: 1876 to the Present*. Rev. ed. New York: Abbeville Press, 1987.
Features extensive bibliography, along with general overview of pottery and porcelain production in the U.S.

Frelinghuysen, Alice Cooney. *American Porcelain 1770-1920*. Exhibition catalog. New York: Metropolitan Museum of Art, 1989.
Well-selected survey of the period, with lengthy catalog descriptions. Extensive bibliography.

Godden, Geoffrey. *British Pottery and Porcelain, 1780-1850*. New York: A.S. Barnes, 1963.

Hillier, Bevis. *Pottery and Porcelain, 1700-1914: England, Europe and North America*. New York: Meredith Press, 1968.
Cross-continent study providing interesting contrasts and comparisons. Part of the *Social History of the Decorative Arts* series.

Jewitt, Llewellynn. *The Ceramic Art of Great Britain*. New ed., rev. Poole, Dorset: New Orchard Editions, 1985.
First published in 1883, this volume provides an interesting contemporary commentary on 19th century ceramics production. Along with a county-by-county survey of England; material on Ireland and Scotland is included.

Jonge, Caroline Henriette de. *Delft Ceramics*. London: Pall Mall, 1970.

Ketchum, William C. *American Stoneware*. New York: Holt, 1991.
Thorough examination by state of stoneware pieces, examining them as both folk art and utilitarian work ware.

_____. *Potters and Potteries of New York State, 1650-1900*. 2nd ed. Syracuse: Syracuse University Press, 1987.
Excellent example of a scholarly and thoroughly researched study that is useful to the less-knowledgable. Extensive tables of potters' biographies, with a bibliography sorted by artisan's name.

Lambert, Gail. *Pottery in New Zealand: Commercial and Collectible*. Auckland: Heinemann, 1985.
A country's ceramics history through a factory-by-factory survey, with regard to outside influences on form and style. Illustrates the fact that nearly every country has been the focus of a regional ceramics study. Marks, glossary, bibliography.

Plinval de Guillebon, Regine de. *Porcelain of Paris, 1770-1850*. New York: Walker, 1972.

Poche, Emanuel. *Bohemian Porcelain*. Prague: Artia. 1957.

Regional Aspects of American Folk Pottery. Exhibition catalog. York, PA: Historical Society of York County, 1974.
Excellent introduction to regional variations and identifying characteristics of New England, Mid-Atlantic, Virginia and North Carolina wares.

Schaffer, Paul, ed. *An Imperial Fascination: Dining with the Czars*. Exhibition catalog. New York: A La Vielle Russie, 1991.
Soviet porcelain is just beginning to become the topic of Western research, and this volume provides an interesting introduction to ceramics designed for use. Good section on factory histories and marks.

Spours, Judy. *Art Deco Tableware: British Domestic Ceramics 1925-1939*. New York: Rizzoli, 1988.
Sets a specific survey of a popular ceramic form against the wider social and design history of the times. Trade names for some patterns provided; appendix lists resource centers where pattern books may be studied.

Webster, Donald Blake. *Decorated Stoneware Pottery of North America*. Rutland, VT: Tuttle, 1971.

Survey of the utilitarian products of a continent, with interesting illustrations of influences, similarites, and characteristic differences.

How

Hamer, Frank. *The Potter's Dictionary of Materials and Techniques*. London: Pitman, 1975.

Morley-Fletcher, Hugo, ed. *Techniques of the World's Great Masters of Pottery and Ceramics*. Seacaucus, NJ: Chartwell, 1984.
Well-illustrated survey of specific techniques, from creating the vessel to its decoration. Useful in establishing guidelines in judging quality as more is known about how various effects are achieved. Lengthy sections on Oriental ceramics.

How Much

Bagdade, Susan and Al. *Warman's English and Continental Pottery and Porcelain*. 2nd ed. Radnor, PA: Wallace-Homestead, 1991.
Covers many of the most commonly found wares, with additional data on museums, references, organizations and company history.

Ball, A. *The Price Guide to Pot-Lids and Other Underglaze Multi-colour Prints on Ware*. 2nd ed. Suffolk: Antique Collector's Club, 1980.
Example of a price guide to a single, specific pottery form in its many variations. Very well-illustrated.

Furniture

Primary Reference Sources

Baker Furniture Museum. East Sixth St., Holland, MI 49423.
Corporate museum of European and Oriental furniture, 17th-20th century, along with collections of tools, hardware, decorative arts and books.

Chipstone Foundation. 777 E. Wisconsin Ave., Ste. 3090, Milwaukee, WI 53202-5373.
Programs support institutions dedicated to the study of American Decorative Arts. Recent areas of interest have included American furniture. Chipstone Foundation publishes a journal of American Furniture, 17th century to the present.

Colonial Williamsburg. Goodwin Building, P.O. Box C, Williamsburg, VA 23185.
Extensive collections in all areas of the decorative, fine and folk arts, including significant holdings of furniture. 55,000+ volume library; research fields include processes, as well as questions of connoisseurship and historical and stylistic development.

Furniture History Society. 1 Mercedes Cottages, St. John's Road, Haywards Heath, W. Sussex, RG16 4EH, England.

Libraries, museums, dealers, historians in 27 countries interested in the study of furniture. Publications include *Furniture History* (annual), which includes archival material and a bibliography, as well as books on furniture and its craftsmen. Sponsors annual conference.

High Point Furniture Library. 1009 North Main, High Point, NC 27262.
7000 volumes relating to furniture history, design, construction and related subjects. Also sells books.

Historic Deerfield. The Street/P.O. Box 321, Deerfield, MA 01342.
Collections and research fields focus on furniture, among other decorative arts, supported by large research library and several historic structures. Past publications have included *The Furniture of Historic Deerfield*.

Public Museum of Grand Rapids. 54 Jefferson S.E., Grand Rapids, MI 49503.
Along with general historical and decorative arts collections, showcases Grand Rapids-made furniture, illustrative of area industry; research fields include the study of 19th and 20th century American furniture.

Bibliographies

Semowich, Charles J., comp. *American Furniture Craftsmen Working Prior to 1920: An Annotated Bibliography*. Art Reference Collection, no. 7. Westport, CT: Greenwood Press, 1984.
Over 2000 citations are arranged into such subject categories as craftsmen biographies, studies of craftsmen groups, general works, trade categories. Appendices include lists of industry-related periodicals and selected manuscript collections.

Vance, Mary A. *Italian Furniture: A Bibliography of Periodical Articles*. Monticello, IL: Vance Bibliographies, 1981.

Indices

Fine Woodworking Comprehensive Cumulative Index. Newtown, CT: Taunton Press, 1985.
Covers issues 1-50 (Winter 1975-Jan./Feb. 1985), listing articles, letters, techniques/methods, queries and photos. *Supplementary Index* covers issues 51 through 65. Subject matter covers craftsmanship, processes and history of form and design, as well as patterns and projects.

Habegger, Jerryll. *Sourcebook of Modern Furniture*. New York: Van Nostrand Reinghold, 1989.
Features designer biographies, including some architect-designed examples.

Sparke, Penny, et al. *Design Source Book*. London: MacDonald, 1986.
Covers 19th and 20th century themes and motifs.

Periodicals

Magazine Antiques. 575 Broadway, New York, NY 10012.

The periodical everyone seems to know about, but it is useful to remember that articles on furniture are emphasized; that it is cited in many indices, including a self-index prepared by the publisher; and that it is often one of the few sources available for information on regional or esoteric forms and studies.

Who

Albers, Marjorie K. *The Amana People and Their Furniture.* Ames, IA: Iowa State University Press, 1990.

Study of the furniture industry within a given community in terms of design characteristics, in how production influenced local economies, and in the specifics of Amana culture and history.

Beard, Geoffrey and Christopher Gilbert, eds. *Dictionary of English Furniture Makers 1660-1840.* London: Furniture History Society, 1986.

Biographical material includes information on commissions and signed or documented pieces.

Bjerkoe, Ethel Hall. *The Cabinetmakers of America.* 2nd ed. Exton, PA: Schiffer, 1978.

The first, and only, attempt to compile such a national biographical list, resulting in this collection of 3000 entries ca. 1680-1900 (and which is still incomplete). A good starting point for research, but other regional studies, monographs and indices should also be utilized.

Fregnac, Claude, ed. *French Cabinetmakers of the Eighteenth Century.* Paris: Hachette, 1965.

Includes information on development of manufacturing techniques and the influences of taste upon form and style.

Heal, Ambrose. *The London Furniture Makers, from the Restoration to the Victorian Era, 1660-1840.*

Records of 2500 cabinetmakers, upholsterers, carvers and gilders, including addresses and dates of activity; many illustrated with reproductions of trade cards. Chapter on challenges of authentication.

Honour, Hugh. *Cabinet Makers and Furniture Designers.* New York: Putnam, 1960.

Profiles of fifty designers and craftsmen from France, England, Italy, France, Holland, Germany, Scandinavia and America.

Ormsbee, Thomas H. *Early American Furniture Makers, A Social and Biographical Study.* Reprint. Detroit: Gale Research, 1976.

Page, Marian. *Furniture Designed by Architects.* New York: Whitney Library of Design, 1980.

Divided into stylistic schools, from Federal to Gothic, Arts and Crafts to Post-War, the designs of major figures in architecture are discussed in detail.

Theunissen, Andre. *Meubles et sieges du xviiie siecle: menuisiers, ebenistes, marques, plans et ornementation de leurs oeuvres.* Paris: Editions "Le Document", 1934.

Biographies and working records of 18th century French cabinetmakers and those in allied trades.

What — Styles, Periods, Materials

Aronson, Joseph. *The Encyclopedia of Furniture.* 3rd ed., rev. New York: Crown Publishers, 1965.

With lists of craftsmen and designers.

Bell, J. Munro. *The Furniture Designs of Chippendale, Hepplewhite and Sheraton.* New York: Arts and Decoration Book Society, 1938.

Reprints of the individual style books, with critical explanatory essays.

Bigelow, Deborah, et al, eds. *Gilded Wood: Conservation and History.* Madison, CT: Sound View Press, 1991.

Based on material presented at a symposium sponsored by the American Institute for Conservation of Artistic and Historic Works.

Boger, Louise Ade. *The Complete Guide to Furniture Styles.* Enl. ed. New York: Scribner's, 1982.

Butler, Joseph. *Field Guide to American Antique Furniture.* New York: Facts on File, 1985.

Expanding upon the idea of a visual dictionary, this volume covers a variety of styles and forms, illustrating the identifying characteristics of each.

Claude-Salvy. *Dictionnaire des meubles regionaux.* [*Dictionary of Regional Furniture.*] Paris: Hachette, 1971.

Duncan, Alastair. *Art Nouveau Furniture.* New York: Crown, 1982.

Edlin, Herbet L. *What Wood is That? A Manual of Wood Identification.* New York: Viking, 1969.

Contains wood samples, with entries for various species which point out characteristics and peculiarities.

Edwards, Ralph. *Dictionary of English Furniture from the Middle Ages to the Late Georgian Period.* London: Antique Collectors Club, 1983.

Definitions and biographies in a three-volume set.

Gloag, John. *A Complete Dictionary of Furniture.* Rev. ed. Woodstock, NY: Overlook Press, 1991.

_____ . *A Short Dictionary of Furniture Containing Over 2600 Entries that Include Terms and Names Used in Britain and the United States of America.* Rev. and enl. London: George Allen and Unwin, 1969.

Emphasis on design; chronology (c. 1100-1950) covers types, construction methods, materials, biographical section on craftsmen.

Hinckley, F. Lewis. *Directory of the Historic Cabinet Woods.* New York: Bonanza Books, 1960.

Discussion of hardwoods used in furniture making c. 1460-1900, with illustrated examples.

Kenney, John Tarrant. *The Hitchcock Chair.* New York: Clarkson Potter, 1971.
History of a specific commercial form, the Hitchcock chair, with examination of style and decoration, technological process and industry development, and the eventual modern restoration of the original factory. Appendices include Lambert Hitchcock estate inventory.

Layton, Edwin J. *Identifying American Furniture: A Pictorial Guide to Styles and Terms, Colonial to Contemporary.* 2nd ed., rev. and exp. Nashville: AASLH, 1989.

Marek, Don. *Arts and Crafts Furniture Design: The Grand Rapids Contribution 1895-1915.* Exhibition catalog. Grand Rapids, MI: Grand Rapids Art Museum, 1987.

Miller, Judith and Martin, eds. *The Antiques Directory: Furniture.* Boston: G.K. Hall, 1985.
International survey of 7000 examples, c. 1500 to late 1800s, with brief introductory section to each form and descriptive caption for each example.

Newman, Bruce M. *Fantasy Furniture.* New York: Rizzoli, 1989.
Illustrates the variety of fantastical forms produced in Europe, the Far East and the U.S. during the 19th and 20th centuries, in styles ranging from "Horn and Antler" to the "Belle Epoque" and utilizing a variety of materials.

Ostergard, Derek E., ed. *Bentwood and Metal Furniture 1850-1946.* Exhibition catalog. New York: American Federation of the Arts, 1987.
Development of technique and industry, tracing roots of design for over a century. Appendix of manufacturers; extensive bibliography cites many trade catalogs.

Penderel-Brodhurst, James. *A Glossary of English Furniture of the Historic Periods.* London: J. Murray, 1925.

Praz, Mario. *An Illustrated History of Furnishing from the Renaissance to the Twentieth Century.* New York: George Braziller, 1964.
History of interior furnishing and arrangement through contemporary visual art.

Rubira, Jose Claret. *Classical European Furniture Design: French, Spanish and English Period Designs.* New York: Gramercy Park, 1989.
Compendium of design elements from the 14th-19th centuries.

Taylor, Henry Hammond. *Knowing, Collecting and Restoring Early American Furniture.* Philadelphia: Lippincott, 1930.

Symonds, R.W. *Victorian Furniture.* London: Country Life, 1962.

The Victorian Cabinet-Maker's Assistant. New York: Dover, 1970.
Contemporary design sourcebook.

White, Anthony and Bruce Robertson. *Furniture and Furnishings: A Visual Guide.* New York: Design Press, 1990.
Detailed visual dictionary for furniture styles, design elements, moldings, hardware, joinings, plus extensive glossary.

When

Cathers, David M. *Furniture of the American Arts and Crafts Movement: Stickley and Roycroft Mission Oak.* New York: New American Library, 1981.
Thoughtful text traces the historical background and offers identification clues to this style; well-illustrated catalog shows a variety of forms.

Cooke, Edward S. *New American Furniture: The Second Generation of Studio Furnituremakers.* Boston: Museum of Fine Arts, 1989.

Dormer, Peter. *The New Furniture: Trends + Traditions.* New York: Thames and Hudson, 1987.

Garner, Philippe. *Twentieth Century Furniture.* New York: Van Nostrand Reinhold, 1980.

Grandjean, Serge. *Empire Furniture 1800-1825.* New York: Taplinger Pub. Co., 1966.

Greenberg, Cara. *Mid-century Modern: Furniture of the 1950's.* New York: Harmony Books, 1984.

Jobe, Brock and Myrna Kaye. *New England Furniture: The Colonial Era.* Boston: Houghton Mifflin, 1984.
Selected from the Society for the Preservation of New England Antiquities collections, well-documented examples serve to illustrate the introductory essays on such topics as craft practice and the rural artisan. Extensive bibliography; list of collections.

Montgomery, Charles. *American Furniture: The Federal Period.* New York: Bonanza Books, 1978.
Detailed catalog of examples from the Winterthur collections, with a section on makers' labels, biographies and a large bibliography. Identification hints in sections that examine characteristic inlays and design elements.

Sparke, Penny. *Furniture: Twentieth Century Design.* New York: Dutton, 1986.

Where

American Manufactured Furniture. West Chester, PA: Schiffer, 1988.
Combines two useful features: utilizes contemporary catalog illustrations and covers an era of machine-made furniture (c. 1920-1940) that is often ignored.

Comstock, Helen. *American Furniture: A Complete Guide to Seventeenth, Eighteenth and Early Nineteenth Century Styles.* New York: Bonanza Books, 1962.
Good pictorial survey is, despite some changes in terminology and scholarship, still a useful tool for locating specific examples.

Cotton, Bernard D. *The English Regional Chair*. Woodbridge, England: Antique Collectors Club, 1990.

Outstanding examples of the study of a specific form and the analysis of regional influences. Exhaustive examination of variations in design and material, with lengthy catalog of woodworkers arranged by location.

Furniture by Harrods. West Chester, PA: Schiffer, 1989.

Reproduction of a c. 1900 commercial catalog provides contemporary terminology and an interesting slant on the significance of this type of material culture.

Jalk, Grete, ed. *Dansk M belkunst gennam 40 aar /40 Years of Danish Furniture Design: The Copenhagen Cabinet-Maker's Guild Exhibitions 1927-1966*. Taastrup, Denmark: Teknologisk instituts forlag, 1987.

Includes indices of cabinetmakers, architects, and periodicals; four-volume set.

Jenkins, Irving. *Hawaiian Furniture and Hawaii's Cabinetmakers*. Honolulu, HI: Daughters of Hawaii, 1983.

Examines regional furniture in the context of a multicultural environment that produced it, with discussion of both European forms adapted to native woods and designs unique to the region. Emphasizes the role of artisans and workshops.

Kreisel, Heinrich. *Die Kunst des deutschen mobels*. [*The Art of German Furniture*.] Munich: Beck, 1974.

Macquoid, Percy. *A History of English Furniture*. Reprint. London: Antique Collectors Club, 1987.

Consists of four volumes: *Age of Oak 1500-1660*; *Age of Walnut 1660-1720*; *Age of Mahogany 1720-1770*; *Age of Satinwood 1770-1820*.

Margon, Lester. *Masterpieces of European Furniture, 1300-1840: A Compendium, with Photographs, Measured Drawings, and Descriptive Commentary*. New York: Architectural Book Pub. Co., 1968.

Puig, Francis J. and Michael Conforti. *The American Craftsman and the European Tradition, 1620-1820*. Exhibition catalog. Minneapolis: Minneapolis Museum of Art, 1989.

Furniture is emphasized in this decorative arts survey, which traces the origin and survival of European influences in the work of U.S. craftsmen.

Riley, Noel, ed. *World Furniture*. Seacaucus, NJ: Chartwell Books, Inc., 1989.

Shimizu, Fumio and David Palterer, eds. *The Italian Furniture*. Tokyo: Graphic-Sha, 1991.

Taylor, Lonn and David B. Warren. *Texas Furniture: The Cabinetmakers and Their Work, 1840-1880*. Austin: University of Texas Press, 1975.

Regional study of vernacular forms trace style and design influences; includes list of regional cabinetmakers and indig-

enous and imported materials. Good example of research conducted from primary sources.

Tomlin, Maurice. *English Furniture: An Illustrated Handbook*. London: Faber and Faber, 1972.

Viollet-le-Duc, Eugene Emmanuel. *Dictionnaire raisonne du mobil-ier francais de l'epoque carlovingienne a la Renaissance*. Saint-Julien: Editions de Saucey, 1980.

Six volume set covers all forms.

How — Materials, Techniques, Tools

Gottshall, Franklin H. *Period Furniture Design and Construction*. Reprint. New York: Bonanza Books, 1951.

Hoadley, R. Bruce. *Understanding Wood: A Craftsman's Guide to Wood Technology*. Newtown, CT: Taunton Press, 1980.

Miller, Judith. *Period Finishes and Effects*. New York: Rizzoli, 1992.

Useful companion to basic wood identification materials.

Salaman, R.A. *Dictionary of Tools Used in the Woodworking and Allied Trades c. 1700-1970*. New York: Macmillan, 1975.

Not only identifies, but also describes, in detail, the application and use of literally hundreds of tools.

Smith, Nancy. *Old Furniture: Understanding the Craftsman's Art. A Guide to Collection, Appreciation and Preservation*. Boston: Little, Brown, 1975.

Discussion of techniques, joinings, carving, hardware, and the consequent effects of time.

Why — Connoisseurship, Ranking

Andrews, John. *British Antique Furniture: Price Guide and Reasons for Value*. Woodbridge, Suffolk: Antique Collector's Club, 1989.

Crawley, W. *Is It Genuine? A Guide to the Identification of Eighteenth Century English Furniture*. New York: Hart Publishing Co., 1972.

Detailed examinations of all components of furniture, from carving to veneers, and how all can be used or changed to create a "period" piece. Marriages and conversions are illustrated in the section entitled "The Museum of Naughty Pieces."

Goggin, Bill. *Understanding and Evaluating Early American Furniture*. New Market, MD: Eagles, 1991.

Jenkins, Emyl. *Emyl Jenkins' Guide to Buying and Collecting Early American Furniture: How to Distinguish Period Pieces from Fakes and Reproductions*. New York: Crown, 1991.

Well-illustrated with photos, the characteristic signs of various tools and techniques are discussed, along with a section on replacements and enhancements. Checklist analysis of selected forms provides guidelines for "acceptable" and "unacceptable" restoration.

Kaye, Myrna. *Fake, Fraud or Genuine? Identifying Authentic American Antique Furniture*. Boston: Little, Brown, 1987.

Clues and tools to aid in determining authenticity.

Montgomery, Charles F. *Some Remarks on the Science and Principles of Connoisseurship*. Reprinted from the 1961 *Walpole Society Note Book*. N.p.: n.pub., 1961.

Sack, Albert. *The New Fine Points of Furniture — Early American*. New York: Crown, 1993.

The classic *Good Better Best* has now been expanded to also encompass "Superior" and "Masterpiece", reflecting some examples that have surfaced in the last 40 years, but the premise remains the same. Examples of a variety of forms are compared and analyzed to determine value points; such judgments are naturally subjective to some degree, but serve to help develop a connoisseur's eye. Emphasis here is on aesthetics and craftsmanship as much as age, rarity and provenance.

How Much

Christie's Pictorial Archive. London: Mindata, 1980+.

Microfiche copies of photos from Christie's sales catalogs or files, issued under various series titles. *Decorative and Applied Art* covers decorative arts, including furniture, sold at London from 1890-1979, but excludes dates and prices; later series, such as *Christie's Pictorial Sales Review* (1985/86+), covers both London and New York sales and includes prices.

Feild, Rachel. *MacDonald Guide to Buying Antique Furniture: Authenticity, Copies, Restoration, Dating, Reproduction, Prices*. Radnor, PA: Wallace-Homestead, 1986.

Includes specific points of authenticity, clues to reproductions, and price ranges for both.

Price Guide Series. Woodbridge, England: Antique Collectors Club.

Series, cited elsewhere, includes several furniture-related titles, including *The Price Guide to 19th Century European Furniture 1830-1910* by Christopher Payne and *The Price Guide to Victorian, Edwardian and 1920s Furniture* by John Andrews.

Rush, Richard H. *Antiques as an Investment*. Englewood Cliffs, NJ: Prentice-Hall, 1968.

Historical data and market analyses for major furniture styles, from Italian Renaissance to Victorian.

Glassware

Primary Reference Sources

Corning Museum of Glass. 1 Museum Way, Corning, NY 14830-2253 (607) 937-5371.

Foremost museum for glass of all areas and periods, from ancient Rome to the contemporary studio artist. Rakow Library is an important reference facility with major reference collections of 45,000+ volumes, including a major trade catalog collection.

Bibliographies

Duncan, George Sang. *Bibliography of Glass: From Earliest Records to 1940*. London: Dawsons of Pall Mall for the Society of Glass Technology, 1960.

Indices/Catalogs

Bush, Louise K. and Paul N. Perrot. *History and Art of Glass: Index of Periodical Articles, 1959-1979*. Corning, NY: Corning Museum of Glass, 1982.

Journal of Glass Studies. Index. Corning, NY: Corning Museum of Glass, 1959+.

Access to scholarly and popular articles on all aspects of glass manufacture, history and connoisseurship. The *Journal* also has published, since 1959, an annual checklist of recently published books and articles on the subject.

Rare Books from the Corning Museum of Glass. Bethesda, MD: University Publications of America, 1990. Microfiche.

A two-part catalog reproduces some of the earliest literature (c. 15th-19th centuries) from the Corning Museum's Rakow Library, with emphasis on the technology of glassmaking and regional variations in style and technique. Includes a printed guide with bibliographic information and title/author indices.

Trade Catalogs from the Corning Museum of Glass. Bethesda, MD: University Publications of America, 1990. Microfiche.

Incomparable collection of over 2300 trade catalogs held in the Rakow Library provides a priced and illustrated inventory of world glass production over the last five centuries. Most materials date post-1850, and are arranged in such categories as tableware, cut glass, bottles, stained and architectural glass, lighting glassware and lamps. Includes a hardcover guide and bibliography with geographical, chronological, company and product indices.

Who — Signatures, Trademarks

Chihuly, Dale. *Chihuly: Form from Fire*. Seattle: University of Washington Press, 1993.

Details the career and work of a contemporary art glass artisan, with list of collections owning his work.

Farrar, Estelle Sinclaire and Jane Shadel Spillman. *The Complete Cut and Engraved Glass of Corning*. New York: Crown, 1979.

Detailed study of the company's history and product line, with well-detailed illustrations that would be useful in identifying Corning pieces.

Pullin, Anne. *Glass Signatures, Trademarks and Trade Names from the Seventeenth to the Twentieth Century.* Lombard, IL: Wallace-Homestead, 1986.
Arranged by mark, identifies company and general era.

Wilkinson, R. *The Hallmarks of Antique Glass.* London: Richard Madley Ltd., 1968.

What

Battie, David and Simon Cottle, eds. *Sotheby's Concise Encyclopedia of Glass.* Boston: Little, Brown, 1991.
Series of essays on a variety of topics, from Islamic glass to twentieth century developments, with a bibliography, biographies and company histories.

Boggess, Bill and Louise. *American Brilliant Cut Glass.* New York: Crown, 1977.
Well-illustrated guide to identifying patterns, signatures and companies.

_____. *Identifying American Brilliant Cut Glass: A Collector's Guide.* Crown: New York, 1984.
Emphasis on identification of manufacturer by pattern analysis.

Duncan, Alastair. *Art Nouveau and Art Deco Lighting.* New York: Simon and Schuster, 1978.
Good example of a secondary source text which would be useful in identifying the glass components of lighting fixtures. Extensive sections on international designers from each period, plus a bibliography that includes a useful section on specific auction catalogs as well as individual bibliographies for the designers themselves.

Heacock, William. *Encyclopedia of Victorian Colored Pattern Glass, Book 5, U.S. Glass from A to Z.* Marietta, OH: Antique Publications, 1978.
One of a nine-volume set, each emphasizing a different form or company product line, all well-illustrated and well-researched using both primary and secondary source material, including trade catalogs. Price guides included with each.

History of Glass. Bethesda, MD: University Publications of America, 1990. Microfiche.
Curator's selection from the collections of the Corning Museum and the Czech Museum of Applied Arts provides an overview of the history of glass in 1700+ images, accompanied by a printed guide. Topics range from Continental Europe 500 to 1980, to Great Britain 1300 to 1980, to Cameo Glass and Glass Paperweights.

Hunter, Frederick William. *Stiegel Glass.* Reprint. New York: Dover, 1967.
Still the most comprehensive study of the early Pennsylvania glassmaker, with discussion of early techniques in general as well as his products in particular.

Jenks, Bill and Jerry Luna. *Early American Pattern Glass 1850-1910.* Radnor, PA: Wallace-Homestead, 1990.

Identification of pressed-glass patterns by photograph, with information on color production, reproductions, and extensive references for each pattern. Price guide included.

Klein, Dan and Ward Lloyd, eds. *History of Glass.* London: Orbis, 1984.

Newman, Harold. *An Illustrated Dictionary of Glass.* London: Thames and Hudson, 1977.
Defines materials, process, products, forms and styles as well as individual designers, decorators and makers.

Perrot, Paul, et al. *Steuben: 70 Years of American Glassmaking.* New York: Praeger, 1974.
Good example of a study of a single company's product line.

When

Arwas, Victor. *Glass: Art Nouveau to Art Deco.* New York: Abrams, 1987.
Emphasizes the work of the individual designers as well as general studio production, with well-illustrated text. Specific physical characteristics are discussed in detail; includes a section on fakes and forgeries. Encyclopedic in scope.

Beard, Jeffrey. *International Modern Glass.* New York: Scribner, 1976.

Davis, Frank. *Early 18th-Century English Glass.* Feltham: Hamlyn, 1971.

Grover, Ray and Lee. *Art Glass Nouveau.* Rutland, VT: Charles Tuttle, 1967.
Well-illustrated with minimal text, emphasizing the form rather than the technique. Useful for identifying glass type, from Amberina to Venetian.

_____. *Contemporary Art Glass.* Crown: New York, 1975.
Although the contemporary studio or art glass movement has gone through a great deal of development since this volume was printed, it remains a useful and interesting study of 20th century international glass art. Provides a country-by-country survey with profiles on individual artists.

National Museum of Modern Art, Kyoto. *Contemporary Studio Glass: An International Collection.* New York: Weatherhill, 1982.
Glasswork and glassworkers, with biographical information.

Pina, Leslie. *Fifties Glass.* Atglen, PA: Schiffer, 1993.
Numerous illustrations of examples from Italy, Scandinavia and elsewhere, with profiles of companies and artists and a section on labels and signatures. Covers a time period which has not been well-researched but is rapidly coming into the marketplace.

Where

Bloch-Dermant, Janine. *Art of French Glass 1860-1914.* New York: Vendome Press, 1980.
Includes useful bibliography.

Charleston, R.J. *English Glass and the Glass Used in England c. 400-1940*. London: Allen and Unwin, 1984.
Covers both the commercial (i.e. manufacture and trade) and the domestic aspects of the subject.

Czechoslovakian Glass 1350-1980. Exhibition catalog. Corning, NY: Corning Museum of Glass, 1981.
History, with glassmakers' biographies, accompanied by a catalog of exhibited examples with detailed notes.

Davis, Derek C. *English and Irish Antique Glass*. New York: Praeger, 1965.

Drahotova, Olga. *European Glass*. New York: Excalibur Books, 1983.

Hajdamach, Charles R. *British Glass 1800-1914*. Woodbridge, Suffolk: Antique Collectors Club, 1991.
Forms, techniques, influences, glass-making regions, marks, patents, the role of expositions, and more. Extensive bibliography.

Hughes, G. Bernard. *English, Scottish and Irish Table Glass*. Boston: Boston Book and Art Shop, 1956.

King, Thomas B. *Glass in Canada*. Erin, Ontario: Boston Mills, 1987.
Good overview of the historic role glass has played in Canada's commercial and cultural history, with emphasis on the output of various glass houses, product lines of all types, and a section on bottle markings and closures. Bibliography.

Klesse, Brigitte and Hans Mayr. *European Glass from 1500-1800: The Ernesto Wolf Collection*. Vienna: Kremayr and Scheriau, 1987.
Exhaustively detailed catalog notes with references, with emphasis on decorated pieces.

Lee, Ruth Webb. *Early American Pressed Glass*. Enl. and rev. Northboro, MA: By the author, 1946.
An early and significant glass researcher, Lee lists here, pattern by pattern, the various products of U.S. companies with commentary on each.

Lindsey, Bessie M. *American Historical Glass*. Rutland, VT: Tuttle, 1967.
Useful in identifying commemorative pressed glass examples.

McKearin, Helen. *American Bottles and Flasks and Their Ancestry*. New York: Crown, 1978.
Examines one of the most common products of the early American glasshouse, with examples from nearly 80 producers. Emphasis on decorative molded designs; section on reproductions. Comprehensive handling of the topic.

_____. *American Glass*. New York: Crown, 1941.
The most comprehensive, single-volume, study of American glass from colonial times to the late 19th century. Provides a chronological history of major factories and glass-producing regions, with a final overview of form and type. Continues to be a major source for glass scholarship.

Revi, Albert Christian. *American Cut and Engraved Glass*. New York: Nelson, 1965.

Shuman, John III. *The Collector's Encyclopedia of American Art Glass*. Paducah, KY: 1988.
Listing, by type, of dozens of forms of art glass, with text on tools, terms, marks, agents, and more. Includes list of museums with significant collections and an international survey of selected contemporary glass manufacturers and sellers.

Slack, Raymond. *English Pressed Glass, 1930-1900*. London: Barrie and Jenkins, 1987.
Well-illustrated, with emphasis on company histories and an extensive table of registry marks. Useful addition to the field, where much has been written on American pressed glass.

Thorpe, William Arnold. *English Glass*. 3rd ed. London: A&C Black, 1961.

_____. *A History of English and Irish Glass*. London: The Medici Society, 1929.
Two-volume set with a lengthy bibliography.

Tsuchiya, Yoshio. *Glass of Japan*. Kyoto: Shikosha Art Books, 1987.
Excellent introduction to a type that only infrequently been the focus of Western studies. This covers both free- and mold-blown glass, as well as regional examples such as Edo and Satsuma cut glass. Interesting illustrations of Western and Japanese influences on form and design.

Warren, Phelps. *Irish Glass: The Age of Exuberance*. London: Faber, 1970.

Welker, John and Elizabeth. *Pressed Glass in America: An Encyclopedia of the First Hundred Years 1825-1925*. Ivyland, PA: Antique Acres Press, 1985.
Detailed history of the subject, with 6800 pattern listings, lists of exhibits, past and present, organizations, and significant figures in the field. Excellent annotated bibliography.

Wilson, Kenneth M. *New England Glass and Glassmaking*. New York: Crowell, 1972.
Good example of a regional study, tracing the industry from the first attempt in the region at the Holmes glass factory in 1639 to the Pairpoint Glass company in the 1970s. Extensively researched.

How

Conservation and Restoration of Stained Glass: An Owner's Guide. New York: Census of Stained Glass Windows in America, 1988.
Useful not only for the specific information given, but for additional information and contacts the organization may be able to provide.

Littleton, Harvey K. *Glassblowing: A Search for Form*. New York: Van Nostrand Reinhold, 1971.
Details the process and techniques of glass blowing and working.

Matcham, Jonathan. *Techniques of Glass Engraving*. New York: Larousse, 1982.

How Much

Acatos, Sylvio. *Acatos: International Ceramics and Glass Auction Price Guide*. New York: Archer Fields, 1990+.
Annual auction report covering glass, pottery and porcelain.

Schroy, Ellen Tischbein. *Warman's Glass*. Radnor, PA: Wallace-Homestead, 1992.
Covers a wide variety of glass types, from art glass to depression glass. Introductory notes to each section are particularly useful, providing information on references, reproduction alerts, periodicals, collector's organizations and museums pertinent to the topic.

Metalware

Associations

Society of American Silversmiths. P.O. Box 3599, Cranston, RI 02910.
Individuals, artisans and students interested in the handcrafting of flatware and holloware, including preservation of the history and art of the craft. Maintains slide and photo library, biographical archives, artisan referral service, speakers' bureau.

Bibliographies

Montgomery, Charles and Catherine Maxwell. *Early American Silver: Collectors, Collections, Exhibitions, Writings*. Reprint from the *Walpole Society Note Book*. Portland, ME: Anthoensen Press, 1969.

Periodicals

Silver. Box 1243, Whittier, CA 90609.
Aimed at collectors, scholars and connoisseurs of English, American and other flatware, holloware and objets.

Sourcebooks

Green, Robert Alan. *The Silver Collector's Address Book: Where to Find Over 500 Dealers, Manufacturers, Auction Houses and Booksellers Specializing in Old Silver*. Key West, FL: By the Author, 1985.

Who

Carpenter, Charles H. *Tiffany Silver*. New York: Dodd, Mead, 1978.
Good example of a company history that sets the products against a social background, with detailed discussions on the hows and whys of holloware, illustrated hallmarks, and more, from the company's founding to modern times.

Cederwall, Sandraline and Hal Riney. *Spratling Silver*. San Francisco: Chronicle Books, 1990.
Traces Spratling's silverwork and its revitalizing effect on the Mexican city of Taxco in the 1920s, which again became a center of silver production. Detailed photo-catalog of his work, with a chronology of hallmarks.

Cotterell, Howard H. *Old Pewter: Its Makers and Marks in England, Scotland and Ireland*. London: B.T. Batsford, 1929.

Culme, John. *The Directory of Gold and Silversmiths: Jewellers & Allied Traders 1838-1914*. London: Antique Collectors Club, 1981.
Two volumes, comprising biographies and marks.

Fallon, John P. *Marks of London Goldsmiths and Silversmiths (c. 1697-1837)*. Rev. ed. Newton Abbot, England: David and Charles, 1988.

Green, Robert Alan. *Marks of American Silversmiths, 1650-1900*. Rev. ed. Key West, FL: By the Author, 1984.
Extensive section of hallmark photos, with additional bonuses of bibliographies.

Grimwade, Arthur. *London Goldsmiths 1697-1837: Their Marks and Lives from the Original Registers at Goldsmith's Hall and Other Sources*. London: Faber and Faber, 1976.
Includes unregistered hallmarks and provincial smiths.

Hamilton, Charles F. *Roycroft Collectibles*. San Diego: A.S. Barnes, 1980.
Includes section on the various metalwares made by this shop, and outlines the philosophy behind the designs.

Jackson, Charles James. *English Goldsmiths and Their Marks: A History of the Goldsmiths and Plate Workers of England, Scotland and Ireland*. 2nd ed. London: MacMillan, 1921.
Listings cover smiths c. 1090-1850.

Jackson, Charles James. *Jackson's Gold and Silver Marks of England, Scotland and Ireland*. Rev. ed. Woodbridge, England: Antique Collectors Club, 1989.

Kolter, Jane Bentley, ed. *Early American Silver and Its Makers*. New York: Mayflower Books, 1979.

Kovel, Ralph and Terry Kovel. *Kovels' American Silver Marks, 1650 to the Present*. New York: Crown, 1989.
Marks listed alphabetically, with each referenced to a bibliographical citation.

Laughlin, Ledlie Irwin. *Pewter in America: Its Makers & Their Marks*. Three volumes in one. New York: American Legacy Press, 1981.
With general historical survey of development and forms, this is essentially a catalog of regional artisans's biographies. (Note that, because this volume is comprised of three previously published volumes, there are multiple bibliographies and indices.)

Paulson, Paul. *Guide to Russian Silver Hallmarks*. Washington: Paulson, 1976.
Slim volume contains detailed info on various hallmarks by city, along with lists of important smiths associated with those locations. Tables of marks, along with a useful Cyrillic-Latin transliteration chart.

Rainwater, Dorothy. *Encyclopedia of American Silver Manufacturers*. New York: Crown, 1975.
Extensive listings of marks and trademarks, with accompanying corporate histories; useful table of troy and silver standard weights.

Renwick Gallery of the National Collection of Fine Arts. *Georg Jensen Silversmithy, 77 Artists, 75 Years*. Washington, D.C.: Smithsonian Institution Press, 1980.
Detailed history of both the workshops and the individual artisans, well-illustrated with selected examples; chronology of marks.

Star, Dagmar. *Pewter Marks of the World*. London: Hamlyn, 1977.

Tardy. *International Hallmarks on Silver*. Paris: By the Author, 1985.

Tardy. *Les poincoins de garantie internationaux pour l'argent*. 13th ed. Paris: Tardy, 1980.

Wright, Barton. *Hallmarks of the Southwest in Cooperation with the Indian Arts and Crafts Association*. West Chester, PA: Schiffer, 1989.
Thoroughly researched study lists silversmiths by name, and their marks by symbol and shop mark. Each biographical entry lists basic career information as well as discussing the style of their individual work.

What

Ash, Douglas. *Dictionary of British Antique Silver*. New York: Hippocrene Books, 1972.

Brett, Vanessa. *Phaidon Guide to Pewter*. Englewood Cliffs, NJ: Prentice-Hall, 1983.

_____ . *Sotheby's Directory of Silver 1600-1940*. London: Sotheby's, 1986.

Clayton, Michael. *The Collectors' Dictionary of the Silver and Gold of Great Britain and North America*. 2nd ed. New York: World, 1985.
Artisan biographies, glossary and bibliography.

Coulter, Lane and Maurice Dixon, Jr. *New Mexican Tinwork, 1840-1940*. Albuquerque: University of New Mexico Press, 1990.
Regional folk art form is thoroughly discussed in this volume, which covers techniques, dating, identification, tinsmiths' biographies and bibliography.

DeVoe, Shirley Spaulding. *Art of the Tinsmith, English and American*. Exton, PA: Schiffer, 1981.
Traces the origins of Cornish tinware and the subsequent importation of those techniques, styles and forms to the U.S.

by immigrants. Useful discussions on characteristics of British and American forms. Techniques, including use of old stencil patterns, emphasized.

Dominy, Arthur L. and Rudolph A. Morgenfruh. *Silver at Your Service: A Collector's Guide to Railroad Dining Car Flatware Patterns*. Huntington Station, NY: D&M Publishing, 1987.
Subject that crosses collecting lines — metalware or railroad collectible? — is covered in this useful volume that identifies potentially obscure patterns.

Jewelers' Circular Keystone. *Sterling Flatware Pattern Index*. 2nd ed., 4th revision. Radnor, PA: Chilton, 1988.
Illustrated with photographs, lists patterns by name and by manufacturer, along with trademarks. Excellent visual identification guide.

Newman, Harold. *An Illustrated Dictionary of Silverware: 2,373 Entries Relating to British and North American Wares, Decorative Techniques and Styles, and Leading Designers and Makers, Principally from c. 1500 to the Present*. London: Thames and Hudson, 1987.

Osterberg, Richard F. and Betty Smith. *Silver Flatware Dictionary*. San Diego: Barnes, 1981.
Useful handbook identifies common and unusual forms of flatware, from asparagus servers to sugar nips, plus section of detailed info on the array of flatware forms issued in selected patterns, all illustrated by photos.

Pickford, Ian. *Silver Flatware, English, Irish and Scottish 1660-1980*. Woodbridge, England: Antique Collectors Club, 1983.
Detailed study, including changes in form through the years, connoisseurship, fakes and forgeries, patterns, and reproduction of a period pattern book.

Rainwater, Dorothy T. and Ivan Rainwater. *American Silverplate*. West Chester, PA: Schiffer, 1988.
Discussion of history and techniques, genesis of form and style (with emphasis on period or unusual types), profusely illustrated with contemporary catalog illustrations.

_____ . *A Collector's Guide to Spoons Around the World*. Hanover, PA: Everybody's Press, 1976.
Illustrated guide to a form of popular collectible, extremely detailed notes on each listed design.

_____ . *Sterling Silver Holloware*. Des Moines, IA: Wallace-Homestead, 1973.
Compiled from nineteenth-century catalogs issued by S. Kirk, Gorham and Unger Bros., this provides a fine photographic record of the various forms and styles: bookmarks, berry bowls, tea balls and teasets. With introductory survey on historical background of holloware.

Schiffer, Peter, Nancy Schiffer and Herbert Schiffer. *Brass Book: American, English and European, Fif-*

teenth Century Through 1850. West Chester, PA: 1978.

Arranged by form, with text on history, processes, fakes; reproduction of 18th century brassmaker's catalog.

Schroder, Timothy. *The National Trust Book of English Domestic Silver 1500-1900.* New York: Viking, 1988.

Examination of various forms and styles of the periods, with particular emphasis given to social and economic factors that affected both patronage and production.

Turner, Noel D. *American Silver Flatware, 1837-1910.* New York: A.S. Barnes, 1972.

Discussion of pieces and patterns, with additional data on U.S., English and Canadian manufacturers. Extensive bibliography is particularly valuable for its numerous citations of early trade catalogs.

Weinstein, Jay. *A Collector's Guide to Judaica.* New York: Thanes and Hudson, 1985.

Liturgical objects, emphasizing metalwares.

Wyler, Seymour B. *The Book of Sheffield Plate, with All Known Makers' Marks including Victorian Plate Insignia.* New York: Crown, 1949.

_____. *The Book of Old Silver: English, American, Foreign, with all Available Hallmarks Including Sheffield Plate Marks.* 2nd ed. New York: Crown, 1937.

Includes hallmarks of North American along with Great Britain, Germany, France, etc.

When

Bruton, Eric. *Hallmarks and Date Letters on Silver, Gold and Platinum.* Rev. London: N.A.G. Press, 1977.

Culme, John. *Nineteenth Century Silver.* London: Hamlyn, 1977.

Hughes, Graham. *Modern Silver Throughout the World 1880-1967.* New York: Crown, 1967.

Profusely illustrated, with biographical section on artisans, designers and firms around the world.

Krekel-Aalberse, Annelies. *Art Nouveau and Art Deco Silver.* New York: Abrams, 1989.

International survey, with hallmarks, biographies and bibliography.

Mulholland, James. *A History of Metals in Colonial America.* University: University of Alabama Press, 1981.

Emphasis on the smelting, refining and smithing processes, with historical overview of the importance of metals to colonization and eventual independence.

Where

Bradbury, Frederick. *British and Irish Silver Assay Office Marks, 1544-1973.* Sheffield: Northend, 1973.

Includes notes on gold maRks, marks on imported foreign silver and gold plate, and Old Sheffield hallmarks.

Crescent City Silver: An Exhibition of Nineteenth-Century New Orleans Silver. New Orleans, LA: The Historic New Orleans Collection, 1980.

Well-documented regional survey, with biographies and bibliography.

Cutten, George Barton. *Silversmiths of North Carolina, 1696-1860.* Raleigh: North Carolina Dept. of Archives and History, 1984.

Davis, Frank. *French Silver 1450-1825.* New York: Praeger, 1970.

Doesen, Gudmund. *Old Danish Silver.* Copenhagen: Hassing, 1949.

Includes hallmarks, names of private owners and goldsmiths.

Ensko, Stephen Guernsey Cook. *American Silversmiths and Their Marks III.* New York: By the Author, 1948.

Covers smiths active pre-1850; chronologically arranged bibliography.

Fales, Martha Gandy. *Early American Silver.* Rev. and enl. New York: E.P. Dutton, 1973.

Often cited as one of the best general surveys on the subject, this covers stylistic and form development, regional characteristics, design sources, features of early materials, tools and techniques.

Forbes, H.A. Crosby, et al. *Chinese Export Silver, 1785 to 1885.* Milton, MA: Museum of the American China Trade, 1975.

Reflects stylistic developments of silver made for Western trade and the attendant artistic exchanges. Useful discussion of hallmarks.

Nederlands Zilver /Dutch Silver. Exhibition catalog. Amsterdam: Rijksmuseum, 1980.

Detailed regional survey of silversmithing, with extensive discussion of individual smiths' work, photo-reproductions of marks, and copious notes, plus a section on unidentified hallmarks.

Poole, T.R. *Identifying British Antique Silver.* London: Bloomsbury, 1988.

Expanded section on hallmarks supplements a series of illustrations designed to identify the obscure piece of silver as to terminology and use.

How

Loyen, Frances. *The Thames and Hudson Manual of Silversmithing.* London: Thames and Hudson, 1980.

Osburn, Burl Neff. *Pewter, Spun, Wrought and Cast.* Scranton, PA: International Textbook Co., 1938.

Smith, Keith. *Practical Silversmithing and Jewelry.* New York: Van Nostrand Reinhold, 1975.

Untracht, Oppi. *Metal Techniques for Craftsmen.* Garden City, NY: Doubleday, 1977.
Discussion of wide array of methods.

Why — Connoisseurship

Feild, Rachel. *MacDonald Guide to Buying Antique Silver and Sheffield Plate: Authenticity, Techniques, Hallmarks, Reproductions, Prices.* London: MacDonald & Co., 1988.
One of the MacDonald Series, emphasizes features of authentic examples with consequent hints on ranking according to various features.

Hood, Graham. *American Silver: A History of Style 1650-1900.* New York: Dutton, 1989.
Classic study of the subject, arranged by style, with emphasis on silver as an art form.

How Much

Dolan, Maryanne. *American Sterling Silver Flatware 1830's to 1990's: An Identification and Value Guide.* Florence, AL: Books Americana, 1993.
Illustrated listings of patterns by company, with additional value data.

Hagan, Tere. *Silverplated Flatware: An Identification and Value Guide.* Rev. 4th ed. Paducah, KY: Collector Books, 1990.
Identifies patterns by line drawings, with general pricing guidelines for various forms and patterns.

Silver Auction Records. Calne, England: Hilmarton Manor Press, 1969/70+.

The Silver Update Guide to Sterling Silver Flatware Prices. Ellicott, MD: N. Monmonier. Vol. 1+.
Issued quarterly; now available also on database for IBM-compatibles.

Fine Art

Research Centers, Libraries, Associations

American Association of Museums. 1225 Eye St. NW, Ste. 200, Washington, D.C., 20005.
Membership comprised of art, history and science museums, historic houses and societies, preservation projects and the affiliated professional personnel. Publications include the *Official Museum Directory*, material on fine arts insurance, etc.

Archives of American Art. Smithsonian Institution, American Art and Portrait Gallery Building, F Street & 8th, Washington, D.C., 20560.
Collects primary and secondary research material on American artists, both native-born and immigrant, with materials totaling over eight million items: letters, journals, scrapbooks, microfilm, interview transcripts. Individuals covered include painters, sculptors, craftsmen, dealers, collectors. Branch offices of the Archives throughout the U.S.

Art Information Center. 280 Broadway, Ste. 412, New York, NY 10007.
Clearinghouse for contemporary fine art, facilitating representation between artists and dealers; aiding collectors, curators and the public in finding works by particular artists or in certain styles; maintains files on 65,000 living artists and on American and foreign galleries and the artists they represent, along with exhibit catalogs.

Art Libraries Society/ARLIS. (Art Libraries Society/North America). 3900 E. Timrod St., Tucson, AZ 85711.
Art librarianship and visual resources curatorship in libraries, galleries, museums, etc.

Avery Architectural and Fine Arts Library. Columbia University, New York, NY 10027.
Outstanding collection of architectural materials, including drawings; also owns the *Marburger Index*, a photographic documentation of fine, applied and decorative art in Germany from the Middle Ages to the present.

Bibliotheca Herziana. Max-Planck-Institut; Via Gregoriana, 28; I-00187 Roma, Italy.
Collections concentrate on Italian art from the early Christian era to the present; several catalogs and guides to the collections have published.

Bibliotheca Medicea-Laurenziana. Piazza San Lorenzo 9; I-50123 Firenze, Italy.
Collections, established c. 1570, now include thousands of manuscripts, books, papyri, illuminations.

Bibliotheque d'Art et d'Archaeologie (Fondation Jacques Doucet). 3 rue Michelet; F-75006, Paris, France.
Part of the University of Paris.

Bibliotheque Forney. Hotel des Archeveques de Sens; 1, rue du Figuier, F-75004 Paris, France.
Maintains reference collection relating to fine, graphic and decorative arts, featuring a collection of 19th-20th century drawings of furniture and fabrics, as well as a major French poster collection.

Bodleian Library. University of Oxford, Broad St., Oxford, OXI 3BG, Oxford, England.
Manuscript collection, founded 1602, numbers over 136,000 pieces, including Medieval, topographical and Oriental examples; numerous publications on the collections have been issued.

Boston Public Library. Art Reference Department, P.O. Box 286, Boston, MA 02117.
Materials on Asian, Classical and Early American arts.

British Library Reference Division. Great Russell St., London, WC1B 3DG.
Depository library with collections of over 10 million books and periodicals, 120,000+ western European and Oriental manuscripts, 100,000 charters and rolls, plus seals, papyri, and more. Researchers must apply for a pass to use the collections.

Canadian Museums Association/Association des musees canadiens. 280 Metcalfe St., Ste. 202, Ottawa, Ontario K2P 1R7.
Publishes *The Official Directory of Canadian Museums and Related Institutions.*

Conway Library. Courtauld Institute of Art, University of London, Somerset House, Strand, London WC2R 2LS.
Significant architecture collections include photographs, drawings, wall and panel paintings, stained glass and metalwork; also Western art from classical Greece to modern times.

Dumbarton Oaks Research Library, Harvard University, 1703 32nd St. NW, Washington, D.C. 20007.
Materials on Byzantine civilization, including the *Dumbarton Oaks Research Archives,* a census of works found in American collections.

Dunlap Society, Lake Champlain Rd., Essex, NY 12936.
Founded in 1974 to visually document all American art, the Society has, to date, produced significant architectural documents. Named for William Dunlap, whose *The Rise and Progress of the Arts of Design in the United States* (1834), was probably the first American art history book.

Frick Art Reference Library, 10 East 71st St., New York, NY 10021.
Collections concentrate on U.S. and Western European artworks, c. AD 325-1930. Extensive collection of visual images of artworks accessible by a variety of indices. Among the country's oldest art libraries.

George Eastman House, 900 East Ave., Rochester, NY 14607.
Houses the International Museum of Photography, along with a significant reference library, collections of images and equipment, and a conservation center.

Getty Center for the History of Art and the Humanities. Library, 401 Wilshire Blvd., Ste. 400, Santa Monica, CA 90401-1455.
Projected to become the world's largest art reference library, it currently specializes in Western European art, archaeology and architecture, with an extensive photograph collection and major indices such as the *Marburger.*

Harvard University Fine Arts Library. Fogg Museum of Art, Quincy St., Cambridge, MA 02138.
Subject areas include Italian Renaissance, Islamic art and architecture, photo history, conservation, and graphic arts.

National Film Information Service. The Margaret Herrick Library of the Academy of Motion Picture Arts and Sciences and Academy Foundation. 8949 Wilshire Blvd., Beverly Hills, CA 90211.
Collections of 60,000 films, 4 million photographs, and significant collections of books, ephemera and vertical files. Research guides and bibliographies available for purchase.

Kunstibibliothek Staatliche Museen Preussicher. Kulturbesitz; Jebensstrasse 2; D-1000 Berlin 12.
Art and culture of Spain, Portugal, Scandinavia and the Anglo-Saxon peoples to 1900; 20th century architecture; Lipperheide Costume Library.

Library of Congress. Prints and Photographs Division. Washington, D.C. 20540.
Contains approx. 12 million graphic items in all media from graphics, prints and photographs to posters and architectural history materials. Several special guidebooks and catalogs to these collections have been issued (i.e. *Guide to the Special Collections of Prints and Photographs in the Library of Congress* (Paul Vanderbilt, 1955) and *Graphic Materials: Rules for Describing Original Items and Historical Collections* (Elisabeth Betz, 1982)).

Metropolitan Museum of Art Libraries. Fifth Avenue and 82nd St., New York, NY 10028.
Consists of the Thomas J. Watson Library with extensive runs of sales and exhibition catalogs; Robert Goldwater Library for art of the Pacific Islands, Africa, Native America; Cloisters Library for Medieval studies.

Museum of Early Southern Decorative Arts. 924 S. Main St., Winston-Salem, NC 27101.
Along with extensive collections of pre-1820 Southern-made decorative arts, maintains the *Index of Early Southern Artists and Artisans*, with 60,000+ entries.

Museum of Modern Art. The Library. 11 W. 53rd St., New York, NY 10019.
Maintains extensive artist files, special collections such as MOMA publications, South American art, artists' books.

National Art Library. Victoria and Albert Museum, South Kensington, London SW7 2RL, England.
Significant collections of materials on fine and applied arts, plus medieval manuscripts, autographed letters, fine bindings.

National Gallery of Art Library. 6th St. and Constitution Ave. N.W., Washington, D.C. 20565.
One of the nation's most important research centers in western European and American art, with collections of artist monographs, *Festschriften*, dissertations, vertical files. Major catalog collections: exhibition, museum, private collection, sale. Also of note are the *Photographic Archives*, again one of the nation's largest, with images supplemented by all of the major microform art and architecture collections.

National Gallery of Canada Library. 380 Sussex Dr., K1N 9N4 Ottawa, Ontario.
Among the collections are extensive vertical files on Canadian artists and subjects.

National Museum of American Art Library. 8th and G Sts. N.W., Washington, D.C. 20560.
Major projects have included inventories of pre-1914 American paintings and American sculpture; index of pre-1877 American art catalogs; along with a 45,000 volume library and extensive manuscript and clipping files.

National Portrait Gallery Library. F St. at 8th N.W, Washington, D.C. 20560.

60,000 volume library complements the institution's mission of collecting images and documents of-and-by significant American personages and artists. Current projects include a census of American portraits and subjects.

National Trust for Places of Historic Interest or Natural Beauty. 36 Queen Anne's Gate, London, SW1H 9AS England.
Formed in 1895 to protect England's heritage, including her historic properties and their contents.

New York Public Library. The Research Library. Fifth Ave. at 42nd St., New York, NY 10018.
With publications on its many collections — including a *Dictionary Catalog, Bibliographic Guide, Artists' Files, Dictionary Catalog of the Prints Division* — and vertical files, this may well be the nation's largest public library.

Rijksbureau voor Kunsthistorische Documentatie. Korte Vijverberg 7, Den Haag ('S-Gravenhage) 2005.
Focus on Dutch and Flemish paintings and drawings. Topographical Department includes a card index of all identified sites depicted by Netherlandish artists. Over one million reproductions and photos. Bibliography of the Netherlands Institute for Art History lists books, exhibition catalogs and other materials dealing with Dutch and Flemish art up to 1830.

Smithsonian Institution. 1000 Jefferson Dr., Washington, D.C. 20560.
Multi-faceted nature of the institution includes a variety of fine arts-related collections, including the Freer Gallery of Art, Hirshhorn Museum and Sculpture Garden, Renwick Gallery, National Museum of American Art, National Portrait Gallery, Arthur M. Sackler Gallery. Research conducted and supported through reference libraries of over 1 million volumes.

University of California, Los Angeles, Art Library. Second Floor, Dickson Art Center, Los Angeles, CA 90024-1392.
Collections include the UCLA Artists' Files, Artists' Bookworks Collections, several major indices such as the *Princeton Index of Christian Art* and the *Marburger Index*. Major television, radio and film archives.

The Warburg Institute Library. Woburn Square, London WC1H OAB.
Collections emphasize the classical tradition in art, literature, religion and science, with large photo collection of ancient art as well as material in the fine and applied arts from antiquity to the 18th century.

Yale University Library. Box 1605 A, Yale Station, New Haven, CT 06520.
Beinecke Rare Book and Manuscript Library features letter and manuscript collections, including some materials from early American artists; Stieglitz archives, Audubon prints; Western Americana collection of early photos; among many others. The Yale Center for British Art maintains research facility of books, dissertations, and travel literature on British art (excluding decorative art and architecture). The Center's Photo Archive maintains an extensive picture collection for two-dimensional works by British artists or foreigners working in the U.K. from c. 1500 to 1945.

Bibliographies

Arntzen, Etta and Robert Rainwater. *Guide to the Literature of Art History*. Chicago: American Library Association, 1980.
Covers over 4000 entries, most published before 1977, in large topic areas: general reference sources (bibliographies, directories, sales records, dictionaries, encyclopedias); general primary and secondary sources (historiography, methodology, histories, handbooks); specific arts fields (two- and three-dimensional art, decorative and applied art, photography); serials (both periodicals and books, plus lectures).

Art and Architecture Book Guide. Boston: G.K. Hall (n.d.) Art Design Photo. Teaneck, NJ: Somerset House, 1972-1976/77.
Annual bibliography of publications on modern art, graphic design, photography, art libraries, etc.

Art Documentation. Tucson, AZ: The Society, 1982+.
Serial from the Art Libraries Society of North America (ARLIS/NA).

ARTBibliographies Modern. Oxford: Clio Press. Vol. 1 (1974+).
Issued semi-annually, providing abstracts of dissertations, exhibition catalogs and over 300 serials on all areas of art, design and photography. From 1974-1988, covered materials from 1800 on; since 1989, coverage was narrowed to art of 1900 to the present, but important influences predating that are also included. (The first three volumes, 1969-1971, were published under the title LOMA: Literature of Modern Art.) Over 150 individual subject headings, with additional author, museum and gallery indices.

Arts in Early American History: Needs and Opportunities for Study. Essay by Walter Muir Whitehill; bibliography by Wendell D. Garrett and Jane N. Garrett. Chapel Hill, NC: University of North Carolina Press for the Institute of Early American History and Culture, 1965.
Bibliography lists the "most important writings" on the arts in America from early colonization to 1826, with annotations and a section on periodicals. Although many new sources have been added to the field in the last three decades, this remains a useful tool.

Bailey, Joyce Waddell, ed. *Handbook of Latin American Art: A Bibliographic Compilation*. Santa Barbara, CA: ABC-CLIO, 1984.
Volume 1 of the proposed three-volume set includes general references and art of the 19th and 20th centuries in North and South America (exclusive of U.S.); Volume 2, Art of the Colonial Period, covers authors, artists and Hispanic art in the U.S.; Volume 3 is projected to be a bibliography of ancient cultures with subject bibliography organized geographically.

Baker, Charles. *Bibliography of British Book Illustrators, 1860-1900*. Birmingham, England: Birmingham Bookshop, 1978.

Barger, M. Susan. *Bibliography of Photographic Processes in Use Before 1880: Their Methods, Processing and Conservation*. Rochester, NY: Rochester Institute of Technology, 1980.

BHA: Bibliography of the History of Art/Bibliographie de l'histoire de l'art. Santa Monica, CA: J. Paul Getty Trust, Getty Art History Information Program, 1991+.
   Quarterly publication combines RILA (Repertoire de la litterature de l'art) and Repertorie de l'art et de l'archaeologie with abstracts from over 4000 serials and museum publications on fine art (sculpture, painting drawing, prints), contemporary art (including video art), photography, popular art, folk art, and material culture. (Among notable exclusions, however, are Native American, Far Eastern, African, Indian and Islamic art.)

Boni, Albert. *Photographic Literature: An International Bibliographical Guide to General and Specialized Literature on Photographic Processes, Techniques, Theory, Chemistry, Physics, Apparatus, Materials, and Applications, History, Biography, Aesthetics, etc.* New York: Morgan & Morgan, 1962.
   First Supplement: 1960-1970, 1972.

Collins, Judith. *Bibliography of Arts Council Exhibition Catalogues, 1942-1980*. London: Arts Council of Great Britain, 1982.
   With indices.

Congressional Information Service, comp. *Early Photography Books*. New York: Clearwater Publishing Co., 1986.
   Microfilm collection of materials covering handbooks and manuals, histories, optics, catalogs, yearbooks and periodicals.

Coulson, William D.E. and Patrician N. Frelert. *Greek and Roman Art, Architecture and Archaeology: An Annotated Bibliography*. 2nd ed., rev. New York: Garland, 1987.

Davis, Lenwood G. and Janet Sims. *Black Artists in the United States: An Annotated Bibliography of Books, Articles and Dissertations on Black Artists 1799-1979*. Westport, CT: Greenwood Press, 1980.

Dawdy, Doris. *Annotated Bibliography of American Indian Painting*. New York: Museum of the American Indian, Heye Foundation, 1968.

Dykes, Jeff. *Fifty Great Western Illustrators: A Bibliographic Checklist*. Flagstaff, AZ: Northland Press, 1975.
   References exhibition and gallery publications, artist-illustrated items (including edition number and ID points), and very useful listing of biographical or other citations for the artist. Dykes was a well-respected bookseller of Western Americana.

Ehresmann, Donald L. *Architecture: A Bibliographic Guide to Basic Reference Works, Histories and Handbooks*. Littleton, CO: Libraries Unlimited, 1983.

_____. *Fine Arts: A Bibliographic Guide to Basic Reference Works, Histories, and Handbooks*. 3rd ed. Littleton, CO: Libraries Unlimited, 1989.
   Annotated entries for over 2000 items, excluding exhibition catalogs and dissertations.

Freedberg, Sydney J., ed. *Connoisseurship, Criticism and Art History in the 19th Century Series: A Selection of Major Texts in English*. New York: Garland, 1978.

Freitag, Wolfgang. *Art Books: A Basic Bibliography of Monographs on Artists*. New York: Garland, 1985.
   International coverage of over 1800 artists, including exhibition catalogs and catalogues raisonnes from all time periods. Majority of entries are for painters; but also includes sculptors, architects, graphic artists and photographers.

G.K. Hall Art Bibliographies Series. Boston: G.K. Hall.
   Series with international scope covers diverse eras, such as *Art and Architecture in the Balkans* (Slobodan Curcic, 1984) and *Italian Romanesque Sculpture: An Annotated Bibliography* (Dorothy Glass, 1983).

Helbing and Lichtenhahn. *Art Kunst: International Bibliography of Art Books*. Basel: Helbing & Lichtenhahn, 1972-1988.
   Annual bibliography in French, German and English.

Hitchcock, Henry Russell. *American Architectural Books: A List of Books, Portfolios, and Pamphlets on Archtecture and Related Subjects Published in American Before 1895*. Minneapolis: University of Minnesota, 1962.
   Includes builders' guides, house pattern books, etc.

Internationale Bibliographie der Kunst Wissenschaft. Berlin: Behr, 1903-1919.

Inuit Art Bibliography. Ottawa: Inuit Art Section, American and Northern Affairs Canada, 1986.

Karpel, Bernard, ed. *Arts in America: A Bibliography*. Washington, D.C.: Archives of American Art, Smithsonian Institution, 1979.
   Four-volume set is the most complete annotated bibliography published to date for American art in 21 divisions, including Native American arts, decorative arts, 19th and 20th century design, painting, graphic art and artists, photography, with each section prepared by a recognized authority in the field. Sources covered include dissertations, theses, serials, general references, bibliographies, trade catalogs and pattern books. Volume 4 includes a comprehensive index to the set, along

with references to artists and subjects listed in the annotated entries.

Kemplon, Richard. *Art Nouveau: An Annotated Bibliography*. Los Angeles: Hennessey & Ingalls, 1977.
Covers all art forms of the period.

Klos, Sheila and Christine Smith, eds. *Historical Bibliography of Art Museum Serials from the United States and Canada*. Tucson, AZ: ARLIS/NA, 1987.
Good source for museum publication titles.

Lincoln, Betty Woelk. *Festschriften in Art History, 1960-1975: Bibliography and Index*. New York: Garland, 1988.
Index to essays included in 344 *Festschriften*, listed by name of subject artist and providing tables of contents, authors and essay titles. Provides information on works issued before publication of *RILA*.

Ludman, Joan and Lauris Mason. *Fine Print References: A Selected Bibliography of Print-Related Literature*. (n.p.): Kraus International, 1982.

McCoubrey, John W. *American Art: 1700-1960. Sources and Documents in the History of Art Series*. Englewood Cliffs, NJ: Prentice-Hall, 1965.

Museum of Modern Art (New York). Library. *Annual Bibliography of Modern Art*. Boston: G.K. Hall, 1987+.
Serial listing of related publications.

Parsons, Christopher and Martha Ward. *A Bibliography of the Salon Criticism in Second Empire Paris*. Cambridge: Cambridge University Press, 1986.

Prescott, Margaret, ed. *Worldwide Art Catalogue Bulletin*. Ithaca, NY: Worldwide Books. Vol. 1, 1963+.
Reviews catalogs issued by approximately 3500 museums and galleries, choosing 700-900 for commercial distribution. Each issue reviews around 200 publications. Geographically arranged, with title, place and date of exhibition, physical details of catalog, review of included material, the bulletin provides further access to the data by such topics as title, artist, media (i.e. ceramics, glass, metalwork or artistic material), topics (decorative arts, illustration, poster art, etc.) Annual index arranged in same manner, with additional indices to museums and galleries in more recent issues.

Print Reference Sources: A Selected Bibliography, 18th-20th Centuries. 2nd ed. (n.p.): Kraus International, 1979.

Reisner, Robert George. *Fakes and Forgeries in the Fine Arts: A Bibliography*. New York: Special Libraries Assocation, 1950.
Still a useful tool, and one of the few to deal with this topic. (Note also the bibliography included in *Fakes and Forgeries* exhibition catalog (Minneapolis Institute of Arts, 1973) for additional recent publications.)

RILA: International Repertory of the Literature of Art. A Bibliographic Service of The J. Paul Getty Trust. Williamstown, MA: Sterling and Francine Clark Institute, 1975+.
Semi-annual abstracts of articles from core collection of about 400 journals, covering books, catalogs, Festschriften, and dissertations, c. 4th century to the present. Sections include journal index; seven principal categories of general topics, i.e. Medieval art, modern art; exhibition list of cross-references to main entries; author and subject lists. Abstracts are arranged in broad categories and subdivisions such as decorative arts, sculpture, pictorial arts, artists, photographers, much of them for Western art. *RILA Cumulative Subject Index* covering the years 1975-1989 available.

Roake, JoAnne. *Women Artists: A Selected Bibliography*. Sacramento, CA: Library, California State University, 1977.
Part of a bibliographic series covering library holdings.

Spalek, John, et al. *German Expressionism in the Fine Arts: A Bibliography*. Los Angeles: Hennessey & Ingalls, 1977.

Sturgis, Russell. *Annotated Bibliography of Fine Art: Painting, Scultpture, Architecture, Arts of Decoration and Illustration*. Boston: Longwood Press, 1977.
Reprint of the 1897 edition.

Weisberg, Yvonne and Gabriel Weisberg. *Japonisme: An Annotated Bibliography on the Japanese Influence on Western Art, 1848-1885*. New York: Garland, 1987.

_____. *The Realist Debate: A Bibliography of French Realist Painting, 1848-1885*. New York: Garland, 1984.

*Handbooks and Directories —
Art Collections and Libraries*

Catalog of the Library of the Museum of Modern Art. Boston: G.K. Hall, 1976+.
Fourteen volumes, updated by the Annual Bibliography of Modern Art (1986+), this collection emphasizes late 19th and early 20th century resources, including the Department of Photography's book collection and material from the Architecture Study Center.

Catalog of the Library of the Whitney Museum of American Art. Boston: G.K. Hall, 1979.
Emphasizes 20th century American art.

Catalogue of the Harvard University Fine Arts Library, The Fogg Art Museum. Boston: G.K. Hall, 1971.
Fifteen volumes cover one of the world's largest university art libraries, with major listings on Romanesque sculpture, Italian primitives, master drawings.

Catalogue of the Library of the National Gallery of Canada. Boston: G.K. Hall, 1973.

Indexes vertical files as well as general library materials. Topic "Artists" gives comprehensive list of entries in the main eight-volume set. Supplemented by a six-volume set published in 1981.

International Museum of Photography. Library Catalog of the International Museum of Photography at George Eastman House. Boston: G.K. Hall, 1982.
Listings by author, title and subject for a major research center, listing books (including those illustrated by photographers), exhibition catalogs and articles.

Library Catalog of the Metropolitan Museum of Art. 2nd ed. Boston: G.K. Hall, 1980. First Supplement, 1982. Second Supplement, 1985. Third Supplement, 1983-1986, 1987.
Among the world's major art museum libraries, this set of over 50 volumes covers all of art history, with emphasis on Near and Far Eastern, classical, European and American art. Sales catalogs only included up to 1982; after that date, they are added to the SCIPIO database.

New York Public Library. Photographica: A Subject Catalog of Books on Photography. Boston: G.K. Hall, 1984.
Collection features a good assortment of 19th-century works.

University of Chicago. *Catalog of the Oriental Institute Library.* Boston: G.K. Hall, 1970.
Sixteen volumes include material on Italian painting (late Middle Ages to the Renaissance), medieval illuminations, Near Eastern archaeology and classical art.

The Victoria and Albert Museum Library: Subject Catalogue. London: Mindata.
Listings on microfiche of over 1.5 million entries, indices to artists and general subjects, with citations for serials and exhibition catalogs.

Indices

American Library Association. *A.L.A. Portrait Index: Index to Portraits Contained in Printed Books and Periodicals.* William Coolidge Lane and Nina E. Browne, eds. Washington, D.C.: American Library Association, 1906. Reprint, New York: Burt Franklin, 1965.
Three-volume set lists famous subjects, with dates and occupations; indices cover over 1000 serials and books.

American Art Annual. New York: R.R. Bowker, 1898+.
Now published as *American Art Directory* and *Who's Who in American Art*, these early issues provided general information including brief artist biographies.

American Art Directory. New York: R.R. Bowker, 1898+. Biennial.
Lists organizations, museums and schools in the U.S., Canada and foreign countries, plus publications, art editors and critics, open exhibitions, and more.

Archives of American Art. *Collection of Exhibition Catalogs.* Boston: G.K. Hall, 1979.
Indexes a microfilm collection of literally thousands of exhibition catalogs issued in America c. 1800 to 1960. This index reproduces card lists of materials held by public, museum and historical society collections, arranged by exhibiting institution and artist or craftsman. The microfilm may be viewed at Archives offices in such places as Boston, New York, Washington or Detroit. Of unmeasurable usefulness, this gives access to a collection that would be impossible to house in a single institution.

Art and Architecture Information Guide Series. Sydney Starr Keaveney, gen. ed. Detroit: Gale, 1974.
Annotated bibliographies, covering individual artists: *American Drawing* (Lamia Doumato, ed., 1979), *American Painting* (Sydney Starr Keaveney, ed., 1974), *American Sculpture* (Janis Ekdahl, ed., 1977).

Art Books. New York: R.R. Bowker. Volume 1: *1876-1949: Including an International Directory of Current Serial Publications.* 1981. Volume 2: *1950-1979: Including an International Directory of Museum Permanent Collection Catalogs.* 1980. Volume 3: *1980-1984: Including an International Directory of Museum Permanent Collection Catalogs.* 1985.
Provides subject, title, author indices, with permanent collection catalogs listed by institution name.

Art Index. New York: H.W. Wilson. Vol. 1, 1929+.
Basic reference, and an initial point of research, this covers over 300 serials and all forms and periods of art. Includes exhibition catalogs only if they are mentioned in book reviews. One of the most commonly and widely used art publications in the U.S.

Artist Biographies: Master Index. Detroit: Gale Research, 1986.
Drawn from *Biography and Genealogy Master Index*, this provides quick reference to over 275,000 artists.

Bancroft Library, University of California, Berkeley: Catalog of Printed Books. Boston: G.K. Hall, 1964. 22 vols. *First Supplement*, 1969. 6 vols. *Second Supplement*, 1974. 6 vols.
Catalog of Western North America and Pacific Islands.

Beall, Karen F. *American Prints in the Library of Congress: A Catalog of the Collection.* Baltimore: Johns Hopkins, 1970.
Provides brief biographical data and information on works including title, date, media, dimensions, edition size, signature, with indices by subject and geographic topic of image as well as by name.

Bell, Doris L. *Contemporary Art Trends 1960-1980: A Guide to Sources.* Metuchen, NJ: Scarecrow Press, 1981.
Divided by trend (mail art, street art) and country, with definitions of terms.

Berger, Stu, ed. *Photography Magazine Index, 1978-1983*. Santa Rosa, CA: Paragon, 1984. Annual looseleaf supplements, 1984-1985.
Index to ten popular serials.

Bibliotheque Nationale: Collections of the Departments of Prints and Photographs. Paris: Studios Photographiques Harcour, n.d.
Microfiche sets reproduce some of the departments' collections of one-quarter million images.

Bronner, Simon J., ed. *American Folk Art: A Guide to Sources*. New York: Garland, 1984.

Canadian Periodical Index: Index de Periodiques Canadiens: An Author and Subject Index. Toronto: Info Globe, 1920+.
Subject/author index, issued monthly, to over 30 serials.

Catalog of Museum Publications and Media. 2nd ed. Detroit: Gale Research, 1980.

Chamberlin, Mary W. *Guide to Art Reference Books*. Chicago: American Library Association, 1959.
Over 2500 annotated entries, with many foreign language works. Significant as the first major Engish language art bibliography, the material remains useful as a source for older materials and for tracking serial title changes.

Clapp, Jane. *Sculpture Index*. Metuchen, NJ: Scarecrow Press, 1970. Vol. 1: *Sculpture of Europe and the Contemporary Middle East*. Volume 2: *Sculpture of the Americas, the Orient, Africa, the Pacific Areas and the Classical World*.
Covers nearly 1000 sources, with indices to subjects, artists and historic persons depicted; often provides current location of work.

Claassen, Lynda Corey. *Finders' Guide to Prints and Drawings in the Smithsonian Institution*. Washington, D.C.: Smithsonian Institution Press, 1984.
Arranged by collection, with description of holdings, finding aids and selected publications.

Coffman, Taylor. *The William Randolph Hearst Collection, Photographs and Acquisition Records*. Morro Bay, CA: Tabula Rasa Press, 1987.

The Courtauld Institute of Art Periodicals Subject Index. Bath, England: Mindata, 1989.
Author-subject listings on microfiche to around 300 serials issued c. 1930-1983. Covers fine and decorative arts and photography.

Courtauld Institute Survey of British Private Collections. London: Courtauld Institute, 1950s+.
The product of a systematic project of photographing artworks (mainly paintings and sculpture) in private collections in the U.K. Occasionally includes interior and exterior views. Adds 800-1000 images annually; currently has upwards of 20,000.

Design and Applied Arts Index. Gurnleys, Burnwash, Etchingham, East Sussex: Design Documentation, 1987+.

DIAL: A Decimal Index to the Art of the Low Countries. The Hague, Netherlands: Rijksbureau voor Kunsthistorische Documentatie.
Series of small black-and-white illustrations of Dutch and Flemish two-dimensional art from the Rijksbureau's photo archive, organized by subject. Total of around 14,000 cards are not indexed by artist name. May be viewed at holding libraries, including the Cleveland Museum, UCLA, Harvard, University of Texas and the National Gallery of Art.

Directory of Vertical File Collections on Art and Architecture Represented by ARLIS M/O/Q. Montreal: ARLIS/MOQ, 1989.
Provides information on serials clipped, subject and name indices, for libraries in Ottawa, Montreal and Quebec.

Fine Art Index. (North American Edition). Chicago: International Art Reference, 1991+.
Serial publication.

Fredericksen, Burton B., ed. *The Index of Paintings Sold in the British Isles during the Nineteenth Century*. Santa Barbara, CA: ABC-CLIO, 1989+.
Volume 1, covering 1801-1805, is the first in a projected annual series of five-year studies. A choronological index of sales, painting index by artist and owner, this goes into further analysis of sales by studying contents, sales prices, names of buyers, etc.

The Frick Art Reference Library Original Index to Periodicals. Boston: Hall, 1983.
Twelve volumes compiled between 1923 and 1969, with author and subject index to 27 serials with emphasis on Western European and American fine and decorative arts.

Gore, St. John., comp. *Royal Academy of Arts Bicentennial Exhibition, 1768-1968*.
Two-volume illustrated catalog.

Hardy, George, ed. *The Concordia University Art Index to Nineteenth Century Canadian Periodicals*. Montreal: Concordia University, 1981.
Index to 26 journals c. 1830 to 1900.

Harvard University, Cambridge, MA. *Catalogue of Auction Sales Catalogues*. Boston: G.K. Hall, 1971.
With 1975 *First Supplement*.

Havlice, Patricia Pate. *Index to Artistic Biography*. Metuchen, NJ: Scarecrow Press, 1973. *First Supplement*, 1981.
Covers 64 biographical dictionaries, c. 1902-1970, in 10 languages, covering some 17,000 artists, with an additional 44,000 artists in the supplement. Variant spellings and alternate names also listed.

_____. *World Painting Index.* Metuchen, NJ: Scarecrow Press, 1977. *First Supplement* 1973-1980, 1982.
References reproductions in 1700+ books and catalogs c. 1940-1973.

Holt, Elizabeth Gilmore, ed. *The Art of All Nations, 1850-73: The Emerging Role of Exhibitions and Critics.* Princeton, N.J.: Princeton University, 1980.
Exhibits in France, England, Germany, Austria and Italy, indexed by artist, critic, title, association, patron.

Horenstein, Henry. *The Photographer's Source: A Complete Catalog — An Annotated and Illustrated Guide to Equipment, Information, Materials, Services, Accessories.* New York: Simon and Schuster, 1989.

Index of Art Sales Catalogs, 1981-1985: A Union List from the SCIPIO Database. Boston: G.K. Hall, 1987.
Chronological lists of sales catalogs, plus index to general subjects (i.e. "Modern Art").

Johnson, Jane. *Royal Society of British Artists 1824-1893.* Woodbridge: Antique Collectors Club, 1975.
Provides addresses and prices realized. Also published as *Works of Art Exhibited at the Royal Society of British Artists 1824-1893 and the New English Art Club 1888-1917.*

Johnson, William S., ed. *International Photography Index.* Boston: G.K. Hall, 1983+.
Index to books, articles and exhibit reviews of over 2000 photographers. (Prior title *1977-78 Index to Articles on Photography.*)

Karpinski, Caroline. *Italian Printmaking. Fifteenth and Sixteenth Centuries: An Annotated Bibliography. G.K. Hall Art Bibliographies Series.* Boston: G.K. Hall, 1987.

Korb, Edward L. *Biographical Index to California and Western Artists.* Lawndale, CA: Old Master Gallery Press, 1983.
References 50+ books and exhibition catalogs as biographical sources.

Korwin, Yala H. *Index to Two-Dimensional Art Works.* Metuchen, NJ: Scarecrow Press, 1981.
Surveys 250 books published between 1960 and 1977.

Lancour, Harold. *American Art Auction Catalogs 1785-1942: A Union List.* New York: New York Public Library, 1944.
Over 7000 catalogs in 21 libraries covering all forms of art sales. Recorded by auction date, with listing of owners' names, auction house, descriptive catalog with title and present location. Microfilm update to 1960.

Lee, Cuthbert. *Portrait Register.* Baltimore: Baltimore Press, 1968.
Lists portraits in the U.S. with sitters' names and dates, painters' names, location of works, and cumulative index of artists cited.

Loeffler, Carl E., ed. *Contemporary Documents: A Series of Comprehensive Resource Books for the New Art.* San Francisco: Contemporary Arts Press.
Series includes *Correspondence Art (International Postal Art),* ed. by Michael Crane and Mary Stofflet, 1984.

Lugt, Frits. *Repertoire des catalogues de ventes publiques interessant l'art ou la curiosite, tableaux, dessins, estampes...* The Hague: Martinus Nijhoff, 1938-1987.
In four volumes, covering the years 1600-1925, and providing locations of sales catalogues in international libraries (including several in the U.S.), totalling over 148,000 entries. Listed choronologically by sales date, with notes as to place of sale, owners, kind and quantities of goods, plus index to collectors of sold works. Numbers assigned to entries often used by compilers of other sourcebooks as references.

McCulloch, Alan. *Encyclopedia of Australian Art.* Updated and corr. Hawthorn, Vic: Hutchinson of Australia, 1984.

McMann, Evelyn de R. *Canadian Who's Who Index 1898-1984.* Toronto: University of Toronto Press, 1986.

McQuaid, James, ed. *Index to American Photographic Collections.* Boston: G.K. Hall, 1982.
Indexes nearly 500 collections and 19,000 photographers.

McShine, Kynaston. *An International Survey of Recent Paintings and Sculpture.* New York: Museum of Modern Art, 1984.

Marburger Index: Photographic Documentation of Art in Germany. Munich: K.G. Saur, 1976+.
Microfiche collection of photographs of art, decorative arts and crafts from the Middle Ages to the present. Exterior and interior views, plus photos c. 1850-1976 of art objects owned by German museums, churches and institutions. Over one million photos, organized topographically, and identifying artists, titles, dates and sizes.

Mason, Lauris and Joan Ludman. *Print Reference Sources: A Selected Bibliography.* White Plains, NY: Kraus International, 1986.
Contains bibliographical citations on 1800 printmakers.

Meyer, George H., ed. *Folk Artists Biographical Index: A Guide to Over 200 Published Sources of Information on Approximately 9,000 American Folk Artists from the Seventeenth Century to the Present Including Brief Biographical Information; a Full Bibliography of Sources; Art Locator, Ethnicity, Geographic, Media, and Type of Work Indexes; and a Directory of Nearly 300 Institutions Where the Works of the Artists are Located.* Detroit: Gale Research, 1987.
Over 200 sources for over 9000 artists from the 17th century to the present, with biographical, bibliographical, location, media, ethnicity and collection information.

Monro, Isabel Stevenson and Kate M. Monro. *Index to Reproductions of American Paintings: A Guide to Pictures Occurring in More than Eight Hundred Books*. New York: H.W. Wilson, 1948; reprint 1966. *First Supplement*, 1964.

Indexes artists, titles of artworks and general subjects from 500 books and 300 catalogs, with an additional 400 works in the supplement.

_____. *Index to Reproductions of European Paintings: A Guide to Pictures in More than Three Hundred Books*. New York: H.W. Wilson, 1956; reprinted 1957.

Moss, Martha. *Photography Books Index: A Subject Guide to Photo Anthologies*. Metuchen, NJ: Scarecrow Press, 1980. *Photography Books Index II*, 1985.

Combined indices to fifty volumes in the areas of photographers, subjects and portraits.

Museum of Modern Art Artists Scrapbooks. Alexandria, VA: Chadwyck-Healey, 1986.

Includes materials on Matisse, Picasso, van Gogh, and others. A projected companion volume, *Museum of Modern Art Artists Vertical Files*, covering around 30,000 contemporary international artists, is currently being prepared.

Myers, Roger, comp. *Guide to Archival Materials of the Center for Creative Photography*. Tucson: University of Arizona, 1986.

The Center contains over 40,000 photographs, acting as a survey of photographic history as an art form. The archives themselves are divided in 76 groups.

National Collection of Fine Arts. *Directory to the Bicentennial Inventory of American Paintings Issued before 1914*. New York: Arno Press for the Smithsonian Institution, 1976.

Contains information on over one-quarter million paintings, 20,000 artists, with 85,000 photographic reproductions of works, including title, statistics and owner or last known sale. Indexed by artist, owner or location, and subject classification. Inquiries may be made through National Museum of American Art, the only depository location.

Parry, Pamela Jeffcott and Kathe Chipman. *Print Index: A Guide to Reproductions*. Westport, CT: Greenwood, 1983.

Lists works by 2100 printmakers.

Photohistorica: Literature Index of the European Society for the History of Photography. Antwerp: European Society for the History of Photography, 1980+.

Includes 80 international titles. Iconography included among the subject listings.

Repertoire d'art et d'archeologie. Under direction of Comite Francais d'Historie et de l'Art. Paris: Centre Documentation Sciences Humaines. Vol. 1, 1910+.

Only indexing service that has covered art serials since 1910, and the pre-1973 issues, which are more difficult to use, are still useful for older material. This international publication abstracts about 400 serials per issue, a high percentage of them Western and Eastern European art serials. Topic areas, which include exhibition catalogs and *Festschriften*, cover 200 AD to the present. (Islamic, Far Eastern, primitive, and post-1940 artworks are excluded, as are artists born after 1920.) Cumulative index to serials, artists, subjects and authors. Ceased in 1989 to form BHA (which see).

Riggs, Timothy A., comp. *The Print Council Index to Oeuvre-Catalogues of Prints by European and American Artists*. Millwood, NY: Kraus, 1983.

Includes 9500 artists, 15th century to the present day.

Robertson, Jack. *Twentieth-Century Artists on Art: An Index to Artists' Writings, Statements and Interviews*. Boston: G.K. Hall, 1985.

Indexes books, serials and exhibit catalogs.

Robinson, Norman H. *Royal Society Catalogue of Portraits*. London: The Royal Society, 1980.

Biographies of and index to the artists and works of art.

Rudisill, Richard. *Photographers: A Sourcebook for Historical Research*. Brownsville, CA: Carl Mautz Pub., 1991.

An annotated worldwide biographical bibliography with sections on regional directory research, methodology and sources.

Schimmelman, Janice Gayle. *American Imprints on Art through 1865*. n.p.: By the author, 1990.

Annotated bibliography of books and pamphlets on painting, drawing, sculpture, aesthetics, art criticism.

Schmidt, Mary. *Index to Nineteenth Century American Art Periodicals*. Princeton, NJ: Princeton University Press, 1986.

Schweers, Hans F., comp. *Paintings in German Museums: Gemalde in Deutschen Museeun*. Munich: K.G. Saur, 1981.

Indexes 350 museums for works by 10,000 artists.

Seifried, Christopher. *Guide to Canadian Photographic Archives/Guides des Archives photographicques canadiennes*. 2nd ed. Ottawa: Public Archives, 1984.

Represents materials from 139 archives.

Smith, Ralph Clifton. *Biographical Index of American Artists*. New York: Williams and Wilkins, 1930; reprint Detroit: Gale Research, 1976.

Entries for approximately 4700 names.

St. Louis Public Library. Index to Black American Artists. St. Louis: St. Louis Public Library, 1972.

Tufts, Eleanor. *American Women Artists, Past and Present: A Selective Bibliographical Guide*. New York: Garland, 1984.

Approximately 500 artists covered.

Wall, John, ed. *Directory of British Photographic Collections*. New York: Camera/Graphic Press, 1977.

Indexes 1600 collections, 1000 photographers.

Wilson, Raymond L. *Index of American Print Exhibitions 1882-1940*. Metuchen, NJ: Scarecrow Press, 1988.
Sorted by name of exhibiting organizations, ranging from The Chicago Society of Etchers to fairs and expositions to the Victoria and Albert Museum.

World Museum Publications: A Directory of Art and Cultural Museums, Their Publications, and Audio-Visual Materials. New York: R.R. Bowker, 1982.
Listed by museum; author and title indices.

Wright, Christopher, comp. *Old Master Paintings in Britain: Index of Continental Old Master Paintings Executed before c. 1800 in Public Collections in the United Kingdom*. New York: Sotheby Parke Bernet, 1976.
Cites institution names in reference to specific Old Masters they may own, providing titles and catalogue citations.

Wright, Christopher, comp. *Paintings in Dutch Museums: An Index of Oil Paintings in Public Collections in the Netherlands by Artists Born before 1870*. New York: Sotheby Parke Bernet, 1980.
Same format and information as above.

Yarnall, James L. and William H. Gerdts, comps. *The National Museum of American Art's Index to American Art Exhibition Catalogues, from the Beginning through the 1876 Centennial Year*. Boston: G.K. Hall, 1986.
Begun as a bicentennial project, and now a basic and key reference work for American art research, these six volumes index the contents of 952 catalogs of art exhibited in the U.S. and Canada. Location, owner, subject, artist, and specific work information are indexed for the contents of each catalog. (Notable exclusions are auction catalogs, museum collections, and panoramas and dioramas.)

Who — Biographies, Signatures and Marks, etc.

Adams, Clinton. *American Lithographers, 1900-1960: The Artists and Their Printers*. Albuquerque: University of New Mexico, 1983.
Coverage of national and regional themes, movements, clubs, and techniques.

Allgemeines Kunstler Lexikon. Leipzig: Seemann, 1983+.
Updates and expands upon *Thieme-Becker* and *Vollmer*, with biographical data on artists and artisans in all fields. Key sections on alphabetizing and romanizing names, use of symbols and abbreviations in entries. Entries are generally longer than either of the two previous publications.

American Institute of Graphic Arts. Membership Directory. New York: American Institute of Graphic Arts. Annual.
Example of one of hundreds of potentially useful membership directories which can supplement or substitute for entries in the more common biographical indices. Access references to such directories in general reference works like the Encyclopedia of Associations.

American Painters Born Before 1900: A Dictionary and Database. Brookline Village, MA: Vose Archive, 1993.
Lists 40,000+ artists with biographical and bibliographical information.

Amstutz, Walter. *Who's Who in Graphic Art: An Illustrated World Review of the Leading Contemporary Graphic and Topographic Designers, Illustrators, and Cartoonists*. Zurich: Amstutz and Herdeg, Graphis Press, 1962.

_____. *Illustrated World Review of Leading Contemporary Graphic Designers*. Dubendorf, Switzerland: De Clivo, 1982.

Archibald, E.H.H. *Dictionary of Sea Painters*. Woodbridge: Antique Collectors Club, 1989.

Art Director's Index to Photographers. Mies, Switzerland: Rotovision, SA, 1989.
North, Central, and South America, Asia and Australia are indexed in part 1; Europe, part 2.

Auer, Michele and Michel Auer. *Photographers Encyclopedia International 1839 to the Present*. Hermance, Switzerland: Camera Obscura, 1985.
References 1600 photographers.

Bartsch, Adam von. *Le Peintre Graveur*. Vienne, France: Degen, 1802-21; reduced size reprinted. Nieuwkoop, Holland: B. de Graaf, 1982.
A major and oft-cited reference, this covers over 500 artists from the 15th to the 18th centuries, with brief biographical information and a listing of prints by media and subject with some state and edition information. Each print is organized by subject, prints based on another artist's work, questionable attributions, prints based on artist's work but engraved anonymously or by another attributed artist. Volumes on Dutch and Flemish, German, and Italian masters. Because Bartsch's original work did not include illustrations, several reference tools, such as *The Illustrated Bartsch*, the *Warburg Institute Project*, *Index Iconologicus*, and *Iconoclas Indexes*, have been proposed and/or developed to provide the needed illustrations. For a more complete discussion to accessing these tools, see Jones' *Art Information: Research Methods and Resources*, 3rd ed., among others.

Benezit, Emmanuel. *Dictionnaire critique et documentaire des peintres, sculpteurs, dessinateurs, et graveurs*. Paris: Librarie Grund, 1976.
Major dictionary containing brief biographical entries, signatures, exhibit history, some bibliographical citations, and a few prices realized. Useful sections on artists known only by initials, as well as a chart comparing the U.S. dollar-franc-pound exchange rate 1901-1973.

Berman, Harold. *Encyclopedia: Bronzes, Sculptors and Founders 1800-1930*. Calne, England: Hilmarton Manor, 1974-80.
Four-volume set, well-illustrated for identification purposes, includes list of foundries, data on sculptors and founders, facsimile signatures.

Bernt, Walther. *The Netherlandish Painters of the Seventeenth Century*. Trans. from the 3rd German ed. by P.O. Falla. London: Phaidon, 1970.
Biographical data and bibliographical references to 800 Dutch and Flemish artists, including signatures. Third volume contains useful list citing teachers, pupils and artists with similar styles for each main entry.

Biographies of Inuit Artists. 3rd ed. Missisauga, Ontario: Tuttavik, 1988.
Expanded four-volume set.

Bles, Arthur de. *How to Distinguish the Saints in Art by their Costumes, Symbols, and Attributes*. New York: Art Culture, 1925; reprint, Detroit: Gale Research, 1975.
Alphabetical list of emblems with associated saints.

Bradshaw, Maurice, comp. *Royal Society of British Artists*. Leigh-on-Sea, England: F. Lewis Publishers, 1973-1977.
Five-volume set covers members exhibiting from 1824 to 1962. Some listings of original asking prices for selected works.

Briquet, Charles Moise. *Les filigranes: dictionnaire historique des marques du papier des leur apparition vers 1282 jusqu'en 1600*. 2nd ed. Paris: A. Picard & Fils, 1907; reprint, New York, Hacker Art Books, 1985.
Illustrates over 16,000 watermarks from the 13th-15th centuries. Arranged by descriptive term, with line drawings; volume four indexes major subjects, paper makers and manufacturers and paper names.

Browne, Turner and Elaine Partnow. *Macmillan Biographical Encyclopedia of Photographic Artists & Innovators*. New York: Macmillan, 1983.
Lists 2000+ major figures, artistic and technical, from the 1800s to the present. Appendix of international museums and galleries.

Bryan, Michael. *Bryan's Dictionary of Painters and Engravers*. Revised and enlarged by George C. Williamson. New York: MacMillan, 1926-34; reprint, New York, Kennikat, 1964.
Five-volume set.

Burbidge, R. Brinsley. *Dictionary of British Flower, Fruit and Still Life Painters*. Leigh-on-Sea, England: F. Lewis, 1974.

Bushnell, George Herbert. *Scottish Engravers: A Biographical Dictionary of Scottish Engravers and Engravers Who Worked in Scotland to the Beginning of the Nineteenth Century with a Chronological Index*. London: Oxford University Press, 1949.

Caplan, H. H. *Classified Directory of Artists' Signatures, Symbols, and Monograms: American Artists with New UK Additions*. New and enlarged edition. London: Grahame, 1987.
5,000+ examples arranged by artists' names, monograms, illegible or indiscernible signatures and symbols.

Castagno, John. *Artists as Illustrators: An International Directory with Signatures and Monograms, 1800-Present*. Metuchen, NJ: Scarecrow Press, 1989.
Biographies and signature facsimiles for 14,000+ artists.

_____. *Artists' Monograms and Indiscernible Signatures: An International Directory, 1800-1991*. Metuchen, NJ: Scarecrow Press, 1991.

Cederholm, Theresa Dickason. *Afro-American Artists: A Bibliographical Directory*. Boston: Trustees of the Boston Public Library, 1973.
Lists approximately 2000 artists from the 1700s to the present.

Churchill, William Algernon. *Watermarks in Paper in Holland, England, France, etc., in the XVII and XVIII Centuries and Their Interconnection*. Amsterdam: Menno Hertzberger and Co., 1935.
Reproductions of watermarks c. 1635-1800, plus brief history of watermarks and papermaking in Europe.

Cirker, Hayward and Blanche Cirker, eds. *Dictionary of American Portraits: 4045 Pictures of Important Americans from Earliest Times to the Beginning of the Twentieth Century*. New York: Dover, 1967.
No extensive biographical data, but does include dates, occupations, some locations.

Contemporary Graphic Artists: A Biographical, Bibliographical, and Critical Guide to Current Illustrators, Animators, Cartoonists, Designers, and Other Graphic Artists. Detroit: Gale Research, 1987.
Indices by artist, occupation and subject are complemented by lists of organizations, awards, media and genre in two volumes.

Cummings, Paul, ed. *Dictionary of Contemporary American Artists*. New York: St. Martin's, 5th ed., 1988.
Revisions every five years update exhibition, commission, collection and bibliographical information for over 900 painters, printmakers and sculptors.

Dawdy, Doris Ostrander. *Artists of the American West: A Biographical Dictionary*. Chicago: Sage Books, 1979-85. 3 vols.
Covers 2700+ artists born before 1900.

Dolman, Bernard, ed. *Dictionary of Contemporary British Artists*. 2nd ed. Woodbridge, Suffolk: Art Collectors' Club, 1981.

Dunford, Penny. *A Biographical Dictionary of Women Artists in Europe and American Since 1850*. Philadelphia: University of Pennsylvania Press, 1989.

Edouard-Joseph, Rene. *Dictionnaire biographique des artistes contemporaines, 1910-1930*. Paris: Art et Edition, 1930-1934. *Supplement*, 1936.
Biographical information for artists active 1910-1930.

Engen, Rodney K. *Dictionary of Victorian Engravers, Print Publishers and their Works*. Teaneck, NJ: Chadwyck-Healey, 1985.

_____. *Dictionary of Victorian Wood Engravers*. Teaneck, NJ: Chadwyck-Healey, 1985.

Falk, Peter H. *Dictionary of Signatures and Monograms of American Artists from the Colonial Period to the mid-20th Century*. Madison, CT: Sound View Press, 1988.

_____, comp. *Who Was Who in American Art*. Madison, CT: Sound View, 1985.
Data on artists active from 1898 to 1947, compiled from contemporary volumes of *American Art Annual* and *Who's Who in America*.

Fine, Elsa Honig. *Women and Art: A History of Women Painters and Sculptors from the Renaissance to the 20th Century*. Montclair, NJ: Allanheld and Schram, 1978.

Fisher, Stanley. *Dictionary of Watercolour Painters, 1750-1900*. London: Foulsham, 1972.
Covers British artists of the era.

Foskett, Daphne. *A Dictionary of British Miniature Painters*. New York: Praeger, 1972.
Two-volume set covers artists active from 1520-1910.

Goldstein, Franz. *Monogramm-Lexikon: internationales Verzeichnis der Monogrammme bildender Kunstler seit 1850*. Berlin: Verlag Walter de Gruyter, 1964.
Supplements Nagler (see below), listing artists active since 1850. Arranged by monogram, includes biographical information; index to artists who used devices such as figures or symbols.

Graham, Mary and Carol Ruppe. *Native American Artist Directory*. Phoenix: Heard Museum, 1985.

Grant, Maurice. *Dictionary of British Etchers*. London: Rockliff, 1952.

_____. *Dictionary of British Landscape Painters from the 16th Century to the Early 20th Century*. Leigh-on-Sea, England: F. Lewis, 1970.

Graves, Algernon. *A Dictionary of Artists Who Have Exhibited Works in the Principal London Exhibitions from 1760 to 1893*. 3rd ed. London: H. Graves, 1991; reprint, New York: Burt Franklin, 1970.

Records of exhibiting artists in 16 societies, including the Royal Academy, the Society of Artists and the British Institution. Does not include titles.

_____. *The Royal Academy of Arts: A Complete Dictionary of Contributors and Their Works from Its Foundation in 1769 to 1904*. London: H. Graves and Co., Ltd., 1905-06.

Groce, George C. and David H. Wallace. *New York Historical Society's Dictionary of Artists in America 1564-1860*. New Haven, CT: Yale University, 1957.
Includes biographies of about 10,000 American artists, draftsmen, engravers, lithographers and those in allied fields.

Gunnis, Rupert. *Dictionary of British Sculptors 1660-1851*. Rev. ed. London: Abbey Library, 1968.
Provides titles, dates, exhibit info, some prices, bibliographical data.

Harper, J. Russell. *Early Painters and Engravers in Canada*. Toronto: University of Toronto, 1970.
Artists pre-1867 are included.

Haslam, Malcolm. *Marks and Monograms of the Modern Movement, 1875-1930*. New York: Scribner, 1977.
Includes identifying marks of artists, designers, retailers and manufacturers, from the Aesthetic Movement to Art Deco and Style Moderne.

Heawood, Edward. *Watermarks Mainly of the 17th and 18th Centuries*. Hilversum: Paper Publications Society, 1969.

Hind, Arthur M. *Early Italian Engraving: A Critical Catalog with Complete Reproductions of All the Prints Described*. New York: Knoedler, 1938-48; reprint, Nendeln, Liechtenstein: Kraus, 1970.

Hollstein, F.W.H. *Dutch and Flemish Etchings, Engravings and Woodcuts, c. 1450-1700*. Amsterdam: Menno Hertzberger, 1949+.
To date, 32 volumes of brief biographies and literary references have been published.

Hook, Philip and Mark Poltimore. *Popular 19th Century Painting: A Dictionary of European Genre Painters*. Woodbridge, Suffolk: Antique Collectors Club, 1986.

Houfe, Simon. *The Dictionary of British Book Illustrators and Caricaturists 1800-1914*. Rev. ed. Woodbridge, Suffolk: Antique Collectors Club, 1981.

Jervis, Simon. *The Facts on File Dictionary of Design and Designers*. New York: Facts on File, 1984.

Johnson, Jane. *The Dictionary of British Artists, 1880-1940*. Suffolk, England: Antique Collectors Club, 1986.

Johnson, Una E. *American Prints and Printmakers*. Garden City, NY: Doubleday, 1980.
Covers data from 1900 onward.

Kobayshi, Terry and Michael Bird. *A Compendium of Canadian Folk Artists*. Erin, Ontario: Boston Mills Press, 1985.

Lami, Stanislas. *Dictionnaire des sculpteurs de l'ecole francaise*. Paris: Champion, 1898-1921; reprint, New York: Kraus, 1970.
Detailed data on sculptors and their work, including Salons, exhibitions, provenance for sculpture from the Middle Ages to the 19th century; the latter is indexed by subject.

Lewis, Frank. *Dictionary of British Bird Painters*. Leigh-on-Sea, England: F. Lewis, 1974.

Lugt, Frits. *Les marques de collections de dessins et d'estampes: marques estampillees et ecrites de collections particuliers et publiques...* Amsterdam: Vereenigde Drukkerij-jen, 1921. *Supplement.* Den Haag: Martinus Nijhoff, 1956. Reprints, San Francisco: Alan Wofsy Fine Arts, 1975. *Supplement,* 1988.
Major resource illustrates and names identification marks from prints and drawings, with accompanying sales information and indexes to collections, artists, dealers and publishers.

MacDonald, Colin S. *Dictionary of Canadian Artists.* Ottawa: Canadian Paperbacks, 1967+.
Seven-volume series, alphabetic divisions, with bibliographical info.

McGlauflin, Alice Coe, ed. *Dictionary of American Artists: 19th and 20th Century.* New York: American Art Annual, 1930; reprint, Poughkeesie, NY: Apollo, 1982.
Artists c. 1850-1950.

McMann, Evelyn de R. *Royal Canadian Academy of Arts/Academie royale des arts du Canada/Exhibitions and Members, 1880-1979.* Toronto: University of Toronto Press, 1981.

Mantle Fielding's Dictionary of American Painters, Sculptors and Engravers. 2nd ed., rev., enl. and updated by Glenn Optiz. Poughkeepsie, NY: Apollo, 1986.
A basic reference source since its introduction in 1926.

Marks, Claude. *World Artists 1950-1980.* New York: H.W. Wilson, 1984.
_____. *World Artists 1980-1990.* New York: H.W. Wilson, 1991.
Basic biographical information for modern artists.

Mason, Lauris and Joan Ludman, eds. *Print Collector's Quarterly: An Anthology of Essays on Eminent Printmakers of the World.* Millwood, NY: KTO Press, 1977.

Murray, Peter and Linda Murray. Rev. ed. *Dictionary of Art and Artists.* New York: Penguin, 1984.
Includes terms used in art.

Nagler, G.K. *Die Monogrammisten.* Nieuwkoop: B. de Graaf, 1991.
Dictionary of 30,000+ artists' signatures, generally for those active pre-1850.

National Academy of Design Exhibition Record 1826-1860. New York: New York Historical Society, 1943.

National Academy of Design Exhibition Record 1861-1900. New York: Kennedy Galleries, 1973.
Indices for artist, owner, subject and place.

Petteys, Chris et al. *Dictionary of Women Artists: An International Dictionary of Women Artists Born Before 1900.* Boston: G.K. Hall, 1985.

Preston, Rupert. *The Seventeenth Century Marine Painters of the Netherlands.* Leigh-on-Sea, England: F. Lewis, 1974.

Pyke, E.J. *A Biographical Dictionary of Wax Modellers.* Oxford: Clarendon Press, 1973.

Reed, Walt. *The Illustrator in America, 1880-1980: A Century of Illustration.* Rev. ed. New York: Society of Illustrators, 1984.

Romero, David, ed. *Directory of American Portrait Artists.* Huntington Harbor, CA: American Portrait Society, 1985.
Good example of accessing an association membership list to find a particular individual or a particular skill.

Rosenak, Chuck and Jan, et al. *Museum of American Folk Art Encyclopedia of Twentieth-Century American Folk Art and Artists.* New York: Abbeville Press, 1990.
Includes bibliographical references.

Royal Academy of Arts. Royal Academy Exhibitors 1905-1970: *A Dictionary of Artists and Their Work in the Summer Exhibitions of the Royal Academy of Arts.* Wakefield, Yorkshire, England: E.P. Publications, 1973-82.
Supplements *Royal Academy of Arts* by Graves, above.

Samuels, Peggy and Harold. *Samuels' Encyclopedia of Artists of the American West.* 2nd ed. Seacaucus, NJ: Castle, 1985.
Good regional survey.

_____. *Contemporary Western Artists.* New York: Doubleday, 1982.
Supplements above volume.

Scheen, Pieter A. *Lexicon Nederlandse beeldende Kunstenaars.* The Hague: P.A. Scheen, 1981.
Covers artists from 1750 to 1950.

Snodgrass, Jeanne O. *American Indian Painters: A Biographical Directory.* New York: Museum of the American Indian, Heye Foundation, 1968.

Stauffer, David McNeely and Mantle Fielding. *American Engravers Upon Copper and Steel*. New York: Burt Franklin, 1964.
Parts 1 and 2, by Stauffer, were originally published in 1907, covering around 700 artists; third section, by Fielding, added about 120.

Tatham, David. *Prints and Printmakers of New York State, 1825-1940*. New York State Studies: Syracuse University Press, 1986.
Good example of a regional study, useful as a supplement to more general, broad biographies.

Thieme, Ulrich and Felix Becker. *Allgemeines Lexikon der bilden-den Kunstler von der Antike bis zur Gegenwart*. Leipzig: E.A. Seemann, 1907-1950; reprint ed. Leipzig, F. Allmann, 1964.
Among the most thoroughly researched and scholarly works, *Thieme-Becker* provides data on painters, sculptors, architects, engravers, some decorative artists, in addition to bibliographical info on older publications. Although many minor artists are represented, many of the 20th century are not. A section on anonymous artists known only by initials or nicknames appears in the last volume. Note that the true, not anglicized, spellings, are used (i.e. "Tiziano", not "Titian"). An essential companion is the *Index to the Most Common German Abbreviations Used in Thieme-Becker's Kunstler-Lexicon* (Valerie D. Meyer. Ann Arbor: University of Michigan Fine Arts Library, 1972.)

Vasari, Giorgio. *Lives of the Most Eminent Painters, Sculptors, and Architects*. London: Macmillan, 1912-15.
This ten-volume edition by one of the first art historians was originally published c. 1568 and covers 300 years of artist biographies. A classic, contemporary reference.

Vollmer, Hans. *Allgemeines Lexikon der bildenden Kunstler des XX Jahrhunderts*. Leipzig: E. A. Seemann, 1953-1962.
Using the same format as *Thieme-Becker*, Vollmer concentrates on artists born after 1870.

Walters, Grant M. *Dictionary of British Artists 1900-1950*. Eastbourne, England: Eastbourne Fine Arts, 1975.

Who's Who in American Art: A Biographical Directory. New York: R.R. Bowker. Vol. 1, 1936-37+.
Brief biographies of over 10,000 artists, collectors, scholars, administrators, art historians and critics. Includes awards and exhibition histories. Indexed geographically and by profession.

Who's Who in Art: Biographies of Leading Men and Women in the World of Art Today: Artists, Designers, Craftsmen, Critics, Writers, Teachers, Collectors, and Curators With an Appendix of Signatures. Havant, Hantsford, England: Art Trade Press, 1927+.
Contains data chiefly on British individuals.

Willis-Thomas, Deborah. *Black Photographers 1940-1940: An Illustrated Bio-Bibliography*. New York: Garland, 1985.

Wilson, Arnold. *Dictionary of British Marine Painters*. Leigh-on-Sea, England: F. Lewis, 1980.

Wood, Christopher. *Dictionary of Victorian Painters*. 2nd ed. Woodbridge, Suffolk: Antique Collectors Club, 1978.
Biographical dictionary of 11,000+ artists active during the Victorian era, with signatures and indices.

Wood, John Clairmont. *Dictionary of British Animal Painters* Leigh-on-Sea, England: F. Lewis, 1973.

Zampetti, Pietro. *Dictionary of Venetian Painters*. Leigh-on-Sea, England. F. Lewis, 1969-79.
Five-volume set, covering the 14th through 20th centuries.

Zigrosser, Carl. *Prints and Their Creators: A World History. An Anthology of Printed Pictures and Introduction to the Study of Graphic Art in the West and the East*. 2nd rev. ed. New York: Crown, 1974.

What — General Art History, Iconography and Symbols, Themes

Castleman, Riva. *Prints of the Twentieth Century: A History*. Rev. and enl. New York: Thames and Hudson, 1988.
Significant survey of styles, including Expressionism, Cubism, Dada, Surrealism, Pop Art.

Cosgrove, Denis. *The Iconography of Landscape*. New York: Cambridge University, 1988.

Daniel, Howard. *Encyclopedia of Themes and Subjects in Painting*. London: Thames and Hudson, 1971.
Surveys artworks from the early Renaissance to mid-19th century.

Eichenberg, Fritz. *The Art of the Print: Masterpieces, History, Techniques*. New York: Abrams, 1976.
Comprehensive and detailed, covers all aspects, from 15th century Far Eastern prints to contemporary Western works.

Encyclopedia of World Art. New York: McGraw Hill, 1958.
Fifteen volumes; good source for general surveys, such as themes and styles, with bibliographies. Supplemented by *World Art in Our Time* (1983) and *New Discoveries and Perspectives in the World of Art* (1987).

Gascoigne, Bamber. *How to Identify Prints: A Complete Guide to Manual and Mechanical Process from Woodcut to Jet Ink*. New York: Thames and Hudson, 1986.
Thorough guide to print processes, with methods of identification through process of elimination.

Greenhill, Ralph and Andrew Birrell. *Canadian Photography 1839-1920*. Toronto: Coach House, 1979.

Hall, James. *Dictionary of Subjects and Symbols in Art.* 2nd ed. rev. New York: Harper and Row, 1979.
References themes and symbols in European art, from Classical Greece; includes bibliography.

Hind, Arthur Mayger. *A History of Engraving and Etching: From the 15th Century to the Year 1914.* 3rd ed., rev. New York: Dover, 1963.
Extensive bibliography, list of monographs, engravings collections with lists of their catalogs.

Hoffer, Thomas W. *Animation: A Reference Guide.* Westport, CT: Greenwood Press, 1981.

Jones, Owen. *The Grammar of Ornament.* Reprint. New York: Van Nostrand, 1972.
Traces design elements and motifs used by an array of civilizations and art historical periods, from Ancient Egypt to the Elizabethan.

Lucie-Smith, Edward. *The Thames and Hudson Dictionary of Art Terms.* London: Thames and Hudson, 1984.
Compact, but complete.

MacKenzie, Donald A. *The Migration of Symbols and Their Relations to Beliefs and Customs.* Detroit: Gale Research, 1968.
Tracks such symbols as the swastika, tree, ear, more through various cultures.

Mathews, Oliver. *Early Photographs and Photographers: A Survey in Dictionary Form.* New York: Pitman, 1973.

Metford, J.C.J. *Dictionary of Christian Lore and Legend.* London: Thames and Hudson, 1983.
Useful reference to symbolism and themes in Christian art.

Morgan, Willard D., ed. *Encyclopedia of Photography.* New York: Greystone, 1974.
Twenty-volume set, originally issued as *The Complete Photographers* (1943).

Pelican History of Art. Baltimore, MD: Penguin.
Extensive list of well-researched, well-illustrated art historical surveys of a variety of places and cultures, from early Christian and Byzantine art to Gothic architecture.

Pinkard, Bruce. *The Photographer's Dictionary.* London: B.T. Batsford, 1982.
Entries on individual photographers, terms, organizations.

Reau, Louis. *Iconographie de l'art chretien.* Paris: Presses Universitaires de France, 1955-59.
Exhaustively detailed in three volumes, with iconography of saints and Testaments, indices to saints' names in various languages, saints' attributes, common scenes or situations with English titles and lists of works that depict said scenes.

_____. *Dictionnaire polyglotte des termes d'art et d'archeologie.* Paris: Presses Universitaires de France, 1953.

Terms and definitions in most Western European languages and Latin.

Ross, John. *The Complete Intaglio Print: The Art and Technique of the Intaglio Print, the Collagraph, Photographic Intaglio, Care of Prints, the Dealer and the Edition, Collecting Prints, Print Workshop, Sources, and Charts.* New York: Free Press, 1974.

_____. *The Complete Screenprint and Lithograph: The Art and Technique of the Screen Print, the Lithograph, Photographic Techniques, Care of Prints...* New York: Free Press, 1974.

Stafford, Maureen and Dora Ware. *An Illustrated Dictionary of Ornament.* New York: St. Martin's, 1974.
Indexes people, places, heraldic devices, plus definitions of related terms.

Stroebel, Leslie and Hollis N. Todd. *Dictionary of Contemporary Photography.* New York: Morgan and Morgan, 1974.

Turner, Jane S., ed. *Dictionary of Art.* London: MacMillan, 1994.
Projected 30-volume set to include international biographies of artists, patrons, critics and collectors, plus entries on styles, subjects and media.

Walker, John Albert. *Glossary of Art, Architecture, and Design Since 1945: Terms and Labels Describing Movements, Styles and Groups Derived from the Vocabulary of Artists and Critics.* 2nd rev. ed. London: Clive Bingley, 1977.

Waters, Clara Erskine Clement. *A Handbook of Legendary and Mythological Art.* 2nd ed. Reprint. Detroit: Gale Research, 1969.
Index arranged by symbolism, legends of places and saints, ancient myths.

Weill, Alain. *The Poster: A Worldwide Survey and History.* Boston: G.K. Hall, 1984.
Includes brief artist biographies.

Witkin, Lee D. and Barbara London. *The Photograph Collector's Guide.* Boston: New York Graphic Society, 1979.
Essays on various aspects of collection and care, material on over 200 photographers, historical and technical chronology, lists of museums, galleries and auction houses.

When — Exhibitions, etc.

The Archives of American Art. *Collection of Exhibition Catalogs.* Boston: G.K. Hall, 1979.
Indexes 20,000+ catalogs c. 1900-1960s, arranged by gallery, museum and personal name; includes group exhibitions.

Art Exhibition Catalogs Subject Index: Collection of the Arts Library, University of California at Santa Barbara. New York: Chadwyck-Healy, 1978+.

Microfiche index includes institution name and location, catalogue title, contents, year, physical data of catalog including inclusion of bibliographies, and authors. Indexed by institution and subject. With 67,000+ entries, this provides an indispensible tool for interlibrary loans of material; UCSB owns much of the cited material.

Art Exhibition Catalogues on Microfiche. New York: Chadwyck-Healey, n.d.
Monumental and important collection covers publications of 3100+ exhibitions in Europe and North America, from the Victoria and Albert 1862-1974 to the Chicago Museum of Contemporary Art 1967-1976.

Cowdrey, Mary Bartlett. *American Academy of Fine Arts and American Art-Union.* New York: New York Historical Society, 1953.
Works listed date from 1816-1852, and includes some sales prices.

Gordon, Donald E., comp. *Modern Art Exhibitions 1900-1916: Selected Catalogue Documentation.* Munich: Prestel-Verlag, 1974.
Lists over 400 painters and sculptors in 850+ exhibitions of modern art, c. 1900-1916, whose catalogues are owned by 52 libraries. Volume 1 contains a chronological catalog list and artist index; second volume has list of catalogs and indexes cities and exhibitors.

Graves, Algernon, comp. *British Institution 1806-1867: A Complete Dictionary of Contributors and Their Work from the Foundation of the Institution.* Reprint: West Orange, NJ: Albert Saifer, 1969.
Indexes portraits, including many examples in sculpture.

_____. *A Dictionary of Artists Who Have Exhibited Works in the Principal London Exhibitions from 1760 to 1893.* Reprint. New York: Burt Franklin, 1970.
Includes shows from 16 societies, including the Royal Academy, Grosvenor Gallery, etc., but does not list by title.

_____. *Royal Academy of Arts: A Complete Dictionary of Contributors and Their Work from Its Foundation in 1769 to 1904.* Reprint. New York: Burt Franklin, 1970.
Reproductions for selected works are included in the serials *Academy Notes* and *Royal Academy Illustrated.*

_____. *Society of Artists of Great Britain 1760-1791: The Free Society of Artists 1761-1783: A Complete Dictionary of Contributors and Their Work from the Foundation of the Societies to 1791.* London: G. Bell & Sons, 1907.
Portrait index and brief histories.

Janson, Horst Woledemar. *Catalogues of the Paris Salon 1673-1881.* New York: Garland, 1977.
In 60 volumes, reprint of all *livrets* issued for this official French art exhibition.

The Knoedler Library of Art Exhibition Catalogs on Microfiche. New York: Chadwyck-Healey, Knoedler Gallery, 1970s.
M. Knoedler and Co., one of New York City's oldest art galleries, maintains a collection of 5200 catalogs. Not all series are complete, but represented exhibitions include the Paris Salons, Royal Academy of Arts Winter Exhibitions, Societe des Artistes Francais, various national and international expositions, and the Knoedler Gallery catalogs. Holdings of U.S. exhibitions are especially comprehensive; year ranges for the collection are approximately 1812 to the present.

McMann, Evelyn de Rostaing, comp. *Royal Canadian Academy of Arts/Academie royale des arts du Canada: Exhibitions and Members 1880-1979.* Toronto: University of Toronto Press, 1981.
Lists over 3000 artists with biographical data and, if available, current location of work.

Mosco, Marilena. *Picture Frames through History/La Cornice attraverso il tempo.* Roma: Federlegno-Arredo, 1984.

National Gallery of Canada Exhibition Catalogues on Microfiche, 1919-1959. Toronto: McLaren Micropublishing, 1980.
Reproductions of 167 catalogs on all types of graphic arts; entries include artist, collectors, galleries, museums, exhibition names. *The National Gallery of Canada: A Hundred Years of Exhibitions, List and Index* (Garry Mainprize) offers an effective indexing system.

Reff, Theodore, comp. *Modern Art in Paris 1855-1900.* New York: Garland, 1981.
Representative catalogs from 200 sources, including Parisian Worlds' Fairs, Salon of the Independants, Post-Impressionist shows, Art Nouveau, Salons des Cent, and many others. Some drawbacks to the indices; individual works can be difficult to cite.

Rinder, Frank. *Royal Scottish Academy 1826-1916.* Glasgow: Maclehose & Sons, 1917.

Rutledge, Anna Wells, ed. *Cumulative Record of Exhibition Catalogues: The Pennsylvania Academy of the Fine Arts 1807-1870; The Society of Artists 1800-1814; The Artists' Fund Society 1835-1845.* Philadelphia: American Philosophical Society, 1955.
Indexes by artist, owner, subject. Illustrative of dozens of other examples produced by various publishers, such as *A History of the Brooklyn Art Association with an Index of Exhibitions, National Academy of Design and the Montreal Museum of Fine Arts...Exhibitions.* Many of the items are available through Interlibrary Loan.

Sandweiss, Martha, ed. *Photography in Nineteenth Century America.* New York: Abrams, 1991.

Stewart, Ann M, comp. *Royal Hibernian Academy of Arts: Index of Exhibitors 1826-1979.* Dublin: Manton, 1985-87.

U.S. Copyright Office. *Catalog of Copyright Entries. Fourth Series, Part 5: Visual Arts Excluding Maps*. Washington, D.C.: U.S. Library of Congress Copyright Office, 1978+.
Useful in dating copyrighted artworks.

Wilson, Raymond L. *Index of American Print Exhibitions, 1882-1940*. Metuchen, NJ: Scarecrow Press, 1988.
Divided by exhibiting organization with individual artists and works indexed. Includes listings for the New York Etching Club, Chicago Society of Etchers, Printmakers Society of California, Fine Prints of the Year, Panama-Pacific International Exposition, New York World's Fair, and more.

Yarnall, James L. and William H. Gerdts, comps. *National Museum of American Art's Index to American Art Exhibition Catalogues: From the Beginning through the 1876 Centennial Year*. Boston: G.K. Hall, 1986.
Accesses 900 catalogs from U.S. and Canadian exhibits, held in cities large and small, all pre-1877, and including private collections, galleries, clubs and fairs. Does not repeat exhibitions cited elsewhere, such as American Academy of Fine Arts, Boston Athenaeum, Pennsylvania Academy of Fine Arts, etc. Copies of catalogues may be obtained with the assistance of the Office of Research Support, National Museum of American Art, Washington, D.C.

Where — Regional Studies, Sources

Best, James J. *American Popular Illustration: A Reference Guide*. Westport, CT: Greenwood Press, 1984.
Includes book and magazine illustration in the U.S. with bibliographic references.

Dockstader, Frederick. *Indian Art in America: The Arts and Crafts of the North American Indian*. 3rd ed. Boston: New York Graphic, 1966.

Evans, Hilary and Mary Evans. *Sources of Illustration 1500-1900*. New York: Hastings House, 1971.

Gerdts, William H. *Art Across America: Two Centuries of Regional Painting, 1710-1920*. New York: Abbeville Press, 1990.
Outstanding and indispensible three-volume set covers major and minor figures in every geographic location, well-illustrated, with detailed notes and good bibliographies. Not only a fine overall resource in itself, but an equally useful means to further research.

Harper, J. Russell. *Painting in Canada: A History*. Rev. ed. Toronto: University of Toronto: 1977.

Johnson, Una E. *American Prints and Printmakers*. Garden City, NY: Doubleday, 1980.
Coverage from 1900 to the present.

How — Techniques, Processes, Tools

Antreasian, Garo Z. and Clinton Adams. *The Tamarind Book of Lithography: Art and Techniques*. New York: Harry Abrams, 1971.

Brunner, Felix A. *A Handbook of Graphic Reproductive Processes*. 3rd ed. New York: Hastings House, 1968.

Chamberlain, Walter. *The Thames & Hudson Manual of Etching and Engraving*. Thames and Hudson, 1978.

Eichenberg, Fritz. *Art of the Print Selections. Lithography and Silkscreen: Art and Technique*. New York: Abrams, 1978.

Goldman, Judith. *American Prints: Process and Proofs*. New York: Harper and Row, 1981.

Goldman, Paul. *Looking at Prints, Drawings and Watercolours: A Guide to Technical Terms*. London: British Museum Publications, 1988.

Huberts, Kurt. *The Complete Book of Artists' Techniques*. New York: Frederick A. Praeger, 1958.
Includes information on recreating historical techniques.

Katlan, Alexander W. *American Artists' Materials Suppliers Directory*. Park Ridge, NJ: Noyes Press, 1987-1992.
Volume 1 references nineteenth century suppliers in New York and Boston; volume 2 is a guide to stretchers, panels, millboards and stencil marks. A useful set for identifying time and place for a work by the materials utilized.

Mayer, Ralph. *The Artist's Handbook of Materials and Techniques*. 4th ed. rev. New York: Viking, 1982.

Pink, Marilyn. *How to Catalogue Works of Art*. Los Angeles: Museum Systems, 1972.

Reilly, James M. *Care and Identification of 19th Century Photographic Prints*. Rochester, NY: Eastman Kodak, 1986.
Excellent guide to identification of prints through analysis of technique.

Senefelder, Alois. *A Complete Course of Lithography*. New York: Da Capo Press, 1977.

Simmons, Rosemary. *The Complete Manual of Relief Printmaking*. New York: Knopf, 1988.

Time-Life Library of Photography Series. New York: Time, 1970-72.
Volumes on all aspects of process, connoisseurship, conservation and history.

Verhelst, Wilbert. *Sculpture: Tools, Materials and Techniques*. 2nd ed. Englewood Cliffs, NJ: Prentice-Hall, 1987.

Wittkower, Rudolf. *Sculpture: Processes and Principles*. New York: Harper and Row, 1977.

Why — Connoisseurship, Ranking, Market Trends and Influences

Allard, Dominic. *Looking at Photographs*. Walton-on-Thames, Surrey: Outposts, 1980.

Donson, Theodore B. *Prints and the Print Market: A Handbook for Buyers, Collectors, Connoisseurs*. New York: Crowell, 1977.

Perrett, Thomas I. *Gold Book of Photography Prices*. Carson, CA: Photography Research Institute, 1989.
Guidelines for pricing and marketing photographs.

Reitlinger, Gerald. *The Economics of Taste, 1961-1970*. New York: Holt, Rinehart and Winston.
Three volumes discuss *The Rise and Fall of the Picture Market 1760-1960*; *The Rise and Fall of the Objets d'Art Market Since 1750*; and *The Art Market in the 1960s* with prices realized for individual items and general market analyses.

Rosenberg, Jakob. *On Quality in Art, Criteria of Excellence Past and Present*. Princeton, NJ: Princeton University Press, 1967.

Shapiro, Cecile. *Fine Prints: Collecting, Buying and Selling*. New York: Harper and Row, 1976.
Includes glossaries of French and German terms.

Simons, Rosemary. *Collecting Original Prints.*. Mountain View, CA: Mayflower Books, 1980.

Taylor, Francis Henry. *The Taste of Angels: A History of Art Collecting from Rameses to Napoleon*. Boston: Little, Brown, 1946.

Zellman, Michael David, ed. *American Art Analog*. New York: Chelsea House Publishers, 1986. Annual supplement, Blue Book, 1987+.
Analyzes the art market for individual artist's works, with discussions of changes in value, record sales and numbers of works sold, etc. Also includes brief artist biographies, essays on subjects and genres, etc.

How Much — Auction Reports, Price Guides, Sales History

Art at Auction in America. Silver Spring, MD: Krax Press, 1989+.
Reports sales information on 10,000 artists and 200,000 works sold through the major houses.

Art Prices Current: A Record of Sale Prices at the Principal London, Continental, and American Auction Rooms. London: William Dawson & Sons, 1907/08-1972/73.
Useful for tracing early sales; Part A includes paintings, drawings and miniatures; Part B covers engravings, etchings, lithographs and prints.

Art Sales Catalogues, 1600-1825. Leiden, Netherlands: Inter Documentation Co., 1989+.
Microfiche reprints of catalogs, largely based on Lugt's *Repertoire* (which see).

Berard, Michele. *Encyclopedia of Modern Art Auction Prices*. New York: Arco Publishing, 1971.
Includes paintings and drawings from 275 artists which represented sales of $2000 or more.

Bibliotheque Forney, Paris. *Catalogue des Catalogues de Ventes d'Art*. [*Catalog of the Catalogs of Art Sales*.] Boston: G.K. Hall, 1972.
Lists 14,000 catalogs, c. 1778-1971, arranged by collector and time and place of auction.

Canadian Art Sales Index. Vancouver, B.C.: Westbridge Publications, 1977/80+.
Annual sales report lists results from 20+ houses in Canada and the U.K. for sales of oils, watercolors, drawings, sculpture, Native art and art books.

Druout: l'art et les encheres en France. Paris: Compagnie des commissaires-Priseurs de Paris, 1988. Annual.
Year in review for the premier Parisian auction house, l'Hotel Drouot.

Fredericksen, Burton B., ed. *The Index of Paintings Sold in the British Isles during the Nineteenth Century*. Santa Barbara, CA: ABC-CLIO, 1989+.
Also called *The Provenance Index of the Getty Art History Information Program*, this is a chronological list of sales, with indexes by artist and owner, plus prices realized. One volume, covering a five-year period, will be issued annually over the next two decades; the first volume includes a discussion of the 19th century European art market.

Graves, Algernon. *Art Sales from Early in the Eighteenth Century to Early in the Twentieth Century (Mostly Old Master and Early English Pictures.)* Reprint. New York: Burt Franklin, 1970.
Major resource for early paintings sold at auction in England.

Hislop, Richard, ed. *Art Sales Index*. Weybridge, Surrey: Art Sales Index, 1968-69+.
Until 1975, this covered only paintings but has gradually added drawings and three-dimensional works including bronzes. Reports sales over a specific period from 400 international houses in 20 countries. Includes sales chronology. *Auction Prices of American Artists* (1978+) is a biennial analysis of the North and South American market.

International Art Market: A Monthly Report on Current World Market Prices of Art, Antique Furniture, and Objects d'Art. New York: Art in America, 1961+.
Covers all manner of fine and decorative arts, often including bought-in prices. Annual index available; back issues available on microfilm. Regular feature on art market conditions.

Karia, Bhupendra, ed. *Artronix: Photographs at Auction*. New York: New York Artronix Data, 1986.
A retrospective survey of the photography market, organized by such topics as photographer, collector, serial, with emphasis on processes used for cited examples. Useful in the careful

recording of provenance, signatures, full-text inscriptions, historical notes, publisher identification, as well as in the statistical and market analysis of selected sales.

Knoedler Library Sales Catalogues. New York: Knoedler Gallery, 1970s.

Sales catalogs from the Knoedler Gallery collection of 13,000 items are organized by country, auction house and date of sale, with particular strengths in the late 19th and early 20th centuries. Microfilm; no index.

Kunstpreis-Jahrbuch. Munich: Weltkunst Verlag. Annual.

Covers a wide variety of properties, but the editors make a subjective decision on which auctions to report. Earlier English editions replaced by German language only since 1980.

Lawrence's Dealer Print Prices. Phoenix: Long and Strider Press, 1992+.

Leonard's Annual Price Index Prints Posters Photographs. Newton, MA: Auction Index Inc., 1992+.

Mireur, Hippolyte. *Dictionnaire des ventes d'art faites en France et a l'etranger pendant les XVIIIeme et XIXeme siecles: tableaux, dessins, estampes, aquarelles, miniatures, pastels...* Paris: Maison d'editions de'oeuvres artistiques, chez de Vincenti, 1911-12.

Fine source for French sales, 18th-19th centuries. Gives standard sales data by artist, plus seller and price.

Photographic Art Market. New York: Photographic Arts Center, 1980/81+.

Comprehensive guide to the market.

Printworld Directory of Contemporary Prints & Prices. BalaCynwyd, PA: Printworld, 1982+.

Useful in providing addresses also.

Redford, George. *Art Sales: A History of Sales of Pictures and Other Works.* London: Redford, 1888.

Useful in tracking provenances: volume 1 gives historical information on sales of major and minor collections and volume 2 cites sales information such as buyer and seller names and prices realized. (The Metropolitan Museum also owns an unpublished document that covers the years 1887-1918, with volumes for British and foreign schools.)

Sotheby and Co.: Catalogues of Sales. Ann Arbor, MI: University Microfilm, 1973.

Includes 15,000+ individual catalogues from the London auction rooms, beginning with the first brochure c. 1734 to the 1970s, and including staff annotations, sales prices, buyers. All types of properties are covered. Chronological arrangement; no index.

Sotheby Parke Bernet. New York. *Art At Auction: The Year at Sotheby's.* London: Sotheby Parke Bernet. Annual.

Collection of articles on various types of works auctioned, published under various titles including *The Ivory Hammer.* Representative of the reviews of the season produced by the larger houses, which can be useful as supplements to individual catalogs and prices realized lists.

Theran, Susan, ed. *Leonard's Index of Art Auctions.* Newton, MA: Auction Index, 1980+.

Indexes two- and three-dimensional works sold at American houses. Particular strength is in its reporting of lower-priced items which may not be mentioned elsewhere. Notes features such as provenance, literature, reproduction or other value factors; notes when reported price includes buyer's premium.

Values of Victorian Paintings: Price Review. Woodbridge, England: Antique Collectors Club, 1979+.

Initially meant to supplement *Dictionary of Victorian Painters* by Christopher Wood.

Wolf, Thomas, ed. *Gordon's Print Price Annual.* New York: Martin Gordon. Vol. 1, 1972+.

Important source for print sales information, with reports from 19 U.S. and European auctions. Detailed information on properties includes edition numbers, condition, signatures; reference to catalogue numbers; bibliography; commissions charged.

World Collectors Annuary. Voorburg: Repro-Holland BV. Vol. 1, 1946/49+.

Reports on drawings, paintings, watercolors, pastels. Occasional references to exhibitions and provenances. *World Collectors Index 1946-1972* is a useful companion.

Chapter 9

Judicial Precedents Affecting Appraisal Practice

Using Legal Citation

The following cases are examined in greater detail in *Fundamentals of Valuation, Level IV*, a course offered by the American Society of Appraisers in its core curriculum. However, anyone wishing to study these cases more closely on their own can obtain a copy of any of these decisions from a law library (at a law school or court). The books in which the cases and decisions are reported are called **reporters**.

The format used in this chapter to abbreviate the citations is from *The Bluebook: A Uniform System of Citation* (Cambridge, Massachusetts: The Harvard Law Review Association, 1991 [fifteenth edition]).

Below is an example of a court citation.

Thus, the decision is recorded in two sources: volume 136 of the *New Jersey Superior Court Decisions*, page 560; and volume 347 of the *Atlantic Reporter, 2nd Series*, page 365. Furthermore, in the second report reference is made to a specific page on which to find the information referred to in the discussion of this case. The year in which the case was decided is listed in parenthesis. It is sometimes preceded by a court citation. In many citations the decision date is followed by a citation of case history (i.e., what happened), e.g., *cert. denied* (*certiorari* denied).

Abbreviations

Following are a list of case reporter abbreviations followed by a list of basic terminology abbreviations used in this chapter. A more comprehensive key to legal abbreviations can be found in *Black's Law Dictionary* (St. Paul, Minnesota: West Publishing Co, sixth edition, 1990) or in Bieber's *Dictionary of Legal Abbreviations*, (Buffalo, New York: William S. Hein Co., third edition 1988).

Reporter Title Abbreviations

A.	=	*Atlantic Reporter* (St. Paul, Minnesota: West Publishing Co.)
A.2d	=	*Atlantic Reporter, 2nd Series* (ibid).
Ark.	=	*Arkansas Reports* (State of Arkansas).
C.	=	*California Reports* (San Francisco: Bancroft-Whitney Co.)
F.	=	*Federal Reporter* (West Publ.).
F.2d	=	*Federal Reporter, 2nd Series* (ibid).
F. Supp.	=	*Federal Supplement* (ibid).
Ga.	=	*Georgia Reports* [Supreme Court of...] (Atlanta: The Harrison Co., State Publisher).
N.E.2d	=	*North Eastern Reporter, 2nd Series* (West Publ.).
NJ	=	*New Jersey Superior Court Decisions* (ibid).
PH Memo T.C.	=	*Tax Court Memorandum Decisions* (Englewood Cliffs, New Jersey: Prentice Hall).

Plaintiff/Appellant	versus	Defendant/Respondent	Reporter Volume	Name	Page
State Com'r. of Transportation	*v.*	*Cooper Alloy Corp.,*	136	N.J. Super.	560,

Reporter Volume	Name	Page	Page Relevant to Citation	Court	Year of Decision	Case History
347	A.2d	365,	368	(6th Cir.	1975)	*cert.'d*

S.Ct.	=	*Supreme Court Reporter* (West Publ.)
S.E.2d	=	*South Eastern Reporter, 2nd Series* (ibid)
S.W.2d	=	*South Western Reporter, 2nd Series* (ibid)
T.C.	=	*Reports of the United States Tax Courts* (Washington, D.C.: U.S. Government Printing Office)
T.C.M. (CCH)	=	*Tax Court Memorandum Decisions* (Chicago: Commerce Clearing House, Inc. [abbreviated CCH])
USCS	=	*United States Code Annotated* (West Publ.)

Other Abbreviations

aff'd.	=	affirmed
aff'g	=	affirming
cert. denied	=	*certiorari* denied (appeal for rehearing refused by higher court, leaving judgment below unchanged)
Cir.	=	Circuit Court (usually cited with number)
rev'd	=	reversed
rev'g	=	reversing
Sup.Ct.	=	Supreme Court
Super.Ct.	=	Superior Court
v.	=	versus (separating "first party" [plaintiff/appellant] and "second party" [defendant/respondent])

Survey of Important Cases to Current Appraisal Practice Divided into Five Categories of Relevance

Fair Market Value

1. *State Com'r. of Transportation v. Cooper Alloy Corp.*,136 N.J. Super Ct. 560, 347 A.2d 365 (1975),

an appellate court reversal of a Superior Court judgment favorable to condemnee in an Eminent Domain case. The appeal was on grounds of trial judge's error in allowing Cooper Alloy to introduce evidence of Reproduction Cost of business. The appellate court held that the evidence was erroneously admitted because it involved speculation and was therefore not relevant to the issue of the property value. Recoverable damage pertains only to land taken and not to any business operating on it. Any "Cost to Cure" method of valuation is irrelevant to the Fair Market Value of compensated property.

2. *Arkansas State Highway Commission v. Delaughter*, 250 Ark. 990 468 S.W.2d 242 (1971),

an appellate court affirmance of a Circuit Court judgment in favor of condemnee in an Eminent Domain case testing "highest and best use." The Commission appealed on the basis of condemnee's expert testimony of value enhancement to compensated land that was being used for cattle grazing because of other potential uses (alleged gravel deposits on the land). Commission argued that since both uses can not be effected simultaneously on the same tract of land, such testimony is inconsistent with "highest and best use" and should have been disallowed. The appellate court affirmed the lower court's justment and in the opinions, stated that since condemnee's experts merely testified to an enhancement of value (for potential mineral use) without actually attempting to assign a separate **monetary expression** to it, no inconsistency with "highest and best use" resulted, and such testimony was permissible and not prejudicial. The court held that "property has but one market value, not one value for one use and another for another."

3. *Sacramento Southern Railroad Company v. Heilbron*,156 C. 408 (1909),

an appellate court affirmance of a state Supreme Court (lower court) judgment adverse to condemnee in an Eminent Domain case. Heilbron appealed arguing that the court erred when instructing the jury upon state law governing the estimation of the damages. Heilbron argued that it was permissible to introduce evidence of value for usage of land, expressed monetarily. The appellate court decided that the judgment being that the damages must be measured by the market value of the land at the time it is taken, and that although evidence of the land being "valuable" for any purpose or usage may always be given, any testimony of a **monetary expression** of this value is inadmissible because it is **speculative**. Hence, the market value is "the highest sum which the property is worth to persons generally purchasing in the open market in consideration of the land's adaptability for any proven use," but such consideration of adaptability cannot extend to include a **monetary expression**.

Relevant Market

4. *Goldman v. Commissioner*, 46 T.C. 136, *aff'd.*, 388 F.2d 476 (6th Cir.1967),

appellate court affirmance of a U. S. Tax Court judgment adverse to taxpayers regarding claimed charitable deductions. Goldman donated bound volumes of outdated medical journals and claimed a deduction figured on the basis of the retail price average for current issues. The IRS disallowed deduction. The tax court later determined the fair market value of the journals to be less than one-third the claimed amount based on expert testimony by a book dealer. The dealer described the market for such items as slow due to the buying patterns of libraries (most subscribe and only purchase second-hand to fill in lost volumes). Therefore, the tax court was persuaded that the only market available to an individual owner of such books was a second-hand book dealer, hence, the price such a person would pay satisfied the court as to the Fair Market Value of the journals. Goldman argued in his appeal that the tax court had applied a wrong criterion in this judgment. The value was determined to be what a book dealer would pay for when purchasing for resale. Such sale would not be to an ultimate consumer, therefore it would be wholesale, not retail, and irrelevant to the fair market value. But since the IRS' witness had clarified his position to the tax court upon cross examination, describing his hypothetical transaction as "a consumer sale" rather than wholesale, the appellate court was unpersuaded by taxpayers' argument.

5. *Anselmo v. Commissioner*, 80 T.C. 872, *aff'd.*, 757 F.2d 1208 (11th Cir. 1985),

an appellate court affirmance of a tax court judgment. The court ruled against a taxpayer who claimed deductions of nearly five times the amount he paid nine months before for 461 colored gems which he donated to the Smithsonian Institution. Taxpayers' claim was based on appraisals treating the stones as components of finished jewelry items and accordingly valuing them at current retail prices charged by jewelry stores for finished jewelry pieces. The IRS' experts argued that the customary buying public for such a large quantity of poor-quality unset colored gems is not the retail jewelry market. They contended that such a group of stones would not even be purchased by a jewelry store but rather by a jewelry manufacturer in a single transaction involving a discount from the usual price. The IRS' experts' convinced the court that the relevant market in which to value such a group of stones was wholesale but rejected their valuation because the appraisers had valued the properties on a **bulk sale basis** with a substantial discount rather than **individually**, as required by the Regulations under Secs. 20.2031-1[b] and 25.2512-1. The IRS was unable to cite any authority directly supporting the necessity of a bulk sale valuation. The tax court observed that neither the taxpayers' nor the IRS' appraisers had established the fair market value of the stones in the relevant market and concluded that the IRS' assessment in the notice of deficiency to taxpayer had failed to be overcome by either party. The regulations (Rule 142[a], Tax Court Rules of Practice and Procedure) stipulate that the taxpayer is to bear the burden of proving a valuation higher than stated in the notice of deficiency.

Since the taxpayers were unable to do so, and since the IRS was unable to establish an aggregate value lower than the amount stated in the deficiency notice (the taxpayers' purchase price plus the fee for appraisal), the tax court held the fair market value of the stones to be the amount determined in the IRS' notice of deficiency. The taxpayers appealed, arguing that the estate and gift tax treasury regulations require the use of the market posited by taxpayers' appraisers rather than the IRS' appraisers. The appellate court rejected this argument that the Tax Court's marketplace selection was a question of law, stating that it was rather a question of **fact**. Therefore, the tax court's finding would be set aside on appeal only if found clearly erroneous. The appellate court found no such clear error. It agreed with the tax court's observation of a major flaw in the taxpayers' argument centered upon an understanding of the word "public" used in the Treasury Regulation. This word refers only to the **customary purchasers** of an item, not all purchasers. Citing the hypothetical example of live cattle, for which the general buying public would be largely slaughterhouses rather than individual consumers, the court observed, "The fair market value of live cattle accordingly would be measured by the price paid at the livestock auction rather than at the supermarket." By extension, the "public" for low-quality, unmounted gems was not the individual consumer of finished jewelry but the jewelry manufacturers and retail stores that create the jewelry items that they sell to the individual consumer. This purchase by the manufacturers is, in this context, a **retail** sale because the manufacturer is the last stage in the chain of distribution, i.e., the ultimate consumer of a specific commodity (unmounted stones of low quality) that would be transformed into a different commodity (a finished piece of jewelry) with a different ultimate consumer.

6. *Hunter v. Commissioner*, 51 T.C.M. (CCH) 1533 (1986-308),

the tax court ruled against taxpayers who claimed a charitable deduction several times more than was paid recently for prints donated as part of a "tax shelter." The IRS argued that a lesser deduction was entitled because the taxpayers were acting as a commercial art dealers, such activity producing ordinary income subject to different treatment under Sec. 1.170-1[c]. They also failed to satisfy the long-term holding requirements relevant to such deductions because they never took physical possession of the prints but rather had them sent directly to the donee. The IRS challenged the ownership of the prints based on these facts. Citing *Skripak v.*

Commissioner, 84 T.C. 285, 316 (1985), the court found the taxpayers to have indeed owned the prints, stating that: "the right of beneficial enjoyment of the property, rather than possession of the property, determines whether a taxpayer is recognized as the owner of property for Federal tax purposes." Furthermore, the court rejected the IRS' allegation that the taxpayers' activity was equivalent to that of a dealer, stating that "Petitioners, who never sold any work of art, are not transformed into dealers by virtue of their donation". However, the court determined the deductible fair market value of the prints to be no more than taxpayers' cost. "The most probative evidence of the fair market value of the prints is the amount petitioners paid for them."

7. *Lio v. Commissioner*, 85 T.C. 56 (1985),

a tax court ruled against taxpayers who claimed a charitable deduction for prints at an amount several times greater than they had paid recently for them as part of a "tax shelter." The IRS limited the deductible amount to what the taxpayers paid. The taxpayers claimed the average of two "independent" appraisals prepared as part of the purchase agreement with the tax shelter promoter that were purportedly based on actual retail market results. Taxpayers argued that the substantial difference in price between their cost and claimed value was explained by the deep discount offered to them by the promoter. The court stated that the taxpayers were not acting as dealers buying wholesale for resale but as collectors and ultimate consumers. Therefore, they purchased the prints at retail, such price being probative evidence of fair market value. An important qualification to evolve from this case is the court's ruling that a sale to an ultimate consumer is "any sale to those persons who do not hold the item for subsequent resale." Also of interest is its description of an appropriate market for valuation purposes as "the most active marketplace for the particular item involved" (i.e., regardless of whether such market is seen to be the **primary** or the **secondary** market).

8. *Sandler v. Commissioner*, 52 T.C.M. (CCH) 563 (1986-451),

a tax court judgment (a) favorable to taxpayer regarding the right to claim a charitable deduction on 30 grave sites donated to a religious organization (in spite of lack of perfected title) and (b) adverse to taxpayer regarding the amount claimed (five times the amount recently paid). The IRS then considered the deduction to be disqualified because the title to sites was not perfected until a later year due to donee's delay. The court disagreed, citing the Income Tax Regs., Sec. 1.170A-1(b), which provide that a contribution is ordinarily made at the time delivery is effected, and gave as an example the contribution of a check to charity, wherein the date of delivery of donation is that of delivery of check to donee rather than date the check clears the bank. Since the donor was unaware of the donee's inadvertence and believed the gift to have been finalized, the court held the former to be entitled to their deduction. However, the court agreed with the IRS that the fair market value of the donation was not what 30 grave sites would sell for on the primary market (from the cemetery). The grave sites should be valued on the secondary market, the only market on which such a large number of sites are customarily bought and sold (indeed the market in which the subject sites were purchased). Because the estate executor from whom the subject sites were purchased was obligated to sell the lots at the highest price available, it was considered probative evidence of the fair market value of these lots. This value was determined to be only slightly higher than cost (including brokerage fee).

9. *Tallal v. Commissioner*, 52 T.C.M. (CCH) 1017 (1986-548),

a tax court ruled against a taxpayer relevant to a claimed charitable deduction of nearly 27 times the amount paid recently for a bulk quantity of bandages donated to the Red Cross, the claimed amount based on taxpayers' alleged findings as to current retail prices for which individual packages of same were customarily sold to the general public from retail vendors. The court found that the subject bandages were not reasonably comparable with the "comparables" (the former being approx. 25 year old government surplus and as such unsuitable for usage by the general public). The IRS' experts testified to an institutional market for such items, as these were often used for training purposes. The court agreed and chose this market as the relevant one to determine the fair market value of the bandages. Taxpayers were allowed a deduction of slightly over their cost (including an inflation factor and storage and shipping costs).

10. *Goldstein v. Commissioner*, 89 T.C. 38 (1987),

a tax court decision (a) favorable to taxpayers' charitable deduction of 42 donated posters that the donor purchased only four days before donation and had not yet paid for in full, (b) adverse to taxpayer regarding the valuation of the deduction and (c) adverse to taxpayer regarding their liability for "negligence" taxes. The IRS argued that no completed gift was made during the subject tax period, hence, no deduction was warranted.

The court disagreed, observing that the three basic requirements defining a gift (donative intent, delivery by donor, acceptance by donee) were indeed satisfied during the subject year, regardless of specific arrangements of payments made by donor for possession of items to be donated. The court therefore turned its attention to determining the fair market value of the posters, disagreeing with taxpayers who claimed that the value should be measured by the current retail prices obtained by galleries for like items in spite of the fact that the taxpayer had paid considerably lower price (one-fifth) recently for the posters. Citing *Lio v. Commissioner* and other relevant market cases, the court found taxpayers to have purchased the posters as ultimate consumers for an undiscounted retail sum. Accordingly, it determined the fair market value of the donated items to be only the "actual price paid" (in this case the cash amount and the discounted value of the promissory notes used). In addition the court agreed with the IRS in holding petitioners liable for additional taxes for negligence (pursuant to section 6653[a]).

Insurance

11. *Orient Ins. Co. v. Dunlap*, 193 Ga. 241, 17 S.E.2d 703 (1941),

an appellate court (Supreme Court of Georgia) reversed a superior court judgment and ruled favorably to an insurance company. Insured (Dunlap *et al*, executors of the estate of Mrs. Ilah D. Little who died during a visit to Germany), upon receiving decedent's personal property via ship from Germany, learned that a pearl necklace had been a thousand times overinsured due to a misidentification as genuine pearls instead of cultured by a German appraiser. The error was exacerbated by a mistranscription of the appraiser's value by two decimals onto the official protocol inventory upon which the insurance was written. The insurer (Orient) refused the insured's request to reform the policy to reflect the true value and refund premiums paid in excess. The insured sued for the refund, arguing that more premiums had been paid unnecessarily due to a "mutual mistake." The appellate court considered whether or not Orient may be charged with bad conscience for failure to pay difference on discovering the truth about the character and value of the necklace (for otherwise no money could be recovered by law). This court ruled that regardless of actual character and value of the necklace, the insurance company had been exposed to a risk comparable with the amount of premium paid. Had the necklace been lost, Orient would have been liable for the insured value without ever

having the opportunity to learn the actual value of the necklace. The exposure to liability endured by the insurance company was not mitigated by the safe arrival of that property at its destination. As a result, the court sided with the insurance company.

12. *Plaza Equities Corp. v. Aetna Casualty and Surety Co.*,372 F.Supp. 1325 (1974),

a U.S. District Court judgment (a) for one insurer (Aetna) against insured (Plaza Equities), entitling the former to dismiss the latter's complaint and (b) for insured against second insurer (Employers' Liability Assurance Corp.). The claims suit was brought by the insured against two "all-risk" insurers refusing settlement on a sustained loss (the collapse of a commercial building complex beneath an insufficiently supported 3 1/2 ton sculpture). The insurer argued the refusal on grounds of specified policy exclusions against defective design. The court was persuaded that Aetna's policy clearly communicated such coverage exclusions to insured but was unpersuaded of the same pertaining to the Employers' policy. The court found the cause of loss to be a misjudgment on the part of the insured in not installing adequate structural support. However, the Employers' policy exclusions for "inherent or latent defect" were communicated in the policy to mean an imperfection in the materials used which could not be discovered "by any known and customary test." As Employers' was unable to present evidence that insured's misjudgment could not have been discovered in time to prevent accident through ordinary stress tests, the court ruled that their policy exclusions were inapplicable here and found no relief from liability to settle claim.

13. *Merchants Fire Assurance Corporation v. Lattimore*, 263 F.2d 232 (9th Cir. 1959),

an appellate court reversed a U.S. District Court judgment favorable to insured regarding a recovery of amount insured on a personal property floater policy. The insurance company's appeal comprised two branches: one pertaining to the recovery on the scheduled fine arts portion of the policy; the other pertaining to the recovery made on the unscheduled portion. In the first branch the insurer argued that the court erred in awarding too high an amount of settlement to the insured due to its allowance of insured's expert witness testimony as to the value of the properties. The insurer claimed that the testimony was "subjective" and, hence, irrelevant and inadmissible. In the second branch the insurer contended that no recovery should have been allowed insured at all on grounds that "concealment and misrepresentation of a material fact" by insured to insurer legally relieved the latter of all contractual obligation. The "subjectivity" allegation in the first branch centered upon the insured's expert's distinction between a **unique** art object (which he believed to retain its identity as art, hence much of its value after damage) and an art object **multiple** (which he believed to be necessarily divested of such identity and hence having lost all or most value by damage, no matter how skillful the subsequent repair). The appellate court observed, that subjective as such testimony doubtlessly was, it was not irrelevant to the estimation of the value of objects. The appreciation of art, hence the value to be attached to it, includes subjective values. The court argued that the loss occasioned by damage would be measured "by the same considerations which gave the art object initial value." Therefore the appellate court held that the trial court had not erred in allowing this testimony on these grounds. (The trial court had discarded other portions of this testimony due to the expert's reliance upon flat-rate depreciation formulae, as it viewed such reliance as an offer of compromise settlement.)

The second branch pertaining to the argument over the unscheduled personal property is more important for appraisal reference. Insured had been awarded by the trial court the full amount on her "all-risk" policy for the insured items because it had been demonstrated that the loss and damage equaled or exceeded the limit. The insurer argued on appeal that the insured knowingly owned properties in this category far in excess of the amount she claimed on her policy to own. They maintained that by neglecting to communicate the excess value of the property to them, insured was directly affecting their risk and was therefore guilty of concealment and misrepresentation of facts material to their contract. State law provided that a contract was made void through such activity. The insurer argued that they were therefore legally relieved of any obligation to the contract. The appellate court ruled that such concealment directly affected the insurer's risk, hence constituted **material** fact. The insurer's witnesses testified that most losses under a personal property floater are partial rather than total, but that this risk of partial losses increases with the total value and amount of property owned. For example, the chance of a $2,000 loss is much greater in the case of a person with $50,000 worth of property than in the case of one with only $2,000. Because of this increased risk, insurance companies customarily ask that coverage be not less than 80% of total value owned. Thus, argued insurer, if they had known the true value of Lattimore's personal property,

they would have insisted on a substantially higher coverage and premium to protect themselves against this higher risk. The court was persuaded that insurer had established a defense of concealment, thereby entitling the insurer to void the personal property floater provision of the policy. The trial court judgment was reversed and the insurer was directed to recover payment from insured.

Taxes

14. *Lampe v. Commissioner*, 49 T.C.M. (CCH) 1505 (1985-236),

a tax court judgment adverse to taxpayer regarding a claimed charitable deduction nearly five times the amount recently paid for donated gems. The claim was based upon an appraisal procured through seller, but the case later revolved around relevant market as the taxpayers' and the IRS' expert witnesses varied drastically in their opinions of the fair market value of the stones. Citing *Anselmo v. Commissioner*, the court observed that the petitioners had indeed paid the retail price for the commodity they had purchased, regardless of the higher amounts obtained further on down the chain of distribution after conversion to a different commodity (see *Anselmo*), and that purchase price was probative evidence of fair market value. Taxpayers' appraiser was obviously using a different market on which to base appraisal than the IRS' appraiser. Taxpayers were allowed a deduction of cost amount rather than appraised amount.

15. *Sammons v. Commissioner*, 838 F.2d 330 (9th Cir. 1988) *aff'g* and *rev'g* 51 T.C.M. (CCH) 1568 (1986),

an appellate court part-affirmance/part-reversal of a tax court judgment adverse to taxpayers regarding a claimed charitable deduction, the actual deductible value of the donation and the liability of taxpayers to pay "negligence" penalty taxes on the resulting tax underpayment. The IRS had disallowed taxpayers' deduction for donation of a collection of American Indian artifacts to a museum on the grounds that (a) the taxpayers had not acquired title to all items included in donation; (b) that they were legally prohibited from taking title to many of these artifacts under a Federal law prohibiting the purchase or sale by an individual of certain bird feathers and appendages; (c) that they had failed to complete the donation transaction in a manner constituting a valid gift as donee supplied donor with back-dated receipt for a portion of collection and (d) that they had failed to establish the value of the donated items, relying upon biased and unsatisfactory appraisals. Furthermore, the resulting substantial income tax underpayment demonstrated negligence on the part of the taxpayers, making them liable for additional "negligence" taxes (as set forth under section 6653[a]). The Tax Court was unpersuaded by the IRS' arguments (a), (b), (c) but sustained (d) and subsequent penalty taxes. This point (d) is the most important to appraisers. The court rejected taxpayers' appraisals on the collection because the only one of the three appraisers to testify in court happened to be vice president of the donee institution, and his independence was therefore questionable. Also the taxpayers' expert witnesses' appraisals, prepared by apparently qualified and independent experts, were considered to be unacceptable by the court because it had been prepared solely from photographs. The Tax Court again found the actual cost the most probative evidence for fair market value and disregarded all appraisals. On appeal of this judgment, taxpayers argued that the Tax Court rejected their experts' appraisal simply because the value conclusions expressed in it was based solely on photographs. The appellate court was unpersuaded and held that the tax court had not abused its discretion in rejecting this appraisal. The tax court rejected the appraisal because the appraisers were forced to make **assumptions** concerning valuation criteria (such as authenticity and condition), not because the appraisals were done from photographs. Because a physical inspection of the properties might have resulted in a different value, the appraisal was seen by the court as insufficient for purposes of determining fair market value. Therefore, the appellate court was persuaded that the tax court had not erred in determining the fair market value of the collection to be the price paid nine months earlier by donor. However, appellate court was unpersuaded by the IRS' argument of taxpayer negligence and the applicability of related penalty taxes. Citing the authority of several cases, it held that when a taxpayer exercises due care in obtaining an appraisal of fair market value and presents "some proof" of the asserted value, reasonable reliance on an appraisal report does not constitute negligence. The appellate court affirmed the tax court's judgment pertaining to taxpayers' underpayment of taxes but reversed the court's judgment against taxpayers for negligence penalty taxes.

16. *Winokur v. Commissioner*, 90 T.C. 733 (1988),
a tax court judgment favorable to taxpayers concerning tax deduction for a charitable contribution of artwork even though donee institution failed to take possession of the artwork for the annual time allotments consistent with the interest portions conferred with gift. The actual deductible value of the artwork was also contested, but this branch of the case will not be discussed here. The IRS cited the Income Tax Regulations identifying a charitable contribution deduction as allowable "whereby the donee is given the right, as a tenant in common with the donor, to possession, dominion, and control of the property for a portion of each year appropriate to its interest in such property." (Sec. 1.170A-7[b][1]) Therefore, the IRS argued, the subject donation should be seen as "future interest" for which deductions are specifically disallowed in the Regulations. However, the court observed "future interest" to involve a donor's temporary restriction of a donee's possession and use. A donee's failure to take advantage of this privilege does not necessarily spring from restrictions imposed by a donor. Therefore the subject case would hardly qualify as an argument of "future interest." In its determination the court paid special attention to "given the right" emphasizing that the regulations specify only that the donee is given the right of possession and use, and that such right no way implies a **requirement** of donee to take advantage of that right. Deduction was allowed, though not at amount claimed.

17. *Koftinow v. Commissioner*, 52 T.C.M. (CCH) 261 (1986),
a tax court judgment (a) favorable to taxpayer pertaining to a charitable contribution deduction allowed on a donated sculpture and (b) adverse to taxpayer as pertained to a disallowance of deduction for donated land upon which sculpture was situated due to failure of taxpayer to make claim or present valuation evidence in time. The branch (a) deals with issues of appraisal persuasiveness and is of interest for appraisers. The court recognized the particular difficulty in appraising the donated sculpture, admitting that the lack of data more indicative of the value was not due to failure on the part of the appraisers, but due to the lack of more probative evidence. The court was unpersuaded by the IRS' appraisers' opinion of the value of this sculpture because the appraisal failed to provide convincing reasons supporting the valuation. The court found the taxpayers' expert's appraisal more persuasive, as it utilized three separate methods to value the sculpture to compensate for the lack of data necessary to the usual comparative sales method. The appraisal considered original production cost, the current production cost by artists of comparable status and an extrapolation of value from extant sales results of smaller works by the same artist. In spite of the overall persuasiveness of taxpayers' appraisal,

the court found it to be in error due to a contradiction between appraiser's demonstration and his value conclusion. Interestingly, the court chose to appropriate the appraisers demonstration for its own purposes of determining the fair market value of the sculpture without utilizing his conclusion. The court determined that the appraiser should have arrived at this value if he had correctly followed the logic of his own argument.

18. *Hecker v. Commissioner*, Sec. 87,296 PH Memo T.C. [56 PH Memo T.C. 1498] (1987-297),

a tax court judgment adverse to taxpayer involving both (a) two claimed charitable contribution deductions over a two year period, each for approximately four times the amount paid recently for donated gems and minerals and (b) additional "negligence" tax imposed by the IRS for resultant tax underpayments. The court was unpersuaded by the taxpayer's expert witness' qualifications to appraise the properties. The expert was not a full time appraiser but a business professor who allocated his free time to an interest in gems and minerals. He had no experience in the buying and selling of such items and he had attended only one gem show during the two year period. The court did not question this appraiser's expertise in evaluating the quality of gemstones, only the dollar value. Furthermore, he had failed to demonstrate to the court his expertise in valuation by means of his appraisal report. The court questioned his methodology and his reliance upon collectors' price lists. The IRS' experts persuaded the court that these price lists were inaccurate and unreliable measurements of market value. The court accepted the IRS' testimony. Citing Section 6659, the court observed that the taxpayer bears the burden of proof in tax deficiency cases resultant from value overstatements. (Subchapter [c] of this Section defines valuation overstatement to include, among other things, a valuation of 150% or more of the correct valuation.) As petitioner failed to meet this burden of proof, and since the acknowledged overstatements resulted in a tax deficiency of over $1,000. each, he was additionally liable for "negligence" taxes, taxes imposed under subchapter (a) of same section wherein taxpayer's underpayment is due to negligence ("a lack of due care or failure to do what a reasonable and ordinarily prudent person would do under the circumstances" [Sec. 6653(a)]) or intentional disregard of rules and regulations. The regulations allow that these penalty taxes may not apply when a taxpayer claims charitable deductions in excess of fair market value in good faith and in reasonable reliance on appraisals performed by qualified experts. Because the petitioner provided no appraisals to support his claims and the claims were significantly higher than the amounts recently paid as retail buyer, the tax court agreed with the IRS as to the taxpayer's liability for the penalty taxes.

19. *United States v. Cartwright* [as Executor of the Estate of Bennett], 411 U.S. 546, 93 S.Ct. 1713 (1973),

a United States Supreme Court affirmance of a Court of Appeals affirmance (457 F.2d 567) of a U. S. District Court (Western District of New York) judgment (323 F.Supp. 769) favorable to taxpayer in a federal estate tax refund action holding the Treasury regulation governing estate-owned assets to be invalid for purposes of valuing mutual funds. Taxpayer (Cartwright), acting as executor of the estate of Ethel B. Bennett, filed a federal estate tax return on which he reported the redemption price of mutual fund shares owned by decedent. The IRS assessed a deficiency in estate taxes based upon this reported value and issued taxpayer a deficiency notice. The deficiency was assessed on the basis of a calculation of the value of the shares at their public offering price, pursuant to Treasury Regulation Sec. 20.2031-8(b). After payment of the deficiency, taxpayer filed a refund claim. When that claim was refused, the taxpayer commenced a refund action in Federal District Court on the ground that the IRS' valuation based on the Treasury Regulation was unreasonable. Had the decedent owned ordinary corporate stock listed on an exchange rather than mutual funds, the taxable value would have been the price the estate could have obtained had it sold such shares on the valuation date. The taxpayer argued that the same treatment should rightly be applied to the valuation of mutual fund shares. Instead, the Regulations single out mutual funds for a contrary basis of valuation. They mandate a valuation based on the public offering price, a price the estate could not obtain on valuation date as the public offering price includes the fixed sales charge ("load") assessed by the fund's underwriter for the service of marketing the fund's share. Mutual fund shares are never traded privately. As "open-ended" funds, they are regulated by a statutory scheme created by the Investment Company Act of 1940 that results in each share having at any given time two distinct prices: that at which the public makes an initial purchase from the fund at the "asked" price including sales load and that at which shareholders may "sell" their shares back to the fund at a fixed, statutorily defined "bid" price excluding sales load paid upon purchase. The Federal Government maintains that due to the statutory obligation of the mutual fund to buy back outstanding shares whenever they are offered, the redemption price does not actually reflect the price paid by a willing buyer. The only market for such funds involving both willing sellers and willing buyers is the public offering market. And since the only price paid in that market is the asking price, such price is an appropriate basis for valuation. The Supreme Court observed, however, that since both the buyer and the seller of mutual fund shares willingly enter into a sales transaction fully aware of the fund's obligation, the "bid" price may be viewed as the final step in a voluntary transaction between a willing buyer and a willing seller. Furthermore, the court observed, when the Government argued that ordinary corporate stocks are also taxed at values above those which could be realized from sale, it fails to distinguish that the fair market price of ordinary stock shares does not make allowance for costs involved in the future sale of same shares. The fair market price of mutual fund shares includes a commission component reflecting the hypothetical **purchase** price of an entity already owned. If ordinary corporate stock would be sold under the regulation governing the mutual funds, it would be taxed on a higher price than that for which it was traded on the date of death. And such, observed the court, would appear to be at odds with the basic notions of value embodied in the Internal Revenue Code. The Government, however, argued that Treasury Regulation Sec. 20.2031-8(b) reasonably values the "bundle of rights" transferred with the ownership of properties and that these rights include not only the right to sell and enjoy the proceeds of sale but also the right **not** to sell and thereby maintain benefits of ownership. Several judicial precedents were relied on for this point, most notably the U.S. Supreme Courts own decision in *Guggenheim v. Rasquin*, 312 U.S. 254, 61 S.Ct. 507, 85 L. Ed. 813 (1941) to uphold the IRS's valuation of gifted life insurance policies at policy cost rather than at the amount that could be received (by donor or donee) if surrendered: the owner of a fully paid life insurance policy has more than the mere right to surrender it; he has the right to retain it for its investment virtues and to receive the face amount of the policy upon the insured's death. That these latter rights are deemed by purchasers of insurance to have substantial value is clear from the difference between the cost of a single-premium policy and its immediate or early cash-surrender value (312 U.S., at 257, 61d S.Ct. at 509). The present court did not hold these cases analogous, due to the distinct differences between the properties compared. Shares in mutual funds are quite unlike insurance policies, especially as concerns redemption. Only the owner of a

single-premium insurance policy has the right to receive the face value of the policy upon the insured's death. This is what makes it so difficult realistically to value the "bundle of rights," hence, the court's deferral to the Commissioner's cost-basis determination in *Guggenheim*. True, there are "investment virtues" and the prospects of capital gains or dividends involved with the prospect of mutual fund shares also, but such is true of ordinary corporate stock as well, and the latter is valued without regard to broker's commissions while the former is so valued. The Supreme Court observed that even if the contested Regulation was not, on its face, technically inconsistent with Sec. 2031 of the Internal Revenue Code, it was "manifestly inconsistent with the most elementary provisions of the Investment Company Act of 1940 and operates without regard for the market in mutual fund shares that Act created and regulates." (93 S.Ct. 1713, 1719.) The judgment of the Court of Appeals holding the Regulation invalid was affirmed.

20. *Estate of David Smith v. Commissioner*, 57 T.C. 650 (1972), *aff'd* on another issue, 510 F.2d 479 (2d Cr. 1975),

a tax court judgment (a) partially favorable to taxpayer relevant to the allowance of a "blockage" discount (though not specified as such by the court) factored into the fair market valuation of a large quantity of artwork included in the taxable gross estate, (b) partially adverse to taxpayer relevant to the amount of discount and (c) adverse to taxpayer in holding that any deductions of selling costs (brokerage commissions) of the artwork are limited to those sales necessary to the generation of funds needed to pay estate taxes, as per Regulations. At the death of the celebrated sculptor David Smith, the executors of his estate filed a return valuing the 425 sculptures by decedent in his estate at $714,000. The IRS responded with a notice of deficiency determining the actual taxable value of the same 425 sculptures to be $5,256,918. The IRS later conceded that they were worth no more than $4,284,000, the same amount the estate executors thought the works would achieve, **if sold on a piece by piece basis**. The taxpayer and the IRS disagreed about the **taxable** value. Smith's executors argued that the taxable value should reflect the practical, attainable value. The estate could never achieve the above hypothetical amount under the constraints of time of estate closing and costs of selling (brokerage commissions). Therefore, they took these considerations into account in their determination of the fair market value entered on the return. They had arrived at the value by taking the hypothetical total of $4,284,000 and discounting it by 75 percent to reflect the discount enjoyed by a bulk purchaser buying for resale, then discounting the result by one-third to compensate for the commissions that would needed to be paid to Smith's dealer in order to achieve such sale. The IRS argued that such value does not reflect the retail market, as mandated by the Estate Tax Regulations (Sec. 2031-1[b]). Taxpayers claimed that the availability of such a large number of items, for which the market is ordinarily limited, would have an adverse affect upon the salability of the items, and that the only purchaser for so many works would be a syndicate acquiring the bulk for resale. The necessarily healthy discount typical to such bulk purchase (a wholesale transaction) should be seen as a relevant and necessary component of the value of the collection as of the date of death. The IRS had rejected this notion of impacted value and had maintained that no such adverse impact would be effected by a simultaneous availability on the market and that indeed the value of each item should be determined simply by the price at which each would sell for separately, in accordance with the Regulations. The tax court disagreed with the IRS on this point, citing a useful analogy in the so-called "blockage" discount principle customarily employed in the valuation of large quantities of securities (i.e., purchased *en bloc*). The court observed that each willing buyer would take into account that 424 other comparable items were being offered for sale in determining the price he would be willing to pay for any item. In the context of sale by public auction such a consideration would be a most material factor. Therefore, the IRS should have given considerable weight to the fact that each item would not be offered in isolation. Nevertheless, this agreement with taxpayers' argument did not result in an acceptance of the discount applied to the collection by the taxpayer. The court found the discount of 75 percent too high (for unsupported reasons) and inapplicable in the specific context of this case: Under the foregoing circumstances, we think that, in this case, the amount which an *en bloc* purchaser for resale would pay and the aggregate of the separate "one-at-a-time" values to be obtained by a variety of dispositions in the "retail market" would be the same. (57 T.C. 650, 658). Furthermore, the court observed the petitioner's one-third discount in consideration of selling costs to be clearly precluded by judicial precedent. Citing *Publicker v. Commissioner* (206 F.2d 250 [1953]) and *Estate of Frank Miller Gould v. Commissioner* (14 T.C. 414 [1950]), the court observed the measure of value as laid down by these cases to be "what could be **received** on, not what is

retained from, a hypothetical sale." The court arrived at its own determination of the taxable value (the fair market value) of these 425 sculptures as of the moment of the artist's death: $2,700,000. The court's value appears to include a discount, as it is significantly lower than the IRS' value, yet it does not reconcile with any of the formulae posited in argument. Such discount appears to support the "blockage" principle (hitherto associated only with the valuation of securities and unrecognized in the courts in the context of artwork), though not so identified. An important lesson to learn from this decision is the freedom with which the tax court is empowered to decide cases (to the extent of including the arbitrary): "We find it unnecessary, in this unusual case, to make any hard and fast choice between the two approaches urged by the parties." (57 T.C. 650, 657)

Copyright

21. *Pushman v. New York Graphic Society, Inc.*, 39 N.E.2d 249 (1942),

an appellate court affirmance of a state Supreme Court judgment adverse to artist, favorable to purchaser/publisher, in a "common law copyright" (or "first right of publication") case. The artist sought injunction against publisher in the trial court case in order to enjoin the publisher from making reproductions of a painting he created and sold to an intermediary party, who sold it to respondent. Since the artist could not evidence any attempt on his part to retain reproduction rights at the time of sale, such sales transaction was seen to have been unconditional, hence, exclusive of any retained rights to the transferred property.

22. *Letter Edged in Black Press, Inc. v. Public Building Commission of Chicago*, 320 F.Supp. 1303 (1970),

a U.S. District Court summary judgment against the defendant (the Commission) in a "common-law copyright" case involving plaintiff's (Commission) right to reproduce images of a monumental sculpture ("the Chicago Picasso") registered for copyright protection by the Commission. The Commission received the sculpture from the artist as an unconditional, unrestricted gift, including full rights to reproduce it, all specifically expressed in a signed deed of gift of August 21, 1966. The maquette for the sculpture was given by the artist to the Art Institute of Chicago on similar terms but with reproduction rights going also to the Commission, the artist's deed of gift describing both sculptures as being given "through them" to the people of Chicago. The Commission embarked soon after upon a publicity campaign for the monumental sculpture (which had yet to be constructed). The campaign involved the dissemination of photographic images of the maquette as well as the aluminum model for the projected monumental sculpture in national and international newspapers and magazines. In conjunction, the maquette was extensively exhibited including the publishing of photographic illustrations in exhibition catalogs. None of these illustrations bore copyright notices. Only two such notices were used in the display of the maquette and the monumental sculpture: one for the maquette posted in the same room with the maquette in the Art Institute of Chicago exhibition and one affixed to the sculpture first seen by the public during the dedication ceremony on August 15, 1967. On January 12, 1968, a year and half after the artist's gift, defendant applied for copyright for the monumental sculpture and, in due time, received a certificate of copyright registration. The Press contended in the suit that the sculpture was in the public domain, not copyrightable and free for anyone to publish. The Commission argued, that attaching notice to the sculpture and registering the copyright were acts sufficient to obtain a copyright under 17 U.S.C. Sections 10 and 11. The court observed that according to Sec. 8 of the same code, any attempts to secure copyright must fail if the work is already in the public domain. Therefore, the court found its chief task to be deciding whether or not this sculpture was in the public domain already by the time of notice. It disagreed with the Commission' contention that copyright notice on the models (including the maquette) was unnecessary before publication of the monumental sculpture. It observed that this contention was based on the Commission' understanding of the copyrightable work of art to be the monumental sculpture only and not its models (as there can be only one copyright in one work of art). Such a notion views the models as mere accessory to the development of the finished artwork. The court pointed out that it is settled by judicial precedent (*Baker v. Selden*, 101 U.S. 99, 25 L.Ed. 841 [1879]) that a copyright can exist only in a perceptible, tangible work and not in a vision. And since the monumental sculpture was not yet created by the time of his deed of gift, the "common law copyright" he had given the defendant was necessarily limited to the only tangible portion of the gift, the maquette; the monumental sculpture was not subject to copyright protection as it was still but a vision. So, observed the court, it was the maquette only that qualified for copyright protection at the time, and since it was published without copyright notice, the artist's work was forever lost to the public domain. Therefore, the completed

monumental sculpture was <u>not</u> copyrightable, as it was itself a copy of a work (the maquette) already in the public domain. The Commission maintained that the maquette was not in the public domain, as its display did not constitute general publication. Three arguments were used in support of this claim: (a) that the Art Institute exhibition was "limited"; (b) that the display of this maquette was inconsequential in that an unpublished work (or a model or copy thereof) needs no copyright notice; and (c) that the Art Institute did not hold the copyright and therefore understandably could not place notice on the maquette. The court was unpersuaded by any of these arguments. It brushed away the first as a meaningless distinction between "limited" and "general" in light of the freedom with which images of the maquette were disseminated at and through the exhibition. The second argument was seen as flawed, as it hinged upon the issue of whether or not there was a general publication. The third argument had no weight because it is the responsibility of the holder of a copyright, rather than that of an intermediary entity such as the museum, to insure that notice is properly posted. The court also rejected the Commission's claim that the doctrine of "fair use" permitted their usage of uncopyrighted material in the publicity campaign (as this doctrine was intended for and historically limited to use as a defense in infringement actions and not as an excuse for the failure to announce copyright intentions). To defendant's further contention that the various newspaper and magazine illustrations of these images (without notice cited) did not amount to publication because they were already protected by copyright secured by the media, the court pointed out that it is settled law that without a separate notice in the name of the copyright holder, any work published in the press is considered to be published without notice. Summary judgment was entered in favor of the Press and against the Commission.

Chapter 10

Policies of the American Society of Appraisers

Professional Parameters

"The American Society of Appraisers is an organization of appraisal professionals and others interested in the appraisal profession. International in structure, it is self-supporting and independent. The Society is dedicated to the benefit of the appraisal profession. It is one of eight major appraisal societies which, in 1987, founded The Appraisal Foundation, a national non-profit organization. It was created to establish uniform criteria for professional appraisers. Since 1989 The Appraisal Foundation has been recognized by The U. S. Congress as the source for the development and promulgation of appraisal standards and qualifications.

"The oldest and only major appraisal organization representing all of the disciplines of appraisal specialists, the Society originated in 1936 and incorporated in 1952. ASA's headquarters are in the metropolitan Washington D. C. area.

"Society members include specialists in real estate (residential, commercial, industrial and agricultural), business valuation, machinery and technical specialties (cost surveys, commercial and pleasure craft marine surveys, machinery, equipment, public utilities, oil, gas, mines, quarries and other properties), personal property (antiques, fine arts, residential contents, automotive specialties, etc.), gems and jewelry, and appraisal review and management; in short, all types of tangible and intangible property, both realty and personalty.

"Each Society member who has earned a professional designation in one or more appraisal specialties is accredited. Such accreditation is predicated upon Society criteria; intensive written examinations, submission of representative appraisal reports and screening of applicant's practice and ethics. With five years or more of full-time valuation experience members are granted the right to use the professional designation ASA (Ac-

credited Senior Appraiser). With more than two years but less than five years of experience members may use the professional designation AM (Accredited Member).

"Accredited Senior Appraisers are required to become reaccredited every five years, through a mandatory continuing education process.

"Ethical practices and conduct required of Society members are defined in *The Principles of Appraisal Practice and Code of Ethics* of the American Society of Appraisers and the *Uniform Standards of Professional Appraisal Practice* as promulgated by The Appraisal Foundation."

International Board of Governors
Resolution #6-71-4
Revised 6-88
Revised 5-94

Membership Requirements

Candidates

Appraisers and persons engaged in the appraisal profession who wish to become designated members join the Society at the Candidate level.

Affiliates

Eligibility for membership is also open to individuals such as attorneys, accountants, museum curators, insurers, bank and trust officials, etc., whose work interrelates with the appraisal profession; they may join ASA as Affiliates. Those joining as Affiliates do not prepare appraisals or hold themselves out to the public as competent to perform appraisals. Membership privilege is personal and cannot be transferred, nor applied to business organizations.

Candidates and Affiliates shall be of legal age, of good character, interested in the activities and objectives of the Society, and shall have established financial responsibility and residence and business experience in the community.

Student-Affiliates

Full or part-time university/college students pursuing a career in Valuation Sciences, are eligible for membership as Student-Affiliates and shall be of legal age, of good character and interested in the activities and objectives of the Society.

Candidates, Affiliates and Student-Affiliates are not professionally designated and may not use the professional designations described under **Professional Status**.

Professional Status

In addition to the examinations and appraisal report requirements, the primary requisites for professional designations include:

1. Investigation, analysis, estimation of cost, forecast of earning power and determination of value of properties of every description;

2. A bachelor's degree or higher degree from a recognized and fully accredited college or university, or such other education, knowledge or experience as may be deemed by the International Board of Examiners to be the equivalent of such professional education;

3. To be of legal age.

Accredited Member (AM) — two years full time appraisal experience. Accredited Members may use the designation AM.

Accredited Senior Appraiser (ASA) — five years full time appraisal experience. Only Accredited Senior Appraisers may use the designation ASA.

Master Gemologist Appraiser — In order to attain the Master Gemologist Appraiser designation, the individual must: (1) have Accredited Senior Appraiser status, (2) be a graduate Gemologist (GG) from the Gemological Institute of America, or hold the designation Fellow, Gemological Association of Great Britain (FGA); (3) must own or be employed by the owner of an ASA registered gemological laboratory; (4) pass the Farnsworth-Munsell 100-hue test for color discrimination; and (5) successfully complete the Master Gemologist Appraiser Program in residence.

Fellow (FASA) — The designation of Fellow may be bestowed upon Accredited Senior Appraisers (ASAs) by the Society's International Board of Governors in recognition of outstanding services to the appraisal profession or the Society. This is the highest designation bestowed by the Society. A Fellow may use the designation FASA.

Mandatory Reaccreditation

To assure that competent, relevant, current valuation counsel will be available to the Public, ASA requires Accredited Senior Appraisers (ASAs) and Fellows (FASAs) to reaccredit every five years. This mandatory program emphasizes professional participation in a continuing education process. The program interfaces with the Society's examination procedures, the Principles of Valuation courses and with the Valuation Sciences Degree Program.

Appraisal Disciplines

For the purposes of identification and efficiency of organization, members of the American Society of Appraisers have been grouped into the following disciplines: Appraisal Review and Management, Business Valuation, Gems & Jewelry, Machinery & Technical Services, Personal Property, and Real Property.

In descriptive material, reference is made to the "professionally qualified" appraiser; this statement distinguishes individuals as having been tested and accredited in their particular field of expertise/specialization, under the auspices of the ASA Board of Examiners.

Personal Property

The tested/accredited personal property appraiser has the specialized knowledge achieved through academic study and practical experience to competently render appraisals for specific valuation purposes such as: insurance, estate, tax, donation, sale, dissolution of marriage and equitable distribution.

Personal property is defined as tangible, movable property which is utilitarian, collectible or decorative, or in combination.

In recognition of the Public's need for professionally qualified appraisers, ASA accredits the personal property appraiser whose sphere of expertise is in one or more of the following: Antiques and Decorative Art; Fine Art; Residential Contents-General and Specialties.

Examination Procedures

ASA has adopted a procedure of Open Group Examinations for members advancing to the grade of Accredited Member or Accredited Senior Appraiser. All examinations are held under the supervision of the ASA

International Board of Examiners and are scheduled throughout the year in various regions of the U. S., annually during the International Appraisal Conference, and during the Mid-Term Board Meeting. Examination fees are waived for individuals sitting for the examination in conjunction with the Conference who are fully registered for the International Conference.

Advancement Requirements

Each candidate must fulfill the following requirements to qualify for professional status in the Society:

Experience

To qualify for Accredited Senior Appraiser, an individual must have a minimum of five years of full time appraisal experience; of that five years, at least three years must be in the discipline or specialty being examined (or discipline if specialties do not exist). At least two years full time appraisal experience is necessary for Accredited Member status; of that two years, at least one-and-one-half must be in the discipline or specialty being examined. Collateral and/or related activities will not be considered as appraisal experience.

Education

A college degree or its equivalent is required. Two years appraisal experience equals one year of college equivalency. Appraisal experience used towards college equivalency must be additional experience and not the same experience accumulated to fulfill the requirement listed above. The International Board of Examiners recognizes career development and non-academic equivalency, e.g., courses, seminars, teaching, administrative/supervisory positions, memberships in professional organizations, etc. Documentation of all academic and non-academic experience is mandatory and must be on file at International Headquarters (copy of diploma, current letter from college or transcript).

Interview and Investigation

The candidate's experience, education, financial background and evidence of personal integrity must be furnished by responsible chapter officers or other designated officials of the Society.

Educational Opportunities

Overview

The Society provides educational opportunities for professional appraisers and allied professionals through formal courses conducted at sites throughout the United States and in other countries. It also sponsors continuing education seminars and special interest workshops and presentations at its regional and international conferences.

Participation in ASA courses and seminars is influenced by both internal and external motivating factors. To accommodate increasingly knowledgeable and discerning clientele, appraisers recognize the need to develop a working mastery of basic and discipline-specific valuation theories and related field practices. To remain competitive and sustain demand for their professional services, appraisers accumulate the education-related hours needed, combined with the required performance documentation and ethical recommendations to quality them to become designated as Accredited Members or Accredited Senior Appraisers in the Society. Once accredited at the senior level, an appraiser must maintain a steady program of continuing education participation in order to meet the Society's mandatory reaccreditation requirements. Such internal motivations to learn are being increasingly complimented by the external reality of federal and state legislated mandates for licensing and certification of appraisal practitioners. Associated with all such mandates are prerequisite numbers of hours of classroom participation in courses covering required topics to prepare enrollees for licensing /certification examinations.

The American Society of Appraisers views its educational programs as its primary and foremost service to its membership and allied professional communities. As a full-service educating, testing and accrediting professional association, it seeks to provide all necessary and appropriate professional continuing education for both early career and senior appraisers and associates.

Following are brief descriptions of the Society's principle educational formats; namely, Valuation Sciences degree programs, the Principles of Valuation course series, and continuing education seminars including annual conferences. Complete information is published in the annual Education Catalogue, which is available without charge from the Education Registrar at International Headquarters.

Valuation Sciences Degree Program

The American Society of Appraisers has, since 1979, cooperated with Lindenwood College in metropolitan St. Louis, Missouri, and Regis University in Denver, Colorado, regarding opportunities for professional appraisers to earn undergraduate or graduate degrees in

Valuation Sciences. Both schools are accredited by the North Central Association of Colleges and Schools and have appropriate programs designed for adult students. Both schools also grant college credit for students successfully completing courses in the Principles of Valuation series. Complete information about the Lindenwood program can be obtained by calling (314)949-4954; and for the Regis program, (303)458-4300 or 1 (800)727-6399.

Principles of Valuation Courses

Principles of Valuation courses provide instruction and examination at successive, accelerating levels across four of the Society's major disciplines: Business Valuation, Machinery/Technical Services, Personal Property and Real Property. All courses are academically defined, yet practitioner oriented. All emphasize strict adherence to high ethical standards of professional practice.

The Personal Property series consists of the following core courses:

PP 201:   Introduction to Personal Property Appraisal
PP 202:   Personal Property Valuation Methodology: Research and Analysis
PP 203:   Personal Property Valuation: Report Writing
PP 204:   Personal Property Valuation: Appraisal Practice and Standards

In addition, there are three higher level courses:

RC 205:   Appraising Residential Contents/General
FD 207:   Appraising Fine and Decorative Art
MG 206:   Master Gemologist Appraiser

The first four courses form an integrated, progressive series designed to introduce personal property appraisers to the basics of appraising all property and to furnish senior appraisers with the leading edge methodology of the profession. The advanced courses apply the basic tenets of appraisal practice to four major ASA specialties; Fine Art, Antiques and Decorative Art, Residential Contents/General, and Gems & Jewelry.

Course examination grades are reported on a pass/fail basis. A score of 75% or higher is necessary for passing. Participants who are Accredited Senior Appraisers receive credit hours for reaccreditation. College credit is also available to students from Lindenwood College and Regis University (see above). Further information can be obtained on the Principles of Valuation courses from the Education Registrar at International Headquarters.

Continuing Education Seminars

The annual Personal Property Appraisal Conference is the longest-running, discipline-specific educational program of the American Society of Appraisers. The program is sponsored by the ASA International Personal Property Committee (see below) and is generally held in the fall. It has been presented at locations throughout the U.S. and in Canada and Great Britain. The locations selected for these conferences provide settings where participants gain knowledge of regional and specialized properties and markets not easily studied from their home practices. This conference includes presentations by leading experts on the issues that affect today's professional appraiser and brings personal property appraisers and allied professionals together to discuss valuation issues and to work together to find solutions to the needs of the Public regarding the appraisal of personal property. This conference is open to all interested parties and provides reaccreditation credit for Accredited Senior Appraisers of personal property.

The annual International Appraisal Conference of the American Society of Appraisers, held in the summer, provides educational seminars on personal property appraisal practice and methodology, alongside similar programs for other appraisal disciplines. The personal property programs are developed by the International Personal Property Committee in conjunction with the ASA International Education Committee. These programs offer a unique opportunity for appraisers from all disciplines to share their knowledge and experiences.

Other activities that take place at the International Conference comprise: (1) reports on activities, (2) membership and financial condition of the Society, (3) open group examinations, (4) meetings of the International Board of Governors and various Society committees, and (5) Society social events. Accredited Senior Appraisers are awarded reaccreditation hours for participation in these programs.

Certification of Appraisers

In June, 1971, the American Society of Appraisers adopted a resolution unanimously supporting certification of all appraisers in order to protect the Public. On August 9, 1989, federal legislation was enacted requiring **real property appraisers** to become state licensed or certified by December 31, 1992, if they wish to make appraisals involving federally related transactions. These licensing and certification processes include prerequisites as well as continuing education provisions. The

American Society of Appraisers reaffirmed in June, 1993, continued support for cooperation with groups and states to license **all appraisers**, including non-real property appraisers.

The Educational Foundation

The American Society of Appraisers Educational Foundation is a separate, non-profit corporation established by ASA to carry on educational, research and charitable activities related to the advancement of the profession. Education grants are awarded for qualified individuals. Applicants should include the following data:

1. A brief history of the applicant's educational background including both scholastic and non-scholastic achievements;
2. Applicant's community and professional involvement;
3. A brief statement by the applicant as to why he or she should be selected;
4. A statement from the chapter regarding their screening of the proposed applicant;

Applications should be forwarded to Educational Foundation c/o International Headquarters.

The International Personal Property Committee of the American Society of Appraisers

The International Personal Property Committee (PPC) of the American Society of Appraisers is dedicated to:

1. fostering the profession of personal property appraisal practice
2. advocating the adherence to guidelines and standards as issued by the American Society of Appraisers and by The Appraisal Foundation
3. providing an educational resource for all personal property appraisers
4. monitoring the legal and political processes that impact personal property appraisers
5. promoting the value of the ASA designation within the profession and to the general public.

All Members, Senior Members and Fellows of the ASA in good standing and accredited in Personal Property as designated in the ASA categories are automatically members of the personal property discipline and eligible to vote for committee members. Candidates in the personal property discipline are non-voting members of the discipline.

The PPC was authorized by administrative rule #10 of the ASA. Its missions beyond the above dedications are to participate in the educational endeavors of the Society by assisting the Professional Development Committee in the development of text books and educational material, providing instructors, and structuring courses and seminars. The PPC assists the International Education Committee by providing technical seminars at the International Conference and the annual Personal Property Appraisal Conference. Additional responsibilities include assisting the International Board of Examiners in review and restructuring of discipline examinations and advising the ASA Board of Governors on issues concerning the personal property discipline.

The PPC is organized in compliance with the ASA Constitution and Bylaws and consists of elected members selected from the eligible voters of the personal property discipline and the immediate past-chair and parliamentarian. The personal property discipline elects four officers; namely, chairman, vice-chairman, secretary and treasurer, for two-year terms with a maximum of two terms for each position. Each year four committee members are elected by the discipline to serve for three-year terms, with a two-term maximum, on the twelve person committee. The PPC meets three times per year, at the annual International Conference, Personal Property Annual Conference, and following the Mid-Term Board Meetings of the ASA. The meetings are conducted under rules of parliamentary procedure and are open to any member of the Society.

The Education Sub-committee

As a part of its mission, the PPC has a standing sub-committee for education which maintains ASA personal property curricula, credentials, and instructors and advises the PPC on all education matters affecting personal property appraisers. This sub-committee consists of a chair, appointed by the PPC chair, who is assisted by members of the discipline serving on the ASA personal property faculty, or in course and examinations review. The Education Sub-committee chair provides support to the PPC chair in its duties as advisor to the Society on ASA education policy and activity.

The Personal Property Journal

The PPC has a standing committee for the publishing and editing of the *Personal Property Journal*, available by subscription to anyone interested in personal property appraisal. The *Personal Property Journal* is published quarterly with articles of interest to personal property appraisers and allied professionals and includes columns regarding political and legislative activity affecting personal property appraisers and their clients, educational programs of the Society, and resource guides and summaries of presentations at ASA International Conferences and Personal Property Appraisal Conferences. The journal serves as the official publication of the personal property discipline along with ASA *Newsline*.

The Nominating Sub-committee

Senior members of the personal property discipline in good standing with the American Society of Appraisers are eligible for nomination to the PPC. Interested members may submit their names to the Nominations Sub-committee of the PPC for consideration. The Nominating Sub-committee is appointed and the call for nominations is published prior to November 1 of each year. A slate is submitted to the PPC at the mid-term meeting of the PPC to be followed by written ballots to the eligible voters of the discipline.

Persons interested in the work of the International Personal Property Committee may contact ASA International Headquarters for further information.

Chapter 11

Business Aspects of a Professional Appraisal Practice

Introduction

The building and maintenance of a successful appraisal practice does not occur by serendipity, but rather is the end result of carefully planned and orchestrated management strategies and procedures, which are goal specific and which encompass both a broad business perspective and a thorough attention to the constellation of details surrounding the implementation of these strategies. The purpose of this chapter is to highlight the most significant elements of successful management through the knowledge and application of skills incorporating the practical mechanics of maintaining a full time and full service appraisal practice.

Time Management

Planning

Many leading appraisal firms consider weekly planning sessions to be of paramount importance, for a variety of reasons, not the least of which is the establishment of basic control over business functions. Regular planning sessions are vital to scheduling of assignments, flow of reports, coordination of research, discussion of difficult assignments and sharing of information with colleagues, as well as contributing to anticipation of cash flow in relation to expenses. The discipline of regular planning sessions enables the growing appraisal firm to set aside time for business analysis and to learn to space assignments appropriately within a given time frame.

Billable Time

A viable appraisal practice must rely upon the consistent performance of tasks which result in income to the company, and the appraiser must learn to manage his time in such a way as to prioritize billable time while at the same time recognizing that many daily tasks and business functions are necessary but not reimbursable.

There may be many worthwhile commitments which represent intangible assets to the company, but it is the billable time which is required for financial viability.

Tasks which are normally considered under billable time include on-site property inspection, cataloging, client consultations, specialized library research, telephone research and telephone consultations, travel, expert witness testimony, professional document preparation and appraisal review. Typical tasks that are not billable include non-productive telephone conversations, study time or learning time not appropriately billed to the client, and field work such as attendance at auctions or antiques shows or professional development opportunities.

Business Development

The largest and most prestigious of appraisal firms often affirm that planned and constant attention to business development is a key to their longevity and success. These well-established firms have insured their niche in the marketplace and their identity in the public's awareness. These accomplishments are not by chance but rather by deliberate and consistent networking with those institutions and individuals who are in a position to refer business to the company on a regular basis, such as insurance companies, law firms, banks, museums, government agencies and other appraisal firms around the country. Many successful appraisers define their identities in terms of their skills rather than their geographical location. When it comes to skills, the appraiser's ability to produce an outstanding document translates to a consistent flow of word-of-mouth referrals to the company and is essentially more effective advertising than various brochures and sell sheets which are routinely distributed to potential clients. Other means of promoting business development may include involvement with professional appraisal associations and making oneself available as a credible guest speaker, course instructor, workshop leader or guest on television or radio programs.

Field Work

An appraiser's obligation to keep current with market developments involves not only keeping up with the literature but also engaging in field work on a regular basis as appropriate opportunities arise. This may include attendance at major and minor auctions, attendance at major exhibitions — both museum and commercial, visits to retail stores, estate sales, research libraries, and other events and opportunities which relate to the appraiser's assignments. The appraiser's budgetary allowances for travel and related expenses of field work should be included in overall financial planning on a monthly or annual basis. The interactive experiences and hands-on opportunities that arise in the course of routine field work enable the professional to be more than an "arm chair" appraiser, and they also provide the added benefits derived from the appraiser's continued visibility in the marketplace, aiding in business development and cultivation of an active professional image.

Professional Development

One of the common traits observed in appraisers who are considered both leaders in their field and high level, credible professionals is the presence of a scholarly attitude and seriousness of purpose. Continuing professional development is considered crucial to the growth of the individual over the span of an entire career and is an integral part of his credibility as an expert in his field. Appraisers are constantly called upon to draw from a foundation of knowledge continually solidified through various aspects of professional development, and it is this scholarly attitude which often separates the professional appraiser from the amateur.

Included under the umbrella of professional development are activities such as participation in professional conferences and symposia, attendance at seminars or lectures on specific appraisal-related issues, participation in museum workshops or courses involving connoisseurship, taking accredited courses at respected universities, and actively participating in appropriate committee work with professional organizations which are respected for their attitudes towards professional development and which are in a position to provide effective learning opportunities commensurate with the appraiser's level. The associated costs of active participation in activities which contribute to such professional growth

are part of overall planned operating costs and should be part of the company's annual budget.

Income and Expense Management

Perspectives on Income

Potential sources of income for personal property appraisers may include consulting fees, professional appraisal fees, appraisal review fees or expert witness testimony fees. Advanced appraisers may also be able to derive income from authorship of articles or books or from appraisal related lectures, although many professional appraisers may write articles for scholarly journals without collecting any fee, or they may deliver a lecture or make an appearance on radio or television primarily for purposes of public education and awareness of the profession rather than for any monetary gain.

Although not mandatory, the collection of a retainer from the client can be essential to the smooth cash flow of the company, particularly if it is in the early stages of growth. Just as in other professions, a retainer is considered appropriate, especially with larger assignments where there will be a sizable length of time between initiation of the appraisal and collection of the balance of the fee. In fact, the term retainer is a legal term and one which clients can relate to as it pertains to business transactions. As with all fee structures, there should be a thoughtful analysis of the retainer in terms of amount required and services rendered in relation to it. Many appraisers expect a retainer in the amount of 50% of the total anticipated fee while others may expect only 25% of the final invoice. Still others may require the retainer to reflect only the amount of time spent on-site during the examination phase of the appraisal. Even though the final invoice may require the balance due upon receipt of statement, most appraisers are not likely to expect payment for at least fifteen to thirty days, depending upon circumstances. Different companies may have varying policies in regard to delivery of the appraisal document, some requiring the balance due prior to actual delivery and others forwarding the document along with the invoice for final payment. Fee structures and payment requirements for testimony as an expert witness or for other specialized services may differ from other payment requirements and serve to illustrate the importance of developing individual office policies which are the result of deliberate and careful analysis and planning rather than chance or guess work.

Professional appraisers are usually extremely aware of the need to devote appropriate time to the analysis of operational costs and to fee structures which reflect not only the value of their time in the marketplace but also reflect the overhead involved in maintaining the office. This is a practical reason why planning sessions can be instrumental in scheduling work as needed to meet monthly or quarterly expenses and operational costs.

Perspectives on Expense

Identification and analysis of key operational costs is essential to the financial viability of the company and is directly related to the resulting need to determine how much income will be required to meet those costs. The typical appraisal office must consider monthly or quarterly expenses such as payment of rent or mortgage; payroll for other appraisers, consultants, research assistance or clerical assistance; cost of employees such as social security or workmen's compensation; payment of taxes, health insurance, automobile insurance or other specialized insurance coverage; and payment of utilities. Additionally, there are expenses related to the purchase and updating of office equipment, continual additions to the in-house library through the purchase of books, price guides, auction catalogs and periodicals related to the appraisal profession and to the appraiser's special field of expertise as well as pertinent marketing or advertising expenses such as advertisement in the telephone book or production of office literature. On-going professional fees such as attorney's fees or accounting fees must also be considered. Finally, a significant portion of overall expenses, though secondary to fixed expenses, is derived from costs of professional development and may include course tuition and materials, travel expenses, conference fees, and numerous incidental costs.

Office Procedures

Forms

The considerable amount of detailed information which the typical appraisal organization must manage makes it critical to provide for the efficient flow and transfer of information, while at the same time keeping a paper trail and permanent record of tasks performed in regard to various appraisal assignments. It is prudent for the new appraisal office to custom-develop a variety of basic office forms which can be revised as required from time to time but which give office personnel a standardized manner in which to record facts and figures in regard to the numerous appraisal assignments which are handled by the company. For example, some companies may choose to develop a standard intake form which provides information on the purpose and function of the assignment, the names, addresses and telephone numbers needed, itemization of expenses and professional fees, payment schedules, special circumstances, deadlines required and other pertinent dates such as the date of death in the case of an estate appraisal. Some appraisers keep a separate time sheet to record hours divided between on-site examination, specialized research, preparation of document, preparation for court testimony and various other billable segments of the appraiser's time. Many appraisers utilize a contractual agreement form which they may revise according to the nature of the assignment and the client involved, while other appraisers may use relatively standardized letters of agreement which again are appropriately revised for each new assignment. Still more specialized are contractual agreements regarding testimony as an expert witness or subcontracting agreements between the appraisal office and specialists who may join a team of appraisers on an as-needed basis. Larger, well-established firms may also have to consider the use of specialized copyright forms. On a daily basis the appraiser is aided by reference to forms which address assignment listings, work plans, travel expense reports, and numerous task specific forms to be used on-site, such as examination forms for silver, ceramics, furniture, graphics, etc.

Equipment

The operating budget for the appraisal firm should address the need for acquiring new office equipment and the maintenance and upgrading of existing equipment. The new firm also needs to think out the fundamental space requirements needed as the business grows, keeping in mind the record keeping requirements stated in the Ethics Provision of *USPAP*, which states:

> An appraiser must retain written records of appraisal, review and consulting assignments — including oral testimony and reports — and retain such records for a period of at least five (5) years after their preparation or at least two (2) years after final disposition of any judicial proceeding in which testimony was given, whichever period expires last.

Space allocations should be planned for proper filing systems, shelving for in-house libraries, computer installations and basic office work regions, conference room equipment and storage units for inactive files. Provision in the budget must be made for the purchase of computer equipment, fax machines, copying machines, answering machines, calculators, typewriters, cameras and other equipment as needed. Because the use of time is a crucial issue for the self-employed professional, such equipment becomes a necessity and aids the appraiser in the attempt to maximize the financial return on the investment of his time and resources.

Clerical Tasks

Experienced business owners will acknowledge that the failure to keep and maintain appropriate records can be a major reason for lack of growth and productivity and even failure. There are many continuing clerical tasks in a busy appraisal office which require constant attention from staff members familiar with these tasks. Record keeping encompasses not only the maintenance of accounting journals such as cash receipts, cash disbursements, profit and loss statements or other relevant financial statements, but also involves the management of client files, clipping files, and other resource files, bibliographies, correspondence, work plans, photographs, computer discs, etc. Equally significant is the need for appropriate personnel to answer telephone inquiries or to follow up on them by forwarding literature or information, to make travel arrangements, to process letters and reports, or to formulate and send invoices or pay bills.

Internships or Apprenticeships

The reality is that a great many appraisal offices are relatively small with minimal personnel to handle the numerous tasks that have been discussed. Thus it is paramount to understand how to prioritize time, to establish office procedures which will ensure effective control over the business and not bog down the appraiser in such a way as to reduce the amount of billable time so substantially that the company no longer can achieve financial viability.

Once a firm is established and more secure, some consideration might be given to the utilization of an intern to assist with research, typing, filing, taking of inventory, measuring and other fundamental tasks. Such interns may typically be graduate students in art history or appraisal studies programs and may be motivated to obtain invaluable experience by working in the field with a seasoned professional. Obviously, the intern will require the expenditure of at least some time in training and orientation, and it is important to weigh the benefits versus the drawbacks of utilizing interns, perhaps depending upon the size and range of the company and the multiple roles which a sole proprietor appraiser plays within his organization.

Attitudes about the use of interns and expenditure of time in training them vary. For example, some companies do not feel that a training program is required nor that interns should be relegated to clerical tasks but rather exclusively used to assist appraisers in functional work.

One leading appraisal firm contacted in the course of preparation for the development of this chapter has organized a formal apprenticeship program with a limited enrollment of apprentices from within the community. These apprentices are already out in the work force and are contemplating the possibility of entering the appraisal profession as a career path. Apprentices in this program must take at least one appraisal course in advance and follow a structured ten-week program in which they are introduced to office procedures and management, taught about the function and use of basic equipment, the use of forms, etc. Later, they are given a project assignment and required to make a presentation. Finally, the cultivation of a polished image is addressed in terms of dress and overall presentation of a professional image to the public. In addition to classroom time, the apprentice is required to devote a specified number of weekly hours to volunteer time in which he or she contributes to the functioning of the company in a meaningful way. Clearly this program is not intended to replace formal academic programs or formal certification procedures, both of which are essential for the professional, but rather this program enables the participant to gain the experience upon which to form a decision on whether or not to seriously pursue a career in appraising and whether or not such a career path is truly appropriate for the participant's needs and expectations.

Subcontracting and Appraisal Administration

A Team Approach

Utilizing a team approach in tackling a large and varied appraisal assignment enables a relatively small firm to become full service. Larger firms or specialty firms may have an in-house staff with diverse capabilities. Occasionally there may be instances when it becomes appropriate to refer a client independently to a particular specialist in another firm, but generally it is possible for many small appraisal firms to act as appraisal administrators, subcontracting other specialist appraisers as needed and including their conclusions within the final appraisal document. This may depend upon the complexity of the assignment and the quantity of property involved. The single authorship of the document by the appraisal administrator promotes a consistency of quality and style in the final product. Additionally, the client is able to deal primarily with a single person in a position to present and interpret the product. If extremely cautious in selecting team members, there is certain satisfaction in being able to provide a span of expertise and a reputation for accuracy. Initially, however, it is essential to think out the details of the roles each specialist will play on the team and also to establish control and specific ground rules as an appraisal administrator. One should not necessarily make the assumption that all those holding themselves out to the public as experts do, in fact, have a strong command of valuation theory and techniques in addition to particular knowledge in a classified specialty. For example, in spite of a specialist's ability to identify property with accuracy and in spite of any intuitive instincts about market value he or she may have as a result of continued exposure to the market, these do not in any way insure a clear and concise command of the various kinds of value and how these concepts are applied in different appraisal scenarios involving insurance, probate, charitable donation, bankruptcy, etc. Many of the well-established firms currently utilizing a team approach are quick to emphasize that the failure to accurately judge a team member's ability to participate effectively in a thoroughly informed and cohesive unit may have disastrous results. Clearly, the new appraiser should not begin subcontracting until the numerous appraisal theories and techniques are well internalized, and the appraisal document is a clear reflection of this.

Subcontracting Agreement

Many companies that subcontract do so only after having developed detailed contractual agreements which clearly establish controls and ground rules concerning fees, individual responsibilities, formatting and quality of reports, billing, copyright, confidentiality, covenants against competition within a geographical region, covenants against solicitation, adherence to specific standards of performance, adherence to specified deadlines, and various other requirements. The company that is just beginning subcontracting may well want to consult an attorney and an accountant, both of whom should be well-informed about the nature and nuances of the appraisal profession in addition to any particulars involving a given firm's specialty. For example, a firm specializing in the appraisal of art may wish to utilize attorneys and accountants specializing in art.

Even a one- or two-person office operating in a comparatively unsophisticated environment needs to clearly understand the concept of subcontracting and how it differs from being an employer. This is particularly true in view of the scrutiny with which the IRS examines the company's tax returns with a view towards its compliance with subcontracting rules and regulations. A competent tax consultant should be able to provide the appraiser with a comprehensive checklist in which characteristics of an independent contractor versus an employee are delineated or perhaps a comparison chart which interprets the revenue laws pertaining to these characteristics. Such a checklist or chart should address topics such as instructions about how the work is to be done, how much training is required, the establishment of hours and payment schedules, the continuity of the working relationship, the furnishing of tools or supplies, whether the worker has an established business of his or her own with office, certification or licensing, business telephone, letterhead, etc. It is the unmistakable responsibility of the appraisal company, no matter how small, to be fully informed about IRS regulations and to issue the required tax forms or handle any other appropriate submissions. Additionally, it is the appraisal company's responsibility to require appropriate paperwork from the worker or team member, such as invoices, signed contracts, etc. Record keeping on subcontracting should be attended to as needed to fulfill requirements and to be prepared at tax time.

Fee Considerations in Subcontracting

A fully staffed appraisal firm will have salaried employees, but most of the smaller scale offices will find the need to develop fee schedules in regard to subcontracting arrangements. The main contractor is likely to control the billing. For payment of appraisal services he may establish his own fee schedule for contracted services of a specialist, but it is just as likely that he may pay the fees previously established by the independent contractor for the utilization of his or her expertise in the appraisal assignment. There may be some instances when a smaller appraisal office may act as the appraisal administrator with the bulk of the work being handled by a designated team of specialists. In this event it may be appropriate to establish a percentage of the appraisal fee to cover administrative costs, but generally speaking the fee will be calculated on the basis of the time, costs, and exposure of the administrator.

A Note about Insurance

It is conceivable that appraisers may be exposed to lawsuits from various third parties involved in assignments with which they have had involvement. For this reason the insurance industry has developed professional liability programs which may be available to an appraiser either directly or through a major appraisal association. This coverage is intended to address errors and omissions of the appraiser in the matter of claims or litigation. As with any other insurance program, the appraiser investigating this coverage should be well aware of what a given policy encompasses and whether it adequately addresses his needs. What is interesting to note on the matter of liability insurance is that one tends to find that many of the more successful appraisal firms do not carry such insurance. This is partially because of the high cost of such coverage, but perhaps more importantly, these firms recognize that the quality of their work, their attention to due diligence in performing appraisals, the thorough professionalism displayed in their documents, and the awareness of the inappropriateness of taking on assignments for which they are not qualified all contribute to a well-founded sense of security in meeting any future conflict or controversy which may arise surrounding an appraisal with which they have been involved.

Professional, Personal and Client Relationships

The Professional Image

The value of a client's perceptions of an appraiser cannot be underestimated, as professional persona is such an integral part of overall ability to achieve real success and satisfaction in the appraisal profession. The projection of this persona is not by accident but rather by the deliberate, daily cultivation of traits and attitudes which come together to form it and eventually become second nature. Those traits and attitudes which contribute positively to the public's perception may include the appraiser's dress and speech; manners and sense of diplomacy; level of preparedness for any task that may be required, including physical tasks; willingness to take initiative; ability to listen and to understand the clients needs, not losing sight of goals and ethical responsibilities; and willingness to educate the client. The consistent display of professional standards from the time of initial phone contact through the delivery of the finished product is a goal which encompasses such individual attitudes and traits.

It is useful to ruminate on certain behavioral characteristics which are perceived negatively by the public and which are extremely detrimental to the appraiser's image as a professional. Among the most glaring of these are displays of unethical conduct such as disclosure of confidential information, engaging in activities which are a clear conflict of interest, failing to recognize and stand behind fiduciary responsibilities to the third party. In a team situation, a negative or egotistical attitude, an unwillingness to cooperate with other team members, or an inability to recognize and be able to discuss potential problems with clients are all perceived as both destructive and unprofessional.

Rapport with Clients On-site

The professional appraiser is aware of how his behavior in a client's home influences not only his own credibility but that of the profession as a whole. Having a certain amount of psychological insight into human nature is just as important to client relationships as having an in-depth knowledge of an appraisal specialty. For example, it is appropriate for the appraiser to recognize and to respect a client's sentimental attachment to family heirlooms, regardless of monetary value, and thus to project to the client a respect for their family historical associations, while at the same time being able to teach the difference between sentimental association and actual monetary value. Also, the manner in which the appraiser handles objects in the home can be a real reflection of the level of respect with which the appraiser treats the client. Similarly, but in a more subtle way, the appraiser's body language in the handling of objects reveals much about the overall aura professionalism commands. Handling objects with care regardless of taste level, monetary value, or even stress level in the face of cataloging multiple objects is essential to forming an atmosphere of trust and comfort which is so desirable in the work environment. Being thoughtful and nonjudgmental in dialogue with the client can go a long way in establishing trust and diplomatic relations. The success achieved by an appraiser through confidence displayed and professional behavior is measured well into the future in terms of whether or not a client's trust and respect have been earned to a point at which the client willingly and unreservedly refers new business to the appraiser in the years to come.

Appendices

Appendix 1
Appraisal Ethics

Each of the appraisal societies which educate, test, and certify qualified appraisers has a code of ethics. This discussion is based on *The Principles of Appraisal Practice and Code of Ethics* promulgated by the American Society of Appraisers, the only multidisciplinary appraisal organization in the United States. It follows the outline of the ethics course presented on audio/video tape which is made available to members through their respective chapters.

To begin with, what is ethics? Possibly the best way to answer this is to explain that a code of ethics is a system by which professional behavior is to be governed. Further, the system of ethics that we use in appraisal practice is designed not only to protect our clients but also to enhance the professional well being of other appraisers.

Why do we require a system of ethics? Perhaps the simplest answer is that it tells us how to act, what actions are right or wrong, good or bad. This could mean that ethics may be defined as a science or practice which deals with conduct insofar as it is considered right or wrong, good or bad.

The appraiser's prime concern is the determination of value. judgment is an important factor in arriving at this determination. Basically, we recognize that there are right or wrong ways of doing things. For instance, there is a right way and a wrong way to build a bridge, a right way and a wrong way to assist in a surgical operation; there are also right ways and wrong ways of doing things in the larger relations of life, in the business of life itself, and it is with these things that ethics is concerned.

Let us look on the other side of the coin. Let us imagine that the need for ethics is not important because human beings already know, without any specific training or education, what is a good thing to do and what is a bad thing to do. However, whether we are so gifted is a matter of judgment. The obligation to understand ethical values is almost the first law of life, and the place where it is in the highest demand is in the world of human and moral relations.

Ethics is not a new idea, it has existed as long as human beings began to think. Plato, Socrates, Aristotle, and Aristotophanes are some of the early philosophers who defined ethics and expressed their opinions on what is good and what is bad.

Appraisers Are Obligated to Attain Competency and to Practice Ethically

One of the differences between a professional and a nonprofessional is the code of ethics to which the professional must subscribe. This is established by a governing body or professional society of which the recipient is a member. By becoming a member of an established, accrediting organization, the professional places himself or herself under the jurisdiction of that governing body and is subject to disciplinary action in the event that the society's code of ethics is not followed.

When accepting an assignment, the accredited appraiser places himself or herself within the code of ethics of the society or organization that granted the designation. It is essential that the purpose of the appraisal be defined so that the appraiser can select the appraisal method and analysis which must be employed to give a logical opinion of the value which is to be found. After selecting the method to be utilized, it is the appraiser's obligation to determine the appropriate and applicable numerical results with as high a degree of accuracy as the particular objectives of the appraisal necessitate.

For example, we assume that the appraiser is determining the market value of an object of personal property. The purpose of the appraisal is stated to be the determination of the fair market value. The appraiser should define fair market value so that whoever reads the appraisal report will know that the value is based on a set of specific conditions. For example, the market value may apply to all the objects to be insured.

In this instance, the appraiser should say that the market value is based on this condition. On the other hand, it may be that the market value is to be determined at auction. In this case, the appraiser should know and understand that market level.

This kind of expertise requires that the appraiser must be competent in his or her field. Competency is obtained by education, training, study, practice, and experience.

The appraiser must also recognize and understand the orderly liquidation market level. Therefore, the appraiser must have information, expertise, and knowledge, which is not normally possessed by a lay person, and this is part of the difference between the professional and a person who cannot make this claim.

The Appraiser's Fiduciary Relationship to Third Parties

The client, recognizing that the appraiser has expertise which is specialized, and which the client himself does not readily have, must depend on the appraiser to accomplish the objectives of the project. There is no *caveat emptor* principle involved in a relationship between a professional appraiser and a client. On occasion, it may be that the client will turn the appraisal report over to a third party. It is essential that the appraiser recognize that the third party or parties have as much right to rely on the validity and objectivity of the appraisal as does the client. This may be the case where the client submits the appraisal to a banker for review as collateral evidence, or to the Internal Revenue Service as tax liability evidence.

The Appraiser's Fiduciary Relationship to the Public

The fiduciary relationship to the public is the same as the appraiser's fiduciary relationship with third parties. This would apply to assignments involving insurance companies, financial institutions taxpayers or any person making a financial decision based on the value conclusion.

The Appraiser's Obligations to the Client

In some cases, the appraiser turns over the report to a reviewer designated by the client. This is a proper procedure, and the appraiser is bound by it inasmuch as this is a condition set forth by the client. On the other hand, the appraiser must keep the appraisal a confidential matter, which involves only the client. The appraiser cannot reveal the property being appraised, the identity of his client, or the results of the appraisal. This is all a matter of confidential information which is to be delivered only to the client.

It is not proper for the appraiser to reveal to anyone other than the client the amount of the valuation of the property. Sometimes the client will give the appraiser approval to release the information to a specific person or body, in which case the appraiser should obtain written notice to this effect in order to protect himself or herself and to ensure that he or she is handling the matter in an ethical manner. An appraiser cannot use an appraisal report made for a client as evidence of professional qualifications to an appraisal or professional society unless the client has given permission for this type of review. When an appraiser accepts an assignment, it is with the understanding that he or she is qualified to do the work for which he or she is engaged and that the appraiser's field of expertise does not lie outside the appraisal problem. It is possible for an appraiser to accept the assignment, provided that he or she acquaints the client with the limitations of his or her own qualification or associates himself or herself with another appraiser or appraisers who possess the required qualification.

The Appraiser's Obligation Relative to Giving Testimony

In the event that the appraiser testifies in court or gives testimony in a deposition, it is necessary to present the data analysis and value without bias regardless of the effect of such unbiased presentation on the client's case. An appraiser must not suppress any facts or opinions which are adverse to the case the client is trying to establish or to overemphasize any facts or opinions which are favorable to the client's case. In other words, the appraiser cannot ethically become an advocate. The appraiser may not properly serve more than one client with respect to the same property, or the same legal action, without the consent of both parties to act in this capacity.

The Appraiser's Obligation to Other Appraisers

The appraiser has obligations to other appraisers. For example, an appraiser should protect the professional reputation of all appraisers who subscribe to and practice in accordance with the principles of appraisal practice of an accrediting organization such as the American Society of Appraisers. It is unethical for an appraiser to injure, or attempt to injure, by false or malicious statement or innuendo, the professional reputation of any other appraiser.

Unethical Competitive Conduct

An appraiser should not reduce a fee which he or she has already quoted to a client to obtain an appraisal contract and thus supplant another appraiser after the latest quotation has been made known. As a matter of fact, it is unethical for an appraiser to supplant, or attempt to supplant, another appraiser after the latter has been engaged to perform a specified appraisal service. It is the obligation of a member of the society who has knowledge of an unethical act on the part of another member, to report that act to the society. Further, it is the appraiser's obligation to cooperate with the society in all matters, including investigation, censure, discipline, or dismissal of members who are charged with violations of the society's code of ethics. An appraiser, acting ethically, cannot indulge in self-laudatory advertising or solicitation of appraisal engagements using unwarranted, inaccurate, or misleading claims or promises. These are acts which are considered detrimental to the establishment and maintenance of public confidence in the results of appraisal work. Advocacy, of course, is another aspect of the same problem. Misrepresentation as to qualifications and membership status are also considered unethical practices and are not to be engaged in by appraisers.

Acceptance of Contingency Fees Is Unethical

If an appraiser were to accept an engagement for which the amount of compensation is contingent upon the amount of an award in a property settlement or a court action where the appraiser's services are employed, or is contingent upon the amount of a tax reduction obtained by a client where the appraiser's services are used, or is contingent upon the consummation of the sale or financing of a property in connection with which the appraiser's services are utilized, or is contingent upon the appraiser's reaching any finding or conclusion specified by the client, then anyone considering using the results of the appraiser's undertaking might well suspect that these results were biased and self-serving and, therefore, invalid. Such suspicion would militate against the establishment and maintenance of trust and confidence in the results of appraisal work generally. Therefore, the society considers that the contracting for, or acceptance of, any such contingent fee is unethical and unprofessional.

As a corollary to the above principle relative to contingency fees, the society considers that it is unethical and unprofessional for an appraiser (1) to contract for or accept compensation for appraisal services in the form of a commission, rebate, division of brokerage commissions, or any similar forms and (2) to receive or pay finder or referral fees.

In the matter of percentage fees, the society takes the position that it is unprofessional and unethical for the appraiser to contract to do work for a fixed percentage of the amount of value, or of the estimated cost (as the case may be) which the appraiser determines at the conclusion of the work.

Disinterested Appraisals

Anyone using an appraisal made by an appraiser who has an interest or a contemplated future interest in the property appraised might well suspect that the report was biased and self-serving and, therefore, that the findings were invalid. Such suspicion tends to break down trust and confidence in the results of appraisal work in general. It is, therefore, necessary and proper that the appraiser be wholly disinterested in the property being appraised.

Interests which an appraiser should avoid in a property being appraised include ownership of the subject property; acting, or having some expectation of acting, as agent in the purchase, sale, or financing of the subject property; and managing, or having some expectation of managing, the subject property. Such interests are particularly apt to exist if the appraiser, while engaged in professional appraisal practice, is also engaged in a related retail business (real estate, jewelry, furs, antiques, fine arts, etc.).

The society professes that, subject to the provision for disclosure given in the following paragraph, it is unethical and unprofessional for an appraiser to accept an assignment to appraise a property In which he or she has an interest or a contemplated future interest.

However, if a prospective client, after full disclosure by the appraiser of his or her present or contemplated future interest in the subject property, still desires to have the appraiser do the work, the latter may properly accept the engagement provided he or she discloses the nature and extent of interest in the appraisal report.

Responsibility Connected with Signatures to Appraisal Reports

The user of an appraisal report, before placing reliance on its conclusions, is entitled to assume that the party signing the report is responsible for the findings, either because he or she did the work or because the work was done under his or her supervision.

In cases where two or more appraisers are employed to prepare a joint report, the user is entitled to assume that if all of them sign it, they are jointly and severally responsible for the validity of all the findings therein, and if all do not sign, the client has a right to know what the dissenting opinions are.

In cases where two or more appraisers have been engaged by a single client to make independent appraisals of the same property, the client has the right to expect that he or she will receive opinions which have been reached independently, and that they may be used as checks against each other and/or have evidence of the range within which the numerical results lie. . To implement these principles, the society says that it is unethical (1) to misrepresent who made an appraisal by appending the signature of any person who neither did the work nor had the work done under his or her supervision; (2) in the case of a joint report to omit any signatures or any dissenting opinions; (3) in case two or more appraisers have collaborated in an appraisal undertaking, for them, or any of them, to issue separate appraisal reports; and (4) in case two or more appraisers have been engaged by a single client to make independent appraisals of the same property, for them to collaborate or consult with one another or make use of each other's findings or figures.

An appraisal firm or corporation may property use a corporate signature with the signature of a responsible officer. But the person who actually did the appraisal for the corporation must sign the corporate appraisal report, or the report must acknowledge the person who actually made the appraisal.

Unconsidered Opinions and Preliminary Reports

If an appraiser gives an opinion as to the value, earning power, or cost estimate of a property without having ascertained and weighed all the pertinent facts, such opinion, except by an extraordinary coincidence, will be inaccurate. The giving of such offhand opinions tend to belittle the importance of inspection, investigation, and analysis in appraisal procedure and lessens the confidence with which the results of good appraisal practice are received, and therefore the society professes that the giving of hasty and unconsidered opinions is unprofessional.

If an appraiser makes a preliminary report without including a statement to the effect that it is preliminary and the figures given are subject to refinement or change when the final report is completed, there is the possibility that some user of the report, being under the impression that it is a final and completed report, will accord the figures a degree of accuracy and reliability they do not possess. The results of such misplaced confidence could be damaging to the reputation of professional appraisers in general as well as to that of the appraiser concerned. To obviate this possibility, the society considers it to be unprofessional appraisal practice to omit a proper limiting and qualifying statement in a preliminary report.

Advertising and Solicitation

It is not unethical to advertise the availability of appraisal services. It is unethical to use any inaccurate, misleading, false, or deceptive claim, promise, or representation in connection with any advertisement. These unethical practices are considered by the society in the results of appraisal work. The society considers that such practices on the part of an appraiser constitute unethical and unprofessional conduct. It would be unethical to do the following:

1. Misrepresent in any way one's connection or affiliation with the American Society of Appraisers or any other organization

2. Misrepresent one's background, education, training, or expertise

3. Misrepresent services available or an appraiser's prior or current service to any client, or identify any client without the express written permission of such client to be identified in advertising

4. Represent, guarantee, or imply that a particular valuation or estimate of value or result of an engagement will be tailored or adjusted to any particular use or conclusion other than that an appraisal will be based on an honest and accurate adherence to the principles of appraisal practice as published by the American Society of Appraisers.

Misuse of Membership Designation

The constitution and bylaws of the society establish three professional grades of membership, namely, Accredited Member, Accredited Senior Appraiser, and (An affiliate or candidate does not hold a professional grade of membership in the society.) Accredited Members may use the designation "AM." Only Senior Members may use the designation "ASA." (Accredited Senior Appraiser). Only Fellows may use the designation "FASA." The society considers it to be unethical for a member to claim or imply the holding of a higher degree of membership than he or she has attained.

Summary

Disciplinary action against the members of the society is taken in the event of violations of specific provisions of the society's constitution and bylaws or of its principles of appraisal practice and the code of ethics incorporated in it. Such actions are under the jurisdiction of the international president, the international ethics committee, and the board of governors. Violations may fall under four categories:

1. Deviations from good appraisal practice
2. Failure to fulfill obligations and responsibilities
3. Unprofessional conduct
4. Unethical conduct

After investigation, the society may take action in the form of suggestion, censure, suspension, or expulsion, in which event the member will be required to surrender his or her certificate, membership pin, and other evidences of membership and to desist from all reference to such membership.

The designated members, affiliates, and candidates making up the American Society of Appraisers are governed by the above code. Moreover, there is the implied obligation on the part of the entire membership to uphold and maintain the integrity which the general public has come to expect from the members of a professional organization. There is a good way to do things in the appraisal profession and the society has taken a stand against the bad ways. By doing so, a right way and a wrong way of making an appraisal have been defined because we aspire to the highest ideals in accomplishment and recognize that professional performance requires strict and steadfast fidelity to ethical behavior. All members, including affiliates and candidates, must fully ascribe to the *Principles of Appraisal Practice and Code of Ethics* as set forth by the American Society of Appraisers. The 1994 Revised Edition is included as Appendix 2 of this publication. For future revisions a copy may be obtained, at no cost, by writing American Society of Appraisers, P.O. Box 17265, Washington, D.C. 20041.

▲

Appendix 2

Principles of Appraisal Practice and Code of Ethics of the American Society of Appraisers

FOREWORD

In a Society which not only permits but encourages the private ownership of productive property and one which also engages in large and multitudinous public works, there appears, on every hand, a necessity for the appraisal of property. In fact, property appraisals are used throughout the economic, governmental, legal, and social activities of such a society.

As the vocation of property appraisal has developed during past decades from a business occupation into a profession, certain concepts have emerged and become clear. The word "property" is now given to physical things and also to the legal rights of ownership of tangible or intangible entities. Appraising is now considered to encompass three classes of operations, namely,

(1) **The estimation of the cost of producing or replacing physical property,**

(2) **The forecasting of the monetary earning power of certain classes of property,**

(3) **The valuation or determination of the worth of property.**

Because of the specialized knowledge and abilities required of the appraiser which are not possessed by the layman, there has now come to be established a fiduciary relationship between him and those who rely upon his findings.

The American Society of Appraisers occupies a unique position among professional appraisal societies in that it recognizes and is concerned with all classes of property: **real, personal, tangible,** and **intangible,** including real estate, machinery and equipment, buildings and other structures, furnishings, works of art, natural resources, public utilities, gems and jewelry, investment securities, and so forth. It is also unique in that it recognizes the threefold character of the appraisal function.

In recognizing the need for the highest professional competence among appraisers, the American Society of Appraisers actively supports recognized institutions of higher learning in their scholastic programs which are designed to provide the necessary academic background to both appraiser aspirants and to the qualified professionals who desire to update and broaden their professional skills.

The Society has established an Educational Foundation to assist those institutions of higher learning which actively provide scholastic training and research in the various appraisal disciplines.

The necessity for a set of authoritative principles and a code of professional ethics, broad enough to cover all classes of property as well as the complexities of the various appraisal procedures, is a pressing one. Previous statements of principles have dealt almost exclusively with real estate. Existing codes of ethics are, in large measure, couched in such general moralistic terms that they are impractical for specific application.

Violation of any provision or rule of the Code should not give rise to a civil cause of action and should not create any presumption or evidence that a legal duty has been breached nor should it create any special relationship between the appraiser or any other person. This Code is designed to provide guidance to appraisers and to provide a structure for regulating conduct of members of the ASA through disciplinary actions. Violations of the Code are not designed or intended to be the basis of any civil liability. (January 1990)

To meet the need for a comprehensive set of guideposts and for a specific code of ethics, the Society has prepared and presents herewith The Principles of Appraisal Practice and Code of Ethics of the American Society of Appraisers.

AMERICAN SOCIETY OF APPRAISERS
Authorized June 30, 1968

Revised January 1994

TABLE OF CONTENTS

1   INTRODUCTION

1.1   Membership Composition of the American Society of Appraisers

The American Society of Appraisers is a professional organization of individuals. Each of its members who has demonstrated, to the satisfaction of the Society, that he is qualified to appraise one or more of the existing kinds of property, has been granted the right to use the identification, Member of the American Society of Appraisers. Members and Senior Members may use the appropriate designations authorized by the Board of Governors.

1.2   Definition of "Appraisal Practice" and "Property"

1.21 The term appraisal practice, as defined by the Society, applies to any of the four following operations, singly or in combination, these operations being executed within a framework of general principles of technical procedure and personal conduct:

(1) Determination of the value of property (the transitive verb *determine* having the meaning: "to come to a decision concerning, as the result of investigation, reasoning, etc.");

(2) Forecasting of the earning power of property;

(3) Estimation of the cost of

(a) Production of a new property (*production* having the meaning: "brought into being by assembly of elements, fabrication, construction, manufacture, or natural growth of living things");

(b) Replacement of an existing property by purchase or production of an equivalent property;

(c) Reproduction of an existing property by purchase or production of an identical property.

(4) Determining non-monetary benefits or characteristics that contribute to value. The rendering of judgments as to age, remaining life, condition, quality, or authenticity of physical property, amenities; an estimate of the amount of a natural resource, population increase, nature of market, rate of absorption, etc.

1.22 In a valuation and in a forecast of earning power, the word *property* is used to describe *the rights to the future benefits of something owned or possessed to the exclusion of other persons.* The "something owned" may be tangible, intangible or both.

In a cost estimation, the word *property* is used to describe the "something owned" without regard to its ownership.

1.3 Purpose of Promulgating the Principles of Appraisal Practice and Code of Ethics

The Principles of Appraisal Practice and Code of Ethics of the American Society of Appraisers are promulgated to :

1.31 Inform those who use the services of appraisers what, in the opinion of Society, constitutes competent and ethical appraisal practice;

1.32 Serve as a guide to its own members in achieving competency in appraisal practice and in adhering to ethical standards;

1.33 Aid in the accomplishment of the purposes of the Society, which include:

    (a) Fosterage of appraisal education,

    (b) Improvement and development of appraisal techniques,

    (c) Encouragement of sound professional practices,

    (d) Establishment of criteria of sound performance for use of employers of staff appraisers,

    (e) Enforcement of ethical conduct and practice by its members;

1.34 Provide means, auxiliary to those used in examining applicants for admission to the grades of Members and Senior Member of the Society, for judging their skill, competence, and understanding of ethical principles;

1.35 Epitomize those appraisal practices that experience has found to be effective in protecting the public against exploitation.

2 OBJECTIVES OF APPRAISAL WORK

2.1 Various Kinds of Objectives of Appraisal Work

An appraisal is undertaken for one or more of several objectives, namely: to determine the value of a property; to estimate the cost of producing, acquiring, altering, or completing a property; to estimate the monetary amount of damages to a property; and to forecast the monetary earning power of a property. In specific instances, the work may have additional objectives, such as: the formulation of conclusions and recommendations or the presentations of alternatives (and their consequences) for the client's actions.

2.2 Objective Character of the Results of an Appraisal Undertaking

The primary objective of a monetary appraisal, is determination of a numerical result, either as a range or most probable point magnitude—the dollar amount of a value, the dollar amount of an estimated cost, the dollar amount of an estimated earning power. This numerical result is objective and unrelated to the desires, wishes, or needs of the client who engages the appraiser to perform the work. The amount of this figure is as independent of what someone desires it to be as a physicist's measurement of the melting point of lead or an accountant's statement of the

amount of net profits of a corporation. All the principles of appraisal ethics stem from this central fact.

3 APPRAISER'S PRIMARY DUTY AND RESPONSIBILITY

The appraiser's duty and responsibility, in each subject case, is twofold.

3.1 Appraiser's Obligation to Determine and Describe the Apposite Kind of Value or Estimated Cost

First, because there are several kinds of value and several kinds of cost estimates, each of which has a legitimate place as the end point of some class of appraisal engagement, it is the appraiser's obligation to ascertain which one of these is pertinent to the particular undertaking. In meeting this obligation, the appraiser may consider his client's instructions and/or may obtain legal or other professional advice, but the selection of the apposite kind of value or estimated cost is the appraiser's sole responsibility. Also, it is his obligation, in this connection, fully to explain and describe what is meant by the particular value or cost estimate which he has determined, in order to obviate misunderstanding and to prevent unwitting or deliberate misapplication. For example, an appraisal engagement which calls for the determination of the replacement cost of a merchant's inventory of goods, for insurance purposes, would not be properly discharged by an appraisal of its retail market value; and an engagement which calls for the determination of the current market value of a multi-tenant office building leasehold estate, would not be properly discharged by a determination of the depreciated new cost of replacement of the improvements.

3.2 Appraiser's Obligation to Determine Numerical Results with Whatever Degree of Accuracy the Particular Objectives of the Appraisal Necessitate

Second, it is the appraiser's obligation to determine the appropriate and applicable numerical results with as high a degree of accuracy as the particular objectives of the appraisal necessitate.

3.3 Appraiser's Obligation to Avoid Giving a False Numerical Result

Obviously, the appraiser has every obligation to avoid giving a false figure. The numerical result of an appraisal could be false for one of two reasons: it could be false because it is a grossly inaccurate estimate of the apposite kind of value or cost estimate, or it could be false, even though numerically accurate, because it is an estimate of an inapposite kind of value of cost estimate.

3.4 Appraiser's Obligation to Attain Competency and to Practice Ethically

In order to meet his obligations, the appraiser must be competent in his field. This competency he attains by education, training, study, practice, and experience. He must also recognize, understand, and abide by those ethical principles that are interwoven with and are an essential part of truly professional practice.

3.5 Professional Character of Appraisal Practice

The members of the Society are engaged in a professional activity. A profession is based on an organized body of specific knowledge—knowledge not possessed by laymen. It is of such a character that it requires a high degree of intelligence and considerable expenditure of time and effort to acquire it and to become adept in its application. An appraiser's client, relies on the appraiser's professional knowledge and abilities to whatever extent may be necessary to accomplish the objectives of the work. Members of the Society recognize this relationship.

3.6 **Appraiser's Fiduciary Relationship to Third Parties**

Under certain specific circumstances an appraisal report may be given by a client to a third party for their use. If the purpose of the appraisal includes a specific use by a third party, the third party has a right to rely on the validity and objectivity of the appraiser's findings as regards the specific stated purpose and intended use for which the appraisal was originally made. Members of the Society recognize their responsibility to those parties, other than the client, who may be specifically entitled to make use of their reports.

4 **APPRAISER'S OBLIGATION TO HIS CLIENT**

The appraiser's primary obligation to his client is to reach complete, accurate, and pertinent conclusions and numerical results regardless of the client's wishes or instructions in this regard. The relationship between client and appraiser is not one of principal and agent. However, the appraiser's obligation to his client go somewhat beyond this primary obligation. These secondary obligations are set forth in the following sections.

4.1 **Confidential Character of an Appraisal Engagement**

The fact that an appraiser has been employed to make an appraisal is a confidential matter. In some instances, the very fact of employment may be information that a client, whether private or a public agency, prefers for valid reasons to keep confidential. Knowledge by outsiders of the fact of employment of an appraiser may jeopardize a client's proposed enterprise or transaction. Consequently, it is improper for the appraiser to disclose the fact of his engagement, unless the client approves of the disclosure or clearly has no interest in keeping the fact of the engagement confidential, or unless the appraiser is required by due process of law to disclose the fact of his engagement.

In the absence of an express agreement to the contrary, the identifiable contents of an appraisal report are the property of the appraiser's client or employer and, ethically, cannot be submitted to any professional Society as evidence of professional qualifications, and cannot be published in any identifiable form without the client's or employer's consent.

4.2 **Appraiser's Obligation to Give Competent Service**

It is not proper for an appraiser to accept an engagement to make an appraisal of property of a type he is not qualified to appraise or in a field outside his Society membership classification, unless (a) he fully acquaints the client with the limitations of his qualifications or (b) he associates himself with another appraiser or appraisers who possess the required qualifications.

As a corollary to the above principle, the Society declares that it is unethical for an appraiser to claim or imply that he has professional qualifications which he does not possess or to state his qualifications in a form which may be subject to erroneous interpretation (See Sec. 7.8)

4.3 **Appraiser's Obligation Relative to Giving Testimony**

When an appraiser is engaged by one of the parties in a controversy, it is unethical for the appraiser to suppress any facts, data, or opinions which are adverse to the case his client is trying to establish; or to over-emphasize any facts, data, or opinions which are favorable to his client's case; or in any other particulars to become an advocate. It is the appraiser's obligation to present the data, analysis, and value without bias, regardless of the effect of such unbiased presentation on his client's case. (Also, see Sec. 7.5)

4.4 **Appraiser's Obligation to Document Appraisal Testimony**

When a member accepts employment to make an appraisal, or to testify as to value of property before a court of law or other judicial or quasi-judicial forums, the appraiser shall, before testifying, complete an adequate written appraisal report, or have complete documentation and substantiation available in his files.

4.5 **Appraiser's Obligation Relative to Serving More Than One Client in the Same Matter**

When two or more potential clients seek an appraiser's services with respect to the same property or with respect to the same legal action, the appraiser may not properly serve more than one, except with the consent of all parties.

4.6 **Agreements and Contracts for Appraisal Services**

It is good practice to have a written contract, or at least a clear oral agreement, between appraiser and client, covering objectives and scope of work, time of delivery of report, and amount of fees. In certain circumstances, it may be desirable to include in the appraisal-service contract a statement covering the objective character of appraisal findings and a statement that the appraiser cannot act as an advocate or negotiator.

5 **APPRAISER'S OBLIGATION TO OTHER APPRAISERS AND TO THE SOCIETY**

5.1 **Protection of Professional Reputation of Other Appraisers**

The appraiser has an obligation to protect the professional reputation of all appraisers (whether members of the Society or not) who subscribe to and practice in accord with the Principles of Appraisal Practice of the Society. The Society declares that it is unethical for an appraiser to injure, or attempt to injure, by false or malicious statements or by innuendo the professional reputation or prospects of any appraiser.

5.2 **Appraiser's Obligation Relative to Society's Disciplinary Actions**

A member of the society, having knowledge of an act by another member which, in his opinion, is in violation of the ethical principles incorporated in the Principles of Appraisal Practice and Code of Ethics of the Society, has the obligation to report the matter in accordance with the procedure specified in the Constitution and Bylaws.

It is the appraiser's obligation to cooperate with the Society and its officers in all matters, including investigation, censure, discipline, or dismissal of members who are charged with violation of the *Principles of Appraisal Practice and Code of Ethics* of the Society.

6 APPRAISAL METHODS AND PRACTICES

6.1 Various Kinds of Value

The Society recognizes that different kinds of property may have different kinds of value depending on the particular attendant circumstances and, further, that there are both basic and subordinate kinds of value. Good professional practice requires that the appraiser describe in sufficient detail, in each case, the nature and meaning of the specific value that he is determining.

6.2 Selection of Appraisal Method

The procedure and method for determining the particular value in question is a matter for the appraiser himself to determine—he cannot be held responsible for the result unless he has a free hand in selecting the process by which that result is to be obtained. However, good appraisal practice requires that the method selected be adequate for the purpose, embrace consideration of all the factors that have a bearing on the value, and be presented in a clear and logical manner.

6.3 Fractional Appraisals

Certain classes of properties (real estate, business enterprise, collections of chattels, for example) can be considered as made up of components (for example, in the case of real estate: land and buildings; in the case of a business enterprise: land, buildings, machinery and equipment, contracts, and goodwill). If an element is considered as an integrated part of the whole property, its value, in general, is different from the value the same element has if considered as a fraction separated from the whole property.

An appraisal of an element of a whole property, considered by itself and ignoring its relation to the rest of the whole property, is called a "fractional appraisal." There are legitimate uses for fractional appraisals (appraisal of buildings for fire insurance purposes; appraisal to determine the value of land as if cleared of existing improvements; appraisal in connection with public utility rate-making, etc.) but good practice requires that a fractional appraisal be labeled as such and that the limitations on its use by the client and/or third parties be clearly stated.

6.4 Contingent and Limiting Conditions Affecting an Appraisal

In many instances the validity of the appraiser's conclusions as to the value of a subject property is contingent upon the validity of statements, information, and/or data upon which he has relied, supplied to him by members of other professions or secured by him from official sources. Such material may be obtained, for example, from architects, engineers, lawyers, accountants, government officials, government agencies, etc. It is proper for the appraiser to rely upon and use such material provided (1) he states in his report that he has done so, (2) he stands ready to make his sources and/or the material itself available for any required verification, and (3) he does not pass to others the responsibility for matters that are, or should be, within the scope of his own professional knowledge.

Good appraisal practice requires that the appraiser state any other contingent or limiting conditions which affect the appraisal, such as, for example, that the value is contingent upon the completion of projected public or private improvements, etc.

6.5 Hypothetical Appraisals

A hypothetical appraisal is an appraisal based on assumed conditions which are contrary to fact or which are improbable of realization or consummation. The Society takes the position that there are legitimate uses for some hypothetical appraisals, but that it is improper and unethical to issue a hypothetical appraisal report unless (1) the value is clearly labeled as hypothetical (2) the legitimate purpose for which the appraisal was made is stated, and (3) the conditions which were assumed contrary to fact are set forth.

A hypothetical appraisal showing the value of a company which it is proposed to form by merging two existing companies would be deemed to serve a legitimate purpose. On the other hand, a hypothetical appraisal of a projected apartment house, based on an assumed rent schedule which is so much above the market that it is practically impossible for it to be realized, would not serve any legitimate purpose and its issuance might well lead to the defrauding of some unwary investor.

6.6 Appraisals In Which Access to Pertinent Data is Denied

Situations sometimes occur in which data that the appraiser considers pertinent to the making of a valid appraisal are in existence but access to them is denied to the appraiser, either by the client or some other party (for example: the past production records of an oil field; the records of prior revenue and expense of a motel property; etc.). In such a case, the appraiser, at his option, may properly decline to carry out the assignment. In the event he considers such data *essential* to the making of a valid appraisal, he may not properly proceed with the assignment.

6.7 Ranges of Value or Estimated Cost and Reliability Estimates

Some appraisal engagements call for the determination of a probable range of value or estimated cost, either with or without a collateral statement of the most probable figure within that range. It is entirely within the scope of good appraisal practice to give a range of value or estimated cost.

Inasmuch as the appraiser's determination of the amount of a value or an estimated cost cannot, by its very nature, be exact, it is good appraisal practice to append to such numerical results a statement as to the degree of reliability to be accorded thereto. Such reliability estimates are usually expressed as plus and minus percentages.

6.8 Values or Estimated Costs Under Different Hypotheses

The objective of an appraisal undertaking may be the determination of different values or different cost estimates based on different hypotheses. It is entirely within the scope of good appraisal practice to give such differing numerical results, provided the appraiser adheres to the principles set forth in Sec. 3.1 and Sec. 6.5

6.9 Inspection, Investigation, Analysis, and Description of Subject Property

The valuation of a property is a procedure based on an analysis of all the characteristics of the property which contribute to or detract from its value; good appraisal practice requires that the appraiser's inspection, investigation, and study be thorough enough to uncover all of the pertinent characteristics.

Good appraisal practice requires that the description of the property, tangible or intangible, which is the subject of a valuation, cover adequately (a) identification of the property (b) statement of the legal rights and restrictions comprised in the ownership, and (c) the characteristics of the property which contribute to or detract from its value.

In the case of chattels and prospective real estate improvements, identification is particularly important in order to prevent unscrupulous persons from representing the appraisal as applying to substituted inferior property.

In general, the legal rights of the ownership of chattels are obvious and need not be stated; but, in the case of real property, statements of zoning restrictions, building codes, easements, leases, etc., are essential elements of the description. It is understood, however, that the legal rights of the ownership of an interest in real property are matters of legal, not appraisal, opinion, and that the appraiser discharges his obligations in this regard by stating the sources of these data. (See Sec. 6.4) In the case of intangible properties (patents, contracts, franchises, etc.) the documentary provisions not only define what the property is, they also set forth the legal rights and descriptions.

The physical condition of chattels or real property is an element contributing to or detracting from their value; good appraisal practice requires adequate inspection and investigation to determine it.

6.10 Collaboration Between Appraisers and Utilization of the Services of Members of Other Professions

Collaboration between appraisers is desirable, in some situations, to expedite the completion of work and, in other situations, to obtain the benefits of combined judgment or combined data. Such collaboration is entirely proper providing all the collaborators sign a joint report or, if there be dissenting opinions, providing these dissenting opinions are made a part of the report.

In some cases, the nature of the appraisal undertaking calls for special professional knowledge and abilities in addition to those possessed by the appraiser. In such an instance, it is both necessary and proper for the appraiser to employ other appraisers and/or members of other professions to obtain data and derive conclusions relative to specific parts of the work. The principal appraiser builds his final conclusions, in part, on these contributions, taking responsibility for the final result but subject to the validity of the underlying or constituent contributions. (See Sec. 6.4)

7 UNETHICAL AND UNPROFESSIONAL APPRAISAL PRACTICES

The principles of appraisal practice given in Sec. 6 relate to the primary objective of an appraisal undertaking, namely the determination of the apposite numerical result with that degree of accuracy required by the attendant circumstances, whereas the principles given in this section (Sec. 7) relate to the establishment and maintenance of the confidence of clients and other interested parties in the validity of the results of appraisal undertakings. To this end, certain practices are declared by the Society to be unethical and unprofessional.

7.1 Contingent Fees

If an appraiser were to accept an engagement for which the amount of his compensation is contingent upon the amount of an award in a property settlement or a court action where his services are employed; or is contingent upon the amount of a tax reduction obtained by a client where his services are used; or is contingent upon the consummation of the sale or financing of a property in connection with which his services are utilized or is contingent upon his reaching any finding or conclusion specified by his client; then, anyone considering using the results of the appraiser's undertaking might well suspect that these results were biased and self-serving and therefore, invalid. Such suspicion would militate against the establishment and maintenance of trust and confidence in the results of appraisal work, generally; therefore the Society declares that the contracting for or acceptance of any such contingent fee is unethical and unprofessional.

As a corollary to the above principle relative to contingent fees, the Society declares that it is unethical and unprofessional for an appraiser (a) to contract for or accept compensation for appraisal services in the form of a commission, rebate, division of brokerage commissions, or any similar forms and (b) to receive or pay finder's or referral fees.

7.2 Percentage Fees

The Society takes the position that it is unprofessional and unethical for the appraiser to contract to do work for a fixed percentage of the amount of value, or of the estimated cost (as the case may be) which he determines at the conclusion of his work.

7.3 Disinterested Appraisals

Anyone using an appraiser who has an interest or a contemplated future interest in the property appraised, might well suspect that the report was biased and self-serving and, therefore, that the findings were invalid. Such suspicion tends to break down trust and confidence in the results of appraisal work, generally.

Interests which an appraiser may have in a property which is to be appraised, include ownership of the subject property; acting, or having some expectation of acting, as agent in the purchase, sale, or financing of the subject property; and managing, or have some expectation of managing, the subject property. Such interests are particularly apt to exist if the appraiser, while engaged in professional appraisal practice, is also engaged in a related retail business (real estate, jewelry, furs, antiques, fine arts, etc.).

The Society declares that, subject to the provision for disclosure given in the following paragraph, it is unethical and unprofessional for an appraiser to accept an assignment to appraise a property in which he has an interest or a contemplated future interest.

However, if a prospective client, after full disclosure by the appraiser of his present or contemplated future interest in the subject property, still desires to have the appraiser do the work, the latter may properly accept the engagement provided he discloses the nature and extent of his interest in his appraisal report.

7.4 Responsibility Connected with Signatures to Appraisal Reports

The user of an appraisal report, before placing reliance on its conclusions, is entitled to assume that the party signing the report is responsible for the findings, either because he did the work himself or because the work was done under his supervision.

In cases where two or more appraisers are employed to prepare a joint report, the user thereof is entitled to assume that, if all of them sign it, they are jointly and severally responsible for the validity of all of the findings therein; and, if all do not sign, he has a right to know what the dissenting opinions are.

In cases where two or more appraisers have been engaged by a single client to make independent appraisals of the same property, the client has the right to expect that he will receive opinions which have been reached independently and that he may use them as checks against each other and/or have evidence of the range within which the numerical results lie.

To implement these principles, the Society declares that it is unethical (a) to misrepresent who made an appraisal by appending the signature of any person who neither did the work himself nor had the work done under his supervision, (b) in the case of a joint report to omit any signatures or any dissenting opinions, (c) in case two or more appraisers have collaborated in an appraisal undertaking, for them, or any of them, to issue separate appraisal reports, and (d) in case two or more appraisers have been engaged by a single client to make independent appraisals of the same property, for them to collaborate or consult with one another or make use of each other's findings or figures.

An appraisal firm or corporation may properly use a corporate signature with the signature of a responsible officer thereof. But the person who actually did the appraisal for the corporation must sign the corporate appraisal report or the report must acknowledge the person who actually made the appraisal.

7.5 Advocacy

If an appraiser, in the writing of a report or in giving an exposition of it before third parties or in giving testimony in a court action suppresses or minimizes any facts, data, or opinions which, if fully stated, might militate against the accomplishment of his client's objective or, if he adds any irrelevant data or unwarranted favorable opinions or places an improper emphasis on any relevant facts for the purpose of aiding his client in accomplishing his objective, he is, in the opinion of the Society, an advocate. Advocacy, as here described, affects adversely the establishment and maintenance of trust and confidence in the results of professional appraisal practice and the Society declares that it is unethical and unprofessional. (Also, see Sec. 4.3).

7.6 Unconsidered Opinions and Preliminary Reports

If an appraiser gives an opinion as to the value, earning power, or estimated cost of a property without having ascertained and weighed all of the pertinent facts, such opinion, except by an extraordinary coincidence, will be inaccurate. The giving of such offhand opinions tends to belittle the importance of inspection, investigation, and analysis in appraisal procedure and lessens the confidence with which the results of good appraisal practice are received, and therefore the Society declares the giving of hasty and unconsidered opinions to be unprofessional.

If an appraiser makes a preliminary report without including a statement to the effect that it is preliminary and that the figures given are subject to refinement or change when the final report is completed, there is the possibility that some user of the report, being under the impression that it is a final and completed report, will accord the figures a degree of accuracy and reliability they do not possess. The results of such misplaced confidence could be damaging to the reputation of professional appraisers, generally, as well as of the appraiser concerned. To obviate this possibility, the Society declares it to be unprofessional appraisal practice to omit a proper limiting and qualifying statement in a preliminary report.

7.7 Advertising and Solicitation

It is not unethical to advertise the availability of appraisal services. It is unethical to use any inaccurate, misleading, false or deceptive claim, promise or representation in connection with any advertisement. These unethical practices are considered by the Society to be detrimental to the establishment and maintenance of public confidence in the results of appraisal work. The Society declares that such practices on the part of an appraiser constitute unethical and unprofessional conduct. It would be unethical to do the following:

(a) Misrepresent in any way one's connection or affiliation with the ASA or any other organization;

(b) Misrepresent one's background, education, training or expertise;

(c) Misrepresent services available or an appraiser's prior or current service to any client, or identify any client without the express written permission of such client to be identified in advertising;

(d) Represent, guarantee or imply that a particular valuation or estimate of value or result of an engagement will be tailored or adjusted to any particular use or conclusion other than that an appraisal will be based upon an honest and accurate adherence to the Principles of Appraisal Practice.

7.8 Misuse of Membership Designations

The Constitution and Bylaws of the Society establish three professional grades of membership, namely, Member, Senior Member, and Fellow. (An Affiliate or Candidate does not hold a professional grade of membership in the Society.) The designation "A.M.," meaning Accredited Member, may be used in the grade of a Member. The designation "A.S.A.," meaning Accredited Senior Appraiser, may be used only in the grade of Senior Member, except those Senior Members certified in the classification of Real Property Residential (1-4 Units) who use the designation "A.S.A Residential." The designation "F.A.S.A." may be used only by Fellows. The Society declares that it is unethical for a member to claim or imply that he holds a higher degree of membership than he has attained. (Also, see Bylaws Art. B-27.)

7.9 Causes for Disciplinary Action by the Society

Disciplinary action against the members of the Society is taken in the event of violations of specific provisions of the Society's Constitution and Bylaws or of its *Principles of Appraisal Practice and the Code of Ethics* incorporated therein. Such actions are under of jurisdiction of the International President, the International Ethics Committee, and the Board of Governors. Violations may fall under six categories:

(1) Deviations from good appraisal practice

(2) Failure to fulfill obligations and responsibilities

(3) Unprofessional conduct

(4) Unethical conduct

(5) Conviction in any judicial tribunal of a) any felony or b) any misdemeanor for which the maximum penalty is three (3) years in jail or more regardless of the actual sentence imposed or c) any misdemeanor involving honesty or veracity, i.e., involving theft or false statement regardless of the actual sentence imposed.

(6) Any unlawful, illegal or immoral conduct (even if not convicted in a judicial tribunal) which would bring disrepute to the appraisal profession or to the American Society of Appraisers.

After due investigation, the Society may take action in the form of suggestion, censure, suspension, or expulsion, in which last event the member will be required to surrender his Certificate, membership pin, and other evidences of his membership after its termination.

8 APPRAISAL REPORTS

In preceding sections it was stated that good appraisal practice, as defined by the Society, requires the inclusion of certain specific explanations, descriptions, and statements in an appraisal report. These are summarized herewith. (These requirements do not apply to reports prepared by a staff appraiser for the exclusive and non-public use of his employer; but do apply to reports prepared by a public appraiser, i.e., one who offers his services for a fee to the general public.)

8.1 Description of the Property Which Is the Subject of an Appraisal Report

It is required that the property with which an appraisal report is concerned, whether tangible, intangible, real, or personal, be fully described therein, the elements of such description being: (a) identification, (b) legal rights and restrictions encompassed in the ownership, where these are not obvious, (c) value characteristics, and (d) physical condition, where applicable. (See Sec. 6.8)

8.2 Statement of the Objectives of the Appraisal Work

It is required that an appraisal report include a statement of the objectives for which the work was performed: to determine a value, to estimate a cost, to forecast an earning power, to ascertain certain facts, to reach conclusions and make recommendations for action in specified matters, etc. (See Sec. 2.1)

It is required that the meaning attached by the appraiser to any specific kind of value or estimated cost which is the objective of the appraisal undertaking be described and explained in the appraisal report. (See Sec. 6.1)

It is required that an appraisal report include a statement as to the date which the value estimate, cost estimate or forecast of income applies.

When appropriate, an analysis of the highest and the best use of the property should be included in the investigation and study.

8.3 Statement of the Contingent and Limiting Conditions to Which the Appraisal Findings Are Subject

It is required that statements, information, and/or data, which were obtained by the appraiser from members of other professions, or official or other presumably reliable sources, and the validity of which affects the appraisal findings, be summarized or stated in full in the appraisal report and the sources given, so that verification desired by any user of the report may be accomplished. (See Sec. 6.4)

If an appraisal is a hypothetical one, it is required that it be labeled as hypothetical, that the reason a hypothetical appraisal was made be stated, and that the assumed hypothetical conditions be set forth. (See Sec. 6.5)

If an appraisal is a fractional appraisal. it is required that it be labeled as fractional and that the limitations on the use of the reported figure be stated. (See Sec. 6.3)

If a preliminary appraisal report is issued, namely, one in which the figures are subject to refinement or change, it is required that the report be labeled as preliminary and that the limitation on its use be stated. (See Sec 7.6)

8.4 Description and Explanation in the Appraisal Report of the Appraisal Method Used

It is required that the method selected by the appraiser as applicable to the subject appraisal undertaking be described and explained in the appraisal report. (See Sec. 6.2)

8.5 Statement of the Appraiser's Disinterestedness

It is required that the appraiser include a statement in his appraisal report that he has no present or contemplated future interest in the subject property or any other interest which might tend to prevent his making a fair and unbiased appraisal or, if he does have such an interest, to set forth fully the nature and extent of that interest. (See Sec. 7.3)

8.6 Appraisers Responsibility to Communicate Each Analysis, Opinion and Conclusion in a Manner that is not Misleading.

The appraiser should state in each report "I hereby certify that, to the best of my knowledge and belief, the statements of fact contained in this report are true and correct, and this report has been prepared in conformity with the Uniform

Standards of Professional Appraisal Practice of The Appraisal Foundation and the Principles of Appraisal Practice and Code of Ethics of the American Society of Appraisers.

8.7 **Mandatory Recertification Statement**

All Senior Member appraisers should state in each report "The American Society of Appraisers has a mandatory recertification program for all of its Senior members. 'I am' or 'I am not' in compliance with that program."

8.8 **Signatures to Appraisal Reports and the Inclusion of Dissenting Opinions**

It is required that the party who makes the appraisal or who has the appraisal made under his supervision sign the appraisal report. (See Sec. 7.4)

It is required that all collaborating appraisers, issuing a joint the report, who agree with the findings, sign the report; and that any collaborating appraiser who disagrees with any or all of the findings of the others, prepare, sign, and include in the appraisal report his dissenting opinion. (See Sec. 7.4)

▲

Appendix 3

Ethics Provision of The Uniform Standards of Professional Appraisal Practice©
Excerpt from the Uniform Standards of Professional Appraisal Practice, 1994 Edition

© 1994 by The Appraisal Foundation

Because of the fiduciary responsibilities inherent in professional appraisal practice, the appraiser must observe the highest standards of professional ethics. This Ethics Provision is divided into four sections: Conduct, management, confidentiality, and record keeping.

Comment: This provision emphasizes the personal obligations and responsibilities of the individual appraiser. However, it should also be emphasized that groups and organizations engaged in appraisal practice share the same ethical obligations.

Conduct

An appraiser must perform ethically and competently in accordance with these standards and not engage in conduct that is unlawful, unethical, or improper. An appraiser who could reasonably be perceived to act as a disinterested third party in rendering an unbiased appraisal, review, or consulting service must perform assignments with impartiality, objectivity, and independence and without accommodation of personal interests.

Comment: An appraiser is required to avoid any action that could be considered misleading or fraudulent. In particular, it is unethical for an appraiser to use or communicate a misleading or fraudulent report or to knowingly permit an employee or other person to communicate a misleading or fraudulent report.

The development of an appraisal, review, or consulting service based on a hypothetical condition is unethical unless: 1) the use of the hypothesis is clearly disclosed; 2) the assumption of the hypothetical condition is clearly required for legal purposes, for purposes of reasonable analysis, or for purposes of comparison and would not be misleading; and 3) the report clearly describes the rationale for this assumption, the nature of the hypothetical condition, and its effect on the result of the appraisal, review, or consulting service.

An individual appraiser employed by a group or organization which conducts itself in a manner that does not conform to these standards should take steps that are appropriate under the circumstances to ensure compliance with the standards.

Management

The acceptance of compensation that is contingent upon the reporting of a predetermined value or a direction in value that favors the cause of the client, the amount of the value estimate, the attainment of a stipulated result, or the occurrence of a subsequent event is unethical.

The payment of undisclosed fees, commissions, or things of value in connection with the procurement of appraisal, review, or consulting assignments is unethical.

Comment: Disclosure of fees, commissions, or things or value connected to the procurement of an assignment should appear in the certification of a written report and in any transmittal letter in which conclusions are stated. In groups or organizations engaged in appraisal practice, intra-company payments to employees for business development are not considered to be unethical. Competency, rather than financial incentives, should be the primary basis for awarding an assignment.

Advertising for or soliciting appraisal assignments in a manner which is false, misleading or exaggerated is unethical.

Comment: In groups or organizations engaged in appraisal practice, decisions concerning finder or referral fees, contingent compensation, and advertising may not be the responsibility of an individual appraiser, but for a particular assignment, it is the responsibility of the individual appraiser to ascertain that there has been no breach of ethics, that the appraisal is prepared in accordance with these standards, and that the report can be properly certified as required by Standards Rules 2-3, 3-2, 5-3, 6-8, 8-3 or 10-3.

The restriction on contingent compensation in the first paragraph of this section does not apply to consulting assignments where the appraiser is not acting in a disinterested manner and would not reasonably be perceived as performing a service that requires impartiality. This permitted contingent compensation must be properly disclosed in the report.

> Comment: Assignments where the appraiser is not acting in a disinterested manner are further discussed in the General Comment to Standard 4. The preparer of the written report of such an assignment must certify that the compensation is contingent and must explain the basis for the contingency in the report (See S.R. 5-3) and in any transmittal letter in which conclusions are stated.

Confidentiality

An appraiser must protect the confidential nature of the appraiser-client relationship.

> Comment: An appraiser must not disclose confidential factual data obtained from a client or the results of an assignment prepared for a client to anyone other than: 1) the client and persons specifically authorized by the client; 2) such third parties as may be authorized by due process of law; and 3) a duly authorized professional peer review committee. As a corollary, it is unethical for a member of a duly authorized professional peer review committee to disclose confidential information or factual data presented to the committee.

Record Keeping

An appraiser must prepare written records of appraisal, review, and consulting assignments—including oral testimony and reports—and retain such records for a period of at least five (5) years after preparation or at least two (2) years after final disposition of any judicial proceeding in which testimony was given, whichever period expires last.

> Comment: Written records of assignments include true copies of written reports, written summaries of oral testimony and reports (or a transcript of testimony), all data and statements required by these standards, and other information as may be required to support the findings and conclusions of the appraiser. The term written records also includes information stored on electronic, magnetic, or other media. Such records must be made available by the appraiser when required by due process of law or by a duly authorized professional peer review committee.

▲

Appendix 4
Examples of Approaches to Value

Income Approach

Heritage Leasing of Texas offers its corporate clients a wide selection of antiques, art and oriental rugs for furnishing their offices. One of the items most in demand is an English mahogany partners' desk with hand carved legs and leather top. How much can they afford to pay for one?

A series of assumptions must be made, based on the record of performance of desks owned and previously leased by Heritage. After buying a "new" desk, they usually have a craftsman refurbish it, which takes three months and costs $400. Usually a month passes between return of a desk to inventory and its installation in a client's office. Delivery and installation cost Heritage $60; insurance costs $20 per year. The terms of a lease are monthly payment for a one year term; the typical client keeps a desk for three years. The expected life of the desk in commercial use is 10 years; after that, Heritage will refurbish it or sell it, but they don't want to count on that now. More pedestrian pedestal desks they lease for $25 per month; they plan to charge $60 per month for a partners' desk. For desks now in service, they paid $1350 to $1600.

The capitalization rate can be derived from the performance of the pedestal desks. The standard formula is:

Present Value = Total Net Income / Period x Factor

The Factor will tell us the capitalization rate achieved, so to isolate it the formula is rearranged as:

Present Value x Period / Total Net Income = Factor

The Present Value is the price paid, $1,350 to $1,600. Since the income is paid monthly, the Period also is expressed in months: 10 years = 120 months. In calculating Total Net Income, there is Vacancy to consider, since the desks typically are returned after three years and it takes one month to place them with another client; one month every three years = 3 months in ten years. A desk generates income for 117 months (120 - 3) in 10 years. The Gross Income from a pedestal desk, then, is $25 per month x 117 months = $2,925. Expenses to be subtracted are refurbishing ($400), installation (3 times @ $60) and insurance ($20 per year x 10 years).

Gross Income	=	$2,925.
less Expenses		
Refurbishing	-$400.	
Installation	-$180.	
Insurance	-$200.	
Total Net Income	=	$2,145.

Substituting in the formula with the lowest price paid,

$1,350 x 120 months / $2,145 = Factor

75.52 = Factor

Looking in the annuity tables, in the monthly column for a 10 year period, we find that 75.67 is the factor in the 10% table. Substituting in the formula with the highest price paid,

$1,600 x 120 months / $2,145 = Factor

89.5 = Factor

Looking in the annuity tables, we find that 90.07 is the factor for a 6% rate, looking again in the monthly column for a 10 year period. Therefore, the record of performance of pedestal desks indicates a rate of 6% to 10% is appropriate.

The Net Income of a pedestal desk would be:

Gross Income =$60/month x

117 months less Expenses,	=	$7,020.
Refurbishing	-$400.	
Installation	-$180.	
Insurance	-$200.	
Total Net Income	=	$6,240.

The value of a partners' desk at the beginning of the lease period at a 10% rate, is:

Present Value = Total Net Income / Period x Factor

Present Value = $6,240 / 120 x 75.67

Present Value = $3,935

At a 6% rate, the value of a partner's desk is:

Present Value = $6,240 / 120 x 90.07

Present Value = $4,684

However, the lease period begins 5 months after they purchase the desk, after refurbishing and marketing. The diminished value due to that waiting period can be calculated by treating the Present Value of the annuity calculations as a Reversion, a lump sum payable 5 months in the future. The appropriate Factor will be found in tables of Reversion Factors, in the monthly column with a 5 month period. At a 10% rate, the Factor is .959; substituting in the formula:

Present Value = Future Value x Factor
Present Value = $3,935 x .959
Present Value = $3,774

At a 6% rate, the Factor is .975; substituting in the formula:

Present Value = $4,684 x .975
Present Value = $4,567

Now we have the answer Heritage Leasing sought: they can pay $3,775 to $4,500 for a desk. The lower the price they pay, the higher the rate of return on their investment. If they pay $3,775, they will earn 10%; if they pay $4,500, they will earn only 6%.

For more complete understanding of this example and approach, see the Annuity and Reversion tables from *Basic Real Estate Appraisal* by Richard Betts and Silas Ely, or the Monthly Compound Interest Tables in Appendix B of *Questions & Answers to help you pass the Appraisal Certification Exams* by Jeffrey Fisher and Dennis Tosh.

Cost Approach

Artist

Material	$ 500.00	Canvas, paint, etc.
Direct Labor	10,400.00	6 mo. @ $10/hr
Overhead	6,000.00	6 mo. @ $1,000 mo.
Subtotal	$ 16,900.00	
Profit	4,200.00	25% rounded
	$ 21,100.00	

Gallery/Dealer — 100% Markup
    Asking Price — $42,200.00

TOTAL COST APPROACH
Breakdown

Overhead	$ 6,000.00	28.44%
Promotion	1,000.00	4.74%
Labor	5,000.00	23.70%
Profit	4,200.00	20.00%
Risk Premium	4,900.00	23.12%
	$21,100.00	100.00%

Reproduction Cost New Estimate: $42,200.00

▲

Appendix 5
Glossary of Terms

Agents of Production

Agents of Production is the market principle that states that all production results from four agents in balance: Labor, Land or Materials, Capital and Coordination. The loss of balance in any of these makes production inefficient.

Annuity

An annuity is a stream of regular payments at regular intervals.

Anticipation

Anticipation holds that value is created by anticipation of future benefits.

Appraisals

Appraisals are written or oral reports which communicate value.

Arbitration

Arbitration is a quasi-judicial proceeding in which a dispute is sumbitted to one or more impartial parties for a binding determination made by the arbitrator(s).

Binding Arbitration

Compulsory Binding Arbitration is the term used when, in following a statute, government arbitrators, not chosen by the parties, impose the award.

Voluntary Binding Arbitration is the term used when both parties select the arbitrators.

Blockage

Blockage is a form of depreciation resulting from a number of similar properties being offered that is too large for the normal market to absorb as of a specific date.

Change

Change is the market principle which recognizes the shifting importance of other principles. It recognizes the interplay progression and regression, contribution, competition, and explains the cycles of market development, stabilization, decline and renewal.

Characteristics of Value

Characteristics of Value are primarily questions of fact and have an objective relationship to the marketplace.

Competition

Principle of Competition states that competition arises from profits and that the reverse is true, i.e., profits create competition.

Concentration Ratio

When a few players are responsible for a high proportion of sales, a market is said to have a high Concentration Ratio.

Conformity

Conformity is a principle that basically has to do with trends, cycles and general market attitudes.

Condition

Condition is the physical description of the property as to its completeness for performing an identified role. Impairments could be any form of damage or loss of components, wear and tear, or inappropriate or unacceptable repairs.

Constant Dollars

Constant Dollars are dollars which have been adjusted for the change in their purchasing power over time.

Consumer Price Index

Consumer Price Index is the total cost of purchasing a large and varied "market basket" of consumer goods, compared to the total cost in other years and expressed as a ratio.

Contribution

Contribution as a principle states that certain attributes contribute to the value of the whole, and the lack of the same particular attributes detracts from the valuation of the whole.

Cost Approach

Cost Approach is research and analysis of the cost of a substitute property with equivalent function and desirability, providing an estimate of the depreciated reproduction, reproduction new or replacement cost new of the property.

Current Dollar

Current Dollar is the unadjusted value of money at any point in time.

Demand

Demand is what buyers are willing and able to pay to possess something.

Depreciation

Depreciation is a loss from the upper limit of value due to any cause contributing to the ultimate retirement of the property.

Economic Obsolescence

Economic obsolescence results from external impairments on a property's ability to meet a function. Examples are changes in optimum use, legislative enactment's restrictring use, and changes in supply and demand relationships.

Elements of Quality

Elements of Quality, are primarily questions of aesthetic judgment, independent of economics and fashion.

Ethics

Ethics is a system of moral principles or values; principles of right or good behavior; study of the general nature of morals and the specific moral choices an individual makes in relating to others; rules or standards of conduct governing the members of a profession.

Expert Witness

Expert witness is a person who by reason of education or special training and experience possesses specialized knowledge in a particular subject area.

Forensic Appraisal

Forensic appraisal is an appraisal that has been prepared for litigation purposes and one which has the qualities suitable for presentation in a court of law.

Functional Obsolescence

Functional obsolescence is measured as the difference between the subject property's ability to produce the intended result and the ability of a new replacement to produce the same result.

Highest and Best Use

Highest and Best Use of a property is the reasonable, probable, feasible and legal use of a property which results in its highest value.

Historical cost

Historical cost is the actual, first cost of the property at the time it was first placed in service.

Identification

Identification as a principle states that if the identifying characteristics of a genuine article have the same characteristics as the subject property, then the subject property is assumed to be genuine.

Income Approach

Income Approach is research and analysis of the present worth of anticipated income.

Increasing and Decreasing Returns

Increasing and Decreasing Returns as a principle states that additional units of production, consumption or investment create an increase in returns or income at first, but eventually at a decreasing rate.

Index Number

Index Number measures the relative cost of purchasing a representative "market basket" of that category of property, expressed as a ratio of the cost in a base year.

Marginal Utility

Marginal Utility as a principle states that we set value of property by measuring the units or utils of satisfaction it generates.

Market Model

Market Model is an analysis of a sample which describes a pattern in the whole population.

Market Sales Comparison Approach

The Market Comparison Approach is research and analysis comparing sales of property similar enough to the property being appraised to permit detailed comparison, estimating value by comparison with properties sold in the relevant market, with adjustments made for all differences which affect value, such as differences in characteristics of value and in time.

Measures of Central Tendency

Measures of Central Tendency comprise:

Mode: the observation which appears most frequently

Range: the difference between the largest observation and the smallest

Median: the middle value when observations are ranked, usually from the least to the greatest

Mean: the statistical average of the observations.

Mediation

Mediation is a process by which parties to a dispute voluntarily select an impartial third party to facilitate a resolution of the issues by the parties themselves.

Obsolescence

Functional Obsolescence is measured as the difference between the subject property's ability to produce the intended result and a the ability of a new replacement to produce the same result, with the subject and replacement of comparable design and category.

Economic Obsolescence results from external impairments on a property's ability to meet a function.

Technological Obsolescence results from changes in the ability to create a new substitute for a property's nction with modern methods or materials.

Original cost

Original cost is the actual cost to the current owner.

Personal Property

Personal property is tangible, movable property which is utilitarian, collectible or decorative, or in combination.

Present Worth

Present worth is a concept of value within time. It is a discount applied to a sum of value where a quantity of very similar properties would impact a market at one time.

Progression and Regression

Progression and Regression states that the value of a property placed in the context of either higher or lesser valued properties will increase or decrease respectively, by association.

Qualitative Ranking

Qualitative Ranking or Qualification as a principle states that appraisers rendering opinions on quality, or artistic merit of a property, do so by comparing the quality and characteristics of the characteristics of the subject property with those of like properties.

Reversion

Reversion is a lump sum to be paid in the future

Scarcity

Scarcity implies there must be somewhat of a limited supply of the product relative to the market demand for it. The principle of scarcity works closely with that of utility.

Stream of Income

Stream of Income is repeated payments in the future.

Substantial Evidence

Substantial Evidence is such evidence as a reasonable mind might accept as adequate to support a conclusion.

Substitution

Substitution is when a property can be easily replaced by another, the value of such property tends to be set by the cost of obtaining an equally desirable substitute property.

Supply

Supply is the amount of a thing that sellers are willing to sell at a given time and price.

Supply and Demand

Supply and Demand states that markets seek a balance between supply—the amount of a thing that sellers are willing to sell at a given price, and demand—what buyers are willing and able to buy.

Surplus Productivity

Principle of Surplus Productivity states that the production left over after a balance between supply and demand is achieved has no value.

Technological Obsolescence

Technological obsolescence results from changes in the ability to create a new substitute for a property's function with modern methods or materials.

Transferability

Transferability is the capacity of any property to change ownership. If a property cannot be sold, demand for it is not effective; thus the property has no market value and is non-marketable and non-transferable.

Value

Value is a social agreement; it is the consensus among people interested in a property of what is a reasonable price for that property.

Value in Exchange

Value In Exchange is the amount of money or things one can receive for a property. It is usually lower than a purchase price new, say a new sofa versus a used sofa.

However, it can be more than one's original investment in the instance of antiques and other works of art.

Value in Use

Value In Use is the amount of money the property is worth to the user, based on the property's ability to produce its contribution to other owned products or the personal requirements of the owner. It is a general category for ways of using things to derive benefits.

▲

About the Contributors

Richard-Raymond Alasko, ASA

Mr. Alasko is principal of The Alasko Company in Chicago. He has authored essays and articles regarding the history of art and the practice of professional appraisal. He earned his undergraduate degree with honors from Ball State University in Muncie, Indiana and his Master of Fine Arts degrees from the University of Notre Dame. He has also pursued post graduate study at Washington University in St. Louis. Mr. Alasko was one of the original developers and is an instructor of the *Principles of Valuation* courses of the American Society of Appraisers. He has also served the Society as a Regional Governor and is currently the International Secretary.

John Alico, PE, FASA, FSVA

Mr. Alico is President, Alico Engineers/Appraisers, Birmingham, MI. He has been honored as a Fellow of the American Society of Appraisers and the Incorporated Society of Valuers and Auctioneers, London, England. A graduate, School of Engineering, Columbia University, he is a registered Professional Engineer in Michigan, New York, Connecticut, and Wisconsin. Mr. Alico serves as an international consultant on metals and processing for the United Nations. He was awarded the first Bachelor of Science-Valuation Sciences Degree issued by Skidmore College. Mr. Alico is the editor of ASA's book, *Appraising Machinery and Equipment*, published by McGraw-Hill in 1988.

David Borodin, ASA

Mr. Borodin is Vice President of Frisk & Borodin Appraisers, Ltd., Philadelphia, PA, with an ASA specialty classification in Asian Art and with seventeen years experience in appraising fine and decorative arts. During that time he also acquired four years experience as an auctioneer and cataloger for The Fine Arts Co. of Philadelphia (1978-81).

Stephen Caudana, ASA

Mr. Caudana is a Southern California-based personal property appraiser accredited in Antiques and Decorative Arts. He is a graduate of the University of California, Berkeley and the London Study Centre for the Decorative Arts and has completed the four level courses of the *Principles of Valuation* series. He currently serves as Parliamentarian of the International Personal Property Committee.

Jessica L. Darraby, JD

Ms. Darraby has a bachelor of arts degree from the University of California, Los Angeles, a master of art degree from the University of California, Berkeley, and a J.D. from Boalt Hall School of Law, Berkeley. She is a member of the California Bar and is author of *Art, Artifact & Architectural Law* (1994), which has a chapter devoted to "Valuation and Appraisal." She is a court-appointed expert in state and federal courts and a judicially referred mediator and arbitrator on arts matters. An adjunct professor of law at Pepperdine University School of Law and the art law columnist for the Los Angeles Daily Journal, Professor Darraby has taught and authored chapters on professional ethics, appraisal practice, and international law and was invited by the Southern California chapter of ASA to teach a class on law and appraisal.

Bernard Ewell, ASA

Mr. Ewell is President of Bernard Ewell Art Appraisals and Restoration, with offices in Colorado Springs and Santa Fe. He is a specialist on Southwestern art, fine art graphics and the works of Salvador Dalí. A recognized national authority on Dalí prints, he serves as a professional expert witness in District, Federal, and Tax Courts and is retained by Federal and State law enforcement agencies. Mr. Ewell writes and publishes extensively.

Carolyn Price Farouki

Ms. Price Farouki is President of Art Advisory Group, an appraisal firm based in the Washington DC area. She specializes in the valuation of fine and decorative arts. She is a graduate of Christie's Fine Arts Program, London, and has completed the four level courses of the *Principles of Valuation* series, as well as the advanced personal property courses. She has written and lectured in the area of fine arts and served three years as the associate editor of the *Personal Property Journal*.

Louise T. Hall, ASA

Ms. Hall is an independent fee appraiser of antique furniture and decorative arts with offices located in Woodstock, Vermont and Cornish, New Hampshire. She has served on the Personal Property Committee, both in the capacity of Senior Editor of the *Personal*

Property Journal and as chairperson of the Personal Property Appraisal Conference. A former Vermont State Director, Ms. Hall is also the founding member and chairperson of the Vermont/New Hampshire satellite branch of the Boston chapter of the American Society of Appraisers. She holds a master's degree from Suffolk University, Boston, Massachusetts.

John W. Housiaux, PE, ASA

Mr. Housiaux is a consulting engineer and professional appraiser with a practice in Shreveport dealing with public utility properties. He is an engineering graduate of the University of Colorado, a registered professional engineer in several states and a Life Member of the American Society of Mechanical Engineers. He has served as a consultant and qualified as an expert witness in many litigated cases involving such matters as condemnations, property tax appeals and rate cases before courts and commissions throughout the United States. He has participated in the activities of the American Society of Appraisers at the chapter and national levels and is a past Governor of Region 4.

Janie M. King, ASA

Ms. King is President of Connoisseur Appraisers, Denver. She received her Bachelor of Arts from Loretto Heights College. She is author of "So You Want To Be An Appraiser?" published in ASA *Personal Property Journal* (1989). She currently serves as Governor of Region 8, is a member of the ASA International Board of Examiners, and is a course developer and instructor for the *Principles of Valuation* courses.

Terry R. King, ASA

Mr. King is Vice-President, Connoisseur Appraisers, Denver, CO. He has served as vice-chairman of the International Personal Property Committee and chairman of the ASA Search for Shelter Committee and is a course developer and instructor for the *Principles of Valuation* courses.

Alyne A. Lacombe, ASA

Ms. Lacombe is a full-time personal property appraiser on Hilton Head Island, SC, with a designation in Antiques and Decorative Arts. She earned a Bachelor of Arts degree in Valuation Sciences from Lindenwood College in St. Charles, Missouri in 1991. Ms. Lacombe has served on the editorial board of the *Personal Property Journal* as Computer Information Review columnist.

John V. Lanterman, ASA

Mr. Lanterman is an independent fee appraiser practicing in the Washington, D. C., Northern Virginia and Suburban Maryland area and is accredited in the specialties of Antiques/Decorative Arts and Residential Contents. He currently serves as Governor Region 3, member of the International Personal Property Committee, Chairman of the Public Relations Committee and as an advisor to the Admissions and Membership Committee.

Dexter DuPont MacBride, FASA

Mr. MacBride is from Diamond Bar, CA, and is Chancellor of the College of Fellows of the American Society of Appraisers, a member of the Virginia Bar Association and a Senior Member of the American Bar Association. He is a Certified Mediator, Claremont Dispute Resolution Center, has served as Administrator of the Diamond Bar Mediation Center and is a member of the Society for Professionals in Dispute Resolution.

Terry Melia, CPA

Mr. Melia is a tax partner for Arthur Anderson & Co., currently head of the tax division in the Albuquerque office. He is a Certified Public Accountant in Arizona and New Mexico and has served as income and estate tax advisor to various artists, including Georgia O'Keeffe and was present throughout the O'Keeffe case. He offers a reflective view of how the results might have been more satisfying by cooperation of the various experts in the application of both market and income approaches to the problem. He presented a review of this case at an ASA Seminar on Blockage in 1993.

Corinne L. Richardson, JD, MVS

Ms. Richardson is an attorney currently employed as the Chief Legal Advisor, St. Louis County Family Court (1966 to date). She was educated at Washington University, St. Louis, Missouri and earned her AB degree in 1958, JD in 1960, and was awarded an MVS from Lindenwood College in 1987. Her articles have been published in the journals of the Missouri Bar, American Bar Association and *Crime and Delinquency*. Her volunteer work includes Past Chair, Advisory Council for the International Valuation Science Institute at Lindenwood College and the Missouri Bar Disciplinary Committee (crisis intervenor).

Maureen Sandstrom, ASA

Ms. Sandstrom is an appraiser in Wheeling, IL, accredited in residential contents. She has a master's degree in education and has completed the four level courses and one advanced course from the *Principles of Valuation* courses. She was a Prospect Heights Education Association negotiator from 1975-1993.

Barbara Shanley, ASA

Ms. Shanley is principal of Barbara Shanley & Associates, San Francisco. She is a full-time independent fee appraiser of antiques and decorative arts, with accreditation in Antique Furniture and Antiques/Decorative Arts. She has a B.A. in Decorative Arts from the University of California, Berkeley. Ms. Shanley is presently the Editor of the *Personal Property Journal* of the International Personal Property Committee. She has published and lectured on the subject of antiques.

Janella N. Smyth, ASA

Ms. Smyth is a full time appraiser and principal of Appraisal Associates, Raleigh, NC, accredited in Antiques and Decorative Arts. She earned her B.A. degree from Texas Tech University and for two years wrote a syndicated column "Antique Wise." She lectures on the subjects of antiques and decorative arts. She is currently a member of the International Personal Property Committee.

Peter Sorlien, ASA

Mr. Sorlien is principal of Sorlien & Associates, Marblehead, MA.. He earned a B.A. degree from Dartmouth College and is the author of "How Good Is Your Ship Model?" He previously served as director of the Mystic Seaport Museum. He serves as a course developer and instructor for the *Principles of Valuation* courses.

Santo J. Sottilare, JD

Mr. Sottilare is a Bar Association Member in Florida and Arkansas and has been a trial attorney in South Florida for 26 years. He attended B. S. Bryant College, Providence, R.I. (1960) and earned his BBA from the University of Miami, Coral Gables (1964) and his J. D. from the University of Miami School of Law, Coral Gables, Fl. (1968) He is co-owner of SanMary Art and Antiques and is a candidate in ASA, having completed *Principles of Valuation* Level Courses I-IV.

Patricia C. Soucy, MVS, FASA

Ms. Soucy, a Fellow in the American Society of Appraisers, is a full-time appraiser of antiques and decorative arts and is designated in four specialties of personal property appraising: Antiques and Decorative Arts, Antique Furniture, Residential Contents-General, and Silver and Metalware. She has her master's in Valuation Sciences, is core-faculty at Lindenwood College in St. Charles, Missouri, teaching Value Theory and Eighteenth Century Material Culture and Decorative Arts. She is Past Chairman of ASA's International Personal Property Committee and is co-developer of four levels of courses in personal property appraisal for ASA's *Principles of Valuation*. Currently she is serving as Governor of Region 7.

Mary Sudar, ASA

Ms. Sudar owns a personal property appraisal and estate sale management business in Tacoma, WA, with designation in Residential Contents-General. She received her B.A. in Art History and French from the University of Peugeot Sound, has completed the *Principles of Valuation* courses, and has lectured on early Northwest art at area historical societies and museums. She has many years experience in public library reference work and her journalistic experiences have ranged from art reviews to restaurant reviews. She is currently a member of the International Personal Property Committee.

NOTES

NOTES

NOTES